Ghosts could walk freely tonight, without fear of the
disbelief of men; for this night was haunted, and it
would be an insensitive man who did not know it.
- John Steinbeck

This book is dedicated with love to George and Lois Taylor. As Lisa's beloved and dedicated parents, they have always encouraged her to go out and learn as much as she can. Writing this book was just another way to learn more. It would be love from Lisa, and Troy's respect for them both, that became the greatest inspirations for this book. It could not have been written without either of them. Lois pointed us in so many directions and whenever we got stuck, needed a date or had to track down an elusive story, we knew that all we needed to do was ask "The George." The community of Jacksonville is lucky to have these two as a part of its rich history and we are truly thankful for their support and guidance.

History & Hauntings of the "Athens of the West"

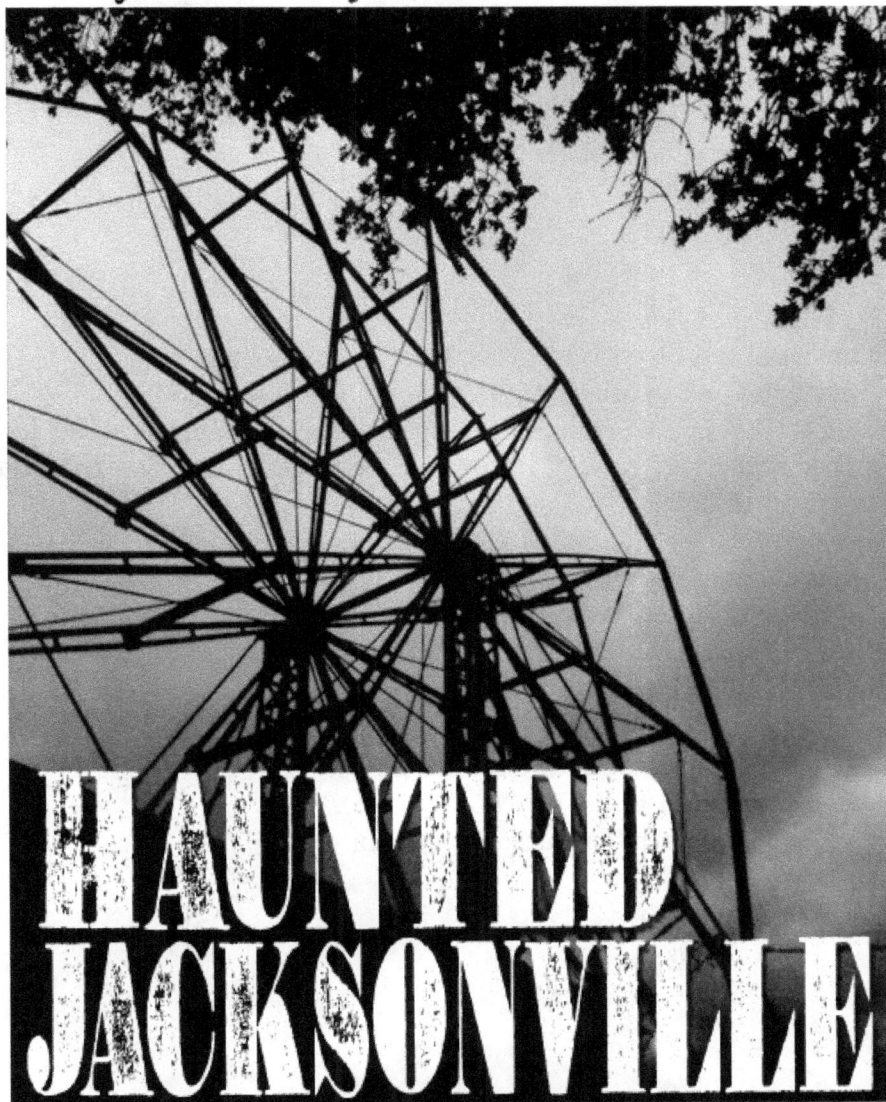

HAUNTED JACKSONVILLE

By TROY TAYLOR
& LISA TAYLOR HORTON

Original Cover Artwork Designed by
© Copyright 2014 by April Slaughter & Troy Taylor

This Book is Published By:
Whitechapel Press
A Division of Apartment 42 Productions
Decatur, Illinois   1-888-GHOSTLY
Visit us on the internet at http: www.whitechapelpress.com

First Edition - October 2014
ISBN: 1-892523-92-2

Printed in the United States of America

TABLE OF CONTENTS

INTRODUCTION

Jacksonville is a town like no other in the state of Illinois. Founded by frontiersmen and settled by farmers, it also became home to an unusual group of New Englanders who set out in the early nineteenth century to bring culture and knowledge to the newly formed states. They were followed by more than 100 families from Yorkshire, England, who made their own impression on the burgeoning settlement. With more colleges, seminaries, and schools than any other town on the prairies, Jacksonville soon acquired the nickname of the "Athens of the West."

During its history, it has been home to three Illinois governors Joseph Duncan, Richard Yates, Richard Yates, Jr. and two presidential nominees Stephen A. Douglas, and William Jennings Bryan and holds a unique place in American history. In 1919, the Eli Bridge Company relocated to the city. W.E. Sullivan, who owned the bridge building business, was so impressed by his ride on the first Ferris Wheel at the 1893 World's Fair in Chicago that he designed the first portable Ferris wheel that could be moved from place to place. The "Big Eli" wheel debuted in Jacksonville's Central Park in 1900. Ferris wheels from Jacksonville can still be found all over the country today.

The city also holds a strange place in America's supernatural history. In 1847, Jacksonville became home to the Illinois State Asylum and Hospital for the Insane, the first such hospital in the state. It was here in 1865 that a young woman named Mary Roff died under mysterious circumstances. More than twelve years later, Mary's spirit allegedly possessed the body of a young girl named Lurancy Vennum and became known as the "Watseka Wonder," a phenomenon that remains one of the most documented supernatural events of all time.

The "Athens of the West" was one of the many nicknames given to the city in years gone by. Today, Jacksonville is considered one of the most haunted towns on the Illinois Prairie. Many ghosts still linger here in the city, but not so much because of pain, horror, trauma, disease and death -- although there is some of that as well.

Most of the ghosts of Jacksonville remain because they simply don't want to leave.

Troy Taylor
& Lisa Taylor Horton
Summer 2014

Haunted Jacksonville

1. BUILDING A CITY

The city of Jacksonville was carved from the rolling "prairie seas of grass" of the Illinois territory in 1825. It was a rich land and one that would be coveted by the streams of settlers and frontiersmen who traveled west from the original American colonies. Those who came to Central Illinois found wide, treeless prairies, with grass taller than any man, formed by the melting of the last ice age. Men, women, and children flocked to these prairies. They came from different places and cultures, but all with the purpose of creating a new life for themselves.

The first men who arrived in what would someday be Jacksonville had been soldiers during the War of 1812. They had fought in the wilderness and on the battlegrounds of the war, during which General Andrew Jackson of Tennessee made a name for himself at the Battle of New Orleans. Many towns became known as "Jacksonville" in the early 1800s. Colonel Seymour Kellogg, his brother, Captain Elisha Kellogg, their families, and Charles Collins, built a camp on the north fork of the Mauvaisterre River in 1819, after the Kickapoo Indians signed a treaty giving up their land in Central Illinois.

In 1825, arguments as to which of several fledging towns would become the county seat were solved by laying out a new town in the center of Morgan County. Jacksonville was soon platted in an orderly fashion with dirt roads and a town square. The first resident, Alexander Cox, was joined by merchants like Joseph Fairfield and George Hackett and before long, settlers and farmers began

8

flocking to the new town after hearing stories of the richness of the Illinois soil. The new residents were convinced that Jacksonville was destined for great things. With a lot of hard work and very little money, they believed that prosperity could be carved from the fertile prairie.

And prosper they did. When the settlers first came to Jacksonville, they needed the basics - food, shelter, and clothing. Because of that, the main way of life for many years was built around farming - but that was almost not the case. The initial would-be farmers were intimidated by the seas of waving prairie grass that surrounded the settlement. Since no trees grew on the prairie, some feared that there was something wrong with the soil. It couldn't possibly be fertile, they thought. They soon found that this was not the case and they began breaking the rich ground to make a living.

The farmers soon found that corn was an ideal crop for the prairie. It was easy to sow and to cultivate and was easily turned into many food products as well as a marketable whiskey. Many farmers owned stills that converted corn mash into a clear but potent whiskey that could then be transported to market via pack horse or river barge. This corn alcohol became a popular western drink and the jug would circulate freely at social events like dances, barn-raisings, and especially at election time.

The secondary crop became wheat, which could be converted to flour, but only at a mill. The mills came a little later, bringing rudimentary mechanics to

9

the frontier. The mills were built along rivers for power, but where dams could not be built, horses and oxen provided the power for the grinding stones. Soon, the mill became the leading establishment in many of the settlements and other businesses, like blacksmith shops and general stores, followed closely behind.

In those days, almost no one on the prairie had money. The settlers made their own clothing by tanning the hides of deer and cattle for shoes while women with spinning wheels and looms produced trousers, shirts and dresses. They grew their own food, or hunted it in the forests, and the small farms provided eggs, milk, and butter. In the general stores, the settlers could trade any surplus goods for whiskey, sugar, salt, tools, crockery, or coffee.

But as idyllic as this all sounds, the frontier was not without its dangers. In the early years, much of that danger came from the Native American populace. The Kickapoo, and other Indians, would keep the settlers in a constant state of alarm for many years. The pioneers died from the many diseases that plagued the region, as well as from the often extreme weather conditions. Terrible thunderstorms on the open plains were not uncommon, and fires were frequently started by lightning strikes, which could burn whole fields, stands of woods, or even entire towns without notice. There were no fire departments to battle these wild blazes in those days.

In the winter, many settlers died from the extreme cold, having little protection from it. Over the winter of 1830-31, Central Illinois was hit with disaster. This terrible season would be remembered for many years as the "deep snow." Early that winter, snow began to fall and continued to come in intervals, sometimes alternating with sleet and freezing rain. This treacherous mixture would form a layer of snow and ice that was three to four feet thick. The snow drifted so high that loaded wagons could be driven over the top of fence rails. Livestock perished and soon game became scarce. It would be years later before the squirrels and prairie chickens could be found to hunt again. Many settlers died in the bitter cold and snow, and that terrible winter offered a grim reminder that life was never easy on the frontier and death and tragedy sometimes triumphed over the hard life of the settlers.

But the people of Jacksonville persevered. Residents were so eager to establish a good education system for the city that, in 1829, they began constructing their first college building, before they even had a faculty or students. Churches were built, railroads were planned and before long, stores, taverns and saloons were flourishing. The first courthouse, constructed from logs, was built on the northwest side of the square in 1825. It burned down two years later and a new courthouse, the first public building made from brick in the city, was built on the square's southwest corner in 1830. There were eleven lawyers and doctors practicing in Jacksonville by 1834. The state of Illinois was settled from south to north, with the initial settlements like Alton along the Mississippi River. With population moving northward, there was a time when Jacksonville was the largest city in the state. In 1833, Chicago was home to only 150 people, while Jacksonville, just one year later, had a population of more than 1,800.

The dedicated creators of the city worked hard to better their own lives and their community. Their efforts paid off, even if it occurred in ways that had not been planned. In 1833, a cholera epidemic swept through the Upper Mississippi Valley region and affected almost half the population of Jacksonville and killed scores of people. Word spread of the afflicted community and people shunned the growing town. Newspapers spread the word that Jacksonville was a "sickly town," and the community was in danger of dying out before it had even really gotten a chance to get started.

Epidemic on the Illinois Prairie

Mrs. Frances Ellis... a lady of rare accomplishments, was taken sick one afternoon and died before six o'clock. She had two little children; one was taken at one o'clock that same night and died before morning; the other, and a niece, Miss Conn, a beautiful young girl of eighteen, died soon after. Mr. Ellis was away at the time, and when he returned he stopped at the church to attend prayer meeting before going to his home. As he entered the door he heard a friend praying for their 'stricken pastor so suddenly bereft of all his family.' He fell to the floor as if he had been struck by a butcher's ax. Immediately after this, forty-seven families, and as many single persons as could leave, fled."

Illinois College Professor Jonathan Baldwin Turner, in an August 28, 1833 letter about the family of Reverend John M. Ellis.

In 1833, a plague swept through the city of Jacksonville. Like the deadly affliction of medieval Europe, it killed without thought and destroyed entire families. Sadly, cholera was just one of the many diseases that faced the settlers of the nineteenth century, but the epidemic that came to Jacksonville nearly wiped the city off the map.

Cholera was probably one of the most terrifying diseases of the past. Spread by carriers of the bacteria, it infected food and water and caused horrible vomiting and diarrhea, which led to rapid dehydration and, without treatment, death. William McPheeters, a doctor who nearly saw St. Louis wiped out by a cholera epidemic in 1849, wrote that the symptoms were "vomiting freely with frequent and copious discharges from the bowels; at first of slight bilious nature, but it soon became pure 'rice water'; cramps in the stomach and lower extremities

11

NOTICE.

PREVENTIVES OF

CHOLERA!

Published by order of the Sanatory Committee, under the sanction of the Medical Counsel.

BE TEMPERATE IN EATING & DRINKING!
Avoid Raw Vegetables and Unripe Fruit !.

Abstain from COLD WATER, when heated, and above all from *Ardent Spirits*, and if habit have rendered them indispensable, take much less than usual.

and tongue cold; skin of blue color and very much corrugated; urinary secretions suspended; eyes sunken and surrounded by a livid hue."

The Illinois outbreak of 1833 actually began the previous summer when federal soldiers from the east were brought to the frontier to help fight the Blackhawk War. In the spring of 1832, the disease, carried by Irish immigrants, had broken out in Quebec and had slowly made its way to New York City. When General Winfield Scott brought troops to Illinois from the northeast in July, they brought the disease with them to Fort Dearborn and the fledgling settlement of Chicago. The epidemic caused the Indian peril to be forgotten. Townspeople and newly-arrived settlers alike took flight and almost overnight, Chicago was emptied of its civilian population. Only the military men remained behind, compelled by orders and a sense of duty, and they spent weeks fighting the epidemic and digging hasty graves for those who died.

Once in Illinois, the disease traveled through the Mississippi Valley, wreaking havoc as it went. Outbreaks occurred in towns like Quincy, Carrolton, and Galena, avoiding Jacksonville - at least at first. But following the deaths of Mrs. Ellis and her children on July 19 and 20, James G. Edwards, the publisher of the Jacksonville newspaper the *Illinois Patriot,* tried to calm his readers. Edwards wrote: "Every requisite attention has been paid to the sick. We hope our country friends will not place dependence on any exaggerated statements they may hear, concerning the ravages of the disease in this place, as the effects may be very injurious. Our accounts, thus far, may be depended on; and, should we be spared, we shall continue to give correct intelligence in regard to this subject."

The *Patriot* revealed that 10 people had died in Jacksonville over the previous three weeks, a secret that had not yet been shared. The first cholera death, Edwards stated, had been a man named John Barber from a town once called Middletown Mills near Exeter in Morgan now Scott County. When he had fallen ill, he had been brought to Jacksonville for treatment, but had died.

Estimates as to the number of deaths that occurred in 1833 vary greatly, but Edwards' published figures for Jacksonville's population and the number sick with cholera are likely the most reliable. On August 10, 1833, Edwards claimed that, according to local doctor's estimates, between 200 and 300 people had contracted cholera. This was at a time when the population was around 1,300 people. Out of that afflicted number, 34 had died - so far. Apparently, many other residents, maybe as many as 600 or 700, fled Jacksonville to escape the epidemic.

Two weeks later, the *Patriot* updated its list of cholera casualties and had some encouraging news for those still around to read the newspaper. Edwards stated, "The cholera - no new case of this disease has occurred in Jacksonville since our last publication. There have, indeed, been two deaths by cholera since last Saturday morning, but they were some days standing. We have now ever inducement to believe that this destroyer of human life has taken its flight, at least for a season, from this place."

By August 24, 1833, cholera had claimed nearly 50 lives in Jacksonville. Over time, that number has changed, ranging from 55 to as many as 100. It's unlikely that we will ever know for sure how many perished. There is no official record of cholera deaths in Illinois. Death records were not required by law until much later in the nineteenth century and newspapers rarely offered obituaries in those days.

However, Jacksonville history did record the efforts of two local men who risked their lives to come to the aid of their afflicted neighbors and who buried the bodies of those who could not be saved. Cabinetmakers John Henry and James Anderson both nursed the sick and prepared the dead for burial. Henry later wrote: "I was in every house where there was a death. I took fifty-three myself to the burying ground and had them buried in a plain, raised lid cherry coffin."

The two men became honored citizens for their brave efforts during the epidemic. Henry's leadership qualities took him all the way to the Illinois House of Representatives, Illinois Senate and on to Congress. Anderson remained in Jacksonville and continued to serve the community as a furniture-maker and undertaker until his death at age 88 in 1899.

The heroism shown by Henry and Anderson is even more remarkable when shown alongside the vivid contemporary account of the cholera epidemic that was recorded by Professor Turner, who had come to Illinois College just a few months before to teach Latin and Greek. He wrote a letter - quoted earlier - on August 28, 1833 that described the grief-stricken community. "From this time the daily yea, the hourly report was 'He is sick,' 'He is dead,' 'He is buried.'" Turner wrote, "To meet a man at night and attend his funeral in the morning has ceased to alarm, much less to surprise. Some die in three hours, seldom do they live twelve, and very rarely twenty-four. As I have walked through the streets in the evening, I have seen through windows and doors the sick and the dying, sometimes four or five in the same room in a log hut, some on the bed, others on the floor, and perhaps one or two sorrow-smitten beings crawling from bed to bed to give a cup of water or brush away the flies. One every face was written 'Woe,' and on every doorpost 'Death,' and not on a few 'Utter Desolation.' For some weeks, not a soul was seen approaching from the country, except here and there a man on a horse upon the full run for 'The doctor! The doctor! For heaven's sake, sir, can't you tell me where is the doctor? My father is dying, my wife is dead, and my children are dying.' All this can be answered at last by stupid stare, or a shake of the head, or perchance, 'They are all sick.' For, at one time, out of eight or ten doctors not one could be had."

A healthy doctor probably would not have helped anyway. The medical world in 1833 had little idea of what caused cholera and had no idea how to treat it. Some people, including many doctors, believed that cholera somehow originated from the decomposition of animals or vegetables and was transmitted through the air. To prevent disease, doctors recommended that decaying food be removed and that lime be thrown into privy pits and sewers once or twice a week. In 1832, New Orleans had been savaged by a cholera epidemic. Those not felled by the disease struggled to find its cause. Days of prayer were organized and cannons were blasted each day to break up the clouds over the city, thinking that perhaps they were responsible for the disease.

Among the "treatments" prescribed by befuddled physicians were calomel pills, a powder used for intestinal worms; laudanum, a solution of opium in alcohol; powdered rhubarb; hot tea of sage; brandy in warm water; and a teaspoonful of crushed charcoal mixed with brandy. Even Professor Turner attempted a cure on a very sick Illinois College student. He gave him laudanum mixed with red pepper, doubling, even quadrupling the dose. "I will either kill him or cure him," Turner wrote. Somehow, the student managed to survive.

But one boy that could not be saved was Alexander Carson, the seven-year-old of Thomas and Catharine Carson - the first male child born in Jacksonville.

He died during the epidemic, which lasted for more than eight weeks and nearly decimated a city that was just beginning to thrive.

Jacksonville Rises Again

The cholera epidemic could have defeated a less determined town. And the same could be said for the loss of the state capital a few years later. In 1837, the city suffered what some called its "most bitter defeat" when it lost the bid to be Illinois' state capital. In truth, Jacksonville had little chance of scoring this political victory. The young city was thoroughly outmaneuvered by Springfield after it was announced that the capital would be moving from Vandalia. Just before a key vote on the capital site, the newspapers in Springfield dredged up the horrible memories of Jacksonville's cholera epidemic. The *Sangamo Journal*, made a point of publishing a doctor's opinion that "moral causes have more to do with spreading cholera than physical," implying that Jacksonville was not spiritually worthy of being the state capital.

While Jacksonville battled the epidemic, Springfield landed a key mail route, further isolating Jacksonville. Finally, the Sangamon County delegation put together the winning package, backed by a group of men known as the "Long Nine" - so named for their height, in part because their ranks included a certain tall, lanky politician named Lincoln.

The head of the Morgan County delegation was a budding politician named Stephen A. Douglas. He had come to Jacksonville in 1833, looking for work. When he found nothing, he moved to Winchester, where he taught school. Douglas voted for Jacksonville to become the capital, but suspiciously to some he was later granted a job at the register of land office in Springfield and was invited to a banquet to celebrate the Long Nine's triumph. Speculation followed that Douglas, a former Morgan County state's attorney, had sold out Jacksonville.

Strangely enough, a few years after the state capital decision, a Springfield newspaper supported Jacksonville in its attempts to move the proposed site of the state insane asylum from Peoria to Jacksonville. Peoria had already won a state Senate vote for the asylum, but the House voted for Jacksonville, which eventually won the asylum.

The city began to recover, and by the time that rumblings over the selection of a site for the new University of Illinois began to be heard, Jacksonville was prepared for a battle. Years earlier, Jacksonville had already become home to Illinois College, but this was a great coup. It was so important to the city that respected and politically connected educator, Illinois College President Julian Sturtevant, was ready and willing to turn Illinois College into the University of Illinois, if needed. The state institution would give the city much greater political clout.

But the decision was postponed until after the Civil War, and that likely ruined Jacksonville's chances. By 1867, other cities had time to bolster their efforts. After the loss of the state capital, Jacksonville had taken up the fight to obtain other state institutions, like the deaf school, the blind school and the state asylum. With pride, it pointed to Illinois College and the Illinois Female Academy later MacMurray College as proof of its intellectual and cultural importance. Unfortunately, all of the other state institutions that Jacksonville had received turned out to lessen the chance of the city getting the University of Illinois. Backers from Champaign-Urbana argued that the west side of the state had already received enough and it was now time for the east side to get its share.

In the end, it all came down to money - or rather, bribes. Jacksonville initially offered more money on the bid than its rivals, but Champaign-Urbana spent money in more productive places, making sure that the right legislators were plied with the right favors and ample amounts of cash.

Jacksonville backers responded with little dignity or restraint, and rightfully so. Johnathan Baldwin Turner wrote: "No men of talent or genius will ever gather around it, nothing above the level of miserable scamps and scallywags whose votes and services were bought up by the capital... No parent from abroad would trust his son there, unless he wanted him to take lessons in the arts of perfidy, imprudence, hypocrisy and drunkenness."

The loss of the University of Illinois seemed to take the fight out of the city. There is no record of Jacksonville making a concerted effort for Illinois State University or Western Illinois University, two schools that could have fit nicely in town. In fact, Jacksonville seemed to resign itself to being a county seat and a premier city of learning. The city seemed to turn its lack of success into a virtue and made it a stable and comfortable place to live, do business, and learn.

Besides, there was no greater school of higher learning in the state at the time than Illinois College. It became Jacksonville's most important education institution and was supportive in establishing other education opportunities like the Jacksonville Female Academy, Jacksonville Public Schools, Whipple Academy, Young Ladies Athenaeum, Illinois Conservatory of Music and, in 1846, the Illinois Conference Female Academy now MacMurray College .

It became a city where higher learning flourished. John Millot Ellis came west from New England to begin Presbyterian churches and soon became more interested in building schools. When Ellis and Thomas Lippincott had reached Jacksonville, they thought the hilltop was perfect, and they constructed the first building for Illinois College in 1829. As luck would have it, seven soon-to-be graduates of Yale read about their work and saw Jacksonville as the answer to their life's ambitions. They came west and became known as the "Yale Band." They came to bring knowledge and culture to the west, and their lives became

16

intertwined with the history of Illinois College and the city of Jacksonville. As Illinois College grew, so did the Illinois Conference Female Academy and soon this dusty town was seen as a beacon of higher learning on the frontier.

Witch Burning at Middle Creek

During the 1830s, the population of Jacksonville continued to grow, reaching as high as 3,000 souls in 1834, with nearly 1,200 of them being college students. By this time, Stephen Douglas had returned to Jacksonville and was now considered a rising star in Illinois politics. Several newspapers were also started in Jacksonville, with the *Illinois State Gazette and Jacksonville News*, edited by S.S. Brooks, becoming the personal mouthpiece of Stephen Douglas.

Meanwhile, the Goudy Print Shop issued "Peck's Gazetteer of Illinois" and "J.A. Wakefield's History of the Blackhawk War," along with prints of almanacs and a few other books. The two books, aside from state publications, were among the first books to be printed in Illinois.

In January 1835, the Jacksonville Female Academy was chartered and a few weeks later, Illinois College was also chartered. In September, Illinois College graduated its first class, Richard Yates and Jonathan E. Spilman, and conferred on them the first college degrees awarded in Illinois. In 1836, Stephen Douglas and John A. Hardin were elected to the legislature, being two of nine men sent to the General Assembly from Morgan County.

Jacksonville was earning its place as city of higher learning, politics, and culture on the Illinois prairie. Thanks to the efforts of city boosters, politicians, and teachers it had acquired the nickname of the "Athens of the West," implying that the city was a step above other settlements that could be found in the rough territory of the west.

But at the same time that Jacksonville was acquiring its cultured reputation, strange things were happening nearby that hearkened back to superstitious days of the past. A strange incident occurred in Morgan County in 1834, near Middle Creek, now in Cass County among a society of religious fanatics that had settled there. The society of about 30 members lived in the Sangamon River bottom about three miles from Chandlerville. They not only believed in witchcraft and communication with spirits, but actually made offerings of themselves, and were burned at the stake to appease the anger of God. The time for offering up their first victim came, and lots were drawn to see who would be sacrificed. It fell upon an old man, who was placed upon an altar, and the wood that had been prepared was set on fire. A man named Elmore was out that day hunting and, hearing the screams of the old man, he ran up and rescued him from the fire, but not before he was badly burned. He'd wasted time having to fight off the cult members so that the old man could be pulled from the blaze. A Morgan

County grand jury indicted the men responsible, and they were brought to this city for trial. The case was tried in the October term of the Circuit Court with Judge Samuel D. Lockwood presiding. The case ended in a guilty verdict and the parties were fined $3 and costs. Or so some of the older records say. More current research into this bizarre tale tells a different story - one even more violent and gruesome than the original legend.

It turns out that what seemed to be an organized cult of fanatics was anything but that - everyone involved, with a few exceptions, were members of one family and all were illiterate and superstitious. The women, some of whom probably were Baptists, were emotional and perhaps hysterical – of the type who always did the loudest shouting at camp meetings – and the men, not then church members, were typical backwoodsmen who regarded the rifle and dog, the axe and jug, as first essentials of the pioneer's cabin equipment. The patriarch of that family was John B. Witty, a native of Tennessee, who married a daughter of John Lucas, and not long thereafter migrated to Kentucky, where he remained several years. As the population in the region increased, he went looking for more space and moved now into the Sangamon country of Illinois. He settled near Middle Creek, six or eight miles south of its confluence with the Sangamon River. There, in the forest, he selected his claim and built his log cabin.

Witty was fairly typical of the pioneers of the day, an average, common man, not well-mannered, nor highly educated, nor very enterprising, nor progressive, but an honest, law-abiding citizen and good neighbor. His family was made up of several sons and daughters, most, or all, of whom were married at the date of the "witch-burning" occurrence. One daughter, Nancy, was living at home with her husband, Pleasant Rose. Another daughter, Polly, of odd and impulsive nature, married to a man named Hickey, and living nearby, was also there at the time. A brother-in-law of Witty, named Bennet, and his wife, were also there, having arrived recently from Kentucky to visit the Witty family.

It was late in the fall or the beginning of winter in 1834, when the Bennets decided to return to Kentucky. A family gathering was arranged at the Witty home to bid them farewell, which offered wild game, garden crops, and a two-gallon jug of whiskey, which social custom made indispensable in those days. That evening, all of the adult sons and their wives, daughters and their husbands, and other kinfolk, assembled there and enjoyed the feast that had been prepared. One of the daughters, Mrs. Berry, recovering from a recent illness, was unable to leave her bed in the corner of the cabin. She could not join them at the table, but she joined in the spirit of the occasion. Outside the cabin, the night was still and cold, but within, the hickory logs briskly blazing in the spacious fireplace diffused a glow of cheerful comfort throughout the room.

The meal ended and the family sat around chatting, occasionally sampling the contents of the jug, hoping to raise their spirits, which had fallen with news of the Bennets' eminent departure. Some of them were good singers, and as their spirits rose, they struck up the old familiar camp-meeting hymns, and sung them with great enthusiasm and force. The effect of the religious music was soon apparent. Mrs. Berry, a young woman of highly nervous temperament, sitting up in bed supported by her mother sitting behind her with arms around her, joined in the singing and became very agitated, overcome by the "spirit." Suddenly, she bit her mother's hand spasmodically, and then leaping out of bed, began shouting and clapping her hands as if she was filled with joy.

Her spiritual excitement was contagious. Some shouted, others prayed, and as their excitement increased, they began working themselves into a religious frenzy. They became wildly upset about their sins and in despair, wailed to the Lord, asking what they should do to be saved. At that time, one member of the party claimed to have a revelation that they would only be spared from God's wrath by offering a human sacrifice.

They prayed for a sign by which they might know who was to be offered as a victim. But with no sign appearing, they concluded that the oldest matron of the family - known through the area as "Granny" Witty - was the fittest member of the clan for sacrifice. Until that moment, they had been marching about the

19

room in single file, the old man leading the procession with his rifle over his shoulder, all loudly singing, shouting, and praying. A halt was called and "Granny" was seized, stripped, tied, and anointed with bear's grease. She was then laid on the stone hearth of the fireplace to await the conclusion of the ceremony. The marching and chanting continued. No one paid attention to her screams as she began to burn. Her eyebrows and hair were scorched away and her cries began to grow weaker as she reached the point of exhaustion and collapse.

Just then, the cabin door was flung open and William Lewis, a neighbor who lived a mile or so away, came into the room. Recovering from his surprise at what he saw taking place, he said, by way of apology for intruding, that he heard a member of the Witty family was sick and he came over to offer to sit up with them or go after a doctor or render any assistance that he could.

No one heard a word that Lewis said. They seized hold of him, thanking the Lord for their new sacrifice. The women at once released the old lady, put on her clothes, and placed her on the bed. After a desperate struggle – in the course of which almost all of Lewis's clothing was torn off – the frenzied men succeeded in securely binding him with strong ropes and then placed him on the stone hearth, in preparation for his incineration in the fire. The men next barred the door, both to prevent the exit of any of their own number and to guard against further intrusion of outsiders. Then resuming their shouting and singing, again marching around as before, and as they passed by their victim each one gave him a kick or prodded him with some sharp instrument. Their actions appeared to be neither angry nor malevolent, but as though they were under the spell of temporary religious lunacy.

Terrified and in great pain, Lewis fought to free himself of his bindings, at the same time calling out vigorously for help. He knew that his death by fire was eminent.

As it happened, three other local settlers -- Julius Elmore, Amos Dick and Philip Hash -- were out raccoon hunting that night, and as they passed near the Witty cabin, they heard the clamor coming from inside. Fearful that the family might be in danger, they hurried to their defense. Elmore was the first to reach the cabin. He knocked and called loudly at the door. Receiving no response, and finding the door fastened on the inside, he seized a fence rail and soon battered it open. By that time his two companions also rushed inside. When they saw Lewis in danger before the fire, they cut away the ropes that held him and were forced into a fight with the delirious mob. When confronted by these three angry and well-armed men, the Witty clan began to quiet down, and they gradually regained their senses.

Mr. Elmore immediately procured a wagon and team from a neighbor to take "Granny" Witty to her home that night. He sent for Dr. Pettit, a physician over on the edge of Menard County, to attend to her and she remained there until she was out of danger.

As for Lewis, he was badly burned, besides having received fourteen puncture wounds, from which he bled so freely that his torn clothing was soaked with blood. Amos Dick and Philip Hash lost no time in getting him to his own home. Then Mr. Dick made such speed in travelling to Chandlerville that he had Dr. Chandler there before daylight the next morning. Lewis was confined to his bed for many days before he recovered.

Quietly, the Bennets set out for Kentucky early the next morning, leaving Illinois far behind.

The bizarre incident, not surprisingly, created a great commotion in the area. Reports of it quickly spread all over the country, and every time repeated – particularly by gossiping women – there was some embellishment or exaggeration added. Many regarded it as merely a drunken revel; but the more thoughtful and religiously inclined saw in it an esoteric working of the spirit guided by supernatural power. There is but little doubt, however, that the inspiration drawn from that jug was the initial excitement. Liquor drinking was then the universal custom, though, in this instance, it was a reasonable assumption that the women there drank none of it, yet they did the wildest and loudest shouting.

What caused this to occur? This was an era of great religious fervor in America. There are many accounts from those years about religious ecstasy actually causing hypnotic hallucinations, similar to the practices of the revivalists, who would shake and dance and utter insane ravings and fall into cataleptic trances at camp meetings and religious gatherings. Such religious movements occurred up and down the frontier in the first half of the nineteenth century.

But religion did not excuse the criminal acts that occurred. The wounding and burning of Lewis shocked the moral sense of the community, and outraged residents called for the punishment of the perpetrators. Attempted murder charges were filed against John B. Witty, his son John L. Witty and Pleasant Rose, his son-in-law. The men were jailed on March 25, 1835, where they waited to stand trial in Morgan County. Indictments were also returned against Nancy Witty, Nancy Rose and Sally Berry for the same offense.

The trial became excruciatingly long, with writs filed and arrest warrants issued for witnesses who failed to appeal. John B. Witty was found guilty and sentenced to a year of punishment in the penitentiary. But a motion was filed when it was discovered that one of the jurors, a man named Doyle, was not a naturalized citizen. A change of venue was gained for the new trial, this time in Sangamon County. Meanwhile, the cases against the three women were stricken from the docket and they were never tried. More subpoenas were issued for other witnesses. Claims were made of self-defense and for the fact that Lewis was never really stabbed at all. By June 1837, more witnesses were sought but could not be found, and then when the scene of the crime was changed from Morgan to Cass County, the entire process had to be started over again.

In the end, it vanished into the convoluted history of the time and nothing more of it ever appeared on the legal record. The cases against the Witty clan were eventually dropped and soon took on the guide of a tall tale. Jacksonville's "witch burning" incident became the stuff of legend.

Beecher Hall at Illinois College

Abolitionists & the Underground Railroad

In the 1830s, the city of Jacksonville became closely associated with the abolitionist movement in Illinois. The movement was popularized by a legal case in Jacksonville, but connections to the abolitionists actually dated back to 1829, when the "Yale Band" arrived in the city to establish what would become Illinois College.

The court case had its beginnings around 1837, when Marcus A. Chinn, who surveyed the Northern Cross Railroad from Jacksonville to Springfield, and Lucy

Jane Hardin Chinn, his wife and sister of local politician John J. Hardin, arrived in town. They had brought with them their two slaves, Robert and Emily Logan. The presence of the two slaves in the community aroused local abolitionists, and they informed the Logans that they were free. The slaves left the Chinns and were hidden in town. At some point, Robert was out running an errand and was kidnapped and sent down the Illinois River by slave traders. Left behind, Emily Logan sued for her freedom. On December 1, 1840, after a trial in which Edward D. Baker and Ninian W. Edwards represented Emily and John J. Hardin represented the Chinns, Emily was declared a free person. The case attracted a lot of attention, although Jacksonville was already known as a haven for abolitionists prior to the arrival of the Chinns and their two slaves in town.

During that era, most Illinois people regarded abolitionists as a fanatical and unpopular minority, a Yankee creation that was unwanted in a state which had not yet managed to rid itself of the remnants of slavery that still existed in the southern parts of the region. The French settlers still had slaves and indentured servants along the Mississippi River and southern slaves were leased to work the salt mines at the southeastern corner of Illinois. Southern Illinois, with its heavy ties to the South, was still the most populous part of the state, and the average person had little interest in allowing New England extremists to upset the status quo and attack an institution that was legal in the neighboring states of Kentucky and Missouri.

Going along with the majority sentiment, the Illinois legislature adopted resolutions that denounced abolitionism in 1837. Senate action was unanimous. Among six dissenting state representatives, Abraham Lincoln and Daniel Stone later recorded a protest in the official journal. They raised a moral point by condemning slavery as both unjust and bad policy, but they agreed with the majority that the "promulgation of abolition doctrines tends rather to increase than abate the evils." Despite the delay and the backpedaling, their protests showed political courage.

There were other exceptions. Many in the southern counties of the state were descendants of men who had left the South because of their hatred of slavery, either on philosophical grounds or because they could not compete economically with the plantation owners. They had come north because Illinois, after 1824, was the only free state with cheap land. Outnumbered and unorganized, they were a silent abolitionist minority that had only a few reinforcements from New England, like the Yale Band in Jacksonville.

Elijah P. Lovejoy - "Martyr to Freedom"
The Yale Band, or the "Illinois Association," had organized at Yale University on February 21, 1829, to establish a school and preach in Illinois. A short time

Elijah P. Lovejoy

later, they combined their efforts with John M. Ellis, who had planned a seminary of learning in Jacksonville. Julian M. Sturtevant, the Yale Band's advance agent, arrived in Jacksonville on November 15, and began organizing Illinois College, as it came to be known after the first meeting of trustees on December 18. Very soon after, construction began on Beecher Hall, the new college's first building. The college was officially opened on January 4, 1830.

The Yale Band was not alone in its support of the abolitionist movement. The American Colonization Society also had a few branches in Illinois. Its members advocated for slaves to be freed, but then to be returned to a colony in Africa. Others were more radical, stating that slavery should be abolished altogether. Perhaps the most outspoken of these men in Illinois was Elijah P. Lovejoy, a Presbyterian minister and newspaper publisher.

Lovejoy was born in Maine and came west as part of a New England movement to uplift the morality and culture of the newly settled states. In St. Louis, he established a classical high school and then edited a political newspaper that covered many reform causes, but ignored slavery. After five years, he experienced a religious conversion, entered Princeton Theological Seminary and obtained a license as a Presbyterian minister. In 1833, he returned to St. Louis and started a newspaper called the *St. Louis Observer.* In it, he opposed Catholics, Baptists, liquor, and slavery with equal intolerance. He came to believe that slavery was a sin and "must cease to exist." Fanatical and stubborn, often in physical danger, he refused to stop his anti-slavery sermons and editorials. Amid growing hostility Missouri was a slave state, after all , he became an unpopular champion of civil rights, including the right to publish, to speak, to petition, and assemble. Editorials that he wrote denouncing the burning at the stake of a free black man in St. Louis resulted in mob action and damage to his printing press. To protect his wife and infant son, Lovejoy moved across the river to Alton, then the largest and most progressive city in Illinois. When it arrived on the Alton docks on Sunday, the unguarded press was destroyed and dumped into the river.

Alton, like Jacksonville, was then dominated by businessmen from New England and as a progressive and comparatively enlightened city, it competed commercially with St. Louis. During the 1830s, it grew steadily as a steamboat and packing center with commission houses that dealt in beef, pork, lard, whiskey, furs, flour, and lead. Much of the town's business was with southern states, and new laborers who arrived during that decade's boom years displayed a not uncommon hostility toward blacks. Nevertheless, Alton city leaders offered moral and financial support to Lovejoy, who planned to call his newspaper the *Alton Observer*. Even though he was now in a free state, he made it clear that he would practice the freedom of the press and continue to fight for the abolition of slavery. And fight he did, angering local residents and even causing some of his supporters to withdraw because of his intolerance. Even so, many admired the raw courage of a man who several times faced down mobs with plans to tar and feather him - or worse. On August 21, 1837, a mob broke into Lovejoy's newspaper office and destroyed his printing press. Contributions from the east helped pay for a third press, which arrived one month later and was immediately hauled out of a warehouse and dumped into the Mississippi.

In September 1837, Lovejoy and Lyman Beecher attended the Illinois College commencement in Jacksonville. They had come to town to rally support for an abolitionist society that he wanted to form in Alton. Edward Beecher, another New England reformer and president of Illinois College, helped to organize the Illinois Anti-Slavery Society, which met in Alton on October 28. Lovejoy had issued a call, signed by 255 men, including twenty-five from Alton, for the convention. Beecher unwisely broadened the call by inviting any "friends of free discussion." Sympathetic delegates came from Quincy and Galesburg. Elihu Wolcott of Jacksonville was chosen as the society's president and delegates from Morgan County were Beecher, Wolcott, William Carter, Jonathan B. Turner, Elijah Jenney, and A.B. Whitlock. Unfortunately, the meeting was taken over by a group of slavery supporters that included Usher F. Linder, the young and brilliant attorney general of Illinois. Compromises failed and Linder and Cyrus Edwards won majority support for a rejection of Lovejoy's constitutional right to publish his newspaper. He was asked to leave Alton, but he refused. He stated before the room, "You can crush me if you will; but I shall die at my post, for I cannot and will not forsake it. The contest was commenced here; and here it must be finished. Before God and you all, I here pledge myself to continue it, if need be, till death. If I fail, my grave shall be made in Alton."

One of Lovejoy's backers was Winthrop S. Gilman, who along with Benjamin Godfrey, was the owner of a massive warehouse on the Alton riverfront. Lovejoy decided that his fourth printing press should be protected there by an armed force of supporters. It arrived by steamer at 3:00 a.m. on November 7. The next night, a mob gathered and gunfire rang out. A man in the crowd fell mortally wounded. Someone carried a flaming torch up a ladder to set fire to the roof. Lovejoy ran out of the warehouse to stop him and was shot five times, falling to the ground and dying almost immediately. His friends fled and the mob put out the fire and destroyed the printing press.

The murder of Elijah Lovejoy in Alton had a tremendous effect on the Abolitionist movement across America, including in Jacksonville, where he had many supporters.

Lovejoy's murder made headlines across the country, even in the South, where his politics were ignored and he became a martyr to freedom of the press. During the wave of indignation that followed, anti-slavery societies gained new members, but the mob leaders went unpunished and State's Attorney Linder even went to the extreme of trying to prosecute Gilman on a charge of starting a riot. Lovejoy, a failure as a reformer in life, had managed to ignite a movement in death that would lead to a civil war just over two decades later.

The Underground Railroad

In the meantime, as slavery continued, the "Underground Railroad" gained importance. The record of this nocturnal passage that helped slaves escape to freedom in the north, is necessarily vague, but it had terminals in river towns like Quincy, Alton, and Chester. The procedure called for white sympathizers to hide fleeing slaves by day and then spirit them on to the next "station" in darkness. The goal was to reach Canada by way of the upper Illinois River and Chicago where public sentiment refused to permit blacks to be taken into custody and returned to the South.

Helping the slaves involved danger. In 1841, Alanson Work, James E. Burr and George Thompson, arrested in Missouri for attempting to aid escaping slaves, were sentenced to 12 years in prison for grand larceny. Slaves were, of course,

26

another man's property. Evidence of the Underground Railroad exists in court records of scattered incidents like the indictment of Owen Lovejoy, brother of the newspaper publisher, who helped two women escape from slavery in 1843. Dr. Richard Eells of Quincy was arrested that same year for aiding a fugitive. Judge Stephen A. Douglas fined him $400 and Eells later became the president of the Illinois Anti-Slavery Society and in 1844, the candidate for governor of the Liberty Party. In March 1842, Julius Willard and Samuel Willard were indicted in the circuit court for hiding an escaped black woman. Julius was found guilty of the charge and fined $25, but Samuel's case never went to trial.

The murder of Elijah Lovejoy and the presence of the Chinn slaves in Morgan County added fuel to the flames of abolitionism in Jacksonville. Reports say that fugitive slaves were safely passed through the county toward Canada as early as 1823. The Underground Railroad in the area was kept very secret but after the Lovejoy murder and the Logan affair, the abolitionists of Jacksonville became much bolder and very active. The city became an important stop on the Underground Railroad in Illinois with fugitives passing through the area almost continuously until the start of the Civil War. During the 1830s, Elihu Wolcott and Ebenezer Carter were the local leaders of the "railroad" and they were assisted by Dr. M.M.L. Reed, Jonathan Turner, Samuel Adams, T.W. Melendy, D.B. Ayers, Daniel C. Pierson, Benjamin Henderson, Julius Willard, Samuel Willard, John Mathers, J.O. King, Henry Irving, David Spencer and many others, including a number of students from Illinois College.

Occasionally, the abolitionists met with resistance from some elements in Jacksonville. In 1843, Sarah Lisle of Louisiana came to Jacksonville to visit two of her sisters and brought a slave girl with her. When the girl was advised that she was free after coming to Illinois, she went to local abolitionists for help and they attempted to send her off to Canada. Before they could do so, however, she was intercepted by a number of pro-slavery men from the community. They were outraged and rallied a number of other pro-slavery residents to their cause. A public meeting was held and handbills were printed calling for a protest against the conduct of the abolitionists.

The meeting was held on February 23, 1843. A resolution was adopted condemning Julius Willard, Samuel Willard, Ebenezer Carter, Chauncey W. Carter and others for their part in the affair, and they promised in the future to protect the property of their acquaintances in the South. Pro-slavery activists planned to form an Anti-Negro Stealing Society and urge Missouri newspapers to print their resolutions so that slaveholders would know that there was an opposing force at work in Jacksonville.

In the end, the Anti-Negro Stealing Society had little effect on the work being done by local abolitionists, and the Underground Railroad continued to operate in the city and in the surrounding area.

There were a number of homes that were used as "stations" on the Underground Railroad in the city. Many of the fugitive slaves came to Jacksonville from the direction of St. Louis with two free black men, Benjamin Henderson and David Spencer, doing most of the driving. They loaded slaves into a wagon at night and took them as far as they could under the cover of darkness. Escaped slaves could be taken to any of a number of locations, depending on which was the safest at the time.

Dr. Bezaleel Gillett was a staunch abolitionist and one of the founders of the Trinity Church, the first Episcopal Church in Illinois in 1832. He was also an original trustee of the Jacksonville Female Academy, which later merged with Illinois College. He was on the first board of trustees of the Illinois State Hospital for the Insane, and he was also a recognized hero for his tireless efforts serving both rich and poor during the cholera epidemic of 1833. Fugitive slaves were often kept in a large shack that was once located south of his home.

The Asa Talcott home today - once a station on the Underground Railroad

Located on Grove Street was the home of Asa Talcott, an abolitionist and one of the founding members of the Congregational Church. The house was built in parts beginning in 1833 and was added onto in 1844 and 1861. Benjamin Henderson, one of Jacksonville's most important Underground Railroad conductors, stated that Talcott was among those he could count on for help when he needed supplies for the fugitives. Asa Talcott was a brick layer and plasterer, and it was reported that he provided refuge for runaways in his barn. One incident that was recorded occurred in February 1844, when Illinois College students brought a fugitive to Talcott after word spread that he was hiding in Jacksonville. Probably like many other escaped slaves, he was hidden under the hay in Talcott's barn.

Woodlawn Farm

Located about three miles east of Jacksonville was Woodlawn Farm, another prominent local station on the Underground Railroad. The farm was established by the Michael Huffaker family in 1824, and soon began to play a prominent role in the development of modern agricultural practices in the region. Huffaker was also an abolitionist and allowed the farm to serve as a hiding place for fugitive slaves. In addition, he was one of the first Morgan County farmers to employ free blacks. Like many other Underground Railroad sites across the country, Woodlawn Farm has been plagued by rumors of ghosts over the years. Stories passed on by visitors to the site recount eerie sounds, voices in empty rooms, and the overwhelming presence of a man on a staircase in the house. One woman that we interviewed was visiting the farm on a bus tour several years ago and stated that she clearly saw the image of a man looking at her from one of the upper windows of the house. He appeared to be dressed in period clothing and was assumed to be was a re-enactor who was present at the house that day. When she asked about him, she was told that not only was no one upstairs in the house, but that there were no re-enactors working at the farm at that time. She

29

was very clear about what she'd seen, but who the man might have been remains a mystery.

General Benjamin Grierson

Another Underground Railroad station in Jacksonville was the home of Benjamin Grierson on East State Street. Grierson was born in July 1826 in Allegheny, Pennsylvania, today a section of Pittsburgh. He was the youngest of five siblings. Grierson became afraid of horses when at age eight he was kicked and nearly killed by a horse. After that, he hated horses, although, ironically, he would become a great Cavalry commander. In 1851, Grierson came west and settled down to become a music teacher and band leader in Jacksonville. In the mid-1850s, Grierson joined the new Republican Party and became friends with one of its leaders, Abraham Lincoln. In 1860, Grierson wrote the campaign music for Lincoln's first presidential campaign, but before that he worked as an abolitionist and conductor on the Underground Railroad. His brick home on East State Street was used as a hiding place for slaves. The house has been greatly expanded today, but the original "station" remains incorporated into the newer structure.

The Grierson House, although not alleged to be haunted, is connected to a ghost story of some endurance, which began in Jacksonville with his marriage to Alice Kirk and the birth of one of their daughters, Edith.

At the start of the Civil War, Grierson enlisted as a volunteer aide-de-camp to Major General Benjamin M. Prentiss. Promoted to major on October 24, 1861, he joined the 6th Illinois Cavalry and was promoted to colonel of that regiment on April 13, 1862. His regiment was engaged in a number of small skirmishes and raids on railroads and facilities in Tennessee and Mississippi that spring and summer. In November, he became a brigade commander in the Cavalry Division of the Army of Tennessee. In December, he participated in the pursuit of Confederate Earl Van Dorn after his Holly Springs raid against the supply lines of General Ulysses S. Grant.

In the spring of 1863, he led Grierson's Raid, a major diversionary thrust deep into the Confederacy, ordered by Grant as part of his Vicksburg Campaign. Over seventeen days, his command marched 800 miles, repeatedly engaged the Confederates, disabled two railroads, captured many prisoners and horses, and destroyed vast amounts of property, finally ending in Baton Rouge on May 2.

General Benjamin Grierson

His raid demoralized the region and diverted the attention of the Confederate defenders of Vicksburg away from General Grant's main attack. General William T. Sherman considered Grierson's raid "the most brilliant expedition of the war." He was promoted to brigadier general of volunteers in June.

Grierson continued his service with the cavalry, battling Nathan B. Forrest's Confederates and leading an attack on the Mobile and Ohio Railroad that resulted in the capture of more than 500 enemy troops. For this expedition Grierson received a brevet promotion to the rank of major general. In the spring of 1865, he took part in the successful campaign to capture Mobile, Alabama.

After the war ended, Grierson decided to remain with the Army and received the rank of colonel. He organized the 10th U.S. Cavalry, one of two mounted regiments composed of black enlisted men and white officers, called the "Buffalo Soldiers." This assignment also made him unpopular with other officers, including his superior, General Philip Henry Sheridan, because of his support for and trust in his troops. His sympathy and courtesy to Native American tribes also led to questions about his judgment.

In spite of this, he later became commander of Fort Concho in San Angelo, Texas, which is where our ghost story has its roots. Fort Concho was built in 1867 to protect settlers and the transportation routes between a chain of forts that stretched across the heartland of Texas. The soldiers stationed at the post frequently battled Comanche and Kiowa Indians until it was abandoned in 1889. The fort has since been designated a national historic landmark. History remains at Fort Concho - and so do the spirits of the past.

One such spirit haunts the officer's quarters at the fort, an area known as "Officer's Row." Located across the parade ground from the enlisted barracks, this row of sturdy stone houses serves as the impetus for most, if not all, of the ghostly tales that are told about the fort.

One of the most distinguished families to occupy the "Row" was that of Colonel Benjamin Grierson. Colonel Grierson's daughter, Edith, died in an upstairs bedroom of Officers' Quarters Number 1 on Sept. 9, 1878, shortly after her thirteenth birthday. Edith was a lively girl who enjoyed riding her pony and going to the dances in the mess hall. She lived at Fort Concho for three years, writing frequently to friends and relatives back home in Jacksonville about regimental life on the frontier, until falling ill from typhoid fever. After thirteen agony-filled days, she succumbed to the illness.

Edith's body was buried with military honors in the fort's graveyard. In the 1930s, the graves were exhumed to make way for city expansion. Edith's body was reburied in San Angelo's Fairmount Cemetery, in the Samuel Smith family plot. Despite the location of her mortal remains, it is said that her spirit never left the house. Over the years, many people have encountered her. In most cases,

Edith Grierson

she is seen quietly playing jacks. Those who have met this spectral girl say that the first thing they notice is that the room where she is playing is substantially cooler than any of the other rooms in the house. Edith is reported to acknowledge the presence of people when they enter the room by turning her head and smiling at them before she turns her attention back to her game of jacks, but she will rarely speak.

One day in the mid-1990s, B.D. Shaffer, a delivery driver who worked for a local florist, dropped off some flowers to the former Grierson home for a reception that was going to be held there. He had been instructed to place two arrangements of flowers in the bedrooms at the top of the stairs, one to the right and one to the left. Reaching the top of the stairs, Shaffer turned and entered the first bedroom on the right. He dropped off the flowers and crossed the hall. From the corner of his eye, as he entered the opposite bedroom, he saw a young girl sitting on the floor of the room he had just left. She looked very real and solid, but as Shaffer turned towards her, she faded away.

The next day, Shaffer had to go to a house at Lake Nasworthy to pick up some artificial flower arrangements. The lady of the house and her husband had been responsible for the restoration of Officers Quarters Number 1 at Fort Concho, the house where Shaffer had his encounter with the ghost. When he told her about his experience in the upstairs bedroom, she said the girl he had seen was Edith Grierson, and she had died in that room.

The following December, Shaffer returned to Officers' Quarters Number 1 for a Christmas event. The docent, upon hearing about his encounter with the ghost of a little girl, took him into another room and showed him a photograph of Edith Grierson. It was the girl he had seen.

Edith Grierson, a young girl from Jacksonville, has never left Fort Concho.

The Railroads Came to Jacksonville

One of the most exciting moments in Jacksonville's history was the arrival of the first steam train on January 1, 1840. It roared into the downtown square with nearly every resident of Morgan County assembled to greet it.

Plans began for a railroad into Jacksonville in 1837. The Northern Cross Railroad, one of the first railroads to use steam power west of the Allegheny

Mountains, was part of what was known as the Internal Improvement Act, passed by the Illinois legislature in February 1837. Nearly everything about the plans for the railroad were politically motivated. Murray McConnel, Jacksonville's first lawyer, was named commissioner of public works, and his job was to oversee the railroad and report its progress back to the state. The contracts for the construction of the Northern Cross were awarded in July 1837 to Myron Leslie, James Dunlap, Thomas T. January, and Charles Collins - all friends of McConnel. Their bid for 57 miles of work was $8,000 and work began on August 1.

McConnel not only pushed through the bid that was offered by his friends, he also made sure that the railroad's route was to the advantage of himself and his allies. The route was planned to pass over lands owned by Joseph Duncan and other close friends, as well as his own property north of Jacksonville.

It was while the grading was being done that many people in town began to question the route of the railroad through the Jacksonville area. Protests were launched and letters were written stating that the route would best benefit the town if the rails ran through the middle of Jacksonville, along West State Street, across the public square and out East State Street. Public meetings were held. Letters were exchanged between McConnel and a committee of merchants and citizens. Accusations were made and bitter tirades were launched from both sides. Finally, the trustees of Jacksonville resolved "that no railroad can be built in Jacksonville unless it ran through the public square and along State Street."

McConnel was sharp in his reply: "You are totally ignorant of the effect of running the road here or there, but I have studied the problem more than you have and much prefer to have trains clattering through the public square, some hundred yards away from my home, than close under my windows." And with that, the rail line was moved away from McConnel's land and swerved south to

33

meet West State Street about 200 feet west of Church Street. The downtown square, the very heart of the city, filled with businesses, offices and homes, would now be linked by both road and rail to the outside world.

On the first day of January 1840, the first steam train arrived. The downtown square was filled with people and horses. When the engine came steaming into the square, making a deafening racket, there was a sudden stampede of horses. Nearly every team broke loose, dragging wagons behind them. Accounts from the time say that a third of the vehicles in the county were broken and that, "many of the people were as scared as the horses at the steaming monster as it came rushing into the square."

The arrival of rail service did not immediately speed up the journey to Jacksonville. Almost as soon as the railroad went into operation, the effects of the national depression that started in late 1837 began to show. The state was practically bankrupt by then, and on February 1, 1840, it suspended all public works, including work on the Northern Cross. The result was that Jacksonville now had a railroad that ran from Meredosia to the center of the square and stopped. For more than two years, the only direction by train out of Jacksonville was west.

Led by John Henry of Jacksonville, the legislature finally allocated enough money to complete the railroad to Springfield. Regular service was established between Jacksonville and Springfield on March 28, 1842. The state now had a completed railroad, but no money to maintain it. The line foundered until February 1847, when it was decided to sell the Northern Cross Railroad to the highest bidder. The legislature also directed that the location of the line through Jacksonville be moved back to the north side of town, as it was originally surveyed.

The railroad was auctioned off on the steps of the courthouse in Springfield for $21,000. The winning bid came from Nicholas Ridgely for a company composed of himself, James Dunlap, Colonel T. Mathers and ex-Governor Joel Matteson. The entire railroad had cost the state more than three-quarters of a million dollars.

The name of the line was changed with the purchase. The Northern Cross soon became known as the Sangamon & Morgan Railroad Co. In addition to moving the route to the north, a better track was laid, repairs were made, and the route was changed at Bluff City to run to Naples rather than to Meredosia.

The first railroad into Jacksonville faded into history, but it was not the last line to come to town. Another railroad line, the Great Western, which became the Wabash, came through Jacksonville and had a station on North Church Street. Many famous people rode that line, including Abraham Lincoln, Stephen Douglas,

The old Chicago & Alton Railroad depot in Jacksonville

and Theodore Roosevelt. Entertainers often made their way into town by rail, including scores of circuses and Buffalo Bill Cody's Wild West Show, which came to Jacksonville several times in the 1890s.

By the early 1900s, there were 28 passenger trains coming in and out of Jacksonville on a daily basis, with 20 trains on Sunday. It was said that you could reach anywhere in the United States from Jacksonville by train during that era. The last passenger train came to town in 1960.

Besides passengers, the trains also carried coal, grain and livestock, and the Wabash used refrigerated cars to bring produce from the West Coast to the East.

Jacksonville was also home to car shops owned by the Chicago, Peoria & St. Louis Railroad, which also had lines going through town. The car shops, which employed as many as 400 people at one point, built and repaired freight and passenger cars. There is nothing left of them today.

Over the years, the railroads have faded across America and in Jacksonville. The only lingering reminder in Jacksonville is the old Chicago & Alton Railroad passenger station that was built back in 1910. It still stands today as Lonzerotti's Italian Restaurant -- and as a monument to the past.

Opening Jacksonville to the World

Traveling to Jacksonville from Springfield today requires no more than 30 minutes in an automobile. In 1800, traveling by wagon, it took all day, from sunrise to sunset. In the 1840s, a train trip took about two hours, provided that the train did not have to stop for fuel or water, which usually required the passengers to hike into the forest for firewood or to the nearest creek for buckets of water.

As mentioned, trains were essential for Jacksonville's growth. They brought passengers, mail and goods and supplies for customers and merchants in town. They also brought delays, smoke, steam, noise, and confused horses. It's no wonder that locals let out a sigh of relief when the trains were rerouted a bit outside of town in 1847.

Traveling about in Jacksonville was done by horse for nearly a century of its existence. Riders on horseback or in carriages, buggies, and wagons were a common sight. Horse-drawn trolleys were also used for many years, and they were later replaced by electric streetcars and early automobiles. In the early 1900s, chaos reigned on the streets of Jacksonville when cars, horse and buggies, trolleys, and pedestrians all navigated the streets with no stop signs, turn signals or right-of-way. Somehow, though, they managed, even on rainy days, when the unpaved streets were turned into a morass of wet, sucking mud.

In 1867, the Street Railway Company was incorporated by Felix Farrell; with the first track laid out on South Main Street. Soon, more track was laid on East State, West State, and North Main. It was taken over by the Hook Company in 1887, and in 1891, they switched to all electric cars. This method of public transportation eased the congestion in the streets and made it easier for everyone to reach the downtown business district.

Even the horse-drawn trolleys were superior to walking downtown on foot. Although since the tracks were laid on dirt streets, they worked much better on sunny days than in the rain. Electric trolleys ran until the development of improved automobiles, whose ability to go anywhere without being restricted to tracks foretold both the demise of the streetcars and the expansion of the city away from downtown.

An early automobile parked in front of Cassell's Cigar Store in downtown Jacksonville.

As automobiles began to become more popular in the early part of the twentieth century, Jacksonville residents eagerly embraced the new-fangled machines. With their popularity came the demand for better roads. Dirt roads were the worst in February and March when the winter thawed and automobiles were simply unable to navigate them. Paving Jacksonville was an expensive but necessary endeavor. In 1913, at a Good Roads meeting, a supporter of the project stated, "Good roads will now increase wealth, happiness, education, religion, civilization, and morality." But not everyone in Jacksonville agreed. Automobiles were often denounced from local church pulpits as a "new tool of the devil" because parishioners often took Sunday joy-rides instead of attending church services. But it was too late to turn back. The automobile soon became an integral part of Jacksonville - and an important way to bring people into the city.

Automobiles could also take residents to other places, including many places they had never been before. Many locals were excited to see the state capital of Springfield for the first time. In 1921, O.M. Olsen, who had moved to Jacksonville to be near his son at the School for the Deaf, started the bus and began making the trip two times each day. It was not quick. He stopped several times to pick up passengers at hotels along the way, but it was a reliable service in the days when not everyone had a car and could not afford the train fare.

The roads were being paved in Jacksonville at the same time that new roads were also being built in other parts of Central Illinois. Eventually, what we consider to be old Route 36 linked the city to other towns, both east and west. In the 1960s, new development began on what would become Interstate 72, an expressway that now connects Indiana to Missouri and links Danville, Champaign, Decatur, Springfield, Jacksonville, and Quincy. The new interstate would be vitally important for traffic flowing east and west, but it also bypassed many towns that had once depended on travelers passing through to spend money locally.

Regardless, planners saw it as a way to attract new business and the first studies for the expressway were started in 1963. Officials in Jacksonville stated that the new road would take the city "out of the boondocks and put you on a highway to the east and west. We're no longer a wide spot on the road; we're a community that has access to the interstate."

On November 15, 1976, Governor Dan Walker officially opened 89 miles of the expressway to traffic. With this opening, which included 27 miles from Jacksonville to Springfield, motorists could drive an uninterrupted, four-lane freeway from the Illinois-Indiana border to Jacksonville. The final segment of the highway was completed in the fall of 1991, and it was officially designated as a federal interstate four years later.

Jacksonville was finally linked to the entire world.

Haunted Jacksonville

2. GHOSTS OF BUSINESS PAST

The rich farmland, booming railroads, and Jacksonville's central location worked as a successful combination for businesses starting in the 1850s. Small stores, taverns, and mercantile shops had been located in the city since the earliest days, but wheat, pork and a highly profitable cattle trade, led by Jacob Strawn, filled the railroad cars heading out of town. Other railroad cars returned with both the necessities and luxuries of life. Around the agricultural products, related businesses took root. A slaughterhouse and a tannery became a part of the cattle industry. The Capps Woolen Mills were a sensible addition to raising sheep. Specialty stores began replacing general stores and cash began to replace the barter system and buying with credit.

One of the greatest challenges to Jacksonville business was the availability of water. A plan in 1868 to develop a waterworks proved to be too costly. Nearly a century later, in 1955, water was still an issue, and an expensive plan to bring water from the Illinois River became a reality. The costly project, built with no state or federal funds, guaranteed a water supply and did manage to bring new industry into the city.

The Jacksonville Square

Business in Jacksonville began in the downtown square, but today, it is a shadow of its former self. As the reader will discover in the pages ahead,

Jacksonville's downtown was a thriving shopping district, dating back to the earliest days of the city. During the heyday of the square, it was dominated by smaller, family-owned stores and businesses, offering anything a customer could possibly want. Through the 1950s, there was rarely a single empty storefront on the square, but all of that soon changed when Highway 36 bypassed from College Avenue and moved the flow of traffic away from downtown to Morton Avenue.

Once local businessmen learned that the bypass would be built on Morton Avenue, it didn't take them long to figure out where the best commercial spots in the city would be located, even though Morton Avenue was just an oil street at that time. Howard "Bud" Walker, who owned the Lincoln Square Shopping Center with partners Martin Newman, J.R. "Junior" Davidsmeyer and Paul Pieper, had a used car lot on Morton Avenue as early as 1956. He moved Walker Motor Co. from North Main to Morton Avenue in 1960. The Jacksonville bypass was much like other bypasses in towns across the country and, as in those communities, it turned the downtown square into a "relic."

The property where Lincoln Square would come to be located was once owned by Ralph and Bill Cruzan, who ran Cruzan Brothers Nursery for many years. They sold the property to Jacob Frohmann of St. Louis, who developed the shopping center. The first store to open was J.C. Penney Co., which moved from downtown to the southeast corner of the shopping center in 1963. At that time, there were no buildings on the east side of the center; it was a parking lot. And parking was one of the conveniences that led people to shop at Lincoln Square rather than downtown. Shoppers could park close to the store and not have to cross the street. The new stores also stayed open later than downtown businesses.

In 1967, the shopping center was sold to Walker, Newman, Davidsmeyer and Pieper, who held onto it until the 1980s, when it was sold to a Chicago company. It remains a centerpiece of the many businesses now found along Morton Avenue - the street that marked the beginning of the end of downtown.

But Morton Avenue was not what nearly killed the downtown square - the city government bears a big responsibility. When businesses started moving out to Morton Avenue, the city of Jacksonville reacted by trying to save the historic downtown with an "urban renewal" program. The decision to change the downtown in the late 1960s changed the city forever. Money was allocated to towns around the country who were trying to rehabilitate their downtowns. By the time the program started in the 1960s, many downtown Jacksonville businesses had already folded or moved elsewhere.

The idea behind the program was that, if you gave the downtown a makeover, businesses would return and the downtown square would become a business center again. Unfortunately, though, things didn't work out that way. There were a number of factors that crippled Jacksonville's plans. There were many forces at work, such as social and economic ones, that encouraged businesses to move to Morton Avenue, but the program itself had its flaws.

The two things that really hurt the whole idea of urban renewal involved access to the buildings. First, the placing of quadrant buildings in the square made it impossible for people driving by to see the storefronts. Second, placing parking lots behind the buildings also hid the storefronts from potential customers. The original idea had people parking behind a business and entering through a back door, but the idea didn't catch on. People simply wanted to see the front of the store.

But the biggest - and most unpopular problem - was the decision to stop traffic from going around the square. The plan was to turn the square into a kind of outdoor shopping mall, and stopping the traffic flow was approved under interesting circumstances.

The city advertised as far away as Chicago, St. Louis, and Indianapolis for an urban renewal contractor. But the only person to step forward for the job was Paul Pieper of Jacksonville, one of the partners in the Lincoln Square development. The original plans for urban renewal called for cutting off the traffic around the square and the construction of "quadrant buildings," large,

41

cheap, squared-off buildings that effectively cut off all traffic. Several city aldermen had reservations about changing the traffic pattern and wanted to go ahead with the project without the quadrant buildings. But Pieper made it clear that he wouldn't take on the project without the quadrant buildings and, by default, a different traffic flow. Because Pieper was the only contractor willing to take on the job, the plan went ahead. He made a lot of money from the construction of the buildings, but even critics of the plan agreed that it was done as an honest decision to help Jacksonville's downtown. Instead, the well-intentioned plan had dire results.

Instead of saving downtown, the plan literally destroyed it. There were 63 buildings demolished as part of the urban renewal program. Plans were made to try and get a large "anchor" store like Kmart to move to the square, but to no avail. The only large stores that remained for a time were True Value and Gillespie's, both of which have long since closed - along with most of the other stores that existed at that time.

Today, while it's unlikely that Jacksonville's downtown will ever rival Morton Avenue as a shopping center, many smaller specialty stores, boutiques, restaurants, coffee shops, and taverns have moved in to fill the gaps created by the migration of decades past. And finally, after a reversal of the poorly planned "urban renewal" of the 1970s, the Jacksonville square is open again and is now considered one of the finest downtown squares in the state.

The hustle and bustle that marked the "heyday" of the downtown square may have passed, but new life has been breathed into this historic part of the city - where denizens of the past still linger behind in rather large numbers.

Jacksonville Business

Business in Jacksonville was born from the land. The earliest settlers were farmers who eked a living from the rich soil of Central Illinois. Thanks to this, most of the business conducted in the area was to supply the farms and the

families who lived on them. The entire town was based around agriculture and most of the residents had more than a passing interest in it.

Jonathan B. Turner, one of the early professors at Illinois College, was a well-known horticulturist and agriculturist. From a stand of seedlings near Webster Avenue, he promoted, developed and sold Osage orange bushes that could be used as fencing by farmers before the invention of barbed wire. The plant was a thorny type of mulberry that withstood the efforts of livestock that tried to pass through it.

Turner's interest in farming was even apparent at his home, which boasted hedge fields, vegetable and flower gardens, and orchards. A grass walk four feet wide extended from the house on College Avenue to State Street. On either side were flower beds of the same width, filled with every variety and color of tulips, hyacinths, crown imperials, jonquils, daffodils and narcissus. Behind them were roses and all kinds of shrubs, with apple, peach, pear, and small-fruit orchards and vineyards. He also kept a large melon patch, which was the delight of children in the neighborhood. Nighttime raids on the patch became so frequent that Professor Turner's older sons often hid in the darkness with shotguns loaded with salt to fire at the legs of trespassers.

A number of city landowners had large farms, either within the city limits or outside of town, with the owners living in Jacksonville. Jacob Strawn, whose family helped found the Strawn Opera House and the Strawn Art Gallery, was a farmer and livestock producer. He owned about 20,000 acres in the Jacksonville area and became extremely wealthy as he continuously sold land and cattle.

Many businesses in town, especially retail stores, were directly tied to income from farmers. As farming ceased to dominate the local economy, its control over the business community started to fade. There were also two grain elevators at one time, but they closed with the loss of large livestock business in the region.

A good example of how that happened can be seen in one of the most successful retail farm equipment companies in Jacksonville. When local residents needed a new buggy or carriage or a new piece of farm equipment in the 1850s, the place to go was John W. Hall's buggy shop. By the time that it closed down

43

in 1969, the Hall Bros. Implement Co. was the oldest continuously running John Deere dealership in America.

John W. Hall was one of a number of British immigrants that came to Jacksonville in the first half of the nineteenth century. In 1850, he and his partner, Elias Keener, established a business that manufactured and sold buggies, wagons, and carriages. In 1856, the partnership ended and Hall went into business with William Guy, setting up a store on College Avenue, between South Main and South Sandy Streets. It remained in the same location for the next 100 years. On January 1, 1864, Hall bought out his partner and renamed the business Hall & Sons in 1890. Although it was a buggy and carriage store, they also sold farm machinery. Not long before the original store opened, John Deere had invented the first plow and the Hall store began selling them, long before there were any established implement dealers around.

After John Hall passed away in 1899, his two sons, William and Harry, took over and changed the name to Hall Bros. They expanded and by the time of both of their deaths in 1936, the company had stores in Chapin, Franklin, Murrayville and, of course, the main store in Jacksonville. The brothers continued their association with John Deere and were local innovators when it came to advertising. They had metal signs printed and convinced local farmers to nail them up on fence posts all around the area. Every farmer recognized them and few did business with anyone other than Hall Bros.

Oddly, though, if John W. Hall had not insisted that his son Harry take over the family business, the younger Hall might have been instrumental in the founding of the Ford Motor Co. Back in the 1890s, Harry was well-known around Jacksonville for an invention that he had dreamed up. He'd taken a motor and attached it to one of the carriages from his father's store and drove it around town. After his contraption had been seen driving up the local streets for a while, he received a letter from a man named Henry Ford, who had heard about the motorized carriage. At the time, Ford was working on a prototype for what would become one of his first automobiles. Ford asked Harry to bring the motorized

carriage to Michigan and come to work for him. But John Hall refused to let him go. He didn't believe there was a future for mechanical engines that did little more than scare horses. Hall sent his son to work for Cyrus McCormick for two summers instead, believing that farm machinery was a more practical use for his son's talents. During that time, McCormick invented the binder, which helped revolutionize the farm industry. After that, Harry returned to Jacksonville, worked in the family business and then took over the store with his brother after John passed away. We'll never know if he regretted not answering Henry Ford's letter.

Harry Lee Hall, Harry's son, took over the business after his father's and uncle's deaths and changed with the times. The business became a full-line implement dealer, selling farm machinery and tools. It was a massive place, filled with every type of tool imaginable, with an elevator that went up to the third and fourth floors.

Harry Lee retired in 1969, and the business ended with his retirement. By that time, the business had changed so much that, even though he loved it, he encouraged his family not to continue it. The John Deere company had control over the dealerships by the late 1960s, stating how many tractors they could sell each year, for instance. In years past, if the store needed tractors, they ordered them, but in time, the company would send a specific number to Hall Bros. and that would be all they were allowed to sell. The company looked at the store's previous year's sales and, based on that figure, would determine the number of tractors slotted for the dealership. Big business had ended the glory days of the Jacksonville store, and like the boom years of the American farmer, its history has faded away with time.

But Hall Bros. was not the only farm implement store in Jacksonville in the late nineteenth century, and they were not the only makers of carriages and buggies, which were always in high demand. Among the other companies were

45

W.S. Richards, Samuel Cobb, Vogel & Co., Day & Dunavan, Phillip Lee and many others.

There were companies like J.L. Padgett's that made shirts and C.H. Dunbrack that made men's suits on a large scale. They hired salesman to go out on the road and sell suits from Iowa to Texas, their advertising stated. E. Hamilton & Sons made fine candies and confectionaries of all kinds. There were a number of companies that made cigars, including B. Pyatt & Sons, Romerman on West State Street and Myers and Knollenberg, which sold over 400,000 cigars in 1874. Several companies milled flour, like E.C. Kreider, Scott & Hackett, Schoonover, and White & Shuff. There were also paper makers, coopers barrel-makers , boot and shoe makers, harness makers, upholsterers, collar makers, and bottling establishments where soda pop, beer, ale and cider were packaged.

Indian Blankets for Indians

One of the Jacksonville companies to receive the most notoriety in the late 1800s and early 1900s was J. Capps & Sons Ltd. By the time it closed down in the mid-1970s, it was the oldest manufacturer in Morgan County and the oldest manufacturer in its line of business in America. It was founded by Joseph Capps, a Kentucky man who moved to Waverly in 1837, where he formed a partnership to card wool. He moved to Jacksonville in 1839, purchased land on the east side of North Church Street between Douglas and Lafayette Avenues, and constructed a building for his machinery and equipment.

His first business was wool carding, a method of gathering wool, cotton, flax and hair lengthwise into rolls of strands, which could then be spun into yarn and made into rough cloth. The yarn could also be used to make sweaters, mittens, and stockings. The first carding machine was powered by oxen walking on a treadmill. Farmers would bring their wool to the plant to be carded and payment for the process was made by either leaving some of the carded wool behind or by bartering with whatever they had of value, like butter, milk, eggs, or meat. A year or so later, spinning equipment was added for spinning wool that had been

46

Jacksonville's J. Capps & Sons' Mill changed from a carding operation to spinning and weaving and then began producing finished blankets, clothing, and uniforms.

received as payment for carding. Farmers soon started to sell their raw wool and purchased the finished yarn.

The carding and spinning business flourished, and in 1852, looms and weaving machinery were added and the manufacture of the company's first rough, unfinished cloth began. For the most part, this meant the making of wool blankets, although they also made some flannel and women's dress material.

In 1857, Capps took his son, Stephen, into the business and the mill then began making blankets and expanded their manufacture of flannel, skirting, cloaks and women's dress goods. In 1862, William E. Capps, the second son, was also made a partner and the company became known as Jacksonville Woolen Mills. They produced blankets for Union troops during the Civil War, and by 1878, the mill was producing 3,000 yards of cloth each day and employing 75 workers. In 1885, they began making men's trousers, hired 25 more workers and had annual sales that exceeded $200,000. J. Capps & Sons manufactured the uniforms for the Army during the Spanish-American War and for World War I. In three weeks, the factory turned out 8,000 uniforms for the forces that invaded Cuba. During World War II, they manufactured the famous Navy pea jacket.

It was in the 1890s and early 1900s, though, that the Jacksonville company achieved its national fame. During this time, they developed an extensive business making Indian blankets. The production and sale of these top-quality blankets made a fortune for J. Capps and Sons. Even the legendary William "Buffalo Bill" Cody endorsed their blankets. In a letter that he wrote to the company in 1911, he stated, "I am very pleased to say, that for characteristic

47

As part of his traveling Wild West show, Buffalo Bill Cody came to Jacksonville and toured the J. Capps Mill. He later gave a printed endorsement for their high quality Indian blankets.

Indian designs, beauty and brilliancy of color, and for quality, the 'Capps Indian Blanket' is superior to any blanket that I am acquainted with, made for the Indian trade. Cody even visited the factory in Jacksonville, further praising the blankets.

Capps capitalized on the early twentieth century fascination with the fading glory of the Old West and the American Indian. At first, in the 1890s, Capps made the blankets only for Native Americans in the western states. They not only used the blankets themselves, but built up a profitable trade on the reservations by reselling them. Tourists sought out the blankets that were "genuine" since they had the Capps label in the corner.

The Capps Indian blankets came in 22 designs and in more than 200 color combinations. They were made from 100 percent pure fleece wool and in 1911, sold for $7.50, not a small sum in those days. Each of the designs was distinguished by the name of a Native American tribe, even though the patterns really had nothing to do with the tribes they were named for.

Capps & Sons stopped making Indian blankets during World War I, when the factory's machinery was turned to the production of army blankets, trousers and other products for the war effort. But even during the short time they were being made, the blankets left their mark on the history of the American West.

After World War I, the company faced a changing world. Due to the inability to secure competent and experienced weavers and dyers and the mill machinery becoming obsolete, the woolen mill division was shut down in 1927. But the company continued making clothing. Capps even used local Jacksonville names to designate its product lines. One of the popular lines of men's clothing, favored by the college crowd, was "Beecher Hall," named for the oldest building on the Illinois College campus. A popular line of men's suits was called "Duncan Park," named for the park where Governor Duncan's home now stands.

In the 1970s, foreign-manufactured clothing from Hong Kong, India, and Central America began flooding the stores. Synthetic and non-union garments were cheap to make and sell. The entire clothing industry, including Capps, was damaged. In 1974, the company decided to get out of the fine clothing business and make "soft body armor" instead. The soft body armor, bullet-and knife-proof vests, were soft and flexible when compared to the lead-lined vests that were then available. Prototypes developed by the company drew great interest from military and law enforcement agencies all over the world. Sadly, though, the armor never got past the development stage. The firm's lack of resources prevented it from accepting any actual orders.

The company closed down in the mid-1970s after being forced into bankruptcy. About 230 workers, mostly from Jacksonville, lost their jobs. The old mill vanished when the land was sold in 1977, and a fascinating part of our local history was lost forever.

Inventing the Wheel

The Eli Bridge Company has been in business for well over a century. In all of those years, it has built only one bridge - and it's not much of a bridge. Located in White Hall, in Greene County, the bridge is a relatively innocuous concrete structure that crosses a small creek. So, how does a bridge company stay in business if it only builds one bridge every 100 years? The answer to that is the story of the most famous company to ever exist in the city of Jacksonville.

William E. Sullivan was born in 1861 in the small town of Roodhouse. His career of choice was farming, although he always had an aptitude for mechanical devices. In the 1880s, he decided to start a bridge company, but it wasn't long before he came to realize that bridges were simply not in his future. It was a visit to the 1893 World's Columbian Exposition in Chicago that not only changed Sullivan's life, but gave Jacksonville a permanent commercial symbol and altered the amusement business in America forever.

It was Sullivan's failure as a bridge builder that led to his trip to Chicago. In order to feed his family, he took a job as a hardware salesman. While in the Windy City in 1893, he paid a visit to the World's Fair and became captivated by the exposition's featured attraction - the Ferris Wheel. Everything about the amazing contraption fascinated him. When he asked for permission to examine it, he was told that if he bought a ticket to ride it, he could look at it all that he wanted. He gladly spent the money, and for hours, he studied the structure, its driving mechanism, the suspension, the giant axle and every other feature. He rode in the passenger cars and absorbed every detail.

The Ferris Wheel was Chicago's answer to the Eiffel Tower, which had been erected for the World's Fair in Paris three years earlier. The giant, rotating wheel of steel that would become a staple for amusement parks everywhere was named for its inventor, George Washington Gale Ferris, a bridge-builder from Galesburg, Illinois. Ferris was always considered to be somewhat of a dreamer. For some reason, as a young boy, the movement of water wheels had fascinated him. Possessing an uncanny mechanical ability, Ferris graduated from a polytechnic institute as a tunnel and trestle builder. He designed and built bridges and also formed a company that experimented with new uses for structural steel.

From the beginning, Ferris knew what design his wheel would have and what it would take to get it built. He was not without his critics, however, as many engineers of the day claimed that the plans for the giant wheel were foolish and impossible. But Ferris persisted. He acquired the financial backing for his design and sold the idea to the planners of the Columbian Exposition. In his mind, it would rival anything that had ever been seen before. And he was right - it truly was the first of its kind.

Nine steel mills were needed to produce the 2,200 tons of metal needed for the giant wheel. Five factories were recruited to forge the many different parts and 175 freight cars were used to haul the parts to the fairgrounds on Chicago's South Side. Four huge towers, anchored in 35 feet of concrete supported the massive axle. When it was completed, the wheel was 264 feet in height, 250 feet in diameter, and 825 feet in circumference. The axle was the largest piece of forged steel in the world at that time, weighing 142,031 pounds. This was heavier than anything that had ever been lifted before. The Ferris Wheel held 36 wooden cars the size of small railroad coaches, each capable of holding sixty people.

The contraption looked very fragile and extremely dangerous. A similar project could never exist today because no company would dream of insuring it. But during each day of the fair, thrill-seekers paid 50 cents each to climb into the cars and soar for 22 minutes above the city. Rumors spread about suicides, but the company denied these allegations. The cars had barred windows to keep people from jumping out, although some passengers discovered their fear of heights a little too late. One man panicked and hurled himself against the bars with such force that he shattered the glass and bent the iron bars. He pushed away everyone who tried to hold him back until a woman to the mixed shock and delight of onlookers lifted her skirt and placed it over the man's head until he calmed down. It was a method that worked with panicked horses and it worked equally well with a panicked human. Needless to say, the man was quickly subdued.

The Wheel was the Exposition's most popular attraction. It was dismantled at fair's end and then rebuilt in St. Louis for the 1904 World's Fair. Unfortunately for Ferris, his subsequent efforts to make the great wheel profitable proved unsuccessful and he died penniless a few years later. In 1906, the first Ferris Wheel was scrapped and portions of it were buried in Forest Park, the St. Louis fairgrounds.

But Ferris' great wheel achieved one thing - it proved an inspiration to William Sullivan. When he returned home to Roodhouse, he told his wife, Julia, that he was going to design and build a portable Ferris Wheel, that is, a wheel that could be dismantled and moved about from fair to fair. Julia believed in his dream. She knew he could build it, but when he did - what would he do with it?

Sullivan had a few years to ponder this question. In the late 1890s, he moved his family to Jacksonville and he set to work on his project. He finished his first wheel on May 12, 1900. It stood 45 feet high and 12 buggy seats for passengers. It was powered by a small gasoline engine and was held together by 521 bolts. It was portable, but it required six men a full day to erect it.

The original Big Eli in 1900

Sullivan received a permit from the city of Jacksonville to operate his wheel and he premiered his creation in Central Park on May 23, 1900. He charged five cents per ride and made $5.56 that day. He wrote about it in his diary but he never explained how he made the extra cent. Legend has it that a child wanted a ride and Sullivan gave it to him for a penny.

A short time later, Sullivan and his friend, J.H. Clements, took the wheel out of town for the first time. They set it up on a sandy street in Beardstown and ran it for a week during the Independence Day celebration. It was a great success, and soon Sullivan began making plans to mass produce the wheels. The only problem was that he had no money with which to do it. So, in 1905, he felt it was necessary to accept stockholders, although few of them felt the wheels would have much of a future. So it was agreed - despite Sullivan's belief in his wheels - the new company would be named to reflect bridge building so that they could avoid the embarrassment of changing the name later when they had to start making bridges instead of portable Ferris Wheels. In 1906, the Eli Bridge Co. was incorporated.

Sullivan chose the name that he had used for his short-lived bridge building company of the late 1800s, but where the name came from has been speculated about ever since. For some reason, Sullivan liked using the phrase, "Get there, Eli!" - a popular expression of the time that meant something like, "hurry up and get it done!" Another possibility is that he chose the name in homage to fellow inventor Eli Whitney. No one knows for sure, but the result was the unique name for a plant that makes Ferris Wheels, or as the company refers to them, Big Eli Wheels.

Sullivan ordered all of the material, made blueprints, attended to correspondence, and wrote the advertising and contracts at his small factory in Roodhouse. This work was mostly done at night or early in the morning so that he could spend most of the day helping his one employee build the first factory-produced wheel. That wheel was sold to C.W. Parker of Sedalia, Missouri for $2,300 in 1906.

As the Eli Bridge Co. grew, the plant in Roodhouse expanded 17 times. In 1919, a factory began operating in Jacksonville with a machine shop, carpentry shop, a structural shop and tool and parts storage areas. In addition, the plant had a 60-foot-tall assembly room built that was large enough to erect and test new Big Eli Wheels.

Different models of the Big Eli were developed, from the 16-seat Aristocrat model to the small, six-seat Baby Eli.

Sullivan gave up active management of the company in 1925 and turned the operation over to his son, Lee, who started working in the shop in 1908 and didn't retired until 1968. As for W.E., he continued to be in the office almost every day until his death in 1932. The family continues to operate the company today. They still make the Big Eli Wheels, even after taking a break to produce war materials during World War II, and in 1955, they introduced a new carnival ride called the Scrambler. Through the years, the company has modernized and introduced new attractions, changing and adapting to keep providing the thrills that will keep the Eli Bridge Co. spinning into the future of the American amusement industry.

"Everyone goes Downtown!"

Since the beginning, the majority of business in Jacksonville was clustered around the downtown square. The square and the streets around it were the place where everyone shopped in the early 1900s. You could find anything you could possibly need within walking distance of the square, from eateries to grocery stores to saloons to even pool halls.

Small grocery stores, precursors to the supermarket, like Schmalz & Sons, sold fresh goods both inside and on the sidewalk. You could buy fresh-baked bread at the Muehlhausen Bakery, where a Yankee loaf was only 10 cents. The Andre & Andre Store offered everything from baby carriages to carpets, stoves, chairs, lamps, and tables. Located downtown were the early banks, like the Hockenhull, King and Elliott Bank, which began in the uncertain years after the Civil War in 1866. It joined the Ayers Bank, the Brown Bank and the First National Bank of Jacksonville when it opened. Merrigan's Ice Cream Parlor was located on West State Street, and it joined a number of other confectionaries in the early 1900s when modern refrigeration techniques came of age. The J.C. Penney store was located on the west side of the square for many years, but became one of the first stores to abandon downtown for Morton Avenue after the Lincoln Square shopping center was opened.

Jacksonville's downtown, like others across the country, began to fade in the 1960s. It was a time of great change in America. In the first decades of the twentieth century, service was a very personal thing, especially for small family businesses. People knew each other, and in most cases, customers were on a first-name basis with the owner of the store. By the 1960s, America had changed. For the first time, women were working outside of the home on a regular basis and operating hours of the downtown stores became inconvenient. Prices became a bigger factor when shopping. With large volumes, chain stores could sell goods cheaper than the small stores downtown, which were, for the most part, family-owned. With more money to advertise and buy in bulk, the chain stores slowly put the "mom and pop stores" out of business. As those stores disappeared, the downtown square went with them.

Luckily, in recent years though, new life has returned to downtown Jacksonville and with it has come stories of ghosts and hauntings.

Hauntings of the Hockenhull Building

On January 15, 1966, seven people were killed when a fire raged through the apartments above Walgreen's drug on the east side of Jacksonville, Illinois' downtown square. This was, by all known accounts, the greatest loss of life from fire in the city's history. Investigation later ruled that the fire had been an accident, started by a burning cigarette, but the eerie result was that it left a haunting in its wake - a chilling presence that still makes itself known in the building today.

An early photo of the Hockenhull Building on the downtown square

Warga's the name of the Walgreens store in Jacksonville was still located on the downtown square in 1966. It had opened in 1935 and was a remnant of what had once been a thriving shopping district during the heyday of the smaller, family-owned businesses that once dominated commerce in every American city. Jacksonville was no exception. After World War II, a shift in where people shopped began to occur, but before that, you could buy everything from suits to dresses, furniture, tools and auto parts in downtown Jacksonville. Many locals purchased toiletries or had prescriptions filled at Walgreens, which was located in what was known as the Hockenhull Building.

John and Robert Hockenhull arrived in Jacksonville in 1839. Both men had been apothecaries in England and they opened a small drug store on the city square. They prospered and soon opened a dry goods store on East State Street. In 1866, Robert branched out further and with Raymond Kind and Edward Elliott, opened the Hockenhull, King and Elliott Bank. By this time, Robert had purchased a home on Grove Street and had become a trustee for Illinois College and for the All-Female Academy, that later became known as MacMurray College. He was one of the most important men in the city and one of the wealthiest. In 1891, he expanded his holdings with the construction of the Hockenhull Building on the east side of the square. The towering stone building

55

still looms above the sidewalk today, although any business that would have been known to Robert Hockenhull has long since vanished from Jacksonville.

Warga's was just one of the many businesses still operating during the fading days of the old square. Before its recent revitalization, the square declined for decades, much like most downtown business districts across the country. As new businesses opened along Morton Avenue, downtown Jacksonville slowly began to die. Many of the remaining stores had apartments over the shops, often cramped and dingy lofts that were as weary as the declining businesses below them. In the Hockenhull Building above Warga's, there were apartments on the second and third floors - apartments that became death traps on a cold winter's night in January 1966.

A photograph taken on the night of the deadly fire in January 1966

According to newspaper reports at the time, the scene at the fire was chaotic. Residents in the building frantically tried to escape the flames while firefighters were working to extinguish the blaze and save the tenants. One man, Robert Lee Brown, 18, who was sleeping with his family in one room of their four-room flat, was rescued by firefighters who used an aerial ladder truck to whisk five people from the upper part of the building within five minutes of their arrival on the scene. The only other member of the Brown family to escape death that night was one of Robert's younger siblings. The rest of them perished from asphyxiation from the smoke.

John Yeager, his wife and two children were trapped in their third floor apartment, but remaining calm, he managed to get them out of a rear window and to a roof below. Tragically, an elderly couple, Alice Leggett and Charles Souza, who lived just on the other side of the Yeagers' wall, were not so lucky.

Authorities believed that about a dozen people escaped from the apartments on the second and third floors, including Kathryn Wease, 19, and her two children, ages 13-months and 6-weeks. The janitor of the building, Virgil Duncan,

56

managed to make it out with two unidentified tenants, who lived above Barney's gift shop. Those who died in the blaze were Leota Mae Brown, 46; her four children, Ray, 15; Donna, 14; Rickey, 10; and Jimmy, 2; along with Leggett and Souza.

Elsie Brannan, 76, was the first to realize that something was wrong in the building around 1:30 a.m. Unable to sleep, she repeatedly thought she smelled smoke, opened her door and saw the flames in the hallway. Although elderly, Elsie reached a window transom, some six feet off the floor, and managed to pull herself up over the door and through the narrow opening. She dropped to the floor in the dense smoke and made her way through a storeroom above the drug store, breaking a window to reach the roof. Several people who escaped from the fire later told reporters that they heard someone yelling "in back, and ringing what sounded like a bell or someone banging on pans."

Mrs. Brannan would later admit that she did what she could to rouse the other sleeping tenants. She then broke out a window at the rear of Birdsell's tailor shop, making her way through the darkness to a window above East State Street, which she promptly shattered. Waving a piece of cloth from the tailor shop, she was eventually spotted by a motorist driving past.

Gary Strubbe, who was driving around the square a few moments later, saw Clara Davis, her daughter, Kathryn Wease, and her two young children frantically screaming for help from an upper floor. He went immediately to the police department and sounded the alarm. Within minutes, the fire department was on the scene. When firefighters arrived, Clara and Kathryn were each holding a child out of the apartment windows and rescue workers at first thought they might throw them from the second floor. Mrs. Davis later explained that they were holding the infants outside of the window to keep them out of the dense smoke. Firefighters used the aerial ladder to save the women, children, and Robert Brown and then to work looking for other survivors.

Led by Assistant Fire Chief Alvin Smith, a crew equipped with oxygen masks groped their way through the smoke to the third floor. Meanwhile, other firefighters battled their way to the second floor, where they discovered the origin of the fire and quickly began trying to douse the flames that were roaring up the wall to the third floor. By this time, nearly 100 people had gathered in the square and many of the men assisted the firefighters in moving hose lines.

A cheer went up as survivors were brought to safety, but then a hush fell over the crowd when someone called out that there were still people trapped on the third floor. By this time, though, the crew led by Assistant Chief Smith had reached the victims and were carrying the bodies out onto a roof at the rear of the building. The departure of several ambulances without their emergency lights bore mute witness to the fact that some of the people trapped in the building had not escaped with their lives. "On Saturday morning," one news reporter wrote, "Jacksonville asked why and how?"

Fire Chief Dale Bond attempted to answer the questions. The fire, he stated, had started in the second-floor apartment, occupied by a woman named Alice McCausland. She had been found semi-conscious in a lower floor hallway between Warga's and Edward's jewelry store. When Police Officer John Irlam asked her at the scene how she escaped the fire, she reportedly told him, "There's no fire up there, I put it out."

According to Chief Bond, the fire spread from McCausland's bedroom up the wall. The intense heat shattered a transom window and spread up the hallway wall to the third floor. Damage to the building was estimated in excess of $50,000.

Later that month, at a coroner's inquest, Chief Bond testified that, during two separate interrogations, McCausland confessed that she had dropped a lighted cigarette in bed, which caught fire, starting the blaze. Bond stated, "She said 'I dropped a cigarette in bed, and when I found it, smoke was coming from the covers. Then I put it out.'" Bond then said that he asked her what she did next and she replied, "'went to bed.'"

During later questioning, the chief said that McCausland would not repeat her earlier confession and firmly told him that she made it a rule not to smoke in bed. According to Charles Runkel, the police chief at the time, no charges were ever filed against McCausland for the deaths of the seven people killed in the fire. Officially, the blaze was listed as accidental.

But accident or not, seven people, including four children, died that night in the rundown apartments above the drug store. According to scores of people who have experienced the haunting that lingers in the Hockenhull Building, those who perished in the fire do not rest in peace.

In the middle 1990s, life began to return to the downtown square. Old buildings saw new activity as coffee shops, art galleries, and small shops began seeking out the nostalgia of yesterday in the brick buildings and ornate structures from Jacksonville's past. The lower portion of the Hockenhull Building was opened as a pet store and later, an art gallery - although the upper floors remained as jarring reminders of the building's tragic past. Evidence of the fire remained starkly visible, from burned floors and walls to even charred clothing that still hung in the closets.

And it wasn't just physical reminders of the past that could still be found. Stories soon circulated of strange shadows, footsteps, laughter, and the eerie voices of children - perhaps the same children who died in January 1966. The artists on the first floor had their own experiences, speaking of cold chills, lights that turned on and off by themselves, office equipment that operated on its own and the smell of cigarettes when no one was smoking in the building.

Our friend Loren Hamilton, who has led American Hauntings ghost hunts in the building, has had more than his share of strange experiences at the Hockenhull. Guests who have accompanied him for these outings have witnessed and recorded many strange things, from disembodied voices, unexplained knocks, unknown shadows, apparitions and more.

To this day, the Hockenhull Building remains one of Jacksonville's most notorious sites. It is a place where the past truly comes back to life and where the dead are unafraid of making their presence known to the living.

27 Public Square: The Ghosts Who Just Won't Leave

Located on the South Side of the downtown Square is an eatery known as Schiraz, a pleasant little bistro with a friendly staff, good food - and a few lurking presences from days gone by that seem to have made the restaurant their permanent home. Our first encounter with the place was several years ago, when it was home to a coffee shop. Troy did a presentation about his book *Weird Illinois* to a packed house and staff members let him know that there were some pretty unusual things taking place in the coffee shop after hours. Apparently, not a lot has changed over the past few years.

The earliest records of 27 Public Square show that it was the first home to the Hopper & Son Shoe Co. in 1887. They remained at the location until 1914, when they moved to a different spot on the square and then remained in business for almost a century. Just a year later, the Farmer's State Bank moved into the spot, and it was the bank that installed the impressive steel vault that is still located in the basement today. The long, narrow building with multiple floors served the bank well until 1942, when they expanded their operations and moved to their current location on the west side of the square.

In 1943, the Hofmann Floral Co. opened in the bank's former location. Florist Harry Hofmann offered arrangements from birth to death and for everything in between, including for just about every wedding in Jacksonville until the early 1980s. The floral company moved out of the building in 1984 and several other businesses followed. From 1985 to 1987, it was home to Country Roads Gifts and Flowers and from 1988 to 1990, it served the square as a bookstore. After a two-year vacancy, the first restaurant opened in the space in 1993. Merrigan's Old Place was a popular spot on the square until 2000, when it closed, leaving 27 Public Square vacant for the next five years.

And while the spot may have been unoccupied, it certainly wasn't empty.

In 2005, Due Gatti Coffee House opened in the space once occupied by a bank, a shoe company, flower shop and a restaurant. And while the "Two Cats" coffee house was quite successful, the first stories of a haunting began to emerge from behind its stone walls. The century-and-a-half building had apparently left behind a number of occupants from years gone by. Staff members whispered strange stories of apparitions that were sometimes seen sitting at tables, of an old land-line telephone that would ring even when it was not plugged in, clanging noises from the building's upper floors, objects that moved around in the kitchen disappearing and returning in different places and even the sound of a woman giggling when no one else is present.

We had several occasions to talk to people who worked at Due Gatti about their experiences. One kitchen worker explained that she often came in very early in the morning and occasionally would walk in to hear hushed voices suddenly stop, as if they realized that someone else had walked into the room. A search of the kitchen, of course, revealed that no one else was present. Another staff member told of how glasses suddenly vanished from on top of the counter. She was in the middle of filling an order, turned around for a moment, looked back, and saw that the half-filled glass that had been sitting there was gone. Assuming that the customer had picked it up too soon, she started to speak up, but then realized they had nothing in their hand. The glass actually turned up later, she recalled, on a high shelf where she could not have accidentally placed it.

It was also not uncommon to sense a presence in the building's basement. One staff member often went down there to bring back supplies and would feel an icy chill come over her, as though the door to a deep freeze had just been opened. This didn't bother her too much - but the ghost that she saw did! One morning, while walking through the basement, she saw the distinctive figure of a man several yards in front of her. He seemed to be standing there, looking in her direction. She couldn't make out any of his features, merely that he was dressed in a business suit that seemed old and dated, perhaps from the 1940s. His face, she recalled, was a blur, but she knew his hair was dark. Before she could let out a cry of surprise, the man darted around a corner and vanished. The staff member scurried up the stairs in fright and convinced another employee to come back downstairs with her to check around. There was no man to be seen and no one else in the building.

Aside from this startling encounter, the events that occurred at the coffee house were not frightening, but they were puzzling. There seemed to be no real reason why the place would be haunted. Perhaps the people who had occupied it in the past simply didn't want to leave.

Due Gatti closed in 2007 and was briefly replaced by another coffee house, the Three-Legged Dog, and finally by Schiraz, which now occupies the space. Stories still linger of otherworldly occupants that don't want to leave the building. Will they always remain here? Who can say? But one thing is sure - they add a little more atmosphere to a building with a history that dates back to the earliest days of business in downtown Jacksonville.

The Emporium

William Norvell, Jr., or Bill as his friends called him, knew his way around tools and equipment. For a good part of his 55 years, he worked as a psychiatric aide at the Jacksonville State Hospital, but his true passion was for gears and machinery and making things work. When not working at the hospital, he could almost always be found at the Emporium, Jacksonville's biggest department store, on East State Street, right off the square. Back in 1926, the Emporium had installed an elevator, the first store downtown to have one. People marveled at the chance to ride from one floor to the next in comfort, but now, 45 years later, the elevator needed almost constant repair. But Bill Norvell didn't mind. He loved tinkering with it and making sure that it ran just the way that his boss, Edward Goldstein, who he always called "Mr. G," wanted it to run.

On a crisp fall morning, October 13, 1969, Bill came to the Emporium after one of the managers called to tell him that the old elevator had stopped working again. He gathered his tools and left his home on South Fayette Street, which he shared with his wife, Loretta, until her death in 1964, and drove downtown. It was around 7:15 a.m. when Bill arrived at the store, well before opening time, and listened to yet another report of how strangely the elevator had been acting. It was a familiar story to the genial man, and with a smile, he climbed the stairs to the highest floor of the building, where the elevator's control box was located. The elevator's car had stopped about 10 feet below, stuck at the third floor.

Bill worked his way through the tangle of gears, pulleys and cables and peered down into the darkness of the elevator shaft. He could plainly see the top of the car below. Bending down, he opened his tool box and reached for a screwdriver. A metal panel would have to be removed before he could get to the electrical wires and see what might be wrong with the controls. But as Bill reached down for that screwdriver -- something happened. We'll never know for

sure what it was, but he lost his balance and for just a split second, his body was suspended in the air at the top of the shaft.

And then he fell.

Plummeting downward, Bill Norvell fell only 10 feet to the top of the car. It wasn't far, but it was far enough. His body slammed onto the top of the metal car and impacted with the gears and brackets that held the cables in place and allowed the car to smoothly travel between floors, when it worked correctly, that is. Bill was probably killed instantly, but we'll never know that for sure either. Nearly two hours passed before anyone thought to check on him and when a fellow employee saw his body crumpled on the top of the elevator car, he immediately called for an ambulance. When firefighters arrived on the scene, they managed to lift Bill's broken body out of the elevator shaft. He was rushed to Passavant Hospital, but it was far too late for him. He was gone.

Over the years, as stories of ghostly activity at the old Emporium building have spread through Jacksonville, it's the legend of the man that fell down the elevator shaft that is always recalled. Few remember his name or even that he was a real person. Most assume that it's nothing but a "ghost story" about a mythical repairman that never existed at all. But Bill Norvell was a real person and he really did die after falling to his death in the Emporium's elevator shaft.

And it's even possible that his ghost still haunts this building. But we believe that if he does, he does not walk here alone.

The building that is known to most Jacksonville residents as the "Emporium" started on East State Street, just off the downtown square, in 1899 as Johnson & Sons, which sold furniture, stoves, furnaces and home furnishing goods. The store was owned by W.H. Johnson and did a thriving business for several years, until Johnson passed away. It was sold to Edwin Galbraith in 1907, who started Galbraith Furniture. The new store was managed by the owner's son, Oliver, who lived in the third floor apartment above the store. The Galbraiths remained in business until 1915, when H.S. Greenstone bought the building and started the Emporium, a women's "ready to wear" clothing store.

The store did very well for several years, but after the passing of Greenstone's wife, Esther, the owner's health began to fail and the business began to suffer. After spending a number of weeks in the hospital in Springfield, Greenstone began looking for a buyer for the business. He found a buyer with Edward Goldstein, whose family owned several retail stores in Central Illinois. Goldstein was familiar with Jacksonville and liked the town, and after receiving a good deal from Greenstone, decided to invest in the Emporium - sight unseen. The contracts were signed in a Springfield hotel lobby in December 1919, and Goldstein drove over to Jacksonville to see his new store for the first time. He would later say, "It wasn't too encouraging," but he planned to make the best of it. Little did he know that the time at the Emporium would become his whole life and that he would spend the next 50 years turning it into the finest department store in the city.

Edward Goldstein, who would affectionately become known as "Mr. G" to his friends and associates, was born in Eastern Europe, the son of Moses and Edith Goldstein, and he came to the United States at the age of four. He had two sisters, Gertrude and Elizabeth, and four brothers, J.W., Harry, Herman and Benjamin. Over the years, the family had operated a number of retail stores and businesses, but Goldstein would leave his greatest mark on Jacksonville with the Emporium.

When the newspapers announced the sale of the store, Goldstein had nothing but praise for the city, which he had visited frequently, and spoke of how much he liked the people. He had big plans for his new store. He told the *Jacksonville Daily Journal*, "I am expecting to offer the women of Jacksonville fine service in ready to wear garments and I am sure they are going to find the Emporium a store where garments correct in style and dependable in quality can be purchased at prices lower than they have heretofore known about."

And the Emporium wasn't going to be just any store. Goldstein planned to make a place that would be talked about by everyone in the city. For starters, it would be the first store in town to offer shopping in air-conditioned comfort. But there were no air-conditioning units available in town and no craftsmen who could install them anyway. Goldstein purchased three systems from buildings that had been torn down in New York and, doing all of the work himself, rigged them together to make one huge unit - much larger than the building even needed. Then he installed the whole thing himself. His jerry-rigged air-conditioning unit continued working until the building was remodeled in 1964, when it was replaced by a modern system. Each time it broke down, Mr. G simply dug out his toolbox and went to work. It wasn't long before the cooling unit would be humming again.

In 1926, Goldstein purchased the three-story building from the Greenstone estate. The business had done so well that he wanted to expand out of the first floor and occupy the entire building. This started an extended period of remodeling, and when it was over, the Emporium had gone from simply a ladies' dress store to a full-fledged department store, which carried clothing for the entire family, furniture, and a shoe department. Later on, the Emporium would serve as the starting place for other businesses that were owned by Goldstein, including Mr. Eddies, Walker Furniture and a number of commercial properties that were leased to other businesses. By the 1940s, the Emporium was the largest department store in Jacksonville and the busiest. At least one well-known local businessman, Martin Newman, got his start working for Mr. G. In the late 1950s,

Newman was the manager of the Emporium's shoe department. He later went on to start his own company, Newman's Shoes, with stores all over Central Illinois.

During his years in business, Goldstein never married. He said, "I've never stopped working long enough to get married." Although a bachelor, he donated both time and money to children's charities, including the YMCA, to which he donated $100,000 during the summer before his death. He was also a leader in the Chamber of Commerce, Jacksonville Industrial Corporation, Intown Merchant's Association, and the initial program to secure an electric plant for the city. He supported many other charitable organizations, like the Salvation Army and the United Fund.

The long hours that he worked and time that he put into the Emporium likely kept him from ever establishing a permanent residence in town. When he first arrived in Jacksonville, he lived at the Colonial Inn and later at the Pacific Hotel for a few years. In the middle 1930s, he lived in an apartment just a few blocks from the store, on State Street, and then moved into the apartment on the top floor of the Emporium in 1941. He stayed there until he became too ill to live alone, moving into the apartment of long-time employee and friend, Louise Cowdin, on East Court Street in 1969.

A rare photo of Eddie Goldstein

On October 30, 1969, Mr. G passed away at Norris Hospital. He had been sick for some time and had been a patient at the hospital for several months. His body was taken to the Williamson Funeral Home and a private service and burial was conducted by Rabbi Meyer Abramowitz. He was buried in Diamond Grove Cemetery.

Goldstein's death left the Emporium without its driving force. His close friend, Louise Cowdin, took over the running of the store after his death, but things were never the same. Even so, the Emporium lasted until 1981, when Louise retired and the Emporium closed for good. The building remained vacant for the next two years - but was it really empty? In a time span of only three weeks, two men connected to the store had died - one tragically in an accident and the other so closely connected to the store that he had spent a lifetime

65

building it into Jacksonville's most successful retail store. What kind of lingering presence had these two men left behind?

In 1983, long after most other downtown businesses had either closed up or had moved out to Morton Avenue, leaving the square a sort-of ghost town, Kruwag's Emporium Mall opened in the old Emporium building on East State Street. Operated by Harold Wagner, Jr. and Michael Kruthaupt, they specialized in one of the most popular furniture items of the day - waterbeds. The store thrived, offering furniture at a discount price, and not surprisingly, getting out of the waterbed business after a few years. They remained in the building until 2001, when the business closed.

For the next five years, the Emporium was abandoned once again. Leaky ceilings, winter months with no heat and summer months with nothing to keep out the dampness took their toll on the old place. The Emporium had turned into a ghost of itself. In early 2006, though, Joe Thomas bought the building with the idea of turning it into a center for troubled youth. He purchased it for a very low price, but quickly found that the deteriorating building would cost much more to repair than he could possibly afford. Even after he rented out the upstairs apartments - Mr. G's old place had been converted into three units - he found that the revenue they generated was not enough to pay for the building's upkeep. Later that fall, he put the building up for sale.

In 2008, the Emporium was converted into a tavern that bears the same name as Edward Goldstein's department store - the Emporium. The clothing racks and shoe departments are long gone now. Pool tables fill the first floor area where the furniture department was once located. The elevator shaft where Bill Norvell fell to his death has been removed - but not all of the remnants of yesterday have vanished.

According to first-hand accounts, spirits of the past still remain.

The first ghost stories about the Emporium building began making the rounds in the 1990s, when it was being used as a furniture store. Staff members spoke of the uncomfortable feeling of being watched and of hearing footsteps in hallways and rooms where no visible person was present. During an interview, one former staff member claimed that she had been touched on the shoulder by an unseen hand. When she turned to see who was trying to get her attention, there was no one there. She quit working at the store that same day.

The stories continued during the time when the apartments on the third floor were being rented out. Tenants complained of hearing footsteps on the stairs and in the hallways. One told of lights that turned on and off by themselves, with no explanation. Oddly, this same occurrence took place during a paranormal investigation of the building in 2006. As ghost hunters moved from floor to floor,

The Emporium today

they discovered that the lights on the first floor kept turning themselves back on again after they were sure they had been turned out.

Our friend Loren Hamilton, who led the group that night, also told of a loud bumping sound that he heard coming from behind the elevator doors on the building's third floor. It was, he explained, like the sound of someone knocking, trying to get out. Of course, this was at the exact spot where Bill Norvell had fallen to his death in 1969 - a fact that Loren did not know at the time! The building's legend claimed that a repairman had fallen down the elevator shaft and died in the basement, after falling three stories. It was not until we did the research for this book that we discovered that Bill had actually only fallen about ten feet and died on top of the elevator car, which was stuck on the third floor at the time. Coincidence? Perhaps, but it seems pretty unlikely based on all of the other stories that have been told.

During the time when the building was being remodeled into the Emporium tavern, the new owners and workers complained about objects that would disappear, move around and reappear while the construction work was being done. Tools vanished, showing up later in strange places where no one had left

67

them, and they often came in certain mornings to find that recently hung drywall was lying on the floor. On one occasion, a "force" was said to have held back a worker's arm as he was drying to nail some woodwork onto the wall - as if someone didn't want the place to be changed.

Are there really ghosts that haunt the old Emporium building? Those who have encountered them certainly think so. Could one of them be Bill Norvell, who fell to his death in the elevator shaft? And if so, is he the only spirit here that doesn't rest? Could Edward Goldstein, who spent most of his life at this building and poured his heart and soul into it, have also remained behind? It certainly seems possible, especially when considering this:

One of the tenants who rented an apartment in the Emporium building in 2006 told a chilling story of waking up in the middle of the night to see a thin man with glasses standing at the end of his bed. Startled into a sitting position on the bed, the tenant watched the man suddenly disappear. He would never think too much of the encounter, telling us a couple of years later that he assumed that it had just been a dream. But we never forgot the story, especially when we were doing research for this book and ran across the first photograph that we'd ever seen of Edward Goldstein -- a thin man who wore glasses his entire life. Could this be the apparition the tenant saw in his apartment that night?

Truthfully, we'd like to think so. If, when someone dies, they have the choice to move on to another place or stay behind in this world, it seems possible - perhaps even likely-- that Mr. G would remain in the one place where he was the happiest during his life. He literally created the Emporium. He designed it, crafted the ideas, lived upstairs, and even built and installed the air-conditioning unit with his own hands. He never had a wife because he was already married in a way to his store.

But if his ghost does not still reside in the building that he loved, there is no question that he left an indelible mark on the place and on the city of Jacksonville itself.

Spirits of Another Sort - KJB's Pint Haus

Although most would never know it when walking down East State Street from the Jacksonville square, they are walking in the footsteps of organized crime in the city. Specifically, someone with an interest in gambling would have to go inside of KJB's Pint Haus, where a "sporting ticker" operated in the 1920s and 30s and offered mob-connected horse racing results to gamblers who placed bets in the bar that existed at that time. A few years later, Harry Herring ran the Jacksonville Novelty Co. upstairs, distributing vending and slot machines around Central Illinois. Most would assume that such businesses were safe to be around - until they discover the bloody history of the racing wire service in Illinois. Could the violence associated with gambling and the mob be the reason that a ghostly presence remains in the building that is now home to KJB's Pint Haus? The reader can be the judge of that after turning the pages ahead.

The site of the current tavern on East State Street has had a long history in downtown Jacksonville, often serving as a restaurant or a saloon, starting as far back as around 1888. The first owner of a saloon at the site was J.F. Coulter, who ran it until 1900, when he sold the business to Daniel Keating. Keating, who lived on West Morgan Street with his wife, Margaret, ran it as a saloon, billiard hall, and cigar shop for seven years. In 1907, he moved his operation to a location on the city square and started a lunch room during a temporary ban on liquor in Jacksonville. Keating never went back into the liquor business. He operated his lunch room and soda fountain until 1915, when he turned it into a restaurant. He retired in 1924.

The building on East State Street became the Batz Café for a time, and was the exclusive distributor for the William J. Lemp Brewing Co. from St. Louis. After that, it was empty for several years and then, in 1915, became the first location for the Williamson and Cody Funeral Home. In 1921, the two undertakers parted ways and it became the C.E. Williamson & Sons Funeral Home. They remained in this building until 1927, when they moved to a former home on West College Street, which is now the location of the Jacksonville Theatre Guild.

In the same year that the undertaker's parlor moved out, the Ogar Cigar Co. moved in. After the end of Prohibition, Paul Aufenkamp turned the place back into a tavern and poolroom. He began offering cigars, light lunches, drinks, billiards, and a "sporting ticker" for gamblers. And it's here where the history of the building starts to get a little shady.

The idea of a race wire service came from John Payne, a former telegraph operator from Cincinnati, Ohio, in the early 1900s. At that time, Payne worked for Western Union, which had recently decided to stop reporting racing results at the urging of one of its principal stockholders. Payne developed his own procedure for dispensing horse race results. He would have someone stationed at the racetrack, and using a mirror, flash back a coded race result to a telegrapher in a nearby building. The results were relayed immediately by the telegrapher to handbooks "bookies" all over the city. One of the benefits of this service was that it allowed bookies to take bets on races where they already knew the results. If they knew the horse being bet on had lost, they would accept the wager. If the horse had won, they would tell the gambler it was too late to place his bet. Is it any wonder that the wire service soon came to the attention of organized crime?

69

Payne had come up with the idea of the wire service, but it took gambler Jacob "Mont" Tennes to spread it across the country, even to Jacksonville. Tennes, a Chicago native, was the son of German immigrants who opened his first saloon and billiard room in the 1890s. By the first decade of the twentieth century, gambling ran wide open in Chicago and was controlled by three syndicates. Mont Tennes and his two brothers, William and Edward, ran the North Side. James O'Leary whose mother owned the cow that allegedly started the Chicago Fire ruled the South Side, and the Loop district was under control of the infamous city aldermen Michael Kenna and John J. Coughlin, better known as "Hinky Dink" and "Bath House John." Of the three, Tennes would become the dominant force.

In 1904, Tennes was running all of the gambling on the West Side of Chicago, backing hundreds of betting parlors. He was indicted for bookmaking that year and fined $200. He would not be found guilty of another crime until 1922. It was also in 1904 that bookmaking at horse tracks in Illinois was made illegal. For the next 18 years, there was no thoroughbred racing in Illinois. However, there was racing in other parts of the country to bet on and the telephone and telegraph gave the gamblers the means to continue betting with the creation of John Payne's race wire.

In 1907, Tennes purchased the "Payne System" exclusively for Illinois for $300 dollars a day. He received the race results at the Forest Park train station using a switchboard consisting of a trunk line with 45 wires. He distributed coded results to several hundred poolrooms and handbooks. The information, which came from tracks around the country was then relayed to the handbook joints. In Chicago, no gambling house could receive horse race results by telephone or telegraph unless Tennes received compensation. Local bookies had to pay him 50 percent of the daily net receipts for the service. As Tennes worked to secure his monopoly with the racing wire, his adversaries initiated a bombing campaign against him. Between July 1 and September 26, 1907, six bombs were detonated at either his home or his businesses. He refused to back down and by 1909 was the absolute dictator of race track gambling and bookmaking in Chicago. He maintained control over the entire operation through violence and terrorism. In 1911, he took things a step further and started his own wire service, the "Tennes General News Bureau," which he planned to use to eliminate the Payne service. Soon, poolrooms in Chicago and elsewhere were using his service and he was receiving a tremendous percent of the profits.

The poolrooms of the early twentieth century including in Jacksonville should not be confused with what we think of as poolrooms today. Places where people went to "shoot" or play pool back then were called "billiard parlors." People went to a poolroom to place illegal bets. A person would use a poolroom to place

70

While men often played billiards while hanging out in "pool rooms" in the early 1900s, they really went there to place illegal bets.

a bet on a horse race much like they would use a bookmaker today. Poolrooms drew a shady group of people and usually served alcohol illegally. While there, men would pass the time gambling, playing cards, shooting dice and playing billiards. The association of shady activities and billiards playing would leave a stigma on poolrooms for decades until they evolved into legitimate establishments.

By 1911, the Interstate Commerce Commission began an investigation into the wire service due to the attention being generated in the struggle between the Payne News Service and Tennes' General News Bureau. The ICC determined there was nothing illegal about the transmission of horse race results. In addition to the results, Tennes' service also provided racing information such as entries, odds, jockeys, and scratches. Tennes was servicing cities all over the country including San Francisco and Salt Lake City in the west, San Antonio and New Orleans in the south, New York City and Baltimore on the East Coast, and scores of cities in the Midwest.

Raids by the police, attacks by rivals, and investigations all failed to slow down the Tennes moneymaking machine. The investigations continued through the 1910s and only seemed to expose crooked cops or politicians after months of work. In 1916, Tennes was under federal investigation and was represented by

71

famed defense trial lawyer Clarence Darrow, who advised him not to answer any questions. However, many others called to testify did talk including some of Tennes' associates, but nothing could be done to legally stop him.

After the investigation, police raids on Chicago gamblers were stepped up. The newspapers helped by publishing the names of the proprietors, but only patrons and office managers seemed to get arrested. During World War I, the public's attention was obviously diverted from the gambling problem, largely because gambling was at an all-time low. It rebounded after the war, though, and Tennes was again in and out of trouble, but never successfully prosecuted.

In 1923, William E. Dever was elected mayor of Chicago. Incorruptible and eager for reform, he started closing down speakeasies and gambling parlors. The John Torrio-Al Capone mob promptly moved their operations to Cicero. Within the first year of Dever's term, his new police chief closed over two hundred handbook joints. The gambling, which enjoyed its greatest success in the Loop area, was said to be "absolutely dead" a year after Dever took office. During this period Tennes avoided arrest claiming he ran a legitimate race wire service dispensing sporting news.

In 1924, Tennes was rumored to have retired from the handbook business. One of the reasons given for this was the pressure being put on him by the Capone mob. Whatever the reason, Tennes' name was seldom seen in print during the mid-1920s. But in 1927, William "Big Bill" Thompson replaced Dever as mayor and Chicago became a wide-open town again. At this point, the city was split in two with Capone controlling the South Side, and the North Side run by George "Bugs" Moran. Tennes was selling his race wire services to both groups.

Tennes was now facing competition from a new race wire service, the Empire News Company. Soon, the new service was being raided by the police and its equipment and telephones were being destroyed. Empire News was undercutting Tennes' prices and he started losing business. He also had to deal with Al Capone, who had started muscling in on his operations. Several of his bookie joints were bombed and Capone began demanding a percent of his business for "protection." Between the competition from the Empire News Service and the Capone gang, Tennes decided it was time to retire for good. In 1927, ownership of the General News Bureau was split into 100 shares. Newspaper magnate, Moses Annenberg purchased 48 shares, current partner Jack Lynch bought 40 shares, and the remainder ended up in the hands of Tennes' three nephews; Edward, Lionel and Mont.

After his retirement from the race wire service, Tennes led a respectable life. He was involved in several real estate ventures and purchased a business. In August 1941, he died in bed of a heart attack. In his will, he bequeathed $10,000 a year for a "character home" for wayward boys named Camp Honor.

It would be newspaper publisher Moses Annenberg who would continue the growth of the wire service. Annenberg had been born in East Prussia and had come to Chicago with his family when he was four-years-old in 1882. His father opened a small grocery store in the "Patch," a tough, mostly Irish neighborhood, which also spawned future race wire owners James M. Ragen and Arthur B. "Mickey" McBride. Developing a love of gambling at an early age from the card and dice games played on the sidewalks of the neighborhood, Annenberg would remain a gambler all his life. Leaving school at the age of twelve to find work to help support the family, he first worked as a messenger boy for Western Union and then took a succession of jobs that offered higher wages. During this time, he worked in a livery stable, sold newspapers, and tended bar for his brother-in-law.

Moses Annenberg

In 1900, William Randolph Hearst launched the *Evening American* newspaper in Chicago. Although the city already had eight newspapers, Hearst with his penchant for hyping newspaper sales with sex, violence, and sensationalism, was not deterred. Hearst needed strong circulation men to fight his battles and one of the first men hired was Moses' brother, Max, who had been working for the *Chicago Tribune*. With Moses' help, they managed to snag scores of subscribers to the new paper. He was so successful that the newly married Moses was made the circulation chief of the *Examiner*, a new morning edition that Hearst started. It was the same position Max held with the *Evening American*. As the competition in the circulation business got tougher and more violent, Moses taught himself how to shoot a gun in the basement of the *Early American* building.

As it turned out, though, he avoided most of the violence that occurred just after he moved to Milwaukee to handle distribution of Chicago papers there. He had left just in time as Hearst's newspapers soon got into a bloody circulation war with Colonel Robert McCormick's *Chicago Tribune*. By the time the battles were over in 1913, 27 news dealers had been murdered and many others injured. Before the bloodshed began, Max had gone back to the *Tribune* and was involved in much of the mayhem that took place. At one point, he was indicted for wounding a man, but McCormick's lawyers got the case dismissed with claims of self-defense.

The Milwaukee News Agency became very profitable for Moses and he quickly invested his money into local businesses like liquor stores, dry cleaners, and bowling alleys. In 1917, he changed careers from newspaper circulation manager to publisher when he took over the *Wisconsin News*. Annenberg soon was credited with increasing the *News* circulation from 25,000 to 80,000. He became personal friends with William Randolph Hearst and was soon on his way to New York City to oversee the circulation of all of Hearst's newspaper and magazine publications. Despite the business empire he had built in Milwaukee, just three days after the offer was made, Moses, his family, and all their belongings were on their way to New York.

Soon, Annenberg was asked to take on the additional responsibility of publisher of Hearst's newest paper, the *New York Daily Mirror*. In the early 1920s, he hired young toughs Charles "Lucky" Luciano and Meyer Lansky to help oversee the circulation of the fledgling *Mirror*.

In 1922, Annenberg discovered a special interest publication devoted to horse racing - the *Daily Racing Form*. The small publication listed the names of the horses that were racing that day along with information about their previous performances. Frank Bruenell, a former sports editor of the *Chicago Tribune*, started the publication in Chicago in 1894. Annenberg approached Bruenell about buying his publication. Bruenell wanted $400,000 in cash and Annenberg delivered it. He then hired Joseph Bannon and Hugh Murray to run it.

Gambling fever seemed to be sweeping the country like no time previously. With the popularity of horseracing on the increase since a "wartime slump," there were now 29 racetracks operating throughout the country and millions of people were eager to bet. Using the shrewd methods he'd developed over the years as a circulation manager for Hearst, he began promoting the new *Racing Form*. He forced retailers to purchase it by threatening to cut off other Hearst publications if they refused. Since the Hearst-distributed magazines and newspapers were a large part of their sales, few refused. His next step in dominating the race information service was to buy out other publications coast to coast. When money didn't work, his army of tough circulation men helped change the minds of would-be holdouts. In 1926, with his *Racing Form* taking up more of his time, Annenberg left Hearst.

In 1927, he purchased the controlling interest in Mont Tennes General News Bureau, known as the race wire service. Annenberg purchased 48 percent of the shares of the General News Bureau. John J. "Jack" Lynch, a former partner of Tennes and a Chicago gambler with a tough reputation, purchased 40 percent. The remainder was bought by Tennes' nephews. Annenberg quickly hired his old "Patch" pal, James Ragen, to run the operation.

Ragen soon mapped out a plan to make General News Bureau the only race wire service in the country. The plan called for strong-arm tactics and bribes. Annenberg's *Racing Form* service initially consisted of seven publications and as the layers of corporations increased, they were arranged to keep a buffer between him and the violence that sometimes took place beneath him. In addition, like Capone, he contributed heavily to political campaigns, especially those of the Democratic machine that ran Chicago. A special fund was set up, referred to as the "widows and orphans" fund, which fed at least $150,000 a year in bribes to police and politicians. The General News Bureau continued to grow in size as smaller operations fell by the wayside. Those that couldn't be bought out were threatened out of business, or had their operations destroyed by the thugs employed by Annenberg and Ragen.

In May 1929, organized crime figures from around the country gathered in Atlantic City for a conference organized by Meyer Lansky, Frank Costello, and John Torrio. At the meeting, a plan was devised to have the syndicate owning its own wire service. What happened next is unclear. Several writers claim that Annenberg was invited to the meeting by Capone and a plan was worked out for the syndicate to get involved in running the wire service. Others say that he was not in attendance but that Capone went to Annenberg with a proposition that he flatly rejected. Whatever happened, within a few years, Annenberg's vision of a national wire service was realized.

By 1932, Annenberg had squeezed out all of the significant competition. He then turned his attention to squeezing out his partners. The first to go were Bannon and Murray who had been running the *Daily Racing Form* since Annenberg had purchased it. He did this by cutting the newsstand price of the *Telegraph*, a racing information publication he had purchased on his own in 1929, and by making sure that his distributors got the *Racing Form* onto the stands late, or not at all. Bizarrely, he went into direct competition with himself. When Bannon and Murray realized what was happening they sold out to Annenberg.

He also began undercutting the wire service so that he could push his partners out of the business completely. He created a printing company that made "wall sheets," which listed races, horses, jockeys, morning odds, and other information that bettors used in deciding how to place their money. The wall sheets were posted on walls of horse parlors for both customers and clerks. To further his gains, he had the wall sheet information printed using the identical codes used by his wire service. This guaranteed that customers buying his printed material also used his wire service and only the bookies who purchased both services were given the key to the codes.

His new service, the Nationwide News Service, started in 1934. When General News Bureau suppliers around the country heard a rumor about the new wire service they called James Ragen to report it. Ragen's response was that he was now employed by Nationwide News and if they were smart they would take the new service. This deception enraged Jack Lynch who contacted the former Capone Outfit for support. Newspapers began reporting that a gang war was eminent. Outfit mobster Frank Nitti approached James Ragen in an attempt to get him to change sides. "If you come along with us, we will kill him Annenberg in twenty-four hours," Ragen was told.

Annenberg was now a marked man. He hired bodyguards to protect him around the clock and quickly decided it was best for him to get out of Chicago. He headed for Miami where he would at least enjoy the protection of old friend Meyer Lansky. In 1936, Annenberg reached an agreement with Lynch and the Outfit. He paid $1 million dollars a year for protection and was free to pursue other interests without being stalked by paid gunmen.

With his race wire problems cleared up, Annenberg returned to the newspaper business that he loved. But his contentment was short-lived and he and his son, Walter, were charged with income tax evasion in 1939. Annenberg made an agreement with the government to drop the charges against Walter in return for a guilty plea. While he was working at the details, Annenberg ended his association with Nationwide News Service on November 15, 1939, by simply walking away from it in an effort to improve his image to the court. He ended up paying $9.5 million in taxes, penalties, and interest and was sent to federal prison for three years. He died from a brain tumor soon after being released from prison in 1942.

Annenberg was dead, but the race wire continued. After he had walked away from Nationwide News Service, it went out of business. Five days later, the Continental Press took its place under the control of Arthur "Mickey" McBride. He was another newspaper man, like Annenberg, and had been involved in the Chicago newspaper wars. McBride, who claimed he never wanted to run Continental, asked James Ragen to take the reins. Ragen declined the offer at the time because he was "having problems with his federal income taxes." Instead, McBride worked out a deal for James Ragen, Jr. to help Tom Kelly operate the service. Within a couple of years, though, the elder Ragen was back in control - and dealing with the mob.

Ragen had been a close associate of Moses Annenberg dating back to his childhood growing up in Chicago's "Patch." When Moses first got involved in Chicago's newspaper circulation battles, he hired James and his brother Frank, who headed the infamous "Ragen's Colts" gang to be head-breaking thugs. Years later, he teamed up with Annenberg to run the General News Bureau. When the Outfit began to muscle Annenberg in the mid-1930s, it was Ragen who the mob

Capone Outfit mobsters   Left to Right : Jake "Greasy Thumb" Guzik, Tony "Batters" Accardo and Murray "The Camel" Humphreys.

contacted to try to persuade him to turn against his boss. Now with Ragen in an ownership position, the Chicago mob was again attempting to gain control.

The initial approach was made by Jake "Greasy Thumb" Guzik, Anthony "Batters" Accardo, and Murray "The Camel" Humphreys. The Outfit wanted to cut itself in on the operation, build up the business and by doing this, they felt they could employ several hundred hoods in the operation. Ragen would continue to be a partner and his share of the profits would increase due to the enhanced income created by the Chicago mob's involvement. Ragen wasn't convinced. He knew that once the mob knew how to run things, he would be expendable. He sought to ease concerns for his own personal safety by meeting with Chicago FBI agents. He also prepared affidavits in which he named Frank Nitti and others involved in the plot to murder Annenberg. He felt these moves would serve as an insurance policy against the mob's efforts.

In 1945, the Outfit established its own wire service, the Trans-American Publishing and News Service, to compete with the Continental Press. As the new wire service established offices around the country, they engaged in a terrorist campaign against the offices of the Continental Press in an effort to force them out of business. In Las Vegas and on the West Coast, Benjamin "Bugsy" Siegel acted as the representative of the Outfit, forcing the new service on bookmakers through strong-arm tactics.

By the spring of 1946, Trans-America was making serious headway. On April 18, Harry "Red" Richmond, a Chicago bookie, was gunned down in front of his home in Chicago. He had recently stopped using the mob's wire service and switched back to Continental. Eleven days later, as Ragen drove from his home, he was followed by another car containing two men. After a fifteen-mile chase, Ragen fled to the safety of the Morgan Park police station. When he told the police who was after him and why, he was given around-the-clock protection, but

77

Ragen soon hired his own bodyguards - but they couldn't protect him from the Outfit.

On June 24, 1946, Ragen was driving on State Street and stopped at the intersection at Pershing Avenue for a red light. Ragen was in the car alone, but was followed by two bodyguards in another vehicle. A few moments later, an old delivery truck, partially loaded with orange crates and boxes and with wooden slat sides and a tarpaulin tossed over the top, pulled alongside of him. As Ragen waited for the light to change, the tarpaulin on the left side of the truck was pulled up and two shotguns were thrust out and aimed at Ragen's vehicle. Two blasts were fired and one tore through Ragen's upper right arm and shoulder. The two bodyguards jumped from their automobile to return fire. One of the guards tried to fire his shotgun, but it jammed, the other emptied his revolver at the truck as it sped away. The truck, which was later found abandoned, had been fitted with quarter inch steel plates to make it bulletproof from the rear.

Ragen was rushed to Michael Reese Hospital. He was in critical condition, suffering from shock and a loss of blood. He was given ten blood transfusions and doctors discussed amputating the mangled arm. The shotgun pellets had shattered Ragen's collarbone, broke his right shoulder, and his right upper arm. On August 8, he had emergency surgery on his kidneys. On August 14, he died at 4:55 a.m. with family members present. It was later reported that Ragen's autopsy showed traces of mercury in his blood indicating that someone had entered his room and poisoned him. The mob wanted to make sure he was dead.

The fighting between Trans-America and Continental continued for months until May 1947, when McBride purchased back the wire service from the Ragen interests. The Continental Press was now under the sole ownership Mickey's son, 23-year-old Eddie McBride, a law student at the University of Miami in Florida. On June 13, 1947, Trans-America suspiciously announced it was going out of business. It was pretty obvious to everyone that the Outfit was now running the racing wire service.

In 1951, the Kefauver Crime Committee made a recommendation to Congress for legislation that would place a ban on the transmission of interstate gambling information. The committee got what it asked for and after a 60-year run, the race wire service in general, and the Continental Press in particular, went out of existence.

Paul Aufenkamp ran the poolroom and betting parlor at 222 East State Street for the next two years and then it was taken over by Harry Herring Liquors. The poolroom and tavern remained in operation, offering betting via the race wires of the Nationwide News Service and then the Continental News Service when the former went out of business. A new form of gambling arrived in 1938 when the Jacksonville Novelty Co. moved into the upper floor of the building. On the surface, it was a vending machine company, but it was also known for distributing slot machines to gambling houses across the area. One of its biggest customers was the Lake Club in Springfield.

The Lake Club in Springfield

The Lake Club opened as a nightclub in 1940 by Harold Henderson and Hugo Giovagnoli. The club soon became one of the hottest nightspots in Illinois, drawing customers from all over the state. It boasted a raised dance floor surrounded by a railing, with curved walls and a swanky atmosphere that made patrons feel as though a New York club had been transported to the shores of Lake Springfield. The owners concentrated on bringing big name entertainment to the club and succeeded. Among the many top performers were Bob Hope, Ella Fitzgerald, Guy Lombardo, Pearl Bailey, Spike Jones, Nelson Eddy, Woody Herman, Mickey Rooney, and many others. The constant stream of entertainers and big bands brought capacity crowds to the club every night. During the height of its popularity, the club even hosted a radio call-in show that broadcast music and entertainment all over the area.

The Lake Club thrived for nearly two decades, becoming known not only for its swinging entertainment, but for its first-rate gambling, as well. Wealthy customers and the society elite of Springfield, Jacksonville and Decatur frequented the club for the musical guests and also for the billiard tables, craps and gaming tables, card games, and slot machines. This part of the club operated in secret in a back part of the building, known only to high rollers and special customers. However, in December 1958, the golden days of the Lake Club came to an end. Two undercover police detectives infiltrated the gambling room and the club was shut down. Newspaper accounts reported the police confiscated all sorts of gambling equipment including tables, dice, slot machines and large quantities of cash.

By that time, though, the Jacksonville Novelty Co. was long out of business. According to rumor, tavern owner Harry Deering was involved in a conflict with Frank Zito, the Springfield-based mobster who controlled organized crime in Central Illinois starting in the 1920s. No one knows for sure if he was the leader

Central Illinois mobster Frank
Zito in the 1960s

of his own crime organization or whether he was connected to the Outfit in Chicago. What is known is that he was born in Sicily in 1893 and came to Illinois with his family. During Prohibition, Zito became involved in bootlegging, prostitution, and illegal gambling in rural Illinois. During this period, Zito was convicted of violating federal liquor laws. While attending the 1957 Apalachin Conference in Apalachin, New York, Zito was captured with numerous other mobsters when the New York State Police raided the meeting. Although indicted in a federal investigation into organized crime in the Midwest, Zito remained in power into the 1970s.

Deering got out of the "novelty machines" business in 1947 after problems with Zito's organization. Fred Steers' Cigar company moved into the upstairs offices vacated by the slot machine company, and by 1950, Deering was out of business altogether.

In 1952, the Continental Tavern opened at 222 East State Street and lasted for the next eight years. After brief stints as an appliance store and an office for City Light and Power, it opened as Andy's Place in 1970. In 1983, it became Wally's place for a decade and then saw a series of operators from 1994 to 2005. In 2006, it became KJB's Pint Haus.

Over the years, rumors of ghostly events have filtered out of the upper floors of the building. This was an area that was rented out as a private apartment, as cigar shops and for a time, as a mob-connected slot machine company. Some stories say that violence occurred here during the time when Frank Zito's operation pushed the novelty company out of business. One story even claimed that one of Deering's men was murdered on the second floor, but there is no record that this ever occurred - which really is not surprising if organized crime was involved. But who - or what – still lurks in the apartment above the current tavern?

There have been a number of people who claim that strange occurrences have taken place in the apartments, from footsteps, to voices to a general "uneasy feeling" that made it hard to keep tenants for any length of time. A search of the records shows this to be the case. After the last cigar company moved out in the 1950s, the upstairs spaces were used as offices and then apartments starting in the early 1980s. Aside from one tenant who remained for about five years and another who stayed for three, records show that the address was mostly vacant.

Reports say that the strange sounds were often to blame for chasing the tenants away. Heavy, plodding footsteps have been described by staff members and short-time occupants, who can't explain where the eerie, disembodied noises are coming from.

Who is it that may haunt the space above KJB's Pint Haus? No one can say for sure, but it just might be one of the unlucky employees of the slot machine company that ran afoul of the mob. With the building's long connection to gambling and sordid business, the candidates for "resident ghost" may just range into some fairly high numbers. Perhaps time will eventually solve this riddle, for the spirit that lingers here seems to have no plans to depart in the near future.

"You Can Check Out Anytime you Like, But You Can Never Leave..."
History & Haunts at the Dunlap Hotel

When Colonel James Dunlap converted a residence on the west side of Jacksonville's downtown into a hotel in 1858, he inadvertently created what would come to be considered "*the hotel* in the city." And while Dunlap may have come up with the idea of enlarging the brick, three-story house with the rear wings of two floors into a hotel, it would be his successor, Captain Alexander Smith, who was the real dreamer and "born hotel keeper." He would create an establishment worthy of luring author Mark Twain to his door and a place that would live on in the history of Jacksonville, long after the original structure was demolished and a new hotel was erected in its place.

And he would also be the kind of figure that would leave a ghost story behind in his wake.

Hotels had an important place in the early history of Jacksonville. While today we think of such places as a room for the night during our travels, they provided much more than that in the middle part of the nineteenth century. Hotels were essential for towns like Jacksonville, which depended on business that was conducted by salesmen and traveling businessmen. A hotel provided not only a room for the night, but a place to live for an extended period of town. It was literally a "home away from home" and in other cases, transient homes for businessmen who knew no other life. They offered a bed, a place to store their belongings, a warm bath and a hot meal. Some were luxurious, some were serviceable, and others, well, for a man with little means, they offered a bed out of the elements and room that may or may not be heated.

Jacksonville had a number of fine establishments for travelers and for businessmen who needed to spend an extended amount of time with clients in the city. Others were more of what we think of as short-term apartments now, often used by young men who came to town to work and had not yet married or started a household. The Park Hotel on the north side of the square was such a place. It was mainly an apartment house, with a restaurant attached, but it was popular for men who had business downtown.

The Rataichak Hotel was built in 1883 by Anton Rataichak and offered better-than-average rooms for business and casual travelers. The brick building was three stories tall, located on East State Street and offered 61 sleeping rooms, as well as longer-term apartments, and a well-appointed parlor. It boasted indoor plumbing, private bathrooms, and steam heat. It was later renamed the Pacific Hotel and aviator Amelia Earhart stayed there when she visited Jacksonville in 1936. It was burned by an arsonist in May 1982.

The Pacific Hotel on East State Street

On West College Avenue, two blocks from the square, was the Southern Hotel, which was built by Elijah Cobb in 1876. Among the other hotels were the Metropolitan, which could accommodate 50 guests; the Northeastern House at East and Court Streets; Transit House at North Main and Washington; Morgan House, a rooming house on North Main that could accommodate 25 guests; Central House, also on North Main; European Restaurant, on the northeast corner of the square; Hilligass' Restaurant and Boarding House on East State Street; Colonial Inn; and others.

In time, such hotels would be replaced by motor lodges and traveler's courts for tourists on the move, and most of the old downtown hotels in every small town began to fade. That shift came about in the early 1900s, when there was a change in the sort of people who used hotels - or motels, as they came to be called. After decades of traveling across America by train, automobiles became popular and people were delighted to be able to choose their own schedule and their route to get to their destination - and they found there was a lot to see on the way. The first overnight lodging for automobile travelers were the tourist camps, where you could pitch a tent outside or even sleep in your car. Tourist cabins and motor courts came along a little later, offering small little hotel rooms that were separate from a main building and could be rented for just a few dollars a night. The motels -- or "motor hotels" - followed. These economical

SMITH'S MODERN CABINS
Class A. A. - On U. S. 36 - 54 - State 104
Jacksonville, Illinois

Smith's Modern Cabins was a popular motor lodge in Jacksonville after World War II

strips of rooms offered easy access to the parking lot, a no-frills bedroom layout and, most importantly, a place to lay your head for the night.

The years that followed World War II were a boom time for the motel industry. After the war, Americans flocked to the highways, and the rush was on to build newer and better facilities for the folks who were putting the miles on their cars again. By today's standards, the motels of the 1940s and 1950s were still pretty primitive affairs. An average establishment had about 25 rooms. Some had swimming pools and restaurants, but few of them had interior public spaces. There might be small registration areas, but no lobbies, lounges or meeting rooms. It would not be the 1960s that chains like Howard Johnson, Travel Lodge, and Holiday Inn would revolutionize the motel business by offering more than just a standard room for the night. Jacksonville had its own Holiday Inn on West Morton Avenue in the 1960s, as well as the Blackhawk Lodge, which is still east of the city, but largely, the downtown hotels were first replaced by clean, comfortable tourist courts like Crain's Motel, Yording's Tourist Court, Smith's Modern Cabins, Smith's Motel, White Haven Motor Court, and the Sandman Motel on West Walnut Street, which became the site of a mysterious disappearance that will be included in a later chapter.

Times changed with the arrival of the new motels, which occurred as the era of grand old hotels of downtown Jacksonville were coming to an end.

But some of the buildings remains - or at least their stories do, like the Dunlap Hotel. The original structure has been gone since 1925, but the New Dunlap now an apartment building took its place, just steps away from the mansion that was converted into traveler's lodging back in 1858. As mentioned, the 80-room hotel had been created by Colonel James Dunlap, a local entrepreneur. The guest rooms were said to be "neat and airy" and each room had a stove and gas fixtures for light. After the hotel's grand opening, local newspaper wrote, "Although this hotel will be a just subject of price to our citizens, and has involved a very heavy expenditure in its erection, it is entirely a private enterprise on the part of Col. Dunlap, and one which entitles him to the commendations of the community for the liberality and public spirit it evinces." The Dunlap soon became the most popular hotel in town, overshadowing the Mansion House, later known as the Park Hotel, as the leading lodging in the city. Mark Twain would be one of the most famous guests of the hotel in its early days. He came to Jacksonville in 1869 during a lecture series about his travels abroad.

The fact that Colonel Dunlap made such of a success of his hotel is likely more because he had already made his fortune and was well-known in Jacksonville than for his qualities as an inn-keeper. Dunlap was a native of Kentucky and had been born on October 30, 1802. He was the son of Reverend

James Dunlap, who had settled in Ohio after leaving Kentucky and spent the remainder of his life in Marietta County. His son left Ohio and settled in Morgan County, Illinois in July 1830. His first business in Jacksonville was on the north side of the square, where he opened a general store. He devoted most of his energy to the store until 1837, when plans were made to bring the railroad into Jacksonville. This would be Dunlap's first brush with scandal, thanks to the political angles involved with the railroad's route and who won the contracts to build it. Murray McConnel, Jacksonville's first lawyer, was the commissioner of public works, and he handed out the contract to Myron Leslie, Thomas T. January, Charles Collins and Dunlap, who were all friends of McConnel. Their bid for 57 miles of work was $8,000 and work began on August 1. Claims of favoritism and bribery made the newspapers for a time, but Dunlap came through the scandal largely unscathed because he did what he had been contracted to do. In 1845, the firm of January & Dunlap had completed the line and made it ready for rolling stock.

This had been Dunlap's first brush with scandal, but not the last. He was also involved in a scandal over nepotism and graft that erupted at the State Hospital for the Insane. Following the 1852 election of Democrat Joel Matteson as Illinois governor, a faction of local Democrats, led by James Dunlap, attempted to seize control of Jacksonville's state institutions. Dunlap first attempted to have his brother appointed hospital superintendent and when that failed, tried to have him made assistant physician instead. When protests were filed by a majority of the seven hospital board members, led by Jonathan Baldwin Turner from Illinois College, the pro-Dunlap minority seized control of the board and replaced the dissenters with their Democrat cronies. The ousted board members used the *Morgan Journal* newspaper to publish letters denouncing the "evil-minded persons" who would "prostitute these trusts to their own selfish ends." Dunlap and several of his supporters entered the office of *Journal* editor Paul Selby and demanded to know who had written one particularly nasty anonymous letter, but he refused to say - even after being threatened with guns and knives and being badly beaten.

The scandal rippled through the state. Under the pretext of investigating graft in public institutions, Governor Matteson encouraged lawmakers to enact reforms. After a series of investigations, the legislature began by expanding the hospital's board of trustees to eight members and replacing the current board with appointees, including only one from Jacksonville. Under the guise of reform, the Democrats had made the state institutions a rich source of patronage for their own party.

The issue continued to aggravate local affairs for some time. In the fall of 1853, Jonathan Baldwin Turner, who continued to speak out against the abuse of local patronage, was the victim of arson. The controversy was still alive even three years later, when *Morgan Journal* editor Paul Selby accused Colonel W.B. Warren a crony of James Dunlap, then treasurer of the State Hospital for the Insane, of shaving $200 off an order to a local carpenter. Selby and Warren exchanged insults in rival newspapers and then one afternoon when Selby was walking with two friends on the downtown square, he encountered Warren with his son and an unidentified relative. Warren, armed with a cane, assaulted Selby, who retaliated by bashing Warren in the head with a revolver. The others joined in and it turned into a blood melee involving canes, bludgeons and horse whips.

The accusations of graft and the trouble that followed the Warren-Selby affair in Jacksonville brought strong official rebukes from the legislature's joint committee of investigation. This led the committee to recommend further controls over local involvement in state institutions - especially in Jacksonville.

Dunlap largely dealt in real estate another way he had profited from the railroad line and was one of the most prominent farmers and stick deals in the area before 1860. He also served on Jacksonville's Board of Trustees for many years. In 1858, he built the Dunlap House, which an 1894 biography called "an ornament to the city, a most inviting and homelike place of accommodation for boarders and travelers."

At the start of the Civil War, he joined the Army and while too old to serve on the battlefield, he used his business talents to serve as the Chief Quartermaster of the 13th Army Corps until 1864. When he was mustered out with the rank of colonel, he returned home to his life and family in Jacksonville.

Colonel Dunlap had been married to Elizabeth Freeman in Greene County, Ohio in November 1823. They had 11 children: Sarah; Mary Jane, who died in infancy; Amanda, who also died as a child; Emily, who married Reverend N.N. Wood of Jacksonville; Mary; Eliza, who married Judge A. H. Robertson of Lexington, Kentucky; Charles, who was a partner in the hardware firm of Conover & Dunlap with a store on the west side of the square; George, who dealt in real estate and livestock in Kansas; and William.

Dunlap never courted political office, but he was elected as a member of the State Constitutional Convention in 1847, to amend the Illinois Constitution. He also served on the Board of Directors of the Illinois School for the Deaf, succeeding General Joseph Duncan. The first school for the blind - the Illinois Institution for the Education of the Blind - was first opened at Dunlap's home, where it rented space until the buildings for which the state legislature had funded could be built. In 1867, he was one of the owners of the Jacksonville Street Railway Co., although it took three years to get the cars moving. The first passengers on the city's streetcars boarded in December 1870. Each car at that time was pulled by a single horse and could accommodate 12 people. They were

The original Dunlap House hotel

popular from the start and were soon bringing in a substantial amount of money. The length of the streetcar system varied over the years, but, generally speaking, it radiated from the public square out the principal streets of East and West State and North and South Main.

The Dunlap House was called the former soldier, farmer, real estate, and railroad man's greatest achievement in Jacksonville, and it remained in business, operated by the Dunlap family, until the patriarch's death on July 8, 1879. As best as we can tell from existing records, the hotel property went into a period of "prolonged litigation" and ended up as the property of the Northwestern Mutual Life Insurance Company. It was from this company that Captain Alexander Smith purchased the hotel in 1880, beginning what has been regarded as the "golden era" of the Dunlap House.

Alexander Smith was born in Eaton, Ohio, in June 1844 and moved to Atlanta, Illinois, in 1859. At the start of the Civil War, he enlisted as a private soldier in Company E, 7th Illinois Infantry, to serve three months. President Lincoln, as well as Federal military officials, never believed the war would last for more than 90 days and so all initial enlistments were only for that time. The company was first at Camp Yates in Springfield, under the governor's call for troops. They were then stationed in Alton, Mound City, and Cairo for the term of enlistment. Smith was bored. He'd learned all he needed to know about light military duty and wanted to see some action. When the company was reorganized, he signed up for three more years and was unanimously elected first-lieutenant of the

Alexander Smith

company - even though he was only 17-years-old. On March 12, 1862, he earned another promotion, this time to captain, for gallantry displayed during the siege of Fort Donelson.

Smith was finally mustered out at Louisville, Kentucky, in 1865. He had served four years and seven months in the Illinois infantry, taking part in all of the Army of Tennessee's great battles, marches and sieges, including Shiloh, Corinth, Altoona Pass, Atlanta, and Sherman's "March to the Sea." He also marched in the last great event of the war, the grand review in Washington, D.C. He received acclaim for this heroic actions at the battle of Altoona Pass in Georgia, during which only 1,200 Union troops were pitted against an overwhelming Confederate force of more than 6,000 men. Captain Smith's company suffered a greater loss, compared with the numbers engaged, than any other during the entire war. He took into battle a company of 51 men, of whom 51 were lost - killed outright or mortally wounded. During the engagement, the flag carried by the regiment was perforated by 217 bullets. It is also worth noting that even though Smith took part in some of the most brutal battles of the war, he was never wounded, captured, or disabled by sickness during his more than four-year enlistment.

Smith returned to Illinois at the end of the war and settled in Mattoon, where he served as a clerk at the Essex House. He was still a very young man at the time, and he quickly learned to love the hotel trade and was determined to make it his life's work. He moved to Jacksonville in 1869 after hearing about an opening at the Dunlap House. He worked there until 1874 and then became the clerk at the Park Hotel for a year before returning to the Dunlap, where he had been lured by the promise of a manager's position. He remained there for one year, before getting the chance to buy the Park Hotel, which he did. In 1880, he purchased the Dunlap as well and became determined to elevate it into the finest hotel in the entire region.

During his time between the two hotels, Captain Smith married Josephine Marie Litzelmen in April 1875. They adopted a son, Alexander Smith, Jr., who fought in the Spanish-American War with the Third Missouri Infantry and later

88

became the manager of the American Hotel in St. Louis, which was erected just in time for the Louisiana Purchase Exposition of 1904.

The first thing that Smith did after taking over the Dunlap was to close the hotel for three months. He began making numerous changes, repairs, and improvements to the building. A veritable army of painters, plasterers and carpenters were brought in to work on the building. It was repainted inside and out, new wallpaper was put up in the public areas, new furnishings were added and more than $10,000 was spent before it reopened on September 2, 1880. The newly remodeled hotel had 75 sleeping rooms for guests, offices, a reading room, several parlors and halls, a billiard room that held six tables, and quarters for the staff. All of the renovated guest rooms were equipped with an electric bell that was connected to the office and, the *Jacksonville Journal* reported, "another feature which few, if any, hotels in our state possess is the ladies private washroom and bathrooms... fitted up in the best possible manner."

Guest rooms now cost about $2 per night, but the newspaper assured their readers that this was a fair price. The paper wrote, "As a guarantee that the house will be ably conducted in such a manner as to satisfy the traveling public, we need only state that Capt. Alex Smith, the proprietor, will have personal supervision of the house and see that the wants of all guests are promptly supplied."

Captain Smith really was a "born hotel keeper," as was often written about him. He spent every waking hour at the hotel and he was thrilled to spend hours in conversations with travelers and businessmen who were passing through Jacksonville. One historian wrote, "Conventions always delighted him and he was happiest when the great lobby and dining room were filled with sociable guests." On one occasion, the Traveler's Protective Association a fraternal organization that helped traveling salesman and advanced charitable causes state meeting was held at the Dunlap House and as each guest went to the desk to pay his bill for himself and his family, the clerk handed him a receipt that stated it had already been paid by Captain Smith. Needless to say, he made many friends for life and frequent travelers through the city went out of their way to insure that they gave their business to the Dunlap House.

Smith also remained the owner of the Park Hotel, although the Dunlap House was his favorite. For the first few years of his proprietorship, he managed both hotels but then leased out the Park Hotel and devoted himself to the Dunlap until January 1, 1904, when he finally retired.

Many wondered what Captain Smith would do without his hotel, but he never considered public office. He had also never taken much interest in any of the secret or fraternal societies in Jacksonville, aside from those organized by veterans of the Civil War. The only one that he joined - in fact, he was a charter

Alexander Smith's home on West State Street, where he died tragically in 1917.

member in Jacksonville - was the Benevolent and Protective Order of Elks. Most of his days began to be devoted to his activities with the Elks, veteran's groups and charities in the city. He leased out the two hotels and settled down in his comfortable home at 1153 West State Street to enjoy his retirement.

But 13 years later, his life would be tragically cut short.

On January 15, 1917, word spread throughout Jacksonville that Captain Smith had burned to death in his home during the night. Although he had been in poor health for several years, he had been improving over the last few months, which made his death even more shocking. His charred remains were found in an upstairs room of his residence some time after his sister, Mrs. F. M. Rule, had been awakened by the smoke, which poured into her bedroom. The coroner's jury returned a verdict of death by burning and suffocation, but what really happened that night has remained a mystery ever since.

The evening before the fire had been pleasant enough. When the captain's wife, Josephine, died in 1915, Smith's sister, Mrs. Rule and her husband, Reverend F.M. Rule, had come to live with and care for the captain. Dr. Rule had been absent for some time in Minnesota, aiding in financial work for a college and later caring for his son, who nearly died from pneumonia but was markedly better. The captain's adopted son, Alex Smith, Jr., had made plans to visit his father, although he had to leave early when news of his father's death arrived. The captain had also received a visit from his close friend Major Vickery, who had been his companion since the war. He would be grief-stricken by his friend's death, as would Major E.S. Johnson, a member of Smith's regiment who lived in Springfield.

The Smith home was two stories tall and the upper part was divided in two by a hall running north and south. On the west side were two rooms, and Captain Smith used the north room as his bedroom. He kept the other as a sort of study and storage room for memorabilia from his war service. There was a door that connected both rooms. On the opposite east side of the hall was the bedroom where Mrs. Rule, Captain Smith's sister, and her granddaughter, Sarah Lee Rule, age 10, both slept. As the captain had been in delicate health for some time, both he and Mrs. Rule left the doors to their rooms open at night so that any sound might be heard by either in case of trouble.

Around 4:00 a.m. on January 15, Mrs. Rule was awakened by the smell of smoke in her room. She hurriedly got out of bed and found the fire. She quickly woke up her granddaughter, who went down and turned in the alarm, while Mrs. Rule was running into the captain's room to rouse him from sleep. But she found that the bed was empty and there was no sign of him in the room. The smoke from the fore, which seemed to be under the room, was so dense that she had to escape. When she started downstairs, the baseboard of the upper part of the stairway was burning and the ends of the bottom steps were almost burned completely through. The fire was burning inside the walls of the house and seemed to be spreading mainly about the west part of the house where the captain was sleeping. She saw it coming out about the door frame and base boards of the room, but after investigating, she found no fire near the floor of the lower story and none at all in the basement kitchen and furnace room.

When the fire department arrived a short time later, Mrs. Rule told Chief Hunt that she felt that the captain was almost certainly trapped upstairs. Capt. Roach of the police department and fireman John Taylor searched the room occupied by the captain but could find no sign of him. Then they took a ladder to the south window of the room that adjoined his, broke their way through the glass, and looked all around the room through the dense smoke but found nothing. Moments later, a bystander arrived and shouted that Captain Smith was safely over at the hotel. Since he couldn't be found in the house, the men turned their energies toward fighting the fire. Rushing water from the steamer engine soaked the house and soon the flames were extinguished. The house was not greatly damaged by the fire but the contents were pretty thoroughly ruined by the water.

After the fire was under control, Chief Hunt told one of his officers, James Hurst, to search the rooms for valuables and place them into safe-keeping for the family. He started his search upstairs and moments later, came bounding down the blackened stairway to announce that Captain Smith had been found. The firefighters surmised that Smith had been roused by the fire several minutes before Mrs. Rule was awakened. Confused and disoriented by a combination of smoke, heat, and illness, he stumbled the wrong direction away from the hallway and into the room south of his own. He staggered into a corner and collapsed, where he was hidden by a door. He was found with his head against the wall and right over the worst part of the fire, which had burned through the floor, burned a part of his body and rendered him almost unrecognizable. Chief Hunt sent his men to fetch a tarpaulin from the hook and ladder wagon and had the body wrapped up in it before removing it to the undertaking parlor of John Reynolds.

Coroner Rose summoned a jury consisting of Dr. W. W. Crane, foreman; C. E. McDougall, J. R. Kirkman, John E. Wright, A. P. Vasconcellos and John Minter. A clerk, S. W. Nichols, assisted by taking down the testimony. All were veterans of the war except Mr. Crane, but even he held Captain Smith with the highest respect. The evidence of Fireman Hurst, Mrs. Rule and Chief Samuel Hunt was heard and the verdict was that death was caused by suffocation and burning. But how did it happen? And why had the fire started?

During the inquest that followed, it was understood that the loss of the house was covered by insurance. It was well built and in good condition, so naturally, the first question was how did the fire originate? In the testimony given Chief Hunt and the deceased's sister, the fire official and Mrs. Rule felt sure it was caused by the electric wires since the fire was almost wholly inside the partition under the stairs at the start and no fire at all was visible in any other part of the house. Mrs. Rule said they had no matches about the place. The kitchen was untouched by fire and the heating plant had not yet been fired and there was at the start no fire below the button in the hall which turns on the electricity in the house. About this Chief Hunt testified, a large hole more than a foot in diameter was burned. On the other hand, S. E. Anderson, inspector for the Jacksonville Railway and Light Company, and G. A. Sieber, an electrical contractor, were certain the fire did not originate there and in proof of it say they had the wires about the button examined and found them intact, which could not be if the fire started there.

So, what caused the fatal blaze? It was never determined and to this day, we still do not know how one of the greatest heroes to ever call Jacksonville home was actually killed.

A funeral followed the death of Captain Alexander Smith, a man described as a genial, whole-souled gentleman who did much good in a quiet manner. He was popular and a man held in high esteem by the legions of guests who called his hotel their home, even for a short time. "Truly a good man has gone and his loss will be deeply felt," wrote the *Jacksonville Daily Journal.*

Hundreds gathered for Captain Smith's funeral, representing every walk of life, from those he had befriended at his hotel, joined in fellowship with at the Elks Lodge, associated with in business or served with in the military, including a large presence from the Grand Army of the Republic.

Dr. Joseph R. Harker, president of the Illinois Women's College, paid great tribute to Captain Smith, a man that he believed stirred more hearts in Jacksonville with his death than any man he could think of. Dr. Harker recalled, "The memory will linger long of the hearty swing of his arm, and the friendly grasp of his hand as he met us, and his genuine interest in us and our families and our work... I have often said that it made the day brighter and the tasks of life lighter to meet the Captain in the morning. He had his inner circle of friends, as everyone has, and of the depth of his affection and the helpfulness of his friendship to these little can be said here... But the captain's capacity for friendship was very wide. Although he never I think held a public office in the community, he was probably for a number of years, one of our best known citizens. His relation to the Dunlap Hotel gave him an unusual opportunity to meet people. And he had a rare quality of meeting you in such a way as to make you feel from the start that he was a sincere and genuine friend. His interest was especially marked in the young men of the community and in the traveling men. He followed the boys of Jacksonville after they had left and gone into other states, and it was a matter of surprise that even in the last two or three years, with impaired health, he would recall so many of our boys and young men, and make constant inquiry about them, always interested in how they are making good."

He cleared his throat as he continued on. "Our beloved Captain is no longer in our midst," he said. "But we are all better men and women, because he has been with us."

But had Captain Smith really left Jacksonville behind? The mystery remained as to what had caused the fire that claimed his life but now another mystery had been added to the strange saga. Was it Captain Smith's ghost who began haunting the Dunlap Hotel in the wake of the fire?

The Dunlap continued to operate after the captain's death, just as it had before. It was leased out and continued to run just as it had until 1925, when the aging building was replaced by a new five-story brick and steel-frame structure that was built just east of the old Dunlap House.

But it was in the years prior to the construction of the new hotel that we are concerned with when it comes to the rumors and legends of ghosts. In those days, after Captain Smith's death, the decline had already started for the grand old hotels of downtown Jacksonville. Crumbling, outdated, and in need of the modern conveniences promised by the new hotels and motels that were taking their place, the old hotels had started to turn into Single Room Occupancy transient hotels that no longer appealed to travelers and salesmen, but men who were down on their luck and had no better place to spend the night.

Sadly, the once grand Dunlap was among those aging denizens of yesterday. The only beautifully-papered walls had grown dim with age. The paint was peeling. The well-appointed rooms were in a state of disrepair and the carpets had grown worn, dirty, and thin. It's no surprise that in those fading years that a handful of ghost stories came to be told about the fading place. Many travelers spoke of being touched by unseen hands. One man even described it as "an affectionate clap on the shoulder" as if someone was wishing him well. Others stated the feeling of someone brushing past them on the staircase, as if being hurried past by someone they could not see. Some guests spoke of hearing a knock at their door in the early hours of the morning. When they looked to see who was in the corridor, it was always empty. Doors did not stay closed, lights turned on and then were switched on again when guests returned to their rooms.

But the greatest - and most often talked about - strange happening had to do with the electric bells that Captain Smith had installed that connected the guest rooms to the front office. Whenever a guest required anything, all he had to do was to ring the bell and a staff member would go up to check on them. It was an ingenious device for the bellmen, who could retrieve bags for departing guests and their promptness always assured them generous tips. For several years, starting around 1905, the electric bells behaved erratically on a regular basis. On many occasions, although normally at night, a guest room bell would ring and a staff member would hurry up the stairs to see what they needed. After a knock, the door would open with a sleepy guest, still in his or her night clothes, wondering why they had been disturbed. When the staff member explained, the guest assured them that they had not rang the bell. This went on for months and eventually, the bell lines were disconnected. They had more than outlived their usefulness, it was thought. Strangely, though, this did not stop them from ringing. On dozens of occasions, the bells would ring in the office as though a guest was summoning a bellmen to pick up luggage or to assist them with some task - even though the bells had been disconnected years ago.

Who haunted the old Dunlap Hotel? Was it, as many suggested, Captain Smith, simply unwilling to leave the place that he loved so much and had devoted his life to? Trapped in his failing body, did he find the freedom that he needed in death to return to the place where he had spent the best years of his life? A number of his former staff members believed that it was this comforting spirit still inhabiting the old place, perhaps still wanting them to know that he was still around and watching over the hotel as she faded into her twilight years.

The New Dunlap Hotel opened in 1925

But if Captain Smith was the lingering resident of the old Dunlap, then who haunts the halls, corridors, and basement of the new building that was raised nearby and took the place of the original hotel. As mentioned, a new modern building took the Dunlap's place in 1925. Called the New Dunlap, it dwarfed the old, outdated mansion-turned-hotel for a few years before wreckers demolished James Dunlap and Alexander Smith's once glorious place.

The New Dunlap promised everything that the old hotel didn't have - modern conveniences, clean rooms, a well-stocked restaurant, elevators, meeting rooms and, after Prohibition ended, a cocktail lounge. In the days that followed the decline of the downtown hotels and the rise of the motor lodges out on Morton Avenue, the New Dunlap was a major draw for upscale travelers, high-powered salesmen and for every convention and meeting that came to Jacksonville. In fact, the place was so ahead of its time that it was completely remodeled less than a decade after it was built.

A bid of $101, 500 resulted in the sale of the hotel in 1936. Built for more than $400,000 in 1925, the rising costs of the hotel forced the owners into the sale of the hotel and its furnishings. The new owners were three Jacksonville men - Judge H.P. Samuell, attorney Walter Bellatti, and Dr. F.A. Norris. A judge had ordered the property to be sold. On June 2, the three men had no idea what they planned to do with the place, but they quickly came to a decision.

In the latter part of 1936, the New Dunlap Hotel underwent a major renovation. The kitchen was completely rehabilitated and the dining room, meeting rooms and lobby were updated and remodeled. A new coffee shop was installed and the cocktail lounge was built alongside the fine-dining restaurant. To further prove that the New Dunlap was an essential part of downtown Jacksonville, the Chamber of Commerce even moved its offices into the lobby of the hotel. Next door to their offices, a dress shop was opened, with large display windows that looked out onto the street. The Jacksonville Auto Club moved into an office next to the Chamber of Commerce, just next to the hotel's gift shop, which sold souvenir postcards, bumper stickers, local books, and memorabilia. Just down the hall was a new barber shop.

Over the next two decades, the New Dunlap remained the finest hotel in downtown Jacksonville. Numerous clubs and local charities used the hotel for their meetings, including the Jeffersonian Club, which planned the Morgan County Fair; board meetings for the Ayers State Bank; the headquarters for the local branch of the Grand Army of the Republic; the Odd Fellows; the Elks; Lion's Club; Democrats and Republicans; Art shows; a Cooking School; special boxing nights over the "Radiola;" huge New Year's Eve parties; the annual crowning of the Queen of the Illinois College Ball; sales presentations for Kelvinators; Rotary Club; Boy Scouts; the Grand Masonic Grotto Balls, after a demand for seats wouldn't let it be held anywhere else; Junior-Senior proms; a taxi service; speakers on everything from the Spanish-American War to Legal matters, the Anti-Horse Thief Association from Oklahoma, politics, books, labor unions, and anything else you can think of; and even a miniature golf course! In short, the New Dunlap was the center of everything in downtown Jacksonville for years and probably the social center for the entire community.

The gamble made by the three local businessmen paid off for many years, but by the 1950s, the New Dunlap was facing the same challenges as the original hotel that had been on the site. Jacksonville's downtown was starting to change and business was moving away from the square and out toward the new Morton Avenue, which offered a more direct route to Springfield, new stores and businesses and, most importantly, shiny new hotels that the aging New Dunlap just couldn't compete with anymore.

As time wore on, the glitter of yesterday faded and soon the hotel was a shadow of its former self, renting rooms on a weekly and monthly basis to transients and down and out types who couldn't afford the monthly rent on an apartment. Eventually, it was converted into public housing. It was during this time that two very gruesome deaths are rumored to have taken place at the Dunlap.

As rumor has it, there was one quiet, single woman who lived in the apartment building after it became Section 8 housing for the city. People that knew of her said that they never saw anyone coming to visit the woman and that she mostly kept to herself. No one thought of her as lonely since she seemed happy and had the company of her many cats. Neighbors guessed she had anywhere from 3-5 cats in her apartment. Because she was a good tenant, and good tenants were hard to come by, the owner ignored her noncompliance with his pet policy. It came as a surprise to the owner when he started to hear of complaints of the cats causing quite an unusual commotion and a great deal of noise. He had recently taken a call from a tenant about a leak in his ceiling, so he had planned to stop by and speak with the woman while he was in the building one day to fix the leak.

Upon entering the tenant's apartment, prepared to quickly repair a leaky pipe, he was puzzled at the location of the leak: in the entranceway near the front door of the man's apartment. He was not a licensed plumber, but he had made enough repairs to know that no pipes or drains ran along that part of the building. He decided to take a look in the apartment directly above to see what could possibly be running through the floor and into this man's apartment. After climbing the stairs to the next floor, he found himself standing in front of the cat woman's door. He knocked at the door. No answer. He fidgeted for his keys and unlocked the door, but when he attempted to enter the apartment, something was stopping the door from opening. The owner pushed harder, and finally, putting all of his weight into it, he heaved the door ajar to find the body of the woman dead and decaying, laying on the other side of the apartment door. It was apparent by the scratch marks on the lower part of the door that the woman had attempted to seek help, but her life was cut short by cardiac arrest. Medical personnel had a difficult time estimating the amount of time the woman may have been laying in that entranceway. It seemed that her body had started to decompose quite rapidly and showed a great deal of trauma from head to toe. It wasn't until someone realized that with their owner now dead, there was no one around to feed the cats.

Although gruesome, the tale of the cat woman is not the most traumatic of events that is rumored to have taken place at the Dunlap during these questionable years. Police officers were often making stops at the apartment building looking for suspects on drug charges or to break up yet another fight. One tenant remembered hearing the familiar sounds of a quarrel taking place in the apartment upstairs. Like many tenants accustomed to hearing the rustling and shouting of the fights, he didn't bother calling the police. It wasn't until he heard the gunshot that he decided that maybe this time was different. While on the phone with the dispatchers, he started to hear more rustling from the floor upstairs, and then silence. Once police arrived on the scene, they had found that a murder had taken place. A man was shot in his living room, but this was not where they found his body. It was quite obvious by the mess that the body had been moved to the apartment's one bathroom. The officers on duty that night would not soon forget what they discovered next, for what they saw was the murder victim, laying lifeless in the bathtub, with the entire handle of a plunger lodged into the man's rectum.

Recently, Jacksonville's revitalized downtown has brought new life to the area, including the historic Dunlap. But one thing that has not changed over the past few years is the stories of the ghosts. For whatever reason, the Dunlap of today is still playing host to the spirits of yesterday. Who are these lingering former residents? No one seems to know and with it being a hotel, the options are almost endless. Think of just how many people pass through a hotel in a single year - hundreds, thousands of people. How many of those people die while spending the night in an unfamiliar bed? That number is a lot higher than most hotel managers would like you to believe and even the most modern, upscale chain hotels see deaths by natural causes, suicides, and even murders. Whether the details of these rumored deaths are completely true or not is still a mystery, but one thing is certain - some extreme energy has been left behind within the walls of the Dunlap Hotel.

A former maintenance worker from the apartment building reflected upon his experiences when renovating the public housing units into up-to-date apartments. He and a small crew of other men would often feel strange sensations while in the building to work. Perhaps finding comfort in horseplay, the men would often tease each other by purposely startling one another during working hours, hiding behind open doors or calling out one another's names. Yet none of the workers could explain their experiences when they would hear their names being called and found no other workers were nearby.

The man would often come to work after hours. Being a student at Illinois College, class times often interfered with a normal workday. Although each time he felt the change in ambiance upon entering the building alone, there was money to be made, needed money that, he felt, could not be frightened away. That is, until the evening he was working at taking up carpet on the top floor of the building. Sweat dripping from his brow, he thought he was imagining things when he heard his name being called out from the distance. When the name-calling became impossible to ignore, he was certain one of his coworkers was in an apartment nearby. He began to hunt for the culprit, ambling down the long stretch of hallway, peeking into each open door. It was a rule that all doors, inside and out of all apartments, were to remain open at all times. Being an uninhabited building with few security measures in place, the owner wanted to take precaution in case any squatters attempted to set up camp within the building. After investigating behind each of the tall, sturdy doors that opened in to each apartment, the man soon discovered he was indeed alone in the building. It was then, standing, perplexed, at the end of the hallway; he felt a force of cold air quickly blast through the wide hallway. Every open door slammed shut simultaneously with a crash. The man exited the building straight away and did not return for several days.

Still, there was much work to be done. Several weeks later, the building owner gave this maintenance worker a new task. He was to clean out the boiler room located in the basement of the apartment building. Over the years, the boiler room had become storage for hundreds of random items hoarded from abandoned apartments. Each day he descended to the boiler room and was overcome with an unsettling sensation. While buried in trash and treasure alike, the maintenance worker sifted through the wall-to-wall stacks of furniture, clothes, pots and pans, and personal items, gradually sensing stronger and stronger feelings that he was not alone in the boiler room. His eerie suspicions became a terrifying reality when the single light bulb mounted above him went dark. Frozen in fear in the still silence and faint glowing red light of a distant exit sign, he heard the slow creak of a child's wooden jewelry box lid as it opened on its own. Finally he mustered enough courage to escape the darkness, leaving the twirling ballerina and her playful tune behind.

3. DOCTORS, UNDERTAKERS & THEATER FOLK
History & Haunts of the old Williamson Funeral Home

The young man saw the little girl as she rounded the corner at the top of the stairs. He knew that no one was supposed to be up in this part of the building. Was she here with her parents? And if so, didn't they notice that she was gone? He climbed the rest of the way up the staircase and looked down the hallway in the direction the girl had run. He saw a flash of her white dress and then she was gone again. Was she laughing? He thought she was - a strange behavior for a child in a funeral home. But she was young and perhaps she didn't know any better. The young man knew that he should escort the girl downstairs and see who she belonged to. There was a service going on in the second parlor and he didn't want her to disturb anyone. She couldn't go too far. He was at the top of the only staircase that led back down to the first floor.

Small footsteps pattered across the floor and a door swung shut. At least he knew where she was now, he thought, and marched down the hall. The door opened and the little girl darted across the corridor to the room on the other side of the hall. He got a good look at her this time - long brown hair in curls, a pink ribbon and a white dress that fell just past her knees. Oddly old-fashioned really, especially for 1989.

He walked to the door of the room that the girl had entered, twisted the knob and pulled it open. The room was too dark for him to see anything. He flicked on the light switch and an overhead bulb flared to life to show - nothing. The room

was empty. There was no little girl. She had simply vanished. It was impossible and yet it happened.

The young man was not the last to see the little girl who lingered in the old house, nor would he be the last. In fact, that particular little girl may not be the only one that people have seen. There are several descriptions of little girls that are there one moment, and gone the next. But whoever they are, the girls aren't leaving the building that stands at 210 West College Street in Jacksonville anytime soon. Their identities remain a mystery. However, it's very possible that the clues as to who they might be can be found in the many layers of this building's past.

Dr. Cochran's Office

The house on College Street, that would go on to become both the Williamson Funeral Home and the headquarters of the Jacksonville Theatre Guild, entered into the public record in 1902 when it became the office and residence of local physician, Dr. Caleb C. Cochran. He was a doctor and surgeon who paid "special attention to the diseases of women and children." Dr. Cochran was a new breed of physician for Jacksonville in that he specialized in both "internal and external cancers; also Gyneatrics," which was the early name for gynecology.

Most doctors of the nineteenth century had been general practitioners, although as far back as the 1840s, many public-minded citizens of the area strived to make Jacksonville a medical center. This resulted in the first medical school at Illinois College in 1843, the first mental hospital in Illinois in 1847, and the first county medical society in 1846.

Jacksonville's first doctor was a land speculator named Ero Chandler, who established a house and office in 1821 before the town was officially founded. Dr. Chandler helped organized the Presbyterian Church in town and, in 1833, gave the land behind his home to establish the Jacksonville Female Academy. His years as a doctor in the city were short-lived. In 1836, he moved to Hancock County and gave up medicine to become a farmer.

Only a few years after Illinois College was founded, the college trustees decided to establish a medical school. The school actually opened in 1843 and had a 16-week course of instruction. Tuition was $60 per term. It generally took two terms to graduate, but the graduate also had to pass an examination before a board of doctors who had already earned their degree. Since there were so few actual doctors in the area, one of the first acts of Illinois College's Medical School was to confer an M.D. degree on several doctors that were already practicing in Jacksonville. The Medical School only lasted until 1848.

The faculty of the school was more distinguished, however. At least two of them achieved national recognition. David Prince was a professor of anatomy and surgery. Except during the time of his service in the Civil War, he remained in Jacksonville and was a pioneer in plastic and orthopedic surgery. He invented a new method for restoring the lower lip and face. He was also well-respected, even beloved, in the community. His medical knowledge far exceeded most doctors of the day and included literature in several foreign languages. He was active in many medical organizations, became Vice President of the American Medical Association, a founder of the American Surgical Association and of the Illinois State Medical Society, and was a delegate to two international medical congresses in Europe. After returning from the war, Price built Jacksonville's first private hospital, the Jacksonville Surgical Infirmary. Better known as the Prince Sanitarium, it opened in 1867 on South Sandy Street.

A colleague of Prince's was Dr. Edward Mead, a professor of material medica and therapeutics. He and Prince had been classmates at the Medical College of Ohio in Cincinnati. Mead was active in promoting Illinois' first insane asylum in Jacksonville, and he later established private mental hospitals in Chicago, Cincinnati and Boston. He is considered today to be one of the founders of American psychiatry.

Another of Prince's colleagues was Dr. Greene V. Black, who developed many of the dental instruments and techniques that are still in use today. He has often been called the "Father of Modern Dentistry."

For the most part, though, doctors in nineteenth century Jacksonville were general practitioners who delivered most of their medical care in people's homes, or in small offices. By the early 1900s, there were more than 50 physicians practicing in Morgan County but only nine of them were specialists like Dr. C.C. Cochran, who established an office at 210 West College Street. He and his family lived upstairs and his offices were on the main floor.

Serving as a medical doctor, and specializing in women and children, Cochran remained in the same office until 1914, when he moved to 309 West College Street. He cared for many people in the community and later, in 1920, he was elected Vice President of the Medical Society of the United States. Dr. Cochran retired in 1929 and he and his wife moved to Denver, Colorado.

Those early years were the only time that the house was ever used as a doctor's office and no records exist to say who visited there, convalesced in the patient's rooms and who may have died on the premises. It's very possible that with his specialty in children's illnesses, that at least one little girl may not have survived her treatment. Could a patient of Dr. Cochran's be one of the spirits that lingers in the building? Perhaps...

But if so, she may not haunt the place alone.

Private Home and Boarding House

The next owner of the house was Ollie Parker, the manager of the LaCrosse Lumber Company, which was located on West College Street, just one block east of the house. He and his family lived in the house for about four years. Little of note occurred during the Parker family's occupancy, other than his son, Ollie Parker, Jr.'s arrest in the early 1920s for liquor violations during Prohibition. Parker managed the lumberyard in Jacksonville for more than 25 years before moving to Louisiana, Missouri, in 1924 and taking over the position of secretary for the company.

Parker died suddenly from an embolism on April 5, 1934, at his home in Missouri. Oddly, he had been in Jacksonville just three days before and, according to the newspapers, had been in "good health." The following day, he entered a Louisiana hospital for an examination and two days later, died from an embolism.

One short-term resident of the house was Dr. S.J. Carter, a veterinarian, who used the house for his office and residence in 1921, before opening a new office with his brother, S.W. Carter, at 112 West College, adjacent to the LaCrosse Lumber Company.

From 1921 to 1926, the building was turned into the Proffit House, a boarding house that offered according to their advertisement "good meals, by day or week; also warm, comfortable rooms; reasonable prices; close to square." The proprietor of the boarding house was L.L. Coker and contrary to local legend, the boarding house did not serve traveling theater performers from the Grand Opera House on the Square. By the time that the boarding house actually opened, the old theater was already showing silent films, having replaced stage performances with moving pictures. In 1927, it was re-named the Illinois Theater.

It was also in 1927 that the house as 210 West College Street went from a boarding house to a funeral home, changing its history forever.

Burying the Dead in Jacksonville

Since the beginning of the city's history, there had been men to bury the dead. During the 1833 cholera epidemic in the city, two furniture-makers, John Henry and James Anderson, became the first unofficial undertakers in Jacksonville. Coffins were made and the dead were buried, but such work was not truly a profession until the funeral industry began in America at the time of the Civil War. It was in the years following the war that American funeral customs became a true business and the local undertaker was no longer merely a cabinetmaker or carpenter. It was the war that really introduced Americans to the art and science of embalming.

Embalming had been around in one fashion or another for centuries. The ancient Egyptians mummified the dead and began the first real rites of burial. The Greeks and Romans devised their own embalming methods so that persons of stature could lie in state for days. They also created wax masks to place over the face of the corpse so that they would appear more life-like. During the Middle Ages, important people were occasionally pickled to preserve their bodies. This usually involved boiling the body in chemicals so that only the skin and bones remained. The Crusaders who went to fight in the Holy Land brought large cauldrons with them so that their bodies could be preserved and then sent home for burial.

In America, though, it took a war to create a real industry. Scores of embalmers appeared in the wake of bloody battles to prepare the dead soldiers to be shipped home when relatives demanded it. They also began to fill a need for more decorative coffins than plain wooden boxes, and most would say that the American funeral industry was born during the war.

The first patent for embalming was granted in 1856. The process involved injecting the body with an arsenic-alcohol mixture, electrically charging it, washing it with chemicals, covering it in oils and then sealing it in a coffin that was filled with alcohol. The body was probably not viewable after such a process,

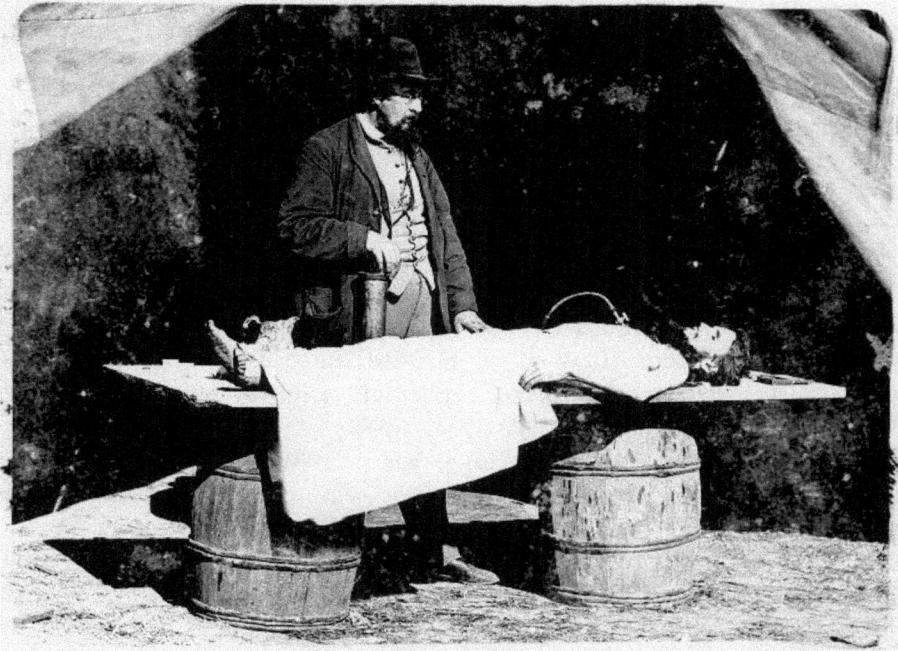

Embalming on the battlefield during the Civil War changed the face of the American funeral industry forever.

but it did effectively preserve the corpse for transportation to far off parts of the country.

Most professional embalmers can trace their start back to Thomas H. Holmes, who thanks to his passion for dissecting corpses and his habit of leaving them around in inappropriate places was expelled from New York University's Medical School before the Civil War. During the war, he received a commission in the Army Medical Corps and spent most of his time embalming soldiers who were killed in battle. He was said to have embalmed 4,028 cadavers in four years. He mostly embalmed officers whose families were willing to pay for the service and charged as much as $100 for each of them. Needless to say, he returned from the war a very rich man. He never revealed his formula for embalming solution, but interestingly, he demanded that his own body not be embalmed when he died. He decided the process was too ghastly.

During the war, military authorities permitted civilian embalmers to work within military controlled areas, and not until the last year of the war did the Army require them to be examined to prove their qualifications. It has been estimated that as many as 30,000 to 40,000 of the Civil War dead were embalmed.

In 1867, August Wilhelm von Hofman discovered a chemical called formaldehyde, the basis for all modern embalming fluids. Embalming would not become commonplace until 1885, but when it did, formaldehyde was almost always used. In 1900, the Massachusetts College of Embalming, the first undertaker's university, was organized and undertakers began advertising in newspapers about their services. Today, embalming is standard practice in America, and the most commonly used method of arterial embalming differs little from the early days. Funeral home operators inject three or four gallons of chemical into the large artery of the corpse, while simultaneously removing the blood from a large vein. They also go through extensive preparations and sometimes even reconstruction to prepare the body for viewing. Modern funeral directors do not have the worries of yesterday when it comes to bad smells or leaking fluids from the corpse.

Although the role of an undertaker had been around for many years prior to the Civil War, this period also marked the beginning of the job being seen as an important position. The word "undertaker" was actually in use as far back as 1698, and it originally meant the one who "undertook" to make funeral arrangements and to keep the body safe. The duties of this person have changed many times through the years and in fact, modern members of the industry dislike the word "undertaker." The term "funeral director" was first coined back in 1885, but it took well over a century for it to catch on. In the early 1900s, the word "mortician" was also devised, but it was never popular.

The undertaker's job began when the doctor's job ended. He performed tasks that quite frankly no one, especially the bereaved family, wanted to do. He cleaned and took care of the corpse and prepared it for burial. Early undertakers usually combined their funeral business with other trades. It was not uncommon for them to be cabinetmakers or furniture makers who made coffins as a sideline. They usually stressed the "furniture" part of undertaking the coffin in their advertising, as this was their major form of income. Businesses that combined furniture sales and funeral directing were common in the Midwest through the middle twentieth century. In most cases, though, undertakers in post-Civil War America began to rely on specialized coffin manufacturers.

By the late nineteenth century, others had joined the ranks as undertakers. Many retired carpenters, gravediggers, and the owners of horse carts saw undertaking as a good way to make a living. Owners of livery stables began to see increasing amounts of business with the rental of wagons, carriages, and coaches that could be used for funerals.

Undertakers gradually began to incorporate embalming into the work, taking over the job from surgeons. The trade later organized as the Undertaker's Mutual Protection Association in Philadelphia in 1864 and by 1881 had organized

in other states as well. By 1900, it had become an acceptable career, and by 1920, the National Funeral Directors Association had nearly 10,000 members.

For years, a social stigma surrounded the local undertaker. While active in the community, many of them were shunned and avoided. They filled a much-needed position, and yet, because of their constant contact with the dead, they were somehow seen as "unclean." This would begin to change as the twentieth century advanced and undertaking was seen as a true vocation. During this time, the practice of embalming and funeral directing also began to move from its early days into modern times. In the late 1800s and early 1900s, embalming was usually done in a private residence with the embalmer bringing his own "cooling board" on which to prepare the corpse. The drainage from the body was funneled right into the kitchen sink. At that time, most funerals took place at home. The bodies were laid out in the front parlor and friends and relatives came to the house for the viewing. The bodies were then transported to the local cemetery for a service and burial.

As times changed, our culture became more and more disconnected from death. People usually didn't die at home anymore; they died in the antiseptic confines of a hospital room. Bodies were no longer washed, embalmed, and laid out at home for viewing. As "funeral director" replaced "undertaker," even the terms for where bodies were once viewed began to change. The word "parlor" was replaced with "living room," so that a person's home was no longer associated with death. The bereaved now traveled to another location - the funeral home -

107

to make their last contact with the dead. Soon, a funeral director had achieved a position of dignity, and the job came to be regarded as a true profession.

There have been a number of undertakers and funeral companies that operated in Jacksonville over the years, most of them starting their business in the latter part of the nineteenth century. The 300 block of East State Street seems to have been a popular place for undertaker's parlors in the early 1900s. John M. Carroll had an undertaking business there, as did O'Donnell and Reavy in the 1930s.

One of the leading firms was that of F.M. Coard, who had a parlor "fitted with all of the modern conveniences and a complete line of funeral supplies on hand." Coard graduated from the Massachusetts College of Embalming, Clark's School of Embalming, and Professor Eckles' Post Graduate Course in Philadelphia. Born and raised in Maine, he was orphaned at age 15 and did farm work to pay for his schooling. After coming west, he attended Shurtleff College in Alton and taught school. He served in the Civil War and then worked in a store in Waverly before coming to Jacksonville. He went into the undertaking business around 1880 and remained in business until his retirement.

Another undertaker's parlor on State Street belonged to S.T. Anderson. He graduated from two schools of embalming, after working as a furniture-maker for many years. He was described in 1905 as a "funeral director of modern methods, experience and known reliability." A specialty of his business was "thorough sanitation and disinfection."

In the fall of 1898, W.W. Gillham and his brother, J.L., moved to Jacksonville from Winchester and established an undertaking business. Both men were graduates of the New York School of Embalming and had opened an undertaking parlor in Winchester. Their new funeral home was established at 226 West State Street in Jacksonville. In the 1920s, W.W. Gillham became the sole proprietor and purchased a large home at 326 West State Street to expand the business. Following his death in 1926, Thomas C. Jenkinson and Fred R. Bailey took over the funeral home. Jenkinson had worked for Gillham for many years and Bailey had been an undertaker in Virginia, Illinois. After Jenkinson passed away in 1948, Clarence H. Muelhausen entered into a partnership with Bailey until his own untimely death in 1950. The following year, Bill W. Buchanan moved to Jacksonville and went into a new partnership with the Gillham Funeral Home, until Bailey retired in 1963.

Under the direction of Bill Buchanan, the funeral home was extensively remodeled and renamed the Gillham-Buchanan Funeral Home. In the years that followed, it remained in the Buchanan family, finally merging in 2007 with the Codys, another family that has long been in the Jacksonville funeral business.

Arthur G. Cody came to Jacksonville from Meredosia in 1903 to serve as an assistant to W.W. Gillham. After eight years, he went into a partnership with C.E. Williamson, who was opening a new funeral parlor on East State Street the current site of KJB's Pint Haus, as detailed in the last chapter . At some point, the two men went their separate ways and Cody went into business for himself at 226 West State Street, then relocated to the former Stice residence at 202 North Prairie Street.

Cody was followed by three succeeding generations, including his son, Willard Cody, his grandsons, Fred and Richard, and his great-grandson, Jon. The two multi-generational firms, Gillham-Buchanan Funeral Home and Cody & Son Memorial Home, were merged in July 2007 to form the Buchanan & Cody Funeral Home and Crematory. While maintaining facilities in Virginia, Meredosia and Ashland, they also moved into a new funeral home on Lincoln Avenue in Jacksonville.

When Robert Reavy opened his funeral home at 551 South Main Street in Jacksonville, it was unlikely that he had any idea of the tragedy and heartbreak that awaited his family in the years to come. Reavy was a well-known funeral director in the city and handled the majority of the Catholic services in town. Born in Galesburg in 1910, he married Josephine Blesse and they had nine children together, including one, Francis, who died in infancy. They attended Our Savior's Church, and as they grew up, the children attended Routt High School.

Tragedy struck the family on July 3, 1961 when the oldest son, Robert, age 21, and his sister, Josephine, 19, were struck and killed by a train at an unmarked railroad crossing outside of Springfield. Robert and Josephine, along with two friends, Mary Ann Chambers, 17, and Carolyn Barnes, 17, were driving home from a night at the drive-in theater and decided to take a different route home to avoid the heavy traffic from Independence Day fireworks celebrations.

Sangamon County Sheriff Hugh Campbell said that their car was struck at the rural crossing by a Gulf, Mobile and Ohio Railroad train out of St. Louis that was traveling between 70 and 75 miles per hour. The station wagon in which they were riding was literally ripped apart by the speeding train in a massive explosion of flesh and steel. The accident was immediately reported by railroad officials, and yet, law enforcement officials were unable to find the wreckage of the car for more than an hour after it happened. The automobile had been destroyed and the pieces of it - as well as the bodies of it unfortunate occupants - were scattered over the tracks for more than a mile.

More family tragedies occurred in the years to come, leaving an indelible mark on the building where the family lived and worked. It has since become a private residence and according to many, one with a haunting past. There are a number of ghosts stories, past residents say, that have yet to be told. At a future time, they undoubtedly will be.

The Williamson Funeral Home

The Williamson name dates back to the late nineteenth century in Illinois. C.E. Williamson, who then lived in Arenzville, was a local purveyor of gas stoves. He decided to expand his business to include furniture and, as was common in those days, undertaking. After briefly moving his business to Beardstown, Williamson came to Jacksonville in 1911 and went into business with Arthur Cody in a funeral parlor on East State Street, just off the square. Their partnership dissolved in 1923, and a few years later, the Williamson family moved into the house at 210 West College Street, which had formerly served as a doctor's office, a private home, a veterinary office and a boarding house.

The Williamson family maintained ownership of the funeral home until 1981, when Harlan Williamson, the third generation of funeral directors, sold the business to the Airsman-Hires funeral company. The Airsman family moved to Jacksonville to take over operations.

The Airsman-Hires story is of a more recent vintage, dating back only to the 1970s in Greene County. Terry and Mary Beth Airsman entered the funeral business in Roodhouse and White Hall after purchasing two facilities from Bill Wolfe, a long-time funeral director in the area. He had given Terry Airsman his first job in the funeral service business, cutting grass, in 1955. Meanwhile, Jess and Niela Hires were operating the Hires Funeral Home in Carrollton and the two families decided to combine operations in March 1979. In addition to other funeral homes, they also purchased the Williamson Funeral Home on West College Street and the business remained at that location until the completion of a new location on Lincoln Avenue in 1998.

Although it's possible that the hauntings at the building date back all of the way to Dr. C.C. Cochran's treatment of sick and dying children in the early 1900s, most believe that whatever occurred to make this place become haunted happened during the occupancy of the funeral home at this location. No records exist to say that anyone actually died in the building, but as most readers know, it does not take a death to occur at a house for a ghost to end up lingering there. Ghosts remain behind because of unfinished business, confusion, sudden trauma, or simply because they refuse to leave the living behind. Many cultures believe that the dead remain with their bodies for hours - even days - after their death. The Native Americans believed this, as did Americans of the Victorian era, when the tradition of covering all of the mirrors in a house after someone has died began. It was believed that if the spirit of the dead person saw his or her reflection in the mirror, it could cause their spirit to remain behind at the place where they died.

There is a funeral home in Decatur, Illinois that became haunted by a spirit that refused to abandon its body. The story tells of an itinerant railroad worker who was killed and brought to the Moran Funeral Home on North Water Street for embalming. His name had been Quincy Mitchell and he had been killed by a train in the Wabash yards. Apparently, he was walking along the tracks when a passenger train and a freight train passed one another. Investigators believed that the rush of air from the two trains somehow threw Mitchell between the cars. His body was horribly mangled and he was killed almost instantly. No one else who worked for the railroad really knew Mitchell. He had worked for the Wabash for only one trip, which was the run from Peru, Illinois to Decatur. All that was known about him was what he had told the engineer of the No. 81 train that had brought him to the city. He stated that he had been born in Tennessee, had been raised in West Virginia, and had since drifted all over the country.

Mitchell's body was taken to the Moran funeral home and an inquest was held into his death. It was ruled accidental and it was suggested that efforts should be made to try and contact his family members. The owner of the funeral home, James Moran, took a personal interest in the plight of the deceased man and led the effort to find the man's family. He passed away himself before the task could ever be completed. Since no relatives were ever found, Mitchell was buried in a pauper's grave.

But Mitchell didn't rest in peace, and accounts say that he has remained at the old Moran building ever since. No one knows what his ghost may be seeking, other than perhaps some peace or some closure to his abruptly ended life. Regardless, he has made his presence known for decades, opening and closing doors, turning lights on and off, and manifesting as cold, unexplainable spots in rooms and doorways. Occupants of the building have also seen him roaming the shadowy corridors of the place, his face masked in an expression of sorrow and grief. He seems stuck at the place where his body was last placed, the victim of a tragic and sorrowful death.

Could such a thing have happened at the former Williamson Funeral Home? It's very possible. Our research has turned up two very different, heartbreaking stories about four young girls, all of whom are likely candidates for the spirits said to linger at the house on College Street.

On Sunday morning, August 23, 1931, the family of Walter Bozarth, a prominent farmer who lived about seven miles southeast of Jacksonville, was on their way to Salem Church, just as they did every Sunday morning. Mr. Bozarth was dressed in his Sunday suit and his wife, Edith, in her nicest dress. Their two daughters, Mildred and Mary Ellen, were in the back seat, looking forward to seeing their friends at Sunday School.

They had a good life. Walter Bozarth was born in Hebron, Nebraska, in 1888, and graduated from the University of Nebraska with a degree in civil engineering. He was a varsity football player while in school. He moved to Morgan County in the 1910s and started working for the Illinois Steel Bridge Factory. He later took up farming, where he was very successful, even in the early days of the Great Depression. He married Edith Ticknor, who grew up in Winchester, in 1918. Although Edith's mother died when she was very young, she was well-looked after by the C.W. Cully family. She attended local schools, as well as Illinois State University and Brown's Business College, eventually working as a teacher in Morgan County schools for five years. The couple's two daughters, Mildred, 11, and Mary Ellen, 9, had a happy life on their family farm and had many friends in school.

It was a Sunday morning, just like any other, but it ended in tragedy.

As Walter drove over a railroad crossing, about a half-mile from the Arnold station, the Wabash No. 29 westbound passenger train slammed into them and totally demolished their car, killing all four of the family members inside.

The bodies of the Bozarth family were taken to the Williamson Funeral Home, where they were later prepared for burial. During the afternoon of Monday, August 24, an inquest was conducted by Coroner C.S. Young to determine what had occurred at that lonely railroad crossing.

Dr. George L. Drennan recounted what he discovered when he examined the bodies. He told the jury that the body of Mr. Bozarth, who he testified died from a crushed skull, revealed many cuts and bruises. The right side of his head was completely crushed and there were deep burns on the right shoulder. Mrs. Bozarth's skull was also fractured, along with her right forearm, pelvis, and right leg. She was also covered in bruises. Both of the young girls died from crushed skulls and Mary Ellen's left arm had been broken.

Joseph A. Cox of Springfield, the engineer of the train, stated that it had been moving at about 50 miles an hour at the time of the accident. This was the average speed of the through train. The engine was about 150 feet from the crossing when he saw the Bozarth automobile drive up on the tracks. He began blowing the whistle and ringing the bell, but the car seemed stuck. He said that he saw it get onto the tracks and then it lurched forward, leaving the rear wheels on the inside of the north rail. When he saw that the car was not moving off the tracks, Cox applied the emergency brakes, but the fast moving train could not be stopped in such a short distance. The pilot at the front of the engine collided with the Bozarth automobile with a screeching, grinding sound, and it was thrown more than 50 feet, completely demolishing the car. Cox said that all of the occupants of the car were thrown clear of the tracks.

More than 850 feet later, the train, with eight passenger cars, was brought to a complete stop. Members of the crew signaled for him to back up to the accident site, and he threw the train into reverse. Nelson Lock, road foreman of engines, was one of those who directed Cox to back up. Lock was with a group of railroad officials who were on the train that morning. He testified that he had been seated on the left side of the train and that he saw the top of a moving automobile above the corn as the car approached the tracks, but he assumed it had time to make it over the crossing. After the crash, Lock said that he was the first man off the train and looking for the bodies. He found Mr. Bozarth under the wreckage of the car and across the body of a little girl. The older girl was found near the car, while the mother was about 40 feet to the west. All of them were dead by the time the crewmen reached the scene of the accident. The four bodies were placed in the baggage coach and brought into Jacksonville, where an ambulance met the train at the depot to take them to the hospital, if any of them could be saved. "It was Mr. Lock's opinion," the newspapers stated, "that all were dead by the time they were placed in the ambulance."

The Bozarth deaths were ruled an accident. There was no way to know what caused their automobile to be stopped on the tracks that day, only that it was unable to make it over the crossing. We'll never know what terrifying thoughts raced through the minds of those four people when they saw the train speeding toward them, but perhaps that moment of abject terror was what helped cause their spirits to linger behind.

The funeral services for the family were conducted at the Williamson Funeral Home on August 25, and they were buried side-by-side in Diamond Grove Cemetery. But do all of them rest in peace? Could the spirits of the young girls that have been seen and experienced in the building be those of Mildred and Mary Ellen Bozarth?

It certainly seems possible, although they were not the only girls in the building's history to experience a horrible death and find themselves on the slab at the Williamson Funeral Home.

It was a cold, clear morning on Friday, February 21, 1947. The Allan sisters, Marilyan, age 12, and Helen, 7, were on their way to Mound School, west of Jacksonville on Route 36. They were being driven to school by Mr. I.S. Dunn, whose son, Ivan, was also in the car, and attended school with the two young girls. The girls often just walked to school, but on especially cold mornings, Mr. Dunn, who lived in Mound Heights, often offered the girls a ride to school.

It would be the last ride to school that the two girls would ever take.

Just a short distance from Mound School, a westbound truck veered out of control on the icy road and slammed into the Dunn car, sending it skidding across into the other lane of traffic. As the truck fish-tailed and then slid into the ditch, a second truck, this one driving eastbound, collided with the Dunn automobile, which had been pushed across the road by the first truck. As the second truck crunched into the car, the sound of twisting metal and shattering glass filled the air - barely covering the sounds of the terrified occupants of the car.

Mary C. Potts, a teacher at the school, heard the crash and looked out the window and saw one truck in the ditch and a second truck sitting at an angle in the yard of the school. She told her students to stay inside, grabbed her coat, and ran outside to investigate. As she neared the mangled Dunn car on the south side of the road, she saw the bodies of the Allan sisters lying in the center of the pavement. Mr. Dunn and his son were also laying nearby and, as far as she could tell, Dunn was unconscious. Blood was spattered and pooling on the icy road and Mary couldn't believe that anyone who had been in the bent and twisted car could possibly still be alive.

Marilyan and Helen had left home at around 8:20 on that Friday morning, their father, J.W. Allan, later testified at the inquest that was held at the Williamson Funeral Home. He didn't know how they were getting to school that day. They usually walked, but often his friend and neighbor, Mr. Dunn, gave them a ride. He trusted his friend with the lives of his daughters. He told the coroner's jury that he felt Dunn was a good driver. When he learned of the accident from Mrs. Dunn, he drove straight to the scene and noted that "the pavement was icy on Friday morning."

One of the witnesses to the accident was Thomas Hardwick of Jacksonville. He was driving west that morning and traveling behind a transport truck. He was about 300 feet behind the truck, he said, and the pavement was slippery. The truck was not traveling fast and, in fact, he gained on it with his own truck. He was driving at about 35 miles per hour. He never saw the Dunn car until it was hit by the westbound truck. The truck slowed down and went about its own length after it struck the car, sliding sideways and into the ditch. Unfortunately, though, the Dunn car did not veer toward the ditch - it spun sharply into the path of oncoming traffic.

A.J. Stewart, who lived just west of the school, was in his back yard when he heard the crash. When he ran out to take a look, and saw how bad things were, he ran into the house and told his wife to call for an ambulance. He then rushed to the scene, and after giving what assistance he could to the injured, he was given a flag by Thomas Hardwick and he went west to flag down traffic.

None of the truck drivers involved in the crash were injured and all of them made every effort to help the injured. Orville Brown and Vernon Smith of

Wichita, Kansas, were in the westbound truck and Scott Arnett or Kansas City was in the eastbound truck. The men were not ticketed or prosecuted since the crash was officially ruled an accident and made unavoidable by the road conditions.

Mr. Dunn and his son survived the crash, but the Allan girls were not so lucky. Sherriff Ralph Bourn investigated the scene and spoke with all three of the truck drivers, noting that the driver of the westbound truck had tried to stop, as evidenced by marks left on the pavement. The sheriff said that both trucks had struck the Dunn car and that the right side of the car was damaged the most. He found blood and brains inside and outside of the car, but the end result was even worse. Sheriff Bourn testified, "I believe the westbound truck hit the Dunn car and knocked it into the path of the eastbound truck and that the Dunn car twirled around and after the girls were thrown out of it, the Dunn car ran over them."

Marilyan's skull was crushed by the impact and her subsequent fall to the pavement. She also had multiple lacerations to her hands, arms and face. Helen's death was even more gruesome. In addition to cuts and lacerations from being thrown through the windows, her legs and her left arm were broken and she was decapitated - either by the window glass or from being run over by the car.

It was a terrible and heartbreakingly sad ending for two young lives that were cut short on the road outside of Jacksonville. Their bodies were prepared for burial at the Williamson Funeral Home, after the inquest and services were held for them on Monday, February 24. They were laid to rest at Diamond Grove Cemetery, and yet, the question again remains: do the two young girls rest in peace?

There are the ghosts of at least two girls - and what may be other spirits as well - who haunt the building at 210 West College Street. The Bozarth and the Allan girls are sadly among the candidates of those whose mortal remains passed through this place on their way to the other side.

Could they be among those who have never left?

The Jacksonville Theatre Guild

After the Williamson Funeral Home moved to its new location on Lincoln Avenue in 1998, the house at 210 West College Street was closed up for a short time and then became the new home of the Jacksonville Theatre Guild. The building may have been silent when the theater group moved in, but it was far from empty.

The JTG was first organized in 1973 and was then called "Summer Theatre '76." Since that time, it has provided an outlet for community members to display their acting talents and take part in a vast number of live shows. In October

1979, the name of the group was changed to the Jacksonville Theatre Guild, but without a headquarters, the group staged productions at the McGee-Spaulding Pavilion in Nichol's Park, the Veteran's Kitchen, the dining room at the Jacksonville Developmental Center, and since 1980, at the Sophie Leschin Building. In 1999, though, the JTG moved into the former Williamson Funeral Home, which it uses as a business office and to showcase small theatrical productions.

It soon became obvious to the office staff, volunteers, board members, performers, and technicians of the Jacksonville Theatre Guild that they were not in the building alone. Strange events began to occur that could not easily be explained. Lights turned on and off, doors opened and closed, things moved about - being left in one place, vanishing and then turning up somewhere else entirely - and most chilling of all were the apparitions and the laughter. People who were in the building alone often claimed to hear what sounded like the laughter of little girls, echoing in empty rooms and hallways. Doors slammed as if someone was nearby but when they checked, they found no one was present. They heard them, however, and saw them too. Young girls, no older than 10 or 12, disappearing around corners, walking through doorways, running down the stairs - there one moment and gone the next. Who were they and why were they in the building? No one knew then, or now.

Over the last several years, the Theatre Guild has been willing to open their doors to us for American Hauntings and we have been in the building for private investigations as well. In nearly every case, our nights behind the locked doors of 210 West College Street have been eventful ones.

One thing that makes this location very unique is that there have been claims of activity in every area of the building, from the garage that housed the funeral car and hearse, to the kitchen that was once used for embalming the dead, to even the wide viewing rooms, now used for seating and stage. There have been several accounts of startled patrons and theatre folk who have caught a glimpse of a woman dressed in a long, pale colored dress, roaming the halls of the first floor. Also on the first floor, people have heard the sound of music being played. Could a spirit be playing a favorite tune on the piano that sits in the northwest corner of the far viewing room? Or could this be the spirit's way of grabbing our attention?

Because of the level of activity throughout this building, and after countless investigations and numerous claims from guests and investigators, we thought no experience was too far out. Even when several people were claiming to see a cat roaming the building, we were not surprised. It is not unusual to feel the tickle of a friendly feline rubbing against your leg or to hear the small footsteps,

116

rustling, or even a meow from the ghost cat that is said to wander from room to room at the Jacksonville Theatre Guild.

The upper floors of the building are packed from floor to ceiling with costumes and props the guild uses for their productions. They have collected thousands of items over their many years and store anything that is not in use on the second and third floors. Is it possible that any of these items could have an attachment that is now haunting the building?

One area of the house that promises significant activity is in the southeast room on the second floor. The room is filled with racks of shoes, antique uniforms, elaborate costumes, and hats. Also unique to the room is a rounded window that looks out on the hustle and bustle of College Avenue. According to the results of several investigations as well as the accounts of two psychics, there seems to be a spirit of a young girl who spends her time in the small alcove. The girl has communicated with many through common ghosting hunting equipment such as K-II meters EMF meters, and her voice has been captured on a digital voice recorder during the team's EVP session in the alcove. Through their spiritual communication with this young girl, she claims to be ill, but is either unable or unwilling to describe her medical condition. She has also revealed her fascination and confusion with the cars going by on the street outside. Other investigators have reported the young girl moving about the second floor, tugging on shirttails or whispering in the darkness. Could this spirit be linked to Dr. Cochran's practice? Or could the young girl be a member of one of the many families that called this building their home?

4. FAMOUS IN JACKSONVILLE

Over the course of nearly two centuries, many well-known people have called Jacksonville home. Some have lived here for extended times, while others first achieved their fame in the city. A number of them were lauded on the national scene, while others were merely names known only by their fellow residents of Jacksonville, but have become locally famous nonetheless. Our city has seen governors, future presidents, former presidents, almost presidents and a great many famous faces who have only passed through the city and yet still managed to leave a mark.

Each and every one of them is worthy of mention within these pages and are all a part of what has continued to make Jacksonville the "Athens of the West."

Jacksonville Politicians Take the National Stage

As mentioned in the introduction to this book, Jacksonville has been home to three Illinois governors and two presidential nominees during its history. One of our local presidential nominees was so determined to get elected that he tried three times - and failed.

Joseph Duncan

Joseph Duncan, the first Illinois governor from Jacksonville, holds a unique place in the history of the state. He was the only Whig party governor of Illinois and was elected in absentia by voters who assumed that he was still a Democrat.

The informal way that elections were held in those days, along with how slow news traveled on the frontier, allowed Duncan's surprise win. The four-term congressman wasn't even in Illinois during the 1834 election because he had stayed in Washington. He didn't make a single campaign speech and yet he won 54-percent of the vote with three other candidates running against him. Meanwhile, he had changed from an admirer to a critic of President Andrew Jackson, which forever changed his political and financial fortunes and changed the direction of state politics. After Duncan ended up in office, Jackson

Joseph Duncan

supporters organized the Illinois Democrats on a statewide level, rallying behind Stephen Douglas. Democrats controlled Illinois politics for the next two decades, until the party was fractured over slavery and the coming of the Civil War.

As the state governor during turbulent times, Duncan was forced to deal with not only the murder of Elijah P. Lovejoy, which gained national attention in 1837, but also with the financial disaster that occurred during the national bank panic that followed that same year. Duncan was conservative when it came to both business and the question of slavery. He had accumulated great wealth from land speculation prior to this term in office, and while he denounced Lovejoy's murder, he blamed the violence and discord on anti-slavery agitators. He was ready to resign as a trustee of Illinois College under the impression that the president and most of the faculty were abolitionists, but he was told it was not true.

Duncan died almost penniless in his Jacksonville home in 1844, but not before creating a name for himself during the early decades of Illinois' history.

Born in Paris, Kentucky, on February 22, 1794, the future governor was the third son of Joseph Duncan, a native of Virginia and an Army major who had settled in Kentucky and built a 20-room stone inn among the log cabins of the area. Unfortunately, his father died when his son was only 12. Rather than going off to school, the young man assumed responsibility of his mother's finances and at age 21, was made guardian of his sister and two younger brothers. But war interfered with his immediate plans and during the War of 1812, he received a military commission. Despite his youth, he gained a sterling reputation in the Battle of Sandusky when he and less than 200 other men repulsed a British and Indian attack. He was involved in a number of other frontier battles during the

119

war. After the British surrendered, he returned home to Kentucky and took up farming.

In 1818, Duncan came to Illinois, largely due to his connections to Ninian Edwards, the Territorial Governor, through an uncle and a brother. He first settled in Jackson County, where his military reputation earned him an appointment to command the local militia, which would later be called into action during the Black Hawk War. In 1923, he was elected to the Illinois Senate and served a four-year term representing Jackson County. During his time in office, he helped introduce a bill that established a system of common schools for the state. It was unpopular at the time - and later repealed - but was a concept that would later be adopted and Duncan remains credited with its creation.

In 1826, one year before his Senate term expired, he was elected as the only representative of the state in the U.S. Congress. He was re-elected every term until 1834, when he won the election to become Illinois' governor. Duncan first went to Congress as a Jacksonian Democrat, but his relationship with President Jackson's party worsened during his career in Congress. By 1834, he voted more often with the opposition Whigs. His final break with the Democrats occurred in June 1834, when he voted to re-charter the Bank of the United States. Of course, the news of this failed to reach Illinois in time for the election and with the help of Democrats - who had no idea of Duncan's change in political leanings - he won the election without even returning to Illinois.

A period of prosperity, marked by optimism and inflated real estate prices, began at the start of Duncan's administration. In his mid-term address in 1836, he asked the legislature to pass a state Internal Improvements Act, which would authorize the construction of numerous roads, railroads, bridges, river and harbor improvements, and canals across the state. But the next year, after the national economic Panic of 1837 began and he saw the cost of those internal improvements beginning to pile up, Duncan asked the legislature to repeal the program. Legislators ignored his advice, adding even more projects to the program. While the number of improvements were few, the program accumulated debt that almost forced the state into bankruptcy. The debt would not be paid off until 1892, long after everyone involved in its creation was dead.

It was also during Duncan's tenure that the state capital was moved from Vandalia to Springfield. This was controversially done in large part by the successful leadership skills of Springfield's representatives, known as the "Long Nine," one of whom was Abraham Lincoln. Lincoln and the eight other members of his delegation won the capital by trading their votes to win the capital for Springfield for projects for other representatives' districts.

Before and after his term as governor, Duncan was wealthy as a result of years of land speculation, but legal problems began to plague him after he retired to Jacksonville. In 1841, claiming that he was being persecuted by Jackson supporters, he fought four court battles, two of which were appealed all the way to the U.S. Supreme Court. Devastated, the government insisted on forced land sales that, at depression prices, wiped out Duncan's fortune. He died a broken man in his Jacksonville home on January 15, 1844, after a short illness. Except for a small trust fund, his wife and seven children were left penniless.

Richard Yates

Richard Yates, Illinois' 13th governor, was one of the most popular and controversial in the state's history. As the "Civil War Governor," serving from 1861 to 1865, he was perhaps the most beloved - and most hated - civilian on the divided Illinois home front. Friendly, handsome, and an eloquent speaker, it was easy for him to convince men to serve in the Illinois regiments during the war. His speeches became regarded as "bugle calls" for more men to march into battle. He mobilized the state behind the war effort, and as a radical Republican, he complained to - and about - Abraham Lincoln, pushing for less delay in the Union's destruction of the Confederacy.

Richard Yates

Emotional, often angry and unable to compromise, he refused to work with his political opposition in the state, which were the Democrats and Southern sympathizers who dominated the legislature. His extreme beliefs in the correctness of the Union cause created many enemies for him within his own government.

Yates was born in Warsaw, Kentucky, on the Ohio River, on January 18, 1815, the fourth child of Henry and Millicent Yates. He was 16 years old when he enrolled at Miami University in Ohio, when his father, who had recently become a widower, moved his family to the free state of Illinois in 1831. After living for a time in Gallatin County, Yates moved to Jacksonville, where he lived for the remainder of his life. In 1835, he was half of Illinois College's first graduating class. He then studied law at Transylvania University in Lexington, Kentucky. He was admitted to the bar in 1837 and opened a law practice in Jacksonville.

Yates made numerous friends. He was of medium height and large build, but he had thick, auburn hair, bright blue eyes, and an appealing manner that won people over. He also had a strong voice that was easily adopted to large, open-air audiences. In that era, this made him an almost irresistible speaker.

121

Yates' political career was almost inevitable. He was the youngest member of the Illinois House of Representatives, to which he was first elected in 1842 and again in 1844 and 1848. In 1850, he was elected as a Whig to the United States House of Representatives where he was the youngest member of the Thirty-second Congress. He was re-elected to Congress in 1852. During Yates' second term in Congress, the repeal of the Missouri Compromise reopened the anti-slavery question. He opposed the repeal and made a forceful speech against the spread of slavery. He also advocated homestead legislation and was regarded as an oddity because he favored women's right to vote. His strong beliefs against slavery, though, soon led him to be connected to the new Republican Party, which may have been a factor when he lost his bid for a third term in Congress.

Six years after losing his congressional seat and one week before Abraham Lincoln won the Republican presidential nomination, Yates became the party's nominee for governor. In 1860, he won the election, and in January 1861, the new governor was too drunk to deliver his inaugural address. Lincoln and other dignitaries were kept waiting for a half-hour before Yates, under escort, staggered down the aisle and collapsed into a chair while the House clerk read his long speech for him. Much different than it would be today, the newspapers printed nothing about the new governor's inebriated condition.

In office, Yates continued to be an outspoken opponent of slavery, and at the opening of the Civil War was very active in raising volunteers. He convened the legislature in extra session on April 12, 1861, the day after the attack on Fort Sumter, and took military possession of Cairo, garrisoning it with regular troops. In Governor Yates's office, General Ulysses S. Grant received his first distinct recognition as a soldier in the Civil War, being appointed by Yates as mustering officer for the state, and afterward colonel of the 21st Illinois regiment. In 1862, he attended the Loyal War Governors' Conference in Altoona, Pennsylvania, which ultimately gave Abraham Lincoln support for his Emancipation Proclamation. Over the course of the war, Illinois contributed six regiments to the fighting, sending 197,360 men into the Federal Army.

After his time in the governor's office ended, Yates was rewarded for his service during the war with election to the U.S. Senate. Following the assassination of President Lincoln, it was Yates who managed to convince Mary Lincoln that her husband should be brought home to Illinois and eventually, to be buried in Springfield. He was a radical voice in the Senate. Determined that the South should be punished for its traitorous ways, he wanted all former slavers to have the right to vote, regardless of their education. Unfortunately, by the time he made it back to Washington, his drinking had gotten the better of him and he spent a great part of his time in an alcoholic haze. Even his supporters considered his time in the U.S. Senate a miserable failure. He lost a bid for a second term and returned home to Jacksonville.

After this loss, he hoped that the new President Ulysses S. Grant would remember the man who gave him his military start in the Civil War, although it was more likely that Grant remembered a more recent occasion when Yates had been "uproariously drunk" at a reception given for General Grant and his wife by President Andrew Johnson. But Yates came home and waited until the mail brought him news of an appointment as a member of a commission that would disband as soon as it inspected a land subsidy railroad in Arkansas. With no other prospects, he took the job.

He was on his way home from this assignment when he died suddenly in a St. Louis hotel on November 27, 1873. It was a sad end to what had been an almost legendary career as a controversial Illinois figure.

Richard Yates, Jr.

The second Richard Yates, Illinois' first twentieth century governor, had many of the same assets as his father - charisma, charm, and the ability to appeal to a mass audience. Unfortunately for the son, who was the first Illinois-born governor, he was a peacetime leader without the stage of a war on which to perform. As a governor, he had no program of his own and made very little mark on the state's history. In fact, he was so forgettable that he ran four times as a candidate for governor and won only his first campaign in 1900. He could never convince the voters to put him back into office again.

It's not surprising considering that one of the main points of his inaugural speech was a confession about how little he knew about running the state. He actually said, "At this time, my knowledge of state affairs is so limited that it would be discourteous to attempt to convey my limited knowledge on the legislature." The bland, pale-faced, dark-eyed man was a University of Michigan law school graduate, but he never practiced outside of Jacksonville and had no administrative experience at all. Before 1900, the highest office he had ever held was as a Morgan County judge.

Richard Yates, Jr. was born on December 12, 1860, in Jacksonville, only a month after his father's election. He would grow up with vague memories of soldiers marching on the

Richard Yates, Jr.

123

lawn of the executive mansion - and in the shadow of his popular father. In the genteel poverty of his widowed mother's home, he attended Jacksonville public schools and hoped for a chance at a military career, but that hope was shattered when President Grant did not appoint him to West Point. He was the city editor of two Jacksonville newspapers, *Daily Courier* in 1878 and 1879 and the *Daily Journal* from 1881 to 1883. Yates graduated from Illinois College in 1880 and from the law department of the University of Michigan at Ann Arbor in 1884.

He returned home to practice law in Jacksonville, and at every opportunity, he made speeches reminding Civil War veterans and other Republicans that he bore a famous name. He was active in local politics, but paid little interest to his legal career. He was city attorney when he married Ellen Wadsworth, who became the mother of his two daughters.

In 1900, Yates was elected governor in his own right, at not yet 40 years of age. There had been better-known men among the Republican candidates, but Yates campaigned as a neutral "dark horse," which won him the support of powerful Senator Shelby Moore. Congressman William Lorimer, who had backed another candidate in a field of well-known men, suddenly switched at the Republican convention, grabbing up a Yates banner and proceeding to stampede the convention. This played out with the results of the third ballot never being announced; Yates was then nominated on the fourth. Since he was at least presentable, he was accepted as being preferable to a split in the Republican ranks.

The keynote legislation signed during the governorship of Richard Yates, Jr., was a new child labor law, the first of its kind in any state, restricting the work week of children to no more than 48 hours. Another significant move of the administration was the signing of a bill permitting municipal ownership of street railways. Yates restricted prison industries, but vetoed a bill calling for a centralized audit of all state agencies. The veto is significant, in light of the Chicago press of the day. Highly critical of the stylish governor, Chicago newspapers reported Yates forced state employees to do campaign work and to contribute to a political "slush fund."

In 1904, Yates did attain a small amount of prominence by being the first Republican west of Ohio to declare for Theodore Roosevelt. But this acclaim didn't last long. Despite being the sitting governor, he did not receive his party's nomination in 1904; no one thought he could win. He did, however, lead the field of six candidates for 58 ballots, before throwing support behind State's Attorney Charles S. Deneen, in order to prevent the nomination of Frank O. Lowden, Yates' chief rival at the convention.

After leaving the governor's office, Yates lived in Springfield and divided his time between the Chautauqua circuit of the day and patronage jobs, such as serving in charge of telephone companies, as a member of the state utility commission. He lost in the 1928 primary for the U.S. Congress but was given the nomination when the man who defeated him died before the election. He went on to win a House seat. Defeated in 1932 when Democrats led by Franklin D. Roosevelt swept the elections, he nevertheless gathered more votes than any other Illinois Republican. His final act of service was to cast a vote in 1933 against the repeal of Prohibition.

After leaving Congress, Yates resided in Harbor Springs, Michigan, where he died while writing his memoirs on April 11, 1936. He was buried in Jacksonville's Diamond Grove Cemetery.

The Men who Ran for President - And Lost

Jacksonville can also hold claim to being the home of two men who may not have won their bids for the highest office in the land, but they made their mark on both Illinois and American history anyway.

Stephen A. Douglas

Stephen Douglas, who became one of the greatest statesmen in American history, first arrived in Jacksonville nearly penniless in 1833. At that time, the 20-year-old, who had been born in Brandon, Vermont, found little opportunity in the city. He spent the next few months in Winchester, where he taught school and earned $3 per pupil. He also studied law and soon returned to Jacksonville, where he set up a practice. He served as the state's attorney and began dabbling in politics. In 1834, he made his first public speech at the Morgan County Courthouse, where he defended President Andrew Jackson's removal of government money from the Second Bank of

Stephen A. Douglas

the United States. Jacksonville citizens carried the short, fiery man on their shoulders around the square, declaring that he was a "Little Giant." The nickname stuck throughout his entire career.

Douglas' popularity led to his election to the state legislature in 1836, and in the next year, he was appointed register of the land office at Springfield, where he moved and truly began his political career. In 1841, at the age of 27, he was appointed an associate justice of the Illinois Supreme Court. However, he resigned from the court after being elected to the U.S. House of Representatives

125

in 1843. He was re-elected in 1844. In Congress, he championed territorial expansion and supported the Mexican War. In 1846, the Illinois General Assembly elected him a U.S. Senator.

While beginning his political rise, Douglas briefly courted Mary Todd, who later married Abraham Lincoln instead. In March 1847, he married Martha Martin, the 21-year-old daughter of wealthy Colonel Robert Martin of North Carolina. The year after their marriage, her father died and bequeathed Martha a 2,500-acre cotton plantation with 100 slaves on the Pearl River in Lawrence County, Mississippi. He appointed Douglas the property manager but, as a senator from the free state of Illinois, and with presidential aspirations, Douglas found the Southern plantation presented difficulties. He created distance by hiring a manager to operate the plantation, while using his allocated 20 percent of the income to advance his political career. Douglas privately told friends that he believed slavery was a "cancer on the nation," he would not offend southerners by publicly condemning it - nor would be choose not to profit from it either.

Douglas moved from Springfield to Chicago the following summer. He and Martha had two sons, Robert and Stephen, Jr. Martha Douglas died in January 1853 after the birth of their third child, a daughter. The girl died a few weeks later, leaving Douglas alone with his sons until he remarried in November 1856. His second wife, 20-year-old Adele Cutts, was the daughter of James Madison Cutts of Washington, D.C., nephew of President James Madison.

Senator Douglas was a strong supporter of popular sovereignty, as doctrine which asserted that residents of territories had the right to decide whether they wanted to have a free state or a slave state. His beliefs, his ties to the south and his support of the Kansas-Nebraska Act of 1854, which applied popular sovereignty to those territories, made him a favorite target of criticism from the new Republican Party. His support of the act made him so unpopular for a time that Douglas joked that he could travel from Washington back to Illinois by the light of burning effigies of him.

In 1856, Douglas was a candidate for the Democratic presidential nomination, and while he received strong support at the convention, he was passed over.

Douglas continued to steer a middle course on the slavery issue. His "popular sovereignty" doctrine that slavery should be decided on locally by states and territories was satisfactory to southerners who didn't want outside interference with slavery and Northerners who didn't want to take sides over it. It was famously said of him that he didn't care "whether slavery was voted up or voted down," as long as it was voted on by the people.

Then in 1857, the U.S. Supreme Court issued the Dred Scott decision, which declared that under the Constitution, neither Congress nor a territorial legislature created by Congress had the power to prohibit slavery in a territory.

This struck down key elements of the Missouri and 1850 Compromises, made the Kansas-Nebraska Act irrelevant, and denied the basis of "popular sovereignty." Pro-slavery Southerners had praised Douglas for relaxing restrictions on slavery in the Kansas-Nebraska Act; now, ardent pro-slavery radicals denounced him for supporting any restrictions at all. At the same time, some Northerners, seeing "popular sovereignty" apparently dead, went over to the Republicans. Douglas faced a dilemma. If he rejected Dred Scott, he would lose Southern support he needed for the presidential election of 1860. If he embraced Dred Scott, he would lose northern support. He tried to avoid both hazards, issuing a tepid endorsement of the decision, while continuing to state that he believed in popular sovereignty without explicitly saying the Court was wrong.

Another issue came up at the same time and Douglas was forced to take a side in the matter. President James Buchanan and his Southern allies tried to get Kansas admitted as a slave state. But the anti-slavery majority in Kansas rejected this, despite efforts to rig the voting there. Douglas strongly opposed Buchanan's maneuvers, and the two became bitter enemies. Even his Republican critics praised him for this stand, and he restored his standing with the moderates of the north. This was critically important, because his Senate term ended in 1859, and he wanted to be re-elected.

It was during this campaign in 1858 that Douglas came up against his friend and political and romantic rival, Abraham Lincoln, who had been picked to run for the Senate seat by the Republicans. Douglas tried to avoid meeting Lincoln directly. He traveled the state, making speeches and was provided with a private train from the Illinois Central, which was then run by his friend and future Civil War General George McClellan. Lincoln followed Douglas around the state, answering each Douglas speech with one of his own a day or two later.

After several such incidents, Douglas agreed to seven formal joint appearances, now known as the Lincoln-Douglas Debates. The events, described at the time as "setting the prairie on fire," were held in Ottawa, Freeport, Jonesboro, Charleston, Galesburg, Quincy, and Alton. In the debates, Douglas reiterated his support of popular sovereignty. He demanded to know whether Lincoln would ever vote to admit a new slave state, even if the majority of settlers favored slavery. He denounced Lincoln for his insistence that slavery was a moral issue that had to be resolved by the nation as a whole. Douglas described this as causing an unnecessary conflict between free and slave states, which threatened to boil up into disunion and war. He also asserted that Lincoln supported civil and social equality between the races, and insinuated that Lincoln even accepted racial intermarriage. For his part, Lincoln criticized Douglas for his moral indifference to slavery, but denied any intention of interference with slavery in the South. He evaded Douglas' question about the admission of a slave state. Lincoln disclaimed the radical views on racial equality attributed to him by Douglas, arguing only for the right of Negroes to personal liberty and to earn their own livings. Like most debates throughout history, the two men attacked each other for allegedly extreme or irresponsible statements by supporters or colleagues, and accused each other of bad faith in denying responsibility for such statements or for inconsistency in their own statements.

In the end, Lincoln lost the election, but two years later, he would win the presidency.

And he faced Stephen Douglas once again. Douglas was the obvious nominee for the Democrats in the election of 1860, despite the opposition of President Buchanan. But Douglas was facing opposition from the south and southern Democrats ran their own opponents against him, essentially splitting the party between north and south. During the subsequent campaign, Douglas broke an unwritten rule by campaigning in person. In those days, it was considered beneath the dignity of a presidential candidate. But Douglas, seeing the dangers facing the country, went on speaking tours across the country. Douglas campaigned energetically, attacking abolitionism in the north, and talk of secession in the south. Despite the vigor of his campaign, Douglas was defeated.

After losing to his old friend, though, Douglas immediately came out in support of Lincoln. He urged the south to accept the results of the election and tried to do what he could to avert secession, which he denounced as criminal. He was one of the strongest advocates of maintaining the integrity of the Union at all hazards.

He was also a loyal friend. He was present at Lincoln's first inauguration. Lincoln took the oath of office, then took off his "stovepipe" hat in preparation for giving his inaugural address. But he had nowhere to set down the hat. Douglas, who was on the platform, stepped forward and took the hat from Lincoln's hands. Moving back, he remarked "If I can't be the President, at least I can hold his hat." It was a symbolic gesture that showed the true character of Stephen Douglas. Though he and Lincoln had long been political rivals, his respect for the man - and the office that he held - overcame any bad feelings he might have had.

After the bombardment of Fort Sumter, Lincoln decided to proclaim a state of rebellion and call for 75,000 troops to suppress it. Douglas looked over the proclamation before it was issued and endorsed it completely. He suggested only one change: Lincoln should call for 200,000 troops, not just 75,000. "You do not know the dishonest purposes of those men as well as I do," he said. He then left on a mission to the border states to raise spirits for Union support, appearing in Virginia, Ohio, and Illinois

It was during this trip that Douglas was infected with typhoid fever, and he died in Chicago on June 3, 1861. He was only 48 years old, and his death left a terrible void in American history. One has to wonder if the Civil War would have dragged on for as long as it did if Douglas had lived to perhaps broker an earlier peace. We will never know.

Strangely, though, Douglas's death would begin a weird and macabre series of events in Chicago that few in Jacksonville know anything about. The events surrounded the monument that had been built for Douglas near the shores of Lake Michigan, and they came to the attention of the public on June 29, 1879, when a man named of Martin Arndt shot himself in the head with a revolver at the monument that had been built in Douglas' honor. Arndt had committed suicide after losing his job earlier that day, leaving a wife and son behind. Arndt was an ordinary man, one of a million sad stories in the Windy City in 1879, but he was not the first man to commit suicide at the Douglas Monument - a place that had a troubled history of its own.

During the last years of his life, Douglas and his second wife, Adele, had resided at Okenwald, their estate on the South Side of Chicago. It was located just east of the present-day intersection of Cottage Grove Avenue and 35th Street. A cornerstone was laid for his monument and tomb on the property in 1866, but it would not be completed until 1881, largely thanks to the war and a long series of funding problems that continued for years.

The U.S. government took control of the property after Douglas' death and constructed a military training camp on part of the property that had once been used as a fairgrounds. It was named in honor of Stephen Douglas. The camp enclosed about 80 acres, which were further divided by interior partitions to create compounds of various sizes. Each of the compounds, or squares, was named according to the purpose that it was used for.

Garrison Square, which was about 20 acres in size, was lined on all four sides by the officers' quarters and the enlisted men's barracks and had a flat parade ground in the center. Hospital Square was about 10 acres in size and served as a medical facility. Whiteoak Square, which was another 10 acres, originally served as the post's prison. When orders were received to prepare the camp for Confederate prisoners, Whiteoak was merged with portions of other squares, creating Prison Square, a compound of 20 acres.

In the early months of the war, the outpost trained thousands of Union troops under the command of General Joseph H. Tucker. Soon, however, the camp became a place of misery for the Confederate prisoners. The camp received its first prisoners in February 1862, after the Battle of Fort Donelson, and soon overcrowding, starvation, scurvy, and a lack of medical attention made the place a living hell. The death toll for the camp during the last three years of the war has been estimated at as many as 6,129 men, which is slightly less than one-third of the entire prison population at the camp. Most perished from scurvy and smallpox, despite the best intentions of relief workers, who organized a fund to care for the men in 1862. The camp was soon dubbed "Eighty Acres of Hell."

The war ended in 1865, and it was closed down that summer. The remaining prisoners were asked to take a loyalty oath to the United States and were then set free. For a short time, the post was used as a rendezvous point for returning federal troops, but by fall, it was deserted.

After the war ended, a drive began to raise the funds to build a monument in Douglas' honor on the former site of the camp. The cornerstone was laid in 1866 with great fanfare, parades and appearances by practically every organized group in Chicago, from the police to Masonic organizations, aldermen and mayors from nearby cities, soldiers from various Illinois units, the Irish societies, the French society, temperance groups, trade unions, various religious groups, singing societies, butchers, and just plain citizens. Speeches were given, flags were waved, and pleas were made for donations. Money came in, but not enough. In the end, the planning committee lost over $1,300 planned for the monument.

Eighteen months passed with little public activity, but Douglas' tomb was now ready to receive his remains. On June 3, 1868, the anniversary of Douglas' death, the body was moved to the tomb. Tickets for the ceremony were sold at twenty-five cents each but the public was allowed two days to view well-preserved features of Douglas through the glass cover of the casket for free. After it was over, the newspapers reported that the monument committee planned to seek $50,000 from the state to complete the work on the structure. That amount was later reduced to $25,000, but delays kept the bill from being voted on.

More time passed. The newspapers waxed sarcastic that nothing more had been done. An article in the *Post* on May 9, 1870 indicated that the masonry on the unfinished monument had cracked because of freezing water. The fence around the site was falling down, and the grounds had become shabby and overgrown. Plans began to be made to move the monument to Chicago University, and Douglas' widow sent letters pleading with the committee to do something or remove the monument.

But matters again dragged. On April 11, 1873 another attempt was made to get the legislature to pass the bill. It passed the House again, but was defeated by the Senate in the winter of 1874. Even bills to move the monument were defeated. Finally, in May 1877, the funding bill was passed and became effective on July 1. Robert T. Lincoln, Potter Palmer and Melville W. Fuller were appointed as a commission to complete the monument, and in July 1877, advertised for bids

Woodland Park, Chicago.
Tomb and Monument of Stephen Douglas.
Cottage Grove Ave., and 35th St.

The Douglas Monument in Chicago - one of the Windy City's macabre suicide spots

on the additional work on walls, sidewalks and limestone walls. It was finally completed in August 1881 - but not before becoming the scene of tragedy.

On November 13, 1877, W.F. Coolbaugh, one of Chicago's leading citizens and President of the Union National Bank, committed suicide at the entrance to the Douglas Monument by shooting himself in the head with a pistol. It seemed that when he left the bank that evening, Coolbaugh went directly to the spot where the tragedy occurred - "the tomb of a man whose political principles he revered," the newspapers stated - and ended his life. There were no witnesses to the suicide, but his body was discovered early the next morning by a patrolman from the Cottage Grove Police Station. Coolbaugh was lying in a pool of blood and next to his body was a silver-plated pistol with his name engraved on it.

The policeman, knowing that attorney Melvin W. Fuller, whose home was nearby, was the son-in-law of Coolbaugh, hurried to the house and alerted Fuller as to what he had discovered. Fuller came immediately to the scene, found the body as described by the police officer, and immediately had the corpse moved to Coolbaugh's home at 120 Calumet Avenue.

As it turned out, a search had been carried out for Coolbaugh the night before. He had been in good spirits when he'd left home in the morning, had stayed away all day, dropping in just briefly later on, but had not returned for supper. When he did not come home that night, Fuller and the dead man's son, James Coolbaugh, searching the city, calling at hotels and anywhere else that the

131

older man might be found. There was no sign of him. They stayed out until 3:00 a.m. before going home. The discovery of the body was the first news that they had of his location.

Coolbaugh's suicide was a bit of a mystery. He left no note behind and no clue as to why he had taken his own life. His health had been bad for several years, though, and his family knew that he had been prone to depression. He had recently returned from a short European tour and had been in better spirits but, as the newspapers noted, "he had undoubtedly become depressed and in a sudden mental aberration committed the deed which in his senses he would have recoiled in horror."

His suicide was a shock to the entire city. Coolbaugh had established himself in Chicago in 1862, but for many years had been a leading merchant and banker in Burlington, Iowa. He was a fiercely loyal Democrat and personal friend of Stephen Douglas. After moving to Chicago, he started the Coolbaugh & Co. bank, which later became the Union National Bank. He was happily married and had six children, but what drove him to his death remains unknown.

Less than two years later, on June 29, 1879, another man - of less social and financial stature - was driven to desperation and death on the same stone steps at the Douglas Monument. His name was Martin Arndt, a 53-year-old tailor, who also shot himself in the head. Unlike Coolbaugh, he had a clear reason for taking his own life, which he had expressed in a letter to his wife that arrived soon after he left the house.

Arndt had left for work on Thursday morning, as he did each day, carrying his lunch with him. But later on that evening, his wife received a letter in the mail, which had been written and posted that same day. In the letter, he explained that he had spoken to the bookkeeper at the company where he worked, Friddart and Sayers, and asked for a raise of a half-cent for each coat that he pressed. Not only was his request refused, but he was fired for asking. In desperation, he learned that his union not only provided death benefits for his family, but additional cash for suicides. He was, he learned, worth far more dead than alive. He begged his wife's forgiveness and asked that, if she remarried, that she make sure that her new husband did not mistreat their son.

After leaving work, he went to the Douglas Monument and shot himself. Apparently, his first shot - fired just below his heart - was not fatal. He deliberately loaded the pistol again and fired this time into his head. His body was found the next morning and taken to his home at 1838 State Street, where he lived with his wife and son. It was a tragic end for a man who only wanted to provide for his family.

This was the beginning of more death and bloodshed at the Douglas Monument. For whatever reason, it became a favorite suicide spot for Chicagoans for a number of years. Perhaps it was the isolated location or something else, but an eerie pull seemed to draw those who wanted to take their own lives. Several other suicides were reported before the monument faded from "popularity," replaced by other strange places in Chicago where suicidal residents could meet their end.

William Jennings Bryan

Presidential campaigns at the dawn of the twentieth century are still remembered today by historians for their fiery rhetoric, venomous attacks, and for the presence of William Jennings Bryan, a man who ran for president in three elections and lost. He may have never achieved the office, but he made a mark on Jacksonville history as a reformer, evangelist, and a man determined to never give up on his beliefs - no matter how unpopular they might have been.

Bryan was born on March 19, 1860, in the Southern Illinois town of Salem. He enrolled in Whipple Academy, Illinois College's preparatory

William Jennings Bryan

school, in 1875 and graduated from Illinois College in 1881. As a student at Illinois College, Bryan finished first in his classes, won prizes for his speaking ability, and was a member of the Sigma Pi literary society. He then studied law at Union Law College in Chicago, which later became Northwestern University School of Law. While preparing for the bar exam, he taught high school and met Mary Elizabeth Baird. The two were married in October 1884, and they settled in Jacksonville, where Mary also became a lawyer and collaborated with him on all his speeches and writings.

Bryan practiced law in Jacksonville from 1883 to 1887, then moved to the boom city of Lincoln, Nebraska. In Lincoln, he found a political base among the farmers who felt abandoned by the Republicans and his political career began. In the landslide election of 1890, Bryan was elected to the U.S. House of Representatives. In the House, Bryan was known for his strong support of the growing Prohibition movement, which would ban liquor in the country, and for issues that affected farmers in the west. His main thrust, though, became "free silver," which became his platform in the presidential election of 1896.

The United States had been on a gold standard since 1873, and Bryan used his innate talents in oratory to try and change that. He gave speeches, organized meetings, and adopted resounding resolutions that impressed farmer's groups

133

that believed by increasing the amount of currency in circulation, commodities would receive higher prices. They were opposed by banks and bond holders who feared the effects of inflation. The ultimate goal was to garner national support for the reinstatement of silver coins, which was popular in the Midwest. At the 1896 Democratic National Convention, Bryan lambasted "Eastern moneyed classes" for supporting the gold standard at the expense of the average worker. His "Cross of Gold" speech made him the sensational new face in the Democratic Party. From the stage, he stated:

Having behind us the producing masses of this nation and the world, supported by the commercial interests, the laboring interests and the toilers everywhere, we will answer their demand for a gold standard by saying to them: You shall not press down upon the brow of labor this crown of thorns, you shall not crucify man upon a cross of gold.

On July 9, 1896, he became the Democratic nominee for president, and in that same year, he became the first presidential candidate to campaign in a car a donated Mueller in Decatur, Illinois. Running against conservative William McKinley, Bryan traveled 18,000 miles and delivered 600 speeches to an estimated 5 million Americans in 27 states. But he lost the election by more than 500,000 votes. The Republicans had characterized him as a madman and a religious fanatic surrounded by anarchists, who would wreck the economy. McKinley had been painted as the man who would bring prosperity to all Americans and he scored solid gains among the middle class, factory and railroad workers, prosperous farmers, and basically anyone who rejected Bryan's wild ideas about the silver standard.

Throughout this time of Bryan's national prominence, he maintained his ties to Jacksonville and Illinois College. He served as the chairman of the college's board of trustees, but resigned when the school accepted a gift of "tainted money" from philanthropist and steel magnate Andrew Carnegie. Angry, Bryan broke off most of his connections with Illinois College and even requested that his name be removed from the list of alumni. He did, however, pay tribute to his alma mater and its founders in a speech that he made during his last visit to Jacksonville in 1925. He also visited with members of the Sigma Pi literary society as well, perhaps softening a little in his later years.

In 1898, when America went to war against Spain, Bryan was forced into speaking about his party's stance on the war. While critical of the military, he did believe in the United States spreading democracy around the world, so he came out in support of the invasion of Cuba. He also agreed with the treaty that was signed with Spain that ended the war, but drew the line at the United States' annexation of the Philippines. He began speaking out against the Republicans' "imperial aspirations," stating that the country was following in the footsteps of Great Britain.

In 1900, he again received the Democratic presidential nomination. He ran on an anti-imperialism platform. Republicans mocked Bryan as indecisive, or a coward, a point which L. Frank Baum satirized viciously in the Bryan-like Cowardly Lion in *The Wonderful Wizard of Oz*, published in the spring of 1900. In the election, President McKinley defeated Bryan by more than 860,000 votes.

The 1908 election was Bryan's third attempt at gaining the presidency. The Democrats nominated Bryan by a wide margin at the Democratic convention held in Denver. Bryan ran against the Republicans, and Theodore Roosevelt's hand-picked nominee William Howard Taft. After another November thrashing, this time by Taft, who beat him by 1.2 million votes, Bryan announced that he would not seek the office again.

After his last defeat, Bryan needed money, and his powerful voice and name recognition made him a popular speaker on the Chautauqua circuit. He delivered thousands of paid speeches on current events in hundreds of towns and cities across the country. He mostly spoke about Christianity, but covered a wide variety of topics. His most popular lecture and his personal favorite was a lecture entitled "The Prince of Peace", which stressed that Christian theology was the solid foundation of morality. He also spoke out against Darwin's theory of evolution and the temperance movement, which wanted to ban alcohol. He traveled the globe with Mary, sightseeing, lecturing, preaching, and avoiding the political chaos of Washington.

However, he did return to the capital to serve as the Secretary of State under President Woodrow Wilson from 1913 to 1915. He resigned, though, when it appeared that Wilson was getting America embroiled in World War I after the sinking of the *Lusitania*.

After leaving his position in the Wilson administration, Bryan campaigned for Constitutional amendments on Prohibition and women's suffrage. He also became an active promoter of Florida real estate, and lived in the Miami area during the colder months. His promotions in print, speeches and even radio talks may have played a role in setting the 1920s Florida real estate boom in motion, and Bryan became rich from his real estate investments. His campaigning for Prohibition had a very real effect on helping Congress pass the 18th Amendment in 1918, which shut down all saloons as of 1920.

Bryan's final appearance on the national stage occurred in the summer of 1925. Earlier that year, fundamentalists had won passage of a law that forbid the teaching of evolution in Tennessee schools and colleges. But John Scopes, a young teacher in Dayton, Tennessee, broke the law and was arrested. In the trial

William Jennings Bryan and Clarence Darrow Left in the heat of the so-called "Scopes Monkey Trial" in Tennessee.

that followed, Bryan joined the prosecution and Clarence Darrow, the most famous trial lawyer in America, headed the defense. When Darrow announced that the trial's real purpose was "to show up fundamentalism to prevent bigots and ignoramuses from controlling education in the United States," an infuriated Bryan vowed to "protect the word of God from the greatest atheist and agnostic in the United States."

Bryan made the mistake of taking the stand and was questioned by Darrow about his views on the Bible. When asked when the biblical Great Flood occurred, Bryan gave the date as 2348 B.C., or 4273 years ago. But Darrow asked him if he knew that the Chinese civilization had been traced back at least 7000 years. Bryan conceded that he did not. When he was asked if the records of any other religion made mention of a flood at the time he cited, Bryan replied: "The Christian religion has always been good enough for me - I never found it necessary to study any competing religion." The national media reported the trial in great detail, with H.L. Mencken ridiculing Bryan as a symbol of ignorance and anti-intellectualism. In a more humorous vein, satirist Richard Armour stated that Darrow had "made a monkey out of" Bryan due to Bryan's ignorance of the Bible.

After the judge retroactively expunged all of Bryan's answers to Darrow's questions, both sides closed without summation. The jury quickly returned a guilty verdict with the defense's encouragement, and Bryan won the case.

However, the state Supreme Court reversed the verdict on a technicality and Scopes went free.

Shocked by his empty victory, Bryan continued to edit and deliver speeches, traveling hundreds of miles in the next few days. On Sunday, July 26, 1925, he returned from Chattanooga to Dayton, where he attended a church service, ate a large meal, and died in his sleep that afternoon - just five days after the Scopes trial had ended. When the news spread, someone remarked to Darrow that Bryan had died from a "broken heart" in the wake of the trial. And perhaps they were right.

The Presidents

While Jacksonville was home to two men who were almost president - or at least who tried to win the office and lost - it's played host to several men during the times before and during their time in the White House.

Abraham Lincoln

Because of his friendship, and sometimes rivalry with men in Jacksonville, Abraham Lincoln is the president most closely associated with our city - even though he never actually set foot here while he was president.

Some of Lincoln's greatest connections with Jacksonville are through Illinois College. He was close friends with Julian Sturtevant, the college's second president. William and Lynne Greene were two brothers who lived with Lincoln in New Salem, and after they were enrolled at Illinois College, they tutored their friend using their class notes and books, making Jonathan Baldwin Turner Lincoln's only college professor. He was also close friends with a number of Illinois College students, including David Rutledge, Harvey Ross, business partner William Berry, law partner William Herndon, and White House secretary Charles Philbrick. Lincoln was also an honorary member of the Phi Alpha and Sigma Pi literary societies at Illinois College.

During his time as a trial lawyer, Lincoln represented clients in a number of court cases in the second Morgan County Courthouse, which was located at the southwest corner of the square. One of Lincoln's close friends in the city was David

As a young man, Abraham Lincoln was often in Jacksonville.

137

A. Smith, a fellow attorney. When Lincoln had legal business in Jacksonville, he used Smith's law office as his headquarters. Records indicate that Lincoln and Smith were associated with 68 cases as either co-counselors or opposing attorneys. In one of their more famous cases, Lincoln represented Jacksonville businessman Colonel James Dunlap, while Smith represented Jacksonville newspaper editor Paul Selby. Selby sued Dunlap for $10,000 in actual and punitive damages after Dunlap and some of his associates allegedly battered him. Ultimately, the jury found for Selby, but only awarded him $300 in damages.

In September 1856, Lincoln delivered a very strong antislavery speech in support of the presidential campaign of John C. Frémont over the course of two hours in the downtown square. He returned for another speech during his 1858 campaign for the Senate against Stephen Douglas. Lincoln arrived in Jacksonville by train from Springfield and was met by large delegations from Morgan, Cass, and Scott Counties. They moved from the depot to the square where Lincoln spoke for more than two and a half hours. It was one of several dozen speeches that he made across the state during the Senate contest.

Lincoln was also friends with Governor Richard Yates, a Jacksonville resident who was the Civil War-era governor of Illinois, who personally recruited thousands of men to the Union Army. James Jaquess, the first president of the Illinois Conference Female Academy now MacMurray College was a Methodist minister who first met Lincoln when he was preaching and Lincoln was practicing law in central Illinois. During the Civil War, Lincoln entrusted Jaquess with important missions. In 1863, Jaquess met with Confederate officials to discuss ending the war. The following year, Jaquess met with Confederate President Jefferson Davis, who declared that the South would accept peace only if it could remain independent. Jaquess gave an oral report to Lincoln that was transcribed and printed as campaign literature for the Union Republican Party.

Civil War hero General Benjamin Grierson had been living in Meredosia in the 1850s when he joined the new Republican Party and became friends with one of its leaders, Abraham Lincoln. The two men met many times at Grierson's home in Jacksonville. In 1860, Grierson, an accomplished musician, wrote campaign music for Lincoln's first presidential campaign. The following year, he joined the service during the Civil War and the musician and bandleader became a nationally-known cavalry commander for the Federal Army.

Jacksonville's second greatest military hero, trailing only Benjamin Grierson in fame, was John J. Hardin. He was a friend of Abraham Lincoln and was in the unique position of being a man that many claimed actually saved the future president's life.

Hardin was born in Frankfort, Kentucky in 1810 into a family of soldiers and statesmen. His grandfather had fought in the Revolutionary War and his father was a U.S. Senator from Kentucky and an officer in the War of 1812. After graduating from Transylvania University in Kentucky and being admitted to the bar, Hardin established a law practice in Jacksonville in 1830. He quickly made a name for himself in the community, and in 1832, was appointed state's attorney for the district. His appointment elevated him to a leadership role in the Whig Party. It was also around this time that Hardin served as an officer in the Illinois militia and was part of Abraham Lincoln's company during the Black Hawk War.

In 1836, he was elected to the Illinois House of Representatives, where he served with Lincoln and his fellow Jacksonville resident, Stephen Douglas. Hardin was re-

John J. Hardin

elected in 1838 and 1840. While he was a state legislator, Hardin opposed the internal improvements bill and voted repeatedly to move the state capital from Vandalia to Jacksonville. Both Hardin and Lincoln left the state legislature at the same time, but remained friends.

In fact, it was in September 1842 that Hardin intervened to stop a duel between Lincoln and a Democrat named James Shields. It was said that Mary Todd, Hardin's cousin, always credited Hardin with saving Lincoln's life - although that's not actually how it happened.

In the summer of 1842, the Illinois banking system collapsed and state officers were forced to suspend the collection of taxes when it became obvious that citizens were only able to pay them with depreciated or worthless bank notes.

A man named James Shields was then auditor of the state and Lincoln and Mary Todd, who he was then courting, decided to use some sharp wit to poke fun at the Democrats who were running the state. They had singled out one man in particular, the pompous State Auditor, James Shields. In August and September, they wrote a number of letters to the *Sangamo Journal* that were supposedly written by a fictitious lady named "Rebecca." The letters not only took aim at Shield's financial policies, but questioned his honesty and mocked his manly courage as well. The letters were obviously meant as satire but many of the Democrats, already feeling public pressure, did not take them that way. Shields was enraged. He demanded to know who had written the letters and when

confronted, Lincoln took the blame. Shields then sent Lincoln a demand - that he could both confess to writing the letters and retract them in full, or face "consequences which no one will regret more than myself."

Lincoln didn't bother with it. He thought the whole thing was a silly joke, but Shields was not satisfied and soon word spread around Springfield of an impending duel between the two men. Lincoln suggested that the two men fight it out with cow pies, but Shields was having none of it. Lincoln, having no desire to fight Shields, was stunned by the whole thing. Hoping to cool tensions, he sent Shields a letter and offered to confess to writing the letters, but only if they could be taken as "political" only and not written in a way to defame Shield's character. If Shields still wanted to have a duel, then Lincoln stipulated that it must be held with cavalry broadswords while standing on a wooden plank that was 10 feet long and 12 inches wide. Most would agree that Lincoln was not really serious about this, and that his stipulations were actually just to show how ridiculous the whole thing was. Others have speculated that Lincoln hoped that Shields would realize that such a duel would have a devastating effect on the smaller man, as Lincoln's blade, with his lanky arms, would have a much longer reach.

Shields still refused to reconsider the idea, and he arranged for the two men to meet in Alton, Illinois, and to hold the duel at a place called "Sunflower Island," which was a short distance away from the city on the Mississippi River. Dueling was illegal in Illinois and so by meeting on neutral ground, they would be able to avoid the authorities.

So, on September 22, Lincoln, Shields, a physician, and a number of friends, including John Hardin, met on the Mississippi River island. Asked to choose weapons, Lincoln, who was much taller than this prospective opponent and with much longer arms, picked up a broadsword and began using it to hack at tree branches that were well out of Shield's reach. With such a vivid demonstration, apologies were renewed between the two men, and Hardin and some mutual friends convinced Shields to listen to Lincoln's explanation. The fight was called off, but if the duel had proceeded, two promising political careers could have ended. Shields later became a Brigadier General in the Mexican and Civil Wars and a U.S. Senator from Illinois, Minnesota and Missouri. In 1855, Lincoln was a favorite to unseat him in Illinois, but Lyman Trumbull defeated them both. The two men later became good friends.

After the matter was settled, the party rowed back to Alton, where those who awaited the outcome of the duel had no idea what had transpired. As the boat carrying the group returned to the river landing, many anxious spectators were startled to see a "bloody corpse" on the floor of the boat. One of the women fainted, but Lincoln and Shields burst into laughter for the "corpse" was actually just a log that was wearing a red shirt. After the "duel", the parties were hosted at the Old '76 Tavern, which was located at Front and Market Streets in Alton.

And while it seemed that the matter ended on a light note, Lincoln was so ashamed of the affair that he never talked about it again. After that, he never published cruel or embarrassing letters either, even for satire. He also became very opposed to physical violence, and when insulted, or if someone tried to pick a fight with him, Lincoln simply laughed and walked away. He would remember how badly things could have turned out for the rest of his life.

Hardin - whatever his role may have been in the duel that never happened - was elected to the U.S. House of Representatives. He also served as a brigadier general of the state militia and led troops against the Mormons, who were causing civil unrest in western Illinois in the fall of 1844 after the murder of their leader, Joseph Smith, in Carthage on June 27.

At the outbreak of the Mexican War, Hardin was commissioned colonel for the 1st Regiment of Illinois Volunteers and was attached to the army that invaded Mexico led by General Zachary Taylor, who later became a U.S. president. Hardin was killed on February 23, 1847, while leading a charge at the Battle of Buena Vista in northern Mexico. His body was returned to Jacksonville that summer and was buried in Jacksonville East Cemetery.

Hardin's funeral was said to have been the largest ever held in Illinois up to that time. Newspaper accounts say that nearly 15,000 people were in attendance, including every leading politician in the state, including his friend, Abraham Lincoln.

Martin Van Buren

On June 20, 1842, former president Martin Van Buren visited Jacksonville. Van Buren was the eighth president of the United States and served from 1837 to 1841. Before he was president, he served as Vice President and Secretary of State, both under Andrew Jackson. Van Buren was a key organizer of the Democratic Party and the first president not of British or Irish descent–his family was Dutch. He was the first president to have been born a United States citizen, since all of his predecessors were born British subjects before the American Revolution. He is the only president not to have spoken English as his first language, having grown up speaking Dutch.

His administration was largely characterized by the economic hardship of his time, the Panic of 1837. He was scapegoated for the depression and called "Martin Van Ruin" by political opponents. Van Buren was voted out of office after four years, losing to Whig candidate William Henry Harrison. In the 1848 election, Van Buren ran unsuccessfully for president on a third-party ticket, the Free Soil Party. He died in 1862.

In 1842, however, after a weekend in Springfield, he spent an afternoon in Jacksonville and then continued by train to Meredosia and by steamboat to St. Louis. His visit to Jacksonville had been arranged by James Dunlap and Murray McConnel.

Theodore Roosevelt

On October 9, 1900, future president and then governor of New York Theodore Roosevelt visited Jacksonville. He was personal friends with local resident James T. King, who hunted with Roosevelt in Africa.

Lyndon B. Johnson

On June 2, 1963, Vice President Lyndon B. Johnson spoke at the MacMurray College commencement program. Of course, no one was aware at the time that just a little over five months later, he would become president after the assassination of John F. Kennedy.

From the Pages of Jacksonville's History

Not all of the great names from this city's history are known throughout America. Many of them are people who have been forgotten by time, only familiar to us because buildings, streets or parks still bear their name. Others achieved a level of fame somewhere else, but trace their beginnings back to the city of Jacksonville.

Dr. Hiram K. Jones

When one thinks of the great thinker of the nineteenth century, one normally considers Henry David Thoreau, Ralph Waldo Emerson and others, but few recall a Jacksonville man named Hiram K. Jones - even though both Emerson and Thoreau considered him one of the great minds of the generation.

Jones who held both a bachelor of arts degree and a medical degree from Illinois College was not only a practicing physician, but was also a lifelong student of philosophy and literature. He, along with Emerson, Thoreau, and Bronson Alcott, founded the Concord Massachusetts School of Philosophy in 1879 as a summer school for the study of philosophy. He often presented lectures at the school, and he also started the Plato Club in Jacksonville, a 30-year organization that encouraged the study of Plato in the classical Greek language. He helped to organize the Jacksonville Historical Society, the Literary Union, the

142

American Akademe, and Jacksonville Microscopial Society. Dr. Jones also played a key role in the life of his cousin, William Jennings Bryan, by providing him with free room and board at his home while Bryan was attending Whipple Academy and Illinois College. Jones also served on the Illinois College faculty as a philosophy professor and was on the board of trustees for 10 years. In 1895, he donated $20,000 toward the construction of a building that housed a chapel, library, classrooms, and offices on campus. The building became a memorial to his late wife, Elizabeth, and the Gothic structure was dedicated in 1897 and used continuously until it was torn down in 1980.

Dr. Jones managed to almost single-handedly put Jacksonville on the map as a place where ancient philosophy and modern thinking was being bridged.

Dr. Greene V. Black

Although mentioned briefly in an earlier chapter, it should be noted that the man who became known as the "father of modern dentistry" was a Jacksonville man whose experiments in the late nineteenth century created the treatments for tooth decay that we still use today. Dr. Greene V. Black advanced the profession of dentistry from a crude mechanical skill that was practiced by blacksmiths to a scientific medical field. He was an investigator, scientist, lecturer, author, and practitioner whose research legitimized the field of dentistry and made it what it is today.

Dr. Greene V. Black

Black was born near Winchester in 1836 and grew up on a farm about seven miles southeast of Virginia. He had little actual schooling but was an avid reader. He studied dentistry under Dr. J.C. Spear, a dentist from Mount Sterling who opened his own office on the Winchester square in 1857. In 1863, Dr. Black opened his own practice in Jacksonville, and it was in his second-floor office on the south side of the square that he invented the belt-driven dental drill.

And he kept experimenting. While working in Jacksonville, he conducted exhaustive tests on the chewing power of the mouth, and he tested the physical and chemical properties of every kind of tooth-filling material used by dentists in the 1880s. With that information, Dr. Black discovered an alloy that would not shrink or expand. This formula for dental amalgam has changed very little since Dr. Black first introduced it. He was also the first dentist to theorize that tooth decay was caused by germs and to see bacteria under a microscope.

143

Black later served as the dean of the Northwestern University Dental School, and he wrote scores of papers on dentistry for professional journals. A replica of Black's Jacksonville dental offices was in the Smithsonian Institution in Washington, D.C. and a statue of him stands in Chicago's Lincoln Park.

He died in 1915 and is buried in Diamond Grove Cemetery.

Frank Haven Hall

Helen Keller

There was a Jacksonville man who often re-told a story about an encounter that he once had with a woman at the World's Columbian Exposition of 1893, which was held in Chicago. The man was working at a booth at the fair where he was displaying a device that he had invented in 1892. The device was called a stereotype, and it was essentially a Braille typewriter, used by those who were visually impaired. The man, whose name was Frank Haven Hall, was showing off the invention when the woman stopped to visit. When she learned that Hall was the inventor of the Braille typewriter that she loved so much, she hugged and kissed him. When Hall told that story in the years that followed, each re-telling of it brought tears to his eyes. And it's no surprise that it did - the woman's name was Helen Keller.

Hall's unusual device came about because of a position that he once held in Jacksonville as the superintendent of the Illinois Institution for the Blind, which started because of mistaken information.

In the middle 1840s, an Ohio man named Samuel Bacon, who had lost his sight to scarlet fever, was on his way to Galena to visit family. While on a boat from Cincinnati to St. Louis, Bacon was talking to a man from Central Illinois, who told him that the Illinois legislature was considering funding a state institution for the blind in Jacksonville. The story actually made sense. Jacksonville was already home to Illinois College, the Illinois Female Academy and an asylum for the insane. If there was going to be a school for the blind in Illinois, surely it would be in Jacksonville. But the story turned out to be a mistake - there was no school for the blind and no one knew of any plans in the works for one.

When Samuel Bacon found out that his information was wrong, he began making plans to correct it. He began working with local politicians who lobbied the state legislature in Springfield for funds to create such a school. His efforts

The Illinois Institution for the Education of the Blind

paid off in 1848, when a special classroom for blind students was created. But this was still not a school. A year later, the legislature authorized $3,000 to be spent to support the school, then known as the Illinois Institution for the Education of the Blind. There were two students in the school as of April 1849, but by July, there were 14, ranging in age from 12 to 30.

In 1850, Bacon turned over the school to a new superintendent, Joshua Rhoads, who remained at the helm through several troubling periods, including a fire that destroyed the building in 1869. It was rebuilt a year later. Dr. Rhoads also made sure that the students were not treated as free labor after a proposal was made to sell items being made in the workshop that taught the blind students life skills. "The legislature intended this as a school, not a manufactury," he said.

A high school was added, and the first students - all male since women were not yet allowed in high school - graduated in 1877. Younger grades were then added and kindergarten started in 1890.

In 1892, the school achieved its greatest fame when superintendent Frank Haven Hall produced the invention that became as important to the visually impaired as the printing press had been for the sighted world.

Hall was born in Mechanic Falls, Maine on February 9, 1841. During the Civil War, he served in the Union Army's 23rd Maine Volunteers, as a hospital steward. After the service, Hall attended Bates College for a short time and began teaching primary school in 1864. Two years later, he moved his family from Maine to Earlville, Illinois, so Hall could advance his career in school administration. He worked as a principal and teacher at public schools in

145

Frank Haven Hall

Earlville, Aurora, Sugar Grove, Petersburg, Jacksonville, and Waukegan. After seven successful years in Aurora, he was asked to head the Sugar Grove Industrial School, a work-and-learn agricultural school near Aurora. He spent the next 12 years there and also owned a general store, a lumberyard, a creamery, and held the political offices of postmaster, township treasurer, and clerk.

Hall's most distinguished post began in 1890, though, when he came to Jacksonville and became superintendent of the Illinois Institution for the Blind. Even though he had no training or experience with education for the blind, he was a quick learner. He visited several schools for the blind on the East Coast, and quickly decided that blind students required vocational and experiential learning much the same as any student. He became an ardent advocate for the visually impaired, persuading school administrators in Chicago to create the first public school class for blind students, for example.

A political shift in Illinois from the Republican to the Democratic Party caused Hall to lose his post. For a few years, he served as the superintendent of the Waukegan Schools but in 1897, was re-appointed to the Illinois Institution for the Blind. He remained at the school until 1902.

In the last ten years of Hull's life he served as superintendent of the Farmers' Institute of Illinois, where he became an advocate for agricultural education. Hall and his wife, Sybill, also remained active in their local church until his death. In the spring of 1910, he was diagnosed with tuberculosis and diabetes. He died the following January and was buried in Aurora.

But his legacy lives on in Jacksonville. On May 27, 1892, while working as Superintendent for the Illinois Institution for the Blind, Hall unveiled the Hall Braille Writer. The typewriter is recognized as the first successful mechanical point writer. Modeled on typewriters of the time, the invention revolutionized Braille communication. It was similar to a typewriter, except that it only had seven keys - upper left dot, upper right, middle left, middle right, lower left, lower right, and space bar.

Prior to his invention, Braille was not widely taught by teachers of the blind because teaching Braille involved writing boards where a student had to push one or more of six Braille character points in reverse. The Hall Braille Writer, along with Hall's own advocacy, helped make Braille the dominant form of

146

written communication for the blind. Hall never patented the machine because he had no interest in profiting from his work for the blind. The Hall Braille Writer was manufactured by the Harrison & Seifried Company in Chicago for $10 - it was sold for $11.

Hall's invention left a mark on the school in Jacksonville too. Gradually, it modernized and female students were allowed to attend starting in

The Hall Braille Typewriter

1906. As the world changed, the name of the school changed with it. The Institute for the Blind became the Braille and Sight-Saving School and then the School for the Visually Impaired, which it remains today.

Samuel Nichols

On October 10, 1903, word leaked out in the *Jacksonville Daily Journal* that an anonymous businessman in town had approached Mayor John R. Davis and offered to provide between $10,000 and $12,000 so that the city could have a beautiful public park. He felt that Jacksonville needed one and he wanted to help the city to get it. He never wanted his name to be revealed, but at the next meeting of the Jacksonville City Council, however, his identity was revealed. His name was Samuel W. Nichols, one of the best-loved residents of the city, and without Nichols Park, which was established in 1904 and now bears his name, Jacksonville would be a much less pleasant place to live.

Excitement over the coming of a new city park was immediate. According to the newspapers, the Retail Merchant's Association told the city council that if Nichols' offer was accepted, the association would also pledge money for the establishment of the park. Once his identity had been revealed, Nichols submitted a letter to the city council outlining his offer, which included a stipulation that 5 percent interest on the money, or $500, be paid back to him for the next 10 years. The offer was immediately accepted by city council members, some of whom raved about it in the newspapers.

Samuel Nichols had a long history in Jacksonville, long before his name appeared on the public park that he built on the city's behalf. The future editor and proprietor of the *Jacksonville Daily Journal* was born near Quincy on February 5, 1844, the son of Warren and Ann Maria Nichols. His father, Warren, was a well-educated man. He received a classical education, and after his graduation from Williams College in 1830, entered Andover Theological Seminary for the purpose of qualifying himself for the ministry in the Presbyterian Church. He graduated in 1833 and moved west, where his health was badly impaired by hard work and a brush with cholera. In 1834, he moved across the river to Illinois and battled with the Mormons for a time. He also became an ardent member worker on the Underground Railroad, helping slaves escape to freedom in the north. He worked as a teacher for years and later moved to Ohio, where he worked as a minister until his health failed in 1862 and he passed away.

Samuel Nichols

His son, Samuel, grew up in Illinois and Ohio, attending public schools. In May 1864, during the Civil War, he enlisted in Company E, One Hundred and Fifty-first Ohio Volunteer Infantry, and served four months in the Army of the Potomac, principally in the defense of Washington.

About two years after the death of his father, he returned to Illinois, and entered Illinois College in the class of 1868. He never finished his four-year course, but was voted graduated anyway and was given his Bachelor's Degree. Entering the Jacksonville Business College in 1866, he became the first graduate of that institution, and during the year that followed, worked there as a teacher. Disliking the work, he relinquished his post to become treasurer and collector for the Jacksonville Gas Company for the next three years. In 1870, he began working as a teller at the First National Bank of Jacksonville and a year later, formed a partnership with Terence Brennan and Joseph DeSilva, under the firm name of Nicholas, Brennan & Co., and sold stoves and tinware for the next six years. From 1877 to 1886, he operated a photographic studio, but during this time, in 1884, was employed as local editor of the *Jacksonville Daily Journal*, devoting his days to his studio and his nights to his newspaper work. In May 1886, he disposed of his studio and worked only for the newspaper. He made scores of friends and became one of the most influential citizens of Jacksonville, turning the paper into one of the most important in Central Illinois during that era.

But he wasn't just a businessman. He became the secretary of Passavant Hospital when it was organized in 1874; a member of the Prudential Committee of the Congregational Church; Superintendent of the colored Sunday School; and

148

of course, donated the money that made the park on Morgan Lake possible in 1904.

It became the foundation of the Jacksonville park system, but it was by no means the limit of his generosity. Nichols often worked with the young and poor and arranged trips and excursions that made it possible for children who had never traveled to see the country. In the late 1890s and early 1900s, he visited Alaska, the Yellowstone Park, the Yosemite Valley, the Grand Canyon of the Colorado, Old Mexico, the Mammoth Cave of Kentucky, the city of Galveston, Niagara Falls, and various other points of unusual interest, both in the East and the West; and on each of these trips he was accompanied by two or more children and appropriate nursemaids, all of whose expenses he paid. During the Louisiana Purchase Exposition in 1904 in St. Louis, he took three small parties of children to that great exhibit, bearing all expenses. On one occasion, he took with him, in a special train, a party of 408, mostly school children. In making up this party he announced that he wanted every poor child in Jacksonville between the ages of 11 and 15 to go so that they could enjoy a memorable visit to the great fair. At Christmas time, he made it a rule to visit the social service agencies and public schools for advice about the children that might be overlooked at the holiday season, and then spent his own money to insure that they had gifts. He was "grandpa" to the little kids and "Uncle Sammy" to the older ones, but they never forgot him.

Few remember the name of Samuel W. Nichols today, except for the fact that there is a park named in his honor and the "Nichols Fund" allows the Jacksonville Police Department to buy candy at Christmas for children in need. But Mr. Nichols probably wouldn't mind. He never wanted the attention anyway. He did the things that he did out of the goodness of his heart, just like he had when he made Nichols Park possible. In 1924, Dr. Frank P. Norbury stated about Nichols Park, "Community life is sweeter, better, more wholesome and constructive because of it. The true humanitarianism of Mr. Nichols is perpetrated for all time."

The Strawn Family

If there is a single family that left the greatest mark on the early history of Jacksonville, it would undoubtedly be the Strawn family. Jacob Strawn owned more than 20,000 acres of land around the city, and he and his family were ultimately responsible for providing Jacksonville with the Strawn Opera House, one of the greatest entertainment venues in the city's history, and the Strawn Art Gallery, which was once the family mansion on West College Street.

Jacob Strawn, one of the most widely-known farmers in Jacksonville history, was born in Somerset County, Pennsylvania on May 30, 1800. He was one of nine

149

Jacob Strawn

sons of Daniel and Rachel Strawn and he also brother to three sisters. Jacob attended the few schools that were offered at the time, but spent much of his time on the farm of one of his aunts. By the time he was 10, he began determining feeding and grazing for her animals and working on profit and loss statements. He was determined to become a stock dealer when he grew up. When he was 17, he moved with his family to Licking County, Ohio and two years later, married Matilda Greene, a daughter of Reverend John Greene. Jacob had been saving money since he was a boy and used $100 to purchase a tract of unbroken land in Licking County. It was his first land purchased, but it would be far from his last.

Jacob and Matilda had three children, who all survived childhood and eventually made a name for themselves in Illinois: William, James and Isaiah. While still living in Ohio, Jacob began dealing in horses and in 1828, made a trip to Jacksonville. Instead of buying horses, though, he bought land. One tract, the Cobb farm, was five miles southwest of town. Later, a family residence was established there. Impressed by Jacksonville and its plans for the future, he returned to Ohio, sold off his interests and returned to Morgan County on May 17, 1831. It was the first step to making him one of the most prominent men in the Illinois stock raising community and allowing him to develop an enterprise of proportions that were unheard of before that time.

For the next few years, Jacob established himself on his Morgan County farm. It was on the farm that Matilda Strawn died on December 8, 1831. Just seven months later, Jacob married again, wedding Phebe Gates, a daughter of Samuel Gates, a prominent settler of Greene County. Her father had been born in Portland, Maine, and had married a relative of Ralph Waldo Emerson. Phebe was only four-years-old when her family moved to the Illinois Territory, which did not become a state until a few months after they arrived. They settled in Bluffdale, eight miles west of Carrollton. The Bluffdale post office was established in the home of John Russell in 1828, and he also founded one of the earliest select schools in Illinois. Russell, a man of great literary ability, offered a school that was even patronized by children from some of the families in St. Louis. He would later become a professor at Shurtleff College in Alton.

Jacob's marriage to Phebe resulted in six children, one of whom died in early childhood. They included Julius, Daniel who was later killed in a mill accident ; Jacob, Gates, David and Martha Amelia. David was engaged in a dental practice in Boston for a time and then returned to Jacksonville to farm and sell livestock as part of the family business. The only daughter, Martha Amelia, spent three years at Dr. Gannett's School in Boston, but fell ill with consumption and died at the age of only 22. Jacob Strawn, Jr., the third son, was diagnosed at a young age with a heart ailment and was advised to go abroad. He made a six month's tour of Europe, Egypt, and Palestine and returned home to wed Mary Jane Patterson. They had three children, but his life was doomed. He died young in 1869.

Meanwhile, Jacob Strawn continued to prosper. For a considerable period, he supplied almost the entire St. Louis market with beef, purchasing and disposing of larger lots of cattle than any dealer in the county. He became known among stockmen all over America. During the first years of his residence in Morgan County, Jacob was engaged in butchering and milling, and furnished the meat and flour supply of Jacksonville. He was the owner of a flour mill, and raised large crops of wheat and corn. He was also one of the most extensive land holders in Illinois, being the owner of 10,000 acres in Sangamon and Morgan Counties, besides his home farm of about 8,000 acres. Around 1850, he made a complete innovation in the customary methods of conducting the stock business, and disposed of his cattle on the ground where he fitted them for market, thereafter confining his attention to the work of grazing and feeding. He was the initiator in Illinois of the system of stall feeding with corn. In 1859, he began the erection of the superb Strawn's Opera House in Jacksonville, which was finished in 1861, and dedicated in March of that year, giving the city the most ornate and imposing structure in the history of Jacksonville. The opera house, stood on the southwest corner of South Main and the square for many years and brought perhaps more entertainment to Jacksonville than any other venue in our history.

During the Civil War, Jacob was a strong supporter of the Union cause, donating vast sums of money to charitable organizations that cared for the sick and wounded. On being informed by a hospital nurse from Vicksburg that the supply of milk for the disabled soldiers was inferior and hard to find, he promptly raised the means to buy 50 cows, which he sent under the care of a special attendant to the hospital stewards of the facility.

Jacob Strawn outlived the end of the war by only a few months. He died on August 2, 1865 at the country home where he first settled and was buried in Diamond Grove Cemetery. Mrs. Strawn spent the last years of her life in the home that she built in Jacksonville as a very wealthy widow. She passed away in February 1906, and besides leaving a fortune to her surviving children, she also

David Strawn donated the family's former home in Jacksonville to be used as the Strawn Art Gallery

made large donations to Illinois College, the Jacksonville Female Academy, and Passavant Hospital.

The family of Jacob Strawn continued his businesses and charitable contributions well into the next century. They traveled widely, supported institutions like Illinois College, and in 1915, David Strawn donated the family mansion on West College to the Art Association of Jacksonville, which had been founded in 1873. The parlor, hallway, and sitting rooms were transformed into gallery viewing spaces, and it is still open today.

Passing Through Jacksonville

During Jacksonville's long history, a great many famous and esteemed people have visited the city. Some of them were asked to come here to speak, lecture or entertain, while others merely dropped by and left a small mark on our history.

One of them was **William "Buffalo Bill" Cody**, the famous western hunter turned entertainer, who created one of the great "Wild West" shows of all time during the days when the west really wasn't wild anymore, but people didn't want to stop remembering the cowboys, shoot-outs, buffalo and Native Americans that had vanished into the sunset by the early 1900s. Buffalo Bill's show played in Jacksonville several times while on tour across the country, but Cody also visited the J. Capps & Sons Woolen Mills in town, where he personally endorsed the Indian blankets that they made.

The famous black educator **Booker T. Washington** explained his efforts to help his persecuted race in a speech he delivered in Jacksonville on January 23,

152

1900. He spoke to a packed audience at the Grand Opera House about the "progress of the colored race in America." Washington was the most influential black leader and educator of his time. He became prominent primarily because of his role as founder and head of Tuskegee Institute, a vocational school for blacks in Tuskegee, Alabama. The school taught specific trades, such as carpentry, farming and mechanics, and trained teachers. Jacksonville had a connection to Tuskegee in that one of its former residents, Alonzo H. Kenniebrew, served as the resident physician and teacher of physiology at Tuskegee from 1897 to 1902. Kenniebrew soon thereafter moved to Jacksonville and founded a surgical hospital and nurse's school in 1908. The

Booker T. Washington

hospital and school, known as New Home Sanitarium, was located near what is now the intersection of West Morgan Street and Dunlap Court. The hospital, which is believed to be the first operated by a black man, was torn down in 1930. Kenniebrew also once served as the personal physician to Washington.

Washington thought that blacks could benefit more from a practical, vocational education rather than a college education. Most blacks lived in poverty in the rural South, and Washington felt they should learn skills, work hard and acquire property. He thought that the development of work skills would lead to economic prosperity. He predicted that blacks would be granted civil and political rights after gaining a strong economic foundation.

During his local lecture, Washington thanked the citizens of Jacksonville for helping blacks and explained how they could overcome their plight. "By carefully explaining the methods and aims of the industrial school, giving numbers of practical examples, he convinced most of the audience that education is the only lasting regenerator," wrote a reporter who covered the speech.

A few months later, on March 14, 1900, nationally known labor leader **Eugene V. Debs**, also spoke at the Grand Opera House on the square. Debs had a very different kind of message to deliver, though. Debs was an American union leader, one of the founding members of the Industrial Workers of the World IWW or the Wobblies , and five times the candidate of the Socialist Party of America for President of the United States. Through his presidential candidacies, as well as his work with labor movements, Debs eventually became one of the best-known socialists living in the United States.

Eugene V. Debs

After working with several smaller unions, including the Brotherhood of Locomotive Firemen, Debs was instrumental in the founding of the American Railway Union ARU , one of the nation's first industrial unions. After workers at the Pullman Palace Car Company organized a wildcat strike over pay cuts in the summer of 1894, Debs signed many into the ARU. He called a boycott of the ARU against handling trains with Pullman cars, in what became the nationwide Pullman Strike, affecting most lines west of Detroit, and more than 250,000 workers in 27 states. To keep the mail running, President Grover Cleveland used the United States Army to break the strike. As a leader of the ARU, Debs was convicted of federal charges for defying a court injunction against the strike and served six months in prison.

In prison, Debs read the works of Karl Marx and learned about socialism. Upon his release, he launched his career as the nation's most prominent Socialist in the first decades of the twentieth century. He ran as the Socialist Party's candidate for the presidency in 1900, 1904, 1908, 1912, and 1920, the last time from a prison cell.

Debs was noted for his oratory, and his speech denouncing American participation in World War I led to his second arrest in 1918. He was convicted under the Espionage Act of 1917 and sentenced to a term of 10 years. President Warren G. Harding commuted his sentence in December 1921. Debs died in 1926, not long after being admitted to a sanatorium.

Admiral George Dewey

On May 3, 1900, an estimated 5,000 visitors arrived in Jacksonville for the "Dewey Day Parade," which was held to celebrate the visit of **Admiral George Dewey** to Jacksonville. Admiral Dewey was a hero for his role in winning the Battle of Manila Bay in May of 1898 during the Spanish-American War in the Philippines. On the night before the parade, the Grand Army of the Republic, an organization of Union veterans, camped out and made speeches and told stories of long ago campaigns.

Admiral Dewey arrived by train at the East State Street station and the parade started there, went west, winding through the square, out College Avenue, down Webster and back east to State to the reviewing

154

stand at the courthouse. Merchants and other vendors set up booths on the square and the arch over East State Street was decorated for the occasion.

At the time of his visit to Jacksonville, Dewey was in the running to be the Democratic candidate for President in the 1900 elections, but later in the month of May he would drop out and declare his support for William McKinley.

Famous evangelist **Billy Sunday** came to Jacksonville in 1908 as part of a scheme by the local churches of the Evangelical Association of Jacksonville to curb drinking and vice in the city. They were convinced that drunkenness, gambling, and immorality in the city could be curbed if all the saloons in town were shut down. They worked together to build support for a "dry law" to be passed, and it worked. Taverns all over Jacksonville were forced to close their doors - for a short time anyway. But the Association had succeeded in their immediate goal, so they next planned a huge camp meeting as a way to save the sinners who had only recently been cavorting in Jacksonville's "dens of iniquity." They built the Tabernacle, a large wooden structure that was like a giant pole barn, in 1908, and invited Billy Sunday to come for a series of revival meetings.

Evangelist Billy Sunday

Sunday had been born in Ames, Iowa, in 1862, and spent his early years in orphanages and with his grandparents. He played major league baseball for Chicago, Pittsburgh, and Philadelphia but then experienced a religious conversion and went to work for the YMCA. He was a Presbyterian minister noted for using slangy language that appealed to the masses and was lauded for his highly developed promotional methods. He was a born showman and believed that he spoke to over 100 million people in his career and converted at least 1 million of them. In rousing sermons, he featured lots of music and denounced "evolution, card players, dance devotees and theatre gadders."

At the Tabernacle in Jacksonville - with 400 lights, two telephones, and bunting and streamers - he was described as a "moral cyclone, a prophet sent by God and the salvation of Jacksonville." Sunday stayed in town for six weeks and spoke before almost 30,000 people. He was paid $8,000 for his work.

Soon after the revival, the Tabernacle was torn down.

Vachel Lindsay, the noted Illinois poet, read some of his poems at the Jacksonville Public Library on January 13, 1915. Lindsay, who was originally from Springfield, is considered the father of modern singing poetry, as he referred to it, in which verses are meant to be sung or chanted. Because of his identity as a performance artist and his use of American Midwest themes, Lindsay became known in the 1910s as the "Prairie Troubadour." For the final twenty years of his life, Lindsay was one of the best-known poets in America. One of his best-known works was a 1914 poem "Abraham Lincoln Walks at Midnight In Springfield, Illinois ," Lindsay specifically places Lincoln in Springfield, with the poem opening:

Vachel Lindsay

It is portentous, and a thing of state
That here at midnight, in our little town
A mourning figure walks, and will not rest...

Lindsay's private life was rife with disappointments, such as his unsuccessful courtship of Sara Teasdale and his constant financial worries. Much of the work that he did -- traveling around the country doing readings - was done because he was desperate for money. In April 1929, Lindsay and his family moved to the house of his birth in Springfield, Illinois, an expensive undertaking. In that same year, coinciding with the Stock Market Crash of 1929, Lindsay published two more poetry volumes. He gained money by doing odd jobs but, in general, earned very little during his travels.

Crushed by financial worry and in failing health from his six-month road trip, Lindsay sank into depression. On December 5, 1931, he committed suicide by drinking a bottle of Lysol. His last words were: "They tried to get me; I got them first!"

During his lifetime, his reputation was high enough to enable him to befriend, encourage, and mentor other poets, such as Langston Hughes and Sara Teasdale. However, his poetry lacked elements that encouraged the attention of academic scholarship, and after his death he became an obscure figure.

In August 1918, famous artist and sculptor **Lorado Taft** spoke for the Women's Club of Jacksonville on the "City Beautiful," which he also presented at the Chautauqua in Nichols Park. Taft was one of the great American sculptors

156

of the late nineteenth and early twentieth centuries. He was born in Elmwood, Illinois, and after being home-schooled by his parents, Taft earned his bachelor's degree and master's degree from the University of Illinois where his father was a professor of geology. In 1880, he left for Paris to study sculpture. Upon returning to the United States in 1886, he settled in Chicago. He taught at the Art Institute of Chicago, a job he would hold until 1929. In addition to work in clay and plaster, Taft taught his students marble carving, and had them work on group projects.

Lorado Taft

In 1892, while the art community of Chicago was preparing for the World's Columbian Exposition of 1893, chief architect Daniel Burnham expressed concern to Taft that the sculptural adornments to the buildings might not be finished on time. Taft asked if he could employ some of his female students as assistants it was not socially accepted for women to work as sculptors at that time for the Horticultural Building. Burnham responded, "Hire anyone, even white rabbits if they'll do the work." From that arose a group of talented women sculptors known as "the White Rabbits": Enid Yandell, Carol Brooks MacNeil, Bessie Potter Vonnoh, Janet Scudder, and Julia Bracken.

In 1898, Taft was a founding member of the Eagle's Nest Art Colony in the small town of Oregon, Illinois. Taft designed the Columbus Fountain at Union Station in Washington, D.C., in collaboration with Daniel Burnham. As Taft grew older, his eloquence and compelling writing led him to the forefront of sculpture's conservative ranks, where he often served as a spokesperson against the modern and abstract trends that developed during his lifetime. Taft's frequent lecture tours for the Chautauqua gave him a broad, popular celebrity status.

Some of Taft's amazing work includes, the 4th Michigan Infantry Monument on the Gettysburg Battlefield; Eternal Silence, Graves Memorial, Graceland Cemetery, Chicago, Illinois; Black Hawk Statue Monument, aka Eternal Indian, Oregon, Illinois; The Solitude of the Soul, Art Institute of Chicago; Columbus Fountain, in front of Union Station, Washington, D.C.; The Soldiers' Monument, Oregon, Illinois; Fountain of Time, Chicago, Illinois; Lincoln the Lawyer, Urbana, Illinois; and many more.

On April 2, 1936, just a year before she vanished without a trace over the Pacific Ocean, aviatrix **Amelia Earhart** came to Jacksonville. She spoke at a banquet sponsored by the Jacksonville Business and Professional Women's Club

Amelia Earhart

at MacMurray College. While she was in town, she stayed at the Pacific Hotel on East State Street.

Earhart was an American aviation pioneer and author. She was the first woman to fly solo across the Atlantic Ocean, for which she received the Distinguished Flying Cross. That was her first record, but not her last. She set many others, wrote best-selling books about her experiences and paved the way for female pilots. A complete record of all of her accomplishments would fill a book of their own, but sadly, hers was a story left unfinished. During an attempt to make a flight that would circumnavigate the globe in 1937, Earhart disappeared over the central Pacific Ocean near Howland Island. To this day, she has never been found.

Robert Wadlow

"America's Gentle Giant," **Robert Wadlow**, came to Jacksonville on September 23, 1937, when he stopped in at Moore's Café on South Main Street to have lunch with his father. It was undoubtedly not an ordinary lunch day for the staff at the café because Robert Wadlow was and still holds the record as the tallest man who ever lived.

Robert was born in the small town of Alton and spent most of his life trying to avoid the limelight that he could never stay out of. While never a sideshow attraction, Robert did earn a living making personal appearances arranged by the Ringling Brothers Circus. In 1940, Robert reached his greatest height at eight feet, eleven-point-one inches. His weight was a massive 490 pounds and he was forced to walk with a cane. Unknown to the quiet young man or his father, a brace that he was forced to wear on his leg had rubbed through his skin he had little feeling in his lower extremities and had become seriously infected while he was in Manistee, Michigan, appearing at a lumbermen's festival on July 4. He began running a high fever from the infection and was rushed to the hospital. He spent 10 days in fever-wracked agony with his family by his bedside. Doctors performed emergency surgery on his foot, but it was too late. In the early morning hours of July 15, Robert died in his sleep.

His remains were returned to Alton and huge crowds came to the funeral home and lined the streets in his honor. A special casket was constructed for his body that was 10 feet long and 32 inches wide. The casket was too big to fit through the doors of the church, so the services were held at the funeral home. Robert was a Freemason and he was buried with full honors in a local cemetery. It required 12 pallbearers and an additional eight men to manage his casket.

Robert Wadlow has been embraced as Alton's native son and is a local folk hero. Have a passing thought about this kind young man today and remember that no matter how much fame he achieved during his lifetime, it was a life that he considered only half-fulfilled. He would gladly have exchanged all of the money and attention for a single day of what he really wanted - an ordinary life.

5. INFAMOUS IN JACKSONVILLE
The City's History of Mystery, Murder & Mayhem

Illinois is the hiding place for villains from every part of the United States, and indeed, from every quarter of the globe. A majority of the settlers have been discharged from penitentiaries and jails or have been the victims of misfortune or imprudence. Many of those will reform, but many, very many, are made fit for robbery and murder.
Milo M. Quaife

Illinois was, in many ways, born in blood. From the Indian massacres of the War of 1812 to the feuds and vendettas in the late 1800s, there is a long history of violence and death written in blood during the early days of the state. But almost every part of the state in its early days of scant population has been the scene of open crime. Outlaws, fleeing in desperation from the restraints of civilization, where the law was strictly enforced, found the wilderness a region where they could carry on their lawless ways. The settlements in those days were small and widely scattered, with broad spaces of unknown forest and prairie lying in between. The beleaguered upholders of the law were unable to be everywhere at once, if they existed at all. It was easy in those days to operate in secrecy, while the very life of the frontier bred a class of rough and desperate men, capable of committing almost any crime.

There is likely no part of Illinois that does not have its local traditions of outlawry during its period of early settlement. These tales that are often weird and gruesome extended over many years until the time came when popular sentiment became too strong to harbor criminals. There are locations that even today are pointed out as murder sites and places where gangs of outlaws once hid. Often these tales are so filled with lore that it is hard to tell when truth ends and fiction begins. Regardless, they paint a vivid portrait of how Illinois came to be and why it gained such a reputation as a lawless place.

The area around Jacksonville was no exception. Despite the reputation that the city would gain in the 1830s and 1840s as a place of higher learning and the "Athens of the West," there were still plenty of lawless elements, dire events, and bloody happenings that took place in the city's history.

"The Regulators of the Valley"

During the 1830s and 1840s, outlaw gangs were so rampant in Illinois that there was no chance that the few, outgunned and overmatched lawmen that existed at the time could possibly keep their activities in check. Murders were committed to keep witnesses from testifying, courthouses were burned and worse. Many counties spent months in a literal state of terror. These events continued unchecked until the people themselves formed bands of "Regulators," vigilante societies that hanged or drove out the worst offenders.

Regulators and vigilance groups began to appear in every corner of the state. As early as 1816, these bands of honest settlers began for the purpose of ridding the country of undesirable characters. While taking the law into the hands of civilians has never been endorsed, these men were largely justified by the circumstances. The entire region had been nearly overrun by counterfeiters, horse thieves, highway robbers, and killers until no traveler was safe and no settler felt sure that his livestock would still be in their pens after a dark night.

It was under these intolerable conditions that the people finally took the law into their own hands. The governor and most of the judges in the region, realizing the necessity of such an action, largely ignored the situation, and for a time, lynch law ruled the entire state and purged it of a great deal of crime. These bodies of Regulators, as Governor Ford described them, were in numbers about equal to a company of soldiers, and their officers were elected as in the militia. Their operations were conducted almost entirely at night and when they assembled for duty, they marched, armed and equipped as if for war. They went to the residence or hideout of a criminal and arrested, tried and punished him on the spot. The usual punishments were whippings and banishment from the region, although there were many instances when offenders were promptly hanged from the nearest tree.

161

During the frontier days, many settlers had to take the law into their own hands to preserve order and to protect their families and farms.

In February 1832, a publication known as the *Illinois Patriot* told the story of similar Regulators that once tried to uphold the law in the Jacksonville area. The story was told by General Murray McConnel -- who would meet his own end at the hands of an outlaw in 1869 - and involved a group of renegades that preyed on some of the law-abiding residents of the area in those early Jacksonville times.

Few of us have any idea of the hardships faced by the settlers who came to our area. Morgan County was mostly unbroken frontier. Farms and homes were few and were often separated by many miles. There was no real law to speak of and the settlers had to do what they could to protect themselves from thieves and bandits.

In 1820, a man named Abraham Williams settled near what would soon be Jacksonville. He carved a home from the fields and forests along the Mauvaisterre Creek and broke ground for planting. Williams' trail was followed by others and soon, about six families made up a small settlement. Cabins were constructed, grain planted, and the woods were hunted for food. The following season, more families came, and the settlement grew. But with the settlers came the unsavory and the lawless. Three men - John Cotrill, Henry Percifield and his brother, Jerry - settled near Williams and in a short time became his friends and associates.

During that autumn, Jerry Percifield, the oldest and the worst of the lot, brought the first two barrels of whiskey into the new settlement. Abraham

162

Williams took possession of it and opened up his home as a tavern of sorts, attracting all of the men of the fledgling settlement. And as author Charles Eames wrote many years later, "From this date the downfall of Williams and the others began."

Robberies began occurring in the area and in neighboring counties, and goods from plundered stores were by rumor said to be hidden near Williams' grove, which made him and his three cronies suspected of being the perpetrators of the crimes. The law-abiding settlers were anxious to have their settlement retain a fair name for honesty and good order, and so warrants were issued, the suspected parties searched, and some of the stolen goods were recovered. When the men were brought before the magistrate, though, they were allowed to testify on each other's behalf, so all were acquitted.

Soon after, horse theft, house breakings, armed robbery, store thefts, and other crimes began to multiply. Williams suddenly became rich, having horses, cattle and more household goods than he could have possibly been able to buy under ordinary circumstances. Shady-looking men began hanging around his property, drinking, gambling, and horse racing during the day and committing crimes at night. Williams, Cotrill, the Percifield brothers, and their assorted ilk soon had the run of the area, beating and bullying the other men of the settlement into going along with their crimes.

Around this time, two new characters emerged on the scene, one of whom was a respectable old gentleman named Lewis G. Newell, who settled south of the Mauvaisterre. He built a fine home, which, of course, caught the attention of Williams and his men. Assuming he had a lot of money hidden away inside, they went to look the place over and ascertain how much money Newell might have, where he might hide it, when he left home, and when he might return. Williams began calling on Newell several times each week. The old man likely assumed that he was being friendly, never realizing that Williams had sinister intentions.

The other new arrival to the area was a Kentucky man whose name was never revealed. He was a backwoodsman and hunter, armed with a knife and a long rifle. His movements were mysterious and he visited every house in the settlements - except that of Williams. No one knew his name but several referred to him as the "wild hunter of the prairie."

One night as Williams and Jerry Percifield were returning from a visit at Newell's home, they saw by the light of the moon that the form of a man was moving toward them on the path. Percifield nudged his friend, asking him if he had seen the "wild hunter." But before Williams could answer, the frontiersman stepped right up to the two men and called on Williams, asking if he recognized him. Williams flinched at the man's voice and cowered behind Percifield.

The hunter spoke again: "Abraham, you know me well; you know, too, that I am acquainted with your unnatural deeds; your ill-gotten wealth shall avail you little. Before many days pass by I will see you again, when circumstances are different, and times more favorable than now." Then the man vanished from sight, slipping silently into the forest.

Percifield was unnerved by the encounter, but nowhere near as frightened as Williams, who refused to speak about the stranger or his identity. Over the course of the next few days, he began selling off his property and he packed up his family and moved to the west side of the Illinois River - very close to the spot where he would soon be buried.

A short time before Williams moved away, Newell left home on business, leaving his wife and young son behind. Two nights after he departed, his house was broken into and all of his money and valuables were stolen. This bold robbery alarmed and aroused the citizens of the settlement. A public meeting was held and a company was formed, consisting of 10 well-armed men. They bound themselves together under the name "Regulators of the Valley." They were determined to rid the area of horse thieves and robbers and not to cease their operations until the outlaws had fled or had been killed. They drew up papers and each of the men signed his name to the contract. After all of this was completed, the party resolved to make Abraham Williams their first target.

The plan was to go to his house in disguise, seize him by force, tie him to a tree and scourge him with whips until he surrendered the money and goods that had been stolen from Newell and others. They wanted him to reveal the names of his associates and accomplices too, but they had no intention of taking his life. With this plan in mind, the regulators rode toward Williams' home across the Illinois River. They crossed the river near the mouth of the Mauvaisterre and rode quietly toward Williams' cabin. As they drew near, a voice whispered to them from the woods. It was a friend, the voice said and the hunter stepped out from the trees. He told the men that he knew their intentions and that Williams was his enemy, having committed a crime that he needed to avenge. He asked the regulators to accept him as their captain, which they did, and then he led the way to Williams' house.

They surrounded the cabin and then the hunter, along with two of the other men, prepared to break open the door and bring Williams outside. Before they could do so, the ferocious barking of Williams' dogs echoed in the night. A light was lit inside of the cabin and the door opened a little, allowing one of the household to peer outside. "Indians!" was the cry from inside, believing that the house was under attack by a raiding party. Williams seized his rifle and rushed outside and the first thing he saw was the mysterious captain. He immediately cried out for the man to stand back or he would shoot him dead. He pulled the trigger and by some unaccountable accident, the weapon snapped but misfired. He was again making ready to shoot when cries went up all around the yard - "Fire! Fire!" A single rifle shot rang out and Williams fell. The other regulators rushed to the door and found the man they had come to question lying on the ground, writhing in his own blood.

They did not stand in silence for long. A woman's screams resounded in the cabin and Williams' wife rushed forward, scratching and clawing at the men, attempting to get to her husband. One of the regulators fired off a shot into the air, hoping to scare her, but it was in vain. She pressed on until she was stopped by the hands of the hunter - a man she had also seen before - and he forced her into the house and closed the door.

The regulators - who were farmers and tradesmen with no knowledge of the law - were frightened and unsure of what to do. They left the house and rode off into the woods. The hunter called a halt. He spoke to them, "My friends, the deed is done. I did it in self-defense. I have rid the world of a monster and myself of an inveterate foe. My conscience acquits me; so I will not regret the act. My advice is for each of you to go your way and I will go mine. You will never see me again. Let every man guard well his secret, and none other will know you were here."

After that, the hunter rode off and vanished into the darkness, leaving the other men behind. The news of Williams' death made the rounds, but there were none who could claim that they knew who had fired the fatal shot, or even who had been there that night. Cotrill, Percifield, and the others left the county with haste and Morgan County was never troubled by such outlaws again. Williams was buried on the left bank of Magee's Creek in Pike County, but no one knows where it is today.

The story of that deadly night was, of course, told a few years later. The tale was penned under the name "J.G.R." but in time it was learned that Murray McConnel was the author of it. One has to wonder just how he knew the details of the events that occurred that night. Was he present? It seems likely that he was. Who was the mysterious stranger who followed Williams from Kentucky with the intention of claiming his life? It's likely that someone in the settlement knew his name - but that was one secret that was never told.

Law and Order
The Jacksonville Police Department
As noted in the beginning of this chapter, when a band of regulators was formed to carry out justice in what became Jacksonville, the city once had an approach to crime prevention that was as confusing as it was colorful. It started

with a piece-rate system for the local tax collector and the preserver of peace, first appointed in 1834, who was paid on a per-case basis. He received an unspecified amount of money for each portion of taxes that he collected on the job and, as a peace keeper, he was given a fee for each arrest he made.

In 1835, things changed a little and the position of town constable was created. He continued to collect taxes but he also took on the job of caring for the streets. For the next year, he continued to be paid on a fee basis, but in 1836, the constable began to receive a decent salary of $200 each year. Although Jacksonville was largely an orderly town, the first jail had been built as early as 1825. The log structure was located on the west side of North Main Street, between the public square and what is currently Douglas Avenue. No records remain as to who exactly was incarcerated there, but there would be more jails to take its place in the years to come.

There were occasionally punishments that had to be handed out, though. A man named Charles King who was indicted by the court for forgery was fined $50, imprisoned in the Morgan County Jail for four months and then received 25 lashes on his bare back as a punishment. The county sheriff was ordered to administer the whipping on the public square in Jacksonville. King was soundly flogged, witnesses later said, but some claimed that the lashes were given with considerable restraint and that the kind-hearted sheriff was actually moved to tears by the punishment.

There are a few other incidents of public floggings - one of Benjamin Crisp for larceny, for one - but the records of the police department in the early and middle 1800s are thin and in many cases, non-existent. However, we do know that by the 1860s, the town's peacekeepers worked out of a small office on the square known as the "calaboose," a not uncommon name for cramped buildings for police operations and holding cells in the nineteenth century. This was where the constables locked up criminals and the fire company stored its equipment. One of the constables, who was also a member of the fire department, was hired to live upstairs in the "calaboose" with his family so that someone could be on duty around the clock.

In 1867, the constables became known as town marshals. The marshal worked during the day and appointed officers, known as night policemen, who patrolled the city after dark. It was around this same time that officers began wearing uniforms while on duty. During the 1870s, the city's marshals patrolled Jacksonville armed with only a nightstick. They worked seven days a week on twelve-hour shifts and if they were ill, they had to find their own replacements. Most of the information from that time period comes from old newspaper reports. In that era, most of the arrests in town were vagrants and drunks, with occasional raids on houses of prostitution. The operators of the bordellos, as well

166

Jacksonville Police Officers in the 1890s. The man in the center is believed to be the police captain who commanded the night shift.

as the customers arrested while patronizing them, were usually fined $3, plus court costs. On many occasions, they were released with a "promise to pay" if they did not have enough money for the fine at the time of their arrest.

The city marshal served as the commanding officer of Jacksonville's police force until 1887, when voters created the position of chief of police. Peter Rabbitt became the city's first chief that same year. The police department then consisted of four other officers, all of whom were appointed by the mayor. The police force was then operating with fairly primitive methods and had a patrol wagon, a rogue's gallery of pictures and arrest records and shoes that got a lot of wear as they continuously walked the beat through Jacksonville's downtown.

In 1893, the police department was moved to the old city hall that was located on West Douglas Avenue. By the 1930s, the city furnished officers with a uniform badge, a cap badge, a flashlight and batteries. Policemen had to buy the rest of their equipment themselves, including uniforms, guns, belts, holsters and nightsticks. They also needed a good pair of shoes because they did a lot of walking. In 1921, Jacksonville police had acquired their first motorcycle, which was used to patrol areas of town out of walking distance from the station until the 1950s. In the 1940s, the department's squad cars - both of them - were only used to respond to calls. They were never used for patrols. The only traffic light in town was at South Main and College, and it was the only stoplight in Jacksonville for years.

The officers also didn't carry radios. Instead, the connection to headquarters was made using a buzzer and a white light mounted on a pole just north of the Civil War monument in Central Park. The desk officer would activate the buzzer and light if he needed to reach one of the officers in the downtown area. An officer would then go to the closest telephone and call the station to find out the problem. If the officer needed to respond, he would then walk to the station and take out one of the squad cars.

By 1950, the department consisted of about 18 officers, including the chief, three desk officers, one motorcycle officer and two who checked parking meters downtown. In those days, the downtown and the square were major traffic and business hubs for the city. Thanks to this, it was also the area with the highest crime rate.

Over time, the Jacksonville Police Department has changed along with the city and has expanded over the years. Today, the police department faces a whole new array of crime problems - problems that could not have been imagined back when the early constables were locking up vagrants in the "calaboose" - but it remains today committed to the safety and protection of the people of Jacksonville.

"Commissioner Killed by Ex-Chief Police!" The Murder of Charles W. Brown

In the late nineteenth and early years of the twentieth century, Jacksonville was still plagued by a fairly disorganized police department, and it was often made up of men who were as rough and violent as the men they were hired to arrest. As was often the case in the civilian world too, alcohol often played a large part in the scandals and problems that damaged the reputation of the department. Even before the Prohibition era and the rampant corruption that touched almost every police department in the country when it came to looking the other way over liquor violations, alcohol played a deadly role in the murder of a Jacksonville city commissioner. His killer? A friend and the former Jacksonville chief of police, Ambrose Hurley.

The murder occurred on Saturday, May 25, 1912, when Hurley walked into his former friend's office on West State Street and shot him in the chest. Brown was dictating a letter at the time and was killed without warning. Hurley then tucked away the gun, walked to the boarding house where he had been staying

168

three blocks away and committed suicide. How had a man who had been once respected as the city's chief of police been driven to murder?

According to accounts from the time, the cause for the murder and suicide dated back to the year before, when Brown had failed to win Hurley a new appointment as police chief. It was at that time that Jacksonville adopted a new form of government and Brown became a commissioner. Prior to that, he had managed to get Hurley the job of police chief, but it all changed with the new election. When Hurley didn't get the position he wanted, Brown tried to make it up to him by appointing him superintendent of the water department, but that wasn't good enough. The two men had a falling out and Hurley, already a heavy drinker, would go on wild liquor sprees, during which he would threaten to kill Brown. Strangely, the two men had been friends for years. In fact, Hurley had worked for Brown's engineering company for nearly a decade. He had been in charge of most of the drainage projects that Brown's company had carried out in the southern part of the state. Perhaps this was the reason why, when mutual friends came to tell him about Hurley's drunken rants, Brown didn't take them seriously. In fact, only a short time before the shooting, the two men had met with their friend D.E. Crabtree, who had smoothed things over between them and later reported that they had settled their differences.

But apparently, they hadn't.

Friends later stated that Hurley had been drinking heavily for several days before the shooting occurred. And when he drank, he began making threats about Brown. Acquaintances warned Brown that his old friend was back in the bottle, but Brown dismissed their concerns. In the early part of the afternoon on May 25, Hurley visited several of the hardware stores in town, trying to buy a pistol. Noting that the man was obviously inebriated, all but one of them refused to sell him one. But it only took one salesman who valued the dollar more than public safety and Hurley walked out of the store with a gun in his pocket.

Hurley then returned home and put on his best suit. He walked back downtown, pistol still in the pocket of his coat, and went to the barber shop for a shave. At 4:15 p.m., he hailed a carriage and was driven to the Scott Building, where Brown's company offices were located. He told the driver to wait and leisurely climbed the stairs.

Hurley walked at once to Brown's office. The door was standing wide open and Brown was seated at his desk, dictating a letter to his secretary. Hurley barged in and uttered, ""You can't break it off into me anymore," and fired the fatal shot into his friend's chest. A second shot was fired, perhaps by accident, and it went into the wall. As Brown slumped onto the floor, Hurley walked out of the office, down the stairs and stepped into the waiting cab. He ordered the man to take him to his boarding house. When he arrived, he went immediately to his room, undressed, lay down on the bed and shot himself in the head. The pistol had fired one last time, claiming the life of the assassin.

To this day, no one can truly say what finally pushed Hurley into carrying out his threats against his old friend. What had occurred between them that finally pushed the former police chief over the edge? Was it the liquor, finally destroying his mind, or were there deeper resentments that none of their mutual friends knew about? We'll never know, but the murder of Charles Brown remains a stain on the history of Jacksonville and on the legacy of the city's police department.

"Murder in Broad Daylight!"
The Unsolved Mystery of Murray McConnel

The slaying of General Murray McConnel may have been one of the most shocking murders that occurred in the early days of Jacksonville, but it was far from the first. What is most puzzling even today is the fact that it has remained unsolved since 1869, when his life was ended in broad daylight in front of his home on North Main Street.

Earlier murders were just as blood-curdling to Jacksonville residents. The first indictment for murder in Morgan County occurred in 1839, when John A. Hall was charged for killing Robert Denny. He had stabbed the other man in the chest with a pair of metal shears. He was tried in November of that year, and even though there were a number of witnesses who saw him commit the act, he was found "not guilty."

The second local murder case was in May 1841, when George Gardner was charged with killing Phillip W. Nash, whom he had shot in the chest. Gardner was found guilty and sentenced to death. He would have been the first man to be executed in the county, but he escaped from jail while his gallows was being built, and he was never heard from again.

The next murder that occurred took place on November 27, 1853, when William Brown was charged with the stabbing death of George Groves. He went on trial in March 1854, and was cleared of the charges. The jury ruled that it had been self-defense.

On July 1, 1858, a man named Cyrus Lake was beaten so badly that his skull caved in. He was found dead at the scene. Two men, Jacob Theby and James Markham, were accused of his murder. The case was tried in October, but the men were both found "not guilty." A year later, another man, William P. Chrisman, was cleared of shooting Charles Krieger to death with a shotgun. Technically, those cases remain unsolved, although officers at the time said they knew the men who had carried out the crimes, they just couldn't prove it in court.

William Swift was killed on February 23, 1859, beaten to death with a wooden stick. Constables tracked down Miles Gibbons, who was indicted for the crime. Gibbons was found guilty at trial and sentenced to five years in the state penitentiary, but he appealed and the verdict was overturned. No one was ever punished for Swift's murder.

In January 1863, William Gordon was indicted for the stabbing death of Frank Sherry. The case lingered in the docket for three years before it was finally dismissed. Sherry's murder was never solved.

In September 1864, Benjamin F. Church was indicted by a grand jury for the murder of Hugh M. Campbell, who had been shot to death. He was found guilty of manslaughter at his trial - a proceeding that many in the area believed was conducted unfairly. In response to public outcry, Church was pardoned by the governor while he was on his way to the prison in Joliet.

One murder that was solved was that of John Murphy in November 1864. He was killed by a shotgun blast, and Robert Pile was indicted for the deed. He eventually entered a guilty plea to manslaughter and received a sentence of 10 years in the penitentiary.

The period of the late 1860s and early 1870s was one of the most prolific eras of murder in the history of Jacksonville and Morgan County. In addition to the killing of Murray McConnel which will be discussed soon , there were many others. It was a time when the "Athens of the West" was soaked in blood.

Henry R. Gillespie was indicted in March 1868 for the murder of John Ruschie, who was killed when his head was beaten in with a fence rail. The case was tried once, ending in a hung jury, and the defendant was given bail. He promptly vanished and never returned to Jacksonville.

Mahon Chapman was indicted for the August 1869 shotgun murder of Jephemiah Rodgers, but escaped from authorities and went into hiding in Missouri. When local law enforcement officers learned of his location, they followed in pursuit. Knowing that he would be arrested - and found guilty of the crime - he chose to commit suicide rather than be brought back to Jacksonville.

In November 1869, Thomas Cantrall was indicted for stabbing his brother, Sampson, in the stomach with a knife. Sampson died and Thomas was sent to trial, where he was found guilty of manslaughter and given a sentence of 10 years.

On July 13, 1870, Charles Atwood got into a fight with Peter Hodin in some woods just northeast of Jacksonville. Atwood stabbed the other man to death with a knife. He was arrested and brought to trial, where he was found guilty and sentenced to 21 years in prison.

George DeWitt was indicted for the shooting death of Edward DeWitt on September 1, 1870, but he took a guilty plea for a lesser sentence and was sent to prison for eight years.

Lewis Maddox, William Maddox and William Knowles were charged with the murder of their father, William Maddox, in August 1870. The case could never be proven and all three men were eventually released.

John Buchin was indicted for the May 27, 1871 murder of his son, Paul. He had shot the younger man in the head with a gun. He went to trial in April 1872 and was found guilty of manslaughter. He received a five-year prison sentence. Around this same time, Henry Henslee was indicted for the murder of his wife, Caroline, by crushing her skull with a flat iron. He was sentenced to serve 20 years in prison.

On May 23, 1872, John H. Douglas was accused of striking Willis J. True in the back of the head with a garden hoe and killing him. A jury found him "not guilty."

During the circuit court term of May 1875, Robert Mayes was indicted for the murder of his wife, Mary. He had hit her repeatedly over the head with a brick and then had hidden her body in the cellar of their house for some time. The trial took place in August 1876 and received a lot of local, even statewide, attention. The jury found the defendant guilty and sentenced him to 22 years in the penitentiary.

William T. Hannas, better known as "Tobe" Hannas, was indicted for the April 14, 1878 murder of William Baker and Clarence Hubbard at an African-American Baptist Church in Jacksonville. The case created a lot of excitement in town and public opinion ran high against the defendant. The jury found him guilty and sentenced him to 20 years in prison. But soon after his arrival at the penitentiary, he was transferred out to the Insane Hospital, where he died a short time later.

On May 20, 1878, Samuel Mathews was indicted for the murder of his father, Richard. He had shot the older man to death with a pistol. However, during the trial, the jury found him guilty of only manslaughter and he was sent to Joliet prison - for only one year.

In August 1878, John and Theodore Angelo were indicted for the murder of Isaac Hamill. During the trial, John was found "not guilty" and Theodor was sent to a reform school. Later, Theodore's case was reversed by the Supreme Court, he was returned to Jacksonville for a new trial and the case was dismissed.

And sadly, the list could go on and on. Murders were not uncommon during this period and they continued on until the dawn of the new century. But there are few murders in Jacksonville's history that affected the town in the way that the murder of Murray McConnel did.

Murray McConnel was no stranger to crime. In the first story in this chapter, we find that he had some involvement with the vigilantes who attempted to keep order in the area before organized law enforcement was established. He may have ridden among their number. At the very least, he told their tale. He was the first attorney to ever practice in Morgan County, and he was the man who arranged to have the city's first railroad line pass over land that belonged to his friends and himself. But no matter what one might think of his motives under some circumstances, there is no question that he was one of the most prominent citizens in early Jacksonville history, and he was also the man with whom Stephen A. Douglas practiced law. When he was murdered on February 9, 1869, it shocked the entire city.

Murray McConnel

McConnel was in his office at home on North Main Street when he was attacked by a perpetrator who still remains unknown. His death was caused by five "mental wounds" caused by blows to the head by an unknown object. He was found murdered, in a pool of his own blood, on the floor of his office by Mary Ryan, a household servant. She had gone into his office - also his bedroom - and found him on the floor. She testified later that she had been in his room to make up the bed and then had gone upstairs. A few minutes later, she heard a loud, sudden sound like a heavy fall. She hurried back downstairs and found that McConnel had been killed. Although it was in broad daylight, the family saw no one entering or leaving the room. The force of the blows had been so vicious that McConnel's jaw was broken and his skull was fractured in several places.

Whoever had killed him certainly seemed to have a grudge against the attorney.

Murray McConnel had been born in September 1798 in western New York. He left home at the age of 15 and headed west, intent on settling on the frontier. By 1815, he had reached Illinois but did not settle in what would become the city of Jacksonville until about 1821. He had been a resident of the city for nearly 50 years at the time of his death and had been deeply interested in almost every facet of the growing community. He was a well-regarded attorney and a fervent Democrat who had been part of county, state and national nominating committees. He was a member of the lower house of the Illinois Legislature, held the office of commissioner of internal improvements, and he also served as fifth auditor of the treasury during the administrations of Presidents Pierce and Buchanan. His last service in political life was the filling of a term of two years in the Illinois Senate, representing the Jacksonville area. He held the title of "general" for his time in the state militia, and he also served as a volunteer during the Blackhawk War. Although he was too old to serve during the Civil War, he stayed true to the Union. Following the example of Stephen Douglas, he spoke with eloquence on many occasions about the need to sustain the government during those trying times.

Could it have been his political beliefs that got McConnel killed? Or had the trouble started much closer to home?

A coroner's inquest was held two days after McConnel's death, and the jury returned a unanimous verdict against William A. Robinson, a 28-year-old grocery store owner who had borrowed money from McConnel. He had apparently been spotted going into McConnel's house that morning by milk man, W.H. Worrell. And while this seems to be rather shaky evidence on which to indict a man for murder, Robinson was arrested and the case went to trial on May 26, 1869.

The trial itself, due to intense public attention to the case, had to be held in the jam-packed Strawn Opera House, with the judge presiding over court from the stage. The prosecutor and the defense attorney interviewed 130 citizens before the jury could be selected. Shortly before the trial began, the local newspapers noted that the public seemed to believe that Robinson was innocent of the crime.

The evidence was, as noted, very circumstantial. Robinson did owe McConnel money. He had borrowed $420 in gold from the attorney to make a start of his grocery business. When McConnel's body was discovered, the books in his office were open to a page of interest rate calculations. There was a black mark in the book next to a set of figures that would have applied to Robinson's debt. In addition to the eyewitness account of the milk man on the morning of the murder, several other people testified that they had seen Robinson in the neighborhood that same day. Also, a few days before the murder, Robinson sold a good chunk of his property and sent his wife and children to his father's house in Lawrence County.

The most damning evidence against the grocery store owner, though, was his own ledger book. It appeared that he was copying his finances into a new book and the new figures showed that the loan from McConnel was paid off, even though it wasn't.

All in all, it was pretty flimsy evidence, and the eyewitnesses at the trial didn't help matters. During cross-examination, the milk man was forced to admit that he would have had to identify Robinson from a distance of about 60 feet and couldn't say for sure what kind of clothes he was wearing. Another witness admitted that she was on the other side of the street when she allegedly saw the suspect. The defense produced a string of witnesses that gave Robinson an alibi. The time of death had been estimated between 8:50 and 9:10 a.m. - when five witnesses stated that they were with Robinson at his store.

The trial went on for a month and ended with Robinson's acquittal. The jury's verdict, according to court records, stated that the evidence was circumstantial and "it is from the evidence that it is possible that some other person may have committed the murder." But was this the case? Could the witnesses have been lying about where Robinson was that day? Or could Robinson have hired someone to commit the murder? We will never know. The case remains unsolved today. Seven years later, a Bloomington man allegedly "confessed" to the murder, but he wasn't taken seriously. By then, public opinion had shifted and many believed that Robinson had, in fact, killed General McConnel after all. But it was too late by then. He had already been acquitted and Robinson had since vanished into the pages of history - leaving the mystery of Jacksonville's most sensational murder in his wake.

"Murder with Penknife!"
The Chilling Slaying of Charles Hastings

It became known as one of the most controversial murder cases in the city's history. On March 31, 1897, an office in downtown Jacksonville was burglarized, and when the owner of the business caught the thief in the act, he was stabbed 172 times. The killer then confessed to the killing, claimed self-defense, and was acquitted. But how? Suffice it to say, he knew all the right people.

On April 2, 1897, a newspaper headline shouted, "Charles L. Hastings of Jacksonville hacked to pieces!" The city was in a frenzy of excitement over the news, and that should come as no surprise given the sensational nature of the crime. Rumors flew about the death of Charles Hastings, who was described as "one of the most exemplary and highly respected citizens" of Jacksonville. Hastings was 50 years old, unmarried, and a native of Vermont. For a number of years, he had been the chief clerk in the law and abstract office of Judge Edward P. Kirby, located at 232 West State Street. This was not Hastings' initial choice of careers, however. At one time, he had been in the real estate business in Minneapolis but the company had failed and he had returned home to Jacksonville. The quiet and unassuming man had been despondent ever since, friends later reported. Perhaps this was the reason why, when it was first learned that he was dead, many feared that he had committed suicide.

175

But when they learned the details of what had occurred in the blood-soaked office, there was no question that Hastings had been brutally murdered.

The body was discovered on the morning of April 1 by a janitor, who walked into the office to see that a struggle had apparently taken place there. The room had been ransacked. Furniture had been overturned and broken, papers were scattered out and, worst of all, the room was sprayed with blood. As a reporter for the *Jacksonville Daily Journal* wrote, "The blood on the wall loosed as it had been smeared there and spurted there as well. It was three or four feet up the wall and presented a ghastly appearance." In the center of the gruesome tableau, Charles Hastings was lying on the floor with blood-soaked clothing and large gashes in his throat, face, hands, and all over his body. The coroner would later reveal that he had been stabbed 172 times with a knife.

An arrest was soon made in the case. Charles Draper was called to testify at the coroner's inquest and was arrested immediately after. Draper, a former employee of the abstract office who had since opened a competing firm, had always been considered a man of great character. He was respected by the community, beloved in church and social circles, and was a quiet man who was held in high esteem. But something had apparently caused him to snap. When he was taken into custody and placed in his cell, the police reportedly found him still wearing clothing with blood on it.

Draper had worked for Hastings at the abstract office for some time, but for some reason, the two men clashed. Witnesses later said that they "disliked each other considerably." Draper had been the judge's chief abstract maker, but he had eventually resigned his position because of the animosity between himself and Hastings. He then set up his own business and was doing quite well - or so it seemed. A short time before the murder occurred, a witness who worked with Hastings in Judge Kirby's office said that Hastings was "anxious" because it appeared that someone had been going through the office files at night. He was determined to catch the intruder, the witness said, and on the night of April 1, he did. It ended up costing him his life.

The next day, Draper tried and failed to hang himself in his jail cell. On April 7, the *Journal* published a copy of a confession that Draper had written to the pastor of the State Street Presbyterian Church, where he attended. In the letter, the accused admitted that he had entered the abstract office the night of March 31 and opened the vault. He had been stealing papers and information to aid his own company. He claimed that in the middle of the burglary, Hastings came into the room "called me by name and rushed upon me, seized me." In the ensuing struggle, which lasted for 15-20 minutes and destroyed the office, Draper claimed that he took out a small knife and "began to use it as best I could to free myself

176

from him." To put it simply, Draper claimed that the 172-stab wound killing had been an act of self-defense.

Needless to say, neither the newspaper nor the general public found Draper's claim very convincing. When the accused's St. Louis attorney, Colonel Patrick Dyer, unsuccessfully requested bail for this client, a member of the courtroom audience stood up and suggested that a lynching might be in order. Local people were upset and unnerved by the brutal, vicious murder - and so was the newspaper. Draper had a contentious relationship with the *Journal* from the start. On April 14, the newspaper carried an editorial that had run in the *Chicago Chronicle* that laid waste to Draper's self-defense claim, saying, "To ask us to believe that the dead man was the attacking party, without having given the intruder a chance to surrender, is to ask too much." On July 9, Draper responded to the editorial - and the *Journal's* printing of it - stating that the Jacksonville paper was "this steaming black hole of Calcutta" and that it was ruining his chances for a fair trial.

The trial was a colorful affair. It began on January 3, 1898, with Judge Robert B. Shirley presiding. Along with Colonel Dyer, Draper had an impressive six-man defense team, including future governor Richard Yates, Jr. and Judge Cyrus Epler. This team went through more than 100 potential jurors, trying to eliminate anyone who had read about the murder in the *Journal.* Draper entered a plea of not guilty, based on self-defense and a claim of temporary insanity. In addition, Dyer even offered a defense on possible burglary charges to explain why Draper was in the office that night in the first place. He wasn't breaking in, Dyer claimed, since Draper had worked for the abstract office for many years and still had a key and the combination for the safe, he felt that he had the right to enter when he wanted to access the information inside. It wasn't burglary - he was simply borrowing the papers from the safe.

Draper enjoyed a steady stream of character witnesses on his behalf, including William Jennings Bryan. The famous orator and unsuccessful presidential candidate returned to Jacksonville to speaker on Draper's behalf. Bryan had attended the same church in Jacksonville as Draper and felt that he knew the man's character. On the witness stand, he defended his favorable opinion of the accused. He said, "My opinion of a person, I make up by what I observe and what others say. If what others say is similar to what I observe, then it makes my impression of that man's character."

Draper also received a number of glowing references from his home state of Missouri, including a U.S. Senator and a former governor. At one point in the trial, a note in the *Journal* stated, "Mr. Draper certainly had some very influential friends in his old home. The array of judges, sheriffs, mayors and aldermen was imposing, and they seemed to be fine men, but does Col. Dyer have the colossal gall to come over here and intimate that it adds to a man's respectability to go to the legislature of poor old Missouri?"

In the end, the Morgan County jury found Draper guilty and sentenced him to life in prison. But this was not the end of the story. Within a month, Draper was granted a new trial and a change of venue because some of the instructions to the jury were allegedly incorrect. The new trial was held in Jersey County, and this time, Draper was acquitted. His claims of self-defense were accepted and he was set free.

Charles Draper was never punished for the heinous murder that he committed and Charles Hastings' death was never avenged. With no wife, children, or family to remember him, he was soon forgotten and he faded away into Jacksonville history.

If you pass by 232 West State Street today, just steps away from the courthouse, have a thought for Charles Hastings, a man who refused to be taken advantage of and who was merely protecting his business on that night in 1897 when his life was abruptly cut short. One has to wonder, even after all of these years, if the quiet, unassuming man has ever been able to rest in peace.

The 1932 Jacksonville Train Wreck
Vandalism, Disaster and Death

On the cold night of December 28, 1932, a Wabash railroad passenger train crossed the cold winter prairie, headed into Jacksonville. The warm glow of the windows in the cars cast a pale light on the snow-covered fields as it steamed along. The cars, filled with passengers still basking in the happiness of Christmas only a few days before, laughed and talked and quieted tired children as the train neared the city. Many of them held packages from post-holiday shopping, while others waited anxiously to meet relatives and friends who waited for them at the station in town.

It was 7:30 in the evening as the train reached the edge of town. The city lights on the horizon meant that the station was near and many of the passengers stirred in their seats, knowing they would be leaving the train very soon. Then, just as the train reached the city limits, it suddenly swerved off the main line and onto a switch track. The engineer tried to stop the train as it neared the North Webster Avenue crossing - but it was too late. The engine slammed into an oil tank car that was on the side track and shuddered at the concussion. As metal sheered into metal, an explosion took place, shooting flames into the sky. The engine and the first passenger car shunted sideways and toppled over, drenched in a flood of burning oil.

Just above the sounds of screaming passengers, alarms and sirens could be heard as emergency workers and fire engines began rushing to the scene of one of the greatest disasters in Jacksonville history - a deadly crash and fire that was caused by a young boy's troubling prank.

The 1932 Wabash Train Wreck remains one of the most disturbing accidents in Jacksonville history, although few recall it today. It took place on December 28, 1932, when a passenger train was re-directed onto a side track and collided with an oil tank car. The accident - which was later deemed to be murder - claimed the lives of two people, injured two others, and endangered the lives of the passengers. Many would consider it a miracle that more people were not killed.

The train's engineer, John Rapp of Springfield, was one of those killed. H.L. Meyer, a passenger on the train from Decatur, also died from injuries. Harry Ross, a baggage handler, and London Simmons, a cook, were both crew members and were both badly hurt. Ross was scalded by escaping steam and Simmons suffered a broken leg. Firefighting equipment was rushed to the scene and workers soon had the blazing oil under control.

The cause of the accident was no mystery. On December 29, the authorities announced that vandalism had been behind it. State's Attorney Wolford H. Asher, who joined the sheriff and railroad officials in a search for answers, told reporters that a preliminary investigation showed that someone had filed open the lock on the switch, threw it wide, and then removed the red danger light that normally would show an engineer that the switch was open. He stated, "There is no question in my mind that this wreck was caused by vandals."

Initially, there was a lot of confusion about who might have been behind the incident. The wreck in Jacksonville followed closely after two other instances of railroad violence in Illinois. About two weeks earlier, a bridge was dynamited near Taylorville, and about the same time, authorities found dynamite hidden under a bridge near Litchfield. The Taylorville bombing, which halted shipments of coal from Christian County mines for a few days, was attributed to mine violence connected to union troubles that were then occurring in the area. For weeks, railroad property and bridges had been guarded and at first, it was assumed that the Jacksonville accident was another case of union violence.

But it would turn out to be something much worse.

Soon after the vandalism occurred, investigators began to realize that the crash had been caused by something much darker than mine trouble. A small saw blade, a sawed rail, and eyewitness accounts that saw a young man in the area of the switch on the afternoon of the accident, soon led to a suspect, but he seemed to have a solid alibi - at first. But as detectives dug into his background, they grew suspicious. He had a troubled past, which connected him to a series of fires in Jerseyville and two different stays at homes for wayward youth. After eyewitness accounts placed him in Jacksonville on December 28, including sightings that put him near the switch that had been tampered with, investigators decided to bring him in for questioning. Sheriff Ivis Johnson and Deputy Sheriff Wendell Johnson, along with G.S. Ward, chief special agent of the Wabash Railway Company, soon tracked the young man down.

On January 21, 1933, mumbling the words, "Something inside me told me to do it. I'm sorry," Charles Stewart Willis, a 16-year-old high school student from Pittsfield, admitted that he had cut the lock, which caused the wreck of the Wabash train. Willis, a former inmate at the Lincoln School for Boys and the Macon Opportunity Home for Boys in Decatur - both reform schools - was arrested in Pittsfield, where he had been living with his aunt, Anna Willis.

The boy was brought back to Jacksonville and after being questioned, admitted that he was in town on the day of the accident. Initially denying that he had anything to do with the crash, investigators soon got him to confess to sawing the lock and throwing the switch that caused the wreck to occur. It was a simple - and ultimately disturbing - solution to a crime that had shocked the community and, according to Wabash detectives, resulted in one of the most determined manhunts in the railroad's history.

After admitting to the crime - and signing three different confessions - he led detectives to the signal where the lock was cut, showed them where he had tossed the saw blade, and guided them to the ditch where he had hidden the frame of the saw. With these articles in their possession, Chief of Police Frank Kiloran filed formal charges of murder against Willis. He was arraigned for the murders

180

of John Rapp and H.L. Meyer, who had died in the crash. He was then locked up in the Morgan County Jail to await grand jury proceedings in February.

The legal proceedings that followed were nearly as disturbing as the crime. Willis was charged and entered a guilty plea, but the question was raised as to whether or not he was responsible for his actions. According to psychiatric tests, the 16-year-old had an I.Q. of only 70, which doctors at the time stated was on the borderline of "feeble-mindedness." The question of his troubled past was raised, including a fire that he started in the barn of his foster mother at the age of eight. Two years later, more fires followed in Jerseyville, destroying a garage and damaging other property. While in a children's home in Decatur, he cut his wrist with a razor blade and nearly bled to death. While living in a group home in Normal, he suffered his first black-out, caused by a disagreement with an older boy. Others would follow, and he would remember nothing that occurred during those incidents. Each of the black-outs, Willis told doctors, were followed by an intense desire for excitement, and after each of them, he had a feeling of relaxation and well-being, followed by horror at the damage he had done.

According to psychiatrists, he spoke freely about the wreck of the Wabash train. At first, he decided not to carry out his plan because he knew he would get into trouble, but then realized that if he didn't do it, he would never know what would happen. With that fevered thought in his mind, he cut the lock, threw the switch, and removed the light that would warn the engineer of danger.

On April 14, Willis returned to court to learn his fate. Circuit Judge Walter W. Wright ignored the recommendations of psychiatrists and sentenced Willis to life imprisonment at the Chester State Penitentiary. Except for a brief jovial mood immediately after the sentence was read, the boy showed no emotion. He became silent and refused to speak to anyone. Officers said that he incessantly paced his cell at the Morgan County Jail until he was transported to Chester.

Charles Stewart Willis appeared only once more in newspapers during his short life. On September 30, 1948, he was released from prison. His release was ordered by the Illinois Supreme Court after ruling in habeas corpus proceedings that had been filed on his behalf by four Madison County attorneys. Willis, then 31-years-old, was removed from the penitentiary after the court found from evidence submitted that he had been "feeble-minded" at the time of his original trial. He was still guilty of the crime that had put him in prison, though, so he was sent to the Lincoln State School and Colony, where he later died.

It was a tragic end to an even more tragic story. One has to wonder what would have happened to Charles Willis if his crimes had been committed today. Would he have been placed out of harm's way before he ever had a chance to cause the wreck - or would he have slipped through the cracks, just as he did in

1932, and perhaps have committed an even more terrible crime? It's an unsettling question to ponder.

"The Man in the Green Pajamas"
Last Seen at the Sandman Motel

Weird things can happen anywhere - including Jacksonville, where one of the greatest American unsolved disappearances of the twentieth century took place in April 1959, when a man named Bruce Nelson Campbell stumbled out of his hotel room one night, dressed only in a pair of green pajamas, and was never seen again. What happened to the New England stockbroker has never been determined - he simply vanished without a trace.

In April 1959, Bruce Campbell, age 57, and his wife, Mabelita, drove to Illinois from Northampton, Massachusetts. The reason for their visit was meant to be a happy one. They had traveled to see their newly-born first grandson, son of Bruce, Jr., who was an assistant professor of chemistry at MacMurray College, in Jacksonville.

For some reason, the long drive to Illinois was especially hard on Campbell, and he began feeling sick while he was in the car. The stock investment counselor became confused and disoriented, and when they arrived in Jacksonville, Mrs. Campbell checked them into the Sandman Motel, a small, family-owned establishment that was typical of motor lodges of the day. It was located on the northwest side of town, on Walnut Street, where a Casey's store now stands.

Each room had a door that opened to the outside and parking was located right outside the guest's room. Campbell was put immediately into bed after they checked into the motel. Bruce, Jr. arranged for Dr. E.C. Bone, a local physician, to visit his father. Dr. Bone gave him some medication to help him sleep, but it didn't seem to work. Two days passed before Campbell seemed to show some signs of improvement.

On the evening of April 14, Campbell visited with his family. Bruce, Jr. later recalled that his father was "rational but still disoriented" during his last visit with him. Twice, later on that night, Mrs. Campbell said her husband asked her if their station wagon, which was parked outside of their room in the motel's parking lot, was locked up. She told him that it was, shortly before going to sleep.

She later woke up at 2:15 a.m. and saw that the other double bed in the room was empty - her husband was gone. She immediately got out of bed to look for him, and when she realized that he was not in the bathroom, hurried to the door of the room, which was unlatched. There was no sign of him in the parking lot and the desk clerk on duty said that he had not seen anyone walking past the office. The Campbells' car was still sitting in the lot. The doors were locked and it was undisturbed.

Because of her husband's weakness and disorientation, Mrs. Campbell quickly called the police. When officers arrived at the motel, she offered a description of the tall, balding man with a slight limp and explained that when he left the motel room, he was wearing only a pair of bright green pajamas, a wrist watch, and a ring with the Delta Upsilon fraternity crest on it. His wallet containing all his money, his shoes, his eyeglasses, and his car keys were still in the motel room.

Police officers searched the surrounding area, the darkened streets and the Jacksonville downtown area, but there was no sign of Campbell. The next morning, a request was put out for information. Theories of murder, suicide, and amnesia led searchers to local creeks, farm buildings, and wells. Jacksonville Police Chief Ike Flynn and Captain Charles Runkel surveyed the entire area, both in a fixed-wing aircraft, and later, by helicopter. They found nothing. The next day, local firefighters joined the search, using a boat to dredge Mauvaisterre Creek. About 150 students from MacMurray College joined the search, too. On the third day, the entire 235-member male population of MacMurray - students and staff - joined with 50 students from Jacksonville High School to help comb the area.

The *Jacksonville Courier* reported that the massive volunteer search team, broken into smaller groups, covered a six-mile-radius around Jacksonville, including creeks and ponds. It was assumed that, since there were no reports of a barefoot man in green pajamas walking around the city, and, since the

Sandman was on the north side, that Campbell must have traveled north into recently planted farm fields. Unfortunately, this assumption turned out to be overly optimistic. Despite the search, no trace of Campbell was found. Dozens of reports of tall hitchhikers from the surrounding area, including White Hall, Murrayville, Woodson, New Berlin and Alexander, kept the police busy for days, but the leads went nowhere.

Police Chief Flynn told the newspaper, "We have looked everyplace that has been suggested and have run out of ideas on what to do next. A fortune teller told us that Campbell was seven miles from Jacksonville, either northeast or northwest of the city. We have even looked there."

Whoever this psychic was, they might have been on to something, however. The newspaper reported that the last solid lead - pretty much the only solid lead - came in when police were about a week into the search. A farmer who lived several miles northwest of the city told investigators that he had been awakened by shouting on or near his property on the night that Campbell went missing. The police checked the area, but nothing was found. Chief Flynn told the *Courier* that the case was "one of the most baffling mysteries that has occurred here."

The search for Bruce Nelson Campbell, the "man in the green pajamas," continued for days and weeks and then it stretched into years. Mabelita Campbell had reluctantly gone home after two weeks of fruitless searching. But the family refused to give up hope that he would be found alive until 1967, when he was finally declared legally dead. Mrs. Campbell passed away in 2004, never learning what had become of her husband.

After several months of extensive searching by the Jacksonville police, the FBI launched its own investigation into the case. On the first anniversary of Campbell's disappearance, it was revealed that the distraught Campbell family had spent almost all of their savings on private investigators who distributed Mr. Campbell's photo and description to police departments around the country. They'd also offered a $5,000 reward for information, which no one ever collected. Unfortunately, this was the only thing that the FBI learned about the disappearance. Like the private investigators who worked the case, the federal agents found no trace of Campbell.

The case of the "man in the green pajamas" turned out to be the last significant case of Police Chief Ike Flynn's career. Just weeks after the vanishing, Flynn retired and Charles Runkel was promoted to succeed him. Runkel later recalled, even though he was off duty, Flynn never let the case go. He died of cancer several months after he retired, haunted to his grave by the missing man. Until the very end of his life, he never stopped checking in at the department to see if any new clues had surfaced. They had not - and even today, the case remains unsolved.

What became of Campbell? No one knows. He simply walked away on the dark nighttime streets of Jacksonville and was never heard from again.

Jacksonville Fires
Bucket Brigades, Fire Companies and City Calamities

It was a night in August 1856 that was finally the last straw for a lot of the people in Jacksonville. Flames raced through Abraham Link's livery stable and caught several nearby buildings on fire before Jacksonville volunteers could finally extinguish them. The blaze reduced five buildings to ashes and, for a short time, threatened most of the buildings on the east side of the square. The danger of losing the entire downtown infuriated a local newspaper editor named James R. Bailey. In a news story that he wrote for the *Jacksonville* Journal, he asked, "Will not the citizens take into serious consideration the propriety of boring an artesian well, organizing bucket companies... to provide against future calamities of his kind?"

The 1856 fire was fought with a primitive fire engine and by people throwing buckets of water at the flames, a usually ineffective firefighting technique called a "bucket brigade." But that was all the city had at the time and it inspired little confidence among business owners and residents of Jacksonville. The volunteer bucket brigade had been organized about 16 years earlier as the city's first attempt at fire protection.

The brigade, the first regularly organized fire company in the city and a predecessor to the current Jacksonville Fire Department, was founded on April 23, 1840, as the result of a legislative act passed five years before that provided for the incorporation of fire companies. At that time, more than 90 Jacksonville men, many of them prominent business and political leaders, joined together to form the volunteer company. The early firefighters used a double-decked hand engine, a manually operated "Philadelphia-style" fire engine, as well as buckets and ladders to extinguish any fires that occurred within the city limits. Most buildings of the time were made from wood, creating hazardous conditions. Jacksonville had no adequate water supply to battle fires, which made things difficult for the company.

One of the first major fires in the city occurred on December 30, 1852. Despite the best efforts of the fire company, the main building of Illinois College, a four-story structure, was destroyed by fire. On October 25, 1855, a fire broke out south of the square, destroying an entire block. About 40 businessmen shared in the loss, which totaled about $65,000. One man and seven horses were killed in a livery stable.

185

It was likely the August 1856 fire that finally spurred the community into action when it came to fire brigades. Even though their efforts continued to be limited by poor equipment and an inadequate water supply, two competing fire companies had appeared in Jacksonville by 1858. Both of them received public funds to battle fires. Union Fire Co. No. 1 and Rescue Fire Co. No. 2 had "considerable rivalry to see which could do the most prompt and efficient service when fires broke out." At first, the fire companies were merely social clubs that were organized by wealthy members of the community to demonstrate their "public spirit" while they protected their property. But the face of the companies began to change and they became true firefighting brigades, responding faithfully to every alarm, despite their lack of good equipment. Those inadequacies became apparent in November 1859, when the *Jacksonville Journal* office, with all of its material, presses, and files were destroyed by fire.

Several other costly fires in 1860 prompted the city to build four water cisterns around the town square and to buy new 300-foot hoses for the Union and the Rescue fire companies.

On December 31, 1861, fire destroyed the First Presbyterian Church, a plain, brick structure that had been built in 1847, but was newly remodeled the years of the fire with new cushions, carpeting, paint and a new organ. The building was completely destroyed, leaving behind only ashes and smoldering ruins.

In the middle 1860s, more devastating fires saw the appointment of fire wardens in each of the town's four quadrants. The fire warden and his assistants were responsible for inspecting houses for potential fire hazards and for making sure that neighbors joined in with any necessary bucket brigades. Additional fire protection measures were undertaken during that decade, leading to the creation of the Jacksonville Fire Department in 1867.

Early the next year, in March 1868, the Bethel African Methodist Episcopal Church burned to the ground, putting the new fire department to its first big test. The building was lost, but the firefighters prevented the blaze from spreading to other buildings nearby.

In April 1869, the main building of the Blind Asylum, now known as the Illinois School for the Visually Impaired, was destroyed by fire. Luckily, no one was hurt in the blaze. The students and teachers were immediately moved to the Berean College building, located west of the asylum, and the following fall, school was resumed at a new location until the institution could be rebuilt. The new building was completed and opened in January 1870.

A month later, on February 28, 1870, the main building of the Illinois Female College, now known as MacMurray College, burned down. The building was insured, but the furnishings were not. Construction costs for the new building exceeded the insurance and the trustees were forced to borrow in order to rebuild. The new building finally went up in January 1871. Built on the same foundation, it was three stories tall, with three towers and a mansard roof. Lit by gas and heated by steam, it contained parlors, a chapel, classrooms, offices, dorm rooms, and an apartment for the president and his family. Best of all, it was built to be fireproof - a claim that it failed to prove when it burned again on November 18, 1872. Another main building was constructed using the same plans and opened for use in December 1873.

One of the most devastating - and yet, forgotten - fires in Jacksonville history took place on Christmas Day, December 25, 1875. The fire broke out at the Jacksonville Stock Yard, located at Sandy and North Streets, around 8:00 p.m. that evening. The stock yards and sale stables belonged to W. Howard Thompson, and the blaze was apparently started by an explosive device that was tossed into a stable for mules. It spread rapidly and soon burned out into the main stables and the stock yards, which were all enclosed under a roof. The horses, mules and cattle managed to be rescued, but large quantities of hay, corn, and oats were burned, adding more fuel to the inferno. High winds fanned the flames, and soon the home of Mrs. Fay on North Street was also burning. The fire jumped from one wooden house to the next, also destroying a second structure on the same lot, the home of George Manseyes, smaller dwellings across the alley that were owned by George Detherdam, and a tenement house where three families lived on Sandy Street. According to news accounts of the time, the fire department had little success putting out the blaze. "Owing to mismanagement and the busting of hose," one story read, "the Fire Department was of little avail. The fire was wholly checked by citizens." No clues were ever discovered as to the identity of the arsonist who started the fire, or why he had done it.

On August 8, 1882 fire destroyed the Wabash, St. Louis & Pacific Railroad passenger depot at the corner of West Lafayette Avenue and North Church Street. The building was a total loss.

On June 27, 1887, a fire broke out in the Wright Furniture store on the south side of the square. The fire started around 11:00 p.m. that night and continued for more than two hours before it could be brought under control. Four stores were destroyed in the blaze, including the furniture store, a drug store, wall paper store and a milliner. Strawn's Opera House was heavily damaged, and the losses on the building were estimated to be around $85,000. The opera house was rebuilt, but this would not be the only time it was struck by calamity. In December 1922, another fire broke out and caused extensive damage to the building. Then, on May 20, 1988, the Strawn building actually collapsed, bringing a rather dramatic end to its history of disasters.

On the night of September 21, 1887, the main, three-story building of Oak Lawn Retreat, a private insane asylum that was operated by Dr. Andrew McFarland, was damaged by fire. The patients and staff members of the building got out safely, but Dr. McFarland was badly injured when a heavy piece of furniture was thrown out of an upper window and struck him on the head.

On the morning of March 28, 1889, fire destroyed the Thompson & Springer's livery stable on West North Street now West Douglas Avenue . At least 50 horses and mules were killed in the blaze.

In 1892, a fire station was built at the east end of City Hall, just north of the square. At that time, fire equipment consisted of hand- and steam-powered water pumpers that were pulled by horses. The brick building was razed in the 1960s and replaced by the current municipal building.

Wadsworth and Matheson's, wholesale and retail dealers in hardware for wagons and buggies, caught fire on the south side of the square on March 22, 1894. The blaze destroyed the building, as well as the china shop owned by C.V. Frankenberg that was located next door. A fireman received a broken leg, and three others were injured when a ladder broke during the fire.

On March 14, 1918, the Jacksonville High School was completely destroyed by fire. The building had been dedicated on West State Street in 1902 and had served hundreds of students during its short history. The blaze broke out around 2:30 a.m. and swept through the building to also destroy the nearby Trinity Episcopal Church.

One of the most famous Jacksonville fires broke out at the Washington Grade School on May 28, 1931. Originating in the upper portion of the building, flames ate away the roof and down into the interior of the structure before firefighters

The old Washington Grade School

could bring the blaze under control. A few seconds after the fire was first discovered, fire alarms sounded and more than 350 children who were in the classrooms marched or slid to safety down stairs and fire escapes. Perfect order was maintained as the boys and girls responded to the alarms and recalled the fire drills of the past. In spite of this, the street outside of the school was soon filled with anxious parents and relatives, filled with terror that their loved ones might be in danger. The school was destroyed, the result, officials believed, of faulty wiring in the old structure.

On Tuesday, October 26, 1937, a shed of lumber caught fire at the Wright Lumber Yard on East College Avenue. The blaze was discovered at about 5:15 p.m. but could not be controlled until after it had swept through an entire warehouse of new lumber. There was no clue about the source of the fire but the owner of the company, Charles N. Wright, said that he was aware of the fact that transients often slept in the shed, which the newspaper colorfully called a "bum's roost." It was suggested that perhaps a fire built by one of the transients had gotten out of control, since the blaze had apparently started in the center of the warehouse. The building and all of its contents were a complete loss.

A fire that started in a locker room at the Urania Odd Fellows hall caused extensive damage to the third floor of the Gallaher Building on West State Street on November 11, 1937. Around 4:00 p.m., two plumbers who were at work in the building smelled smoke and informed members of the lodge, who were in a

189

recreation room playing billiards. The investigation that followed discovered the fire in the locker room. When the door was opened, flames poured out. Lodge member John Wilbur tackled the blaze with buckets of water until firemen could arrive. The fire was put out in a few minutes, but firefighters remained on the scene for more than an hour to make sure that there were no "hot spots" in the false ceiling on the top floor. Most of the damage to the building was caused by smoke and water.

On January 15, 1966, a fire broke out in the Hockenhull building on the east side of the downtown square. Seven people who lived above the Walgreen's drug store were killed in the fire, which was detailed in an earlier chapter. The building is considered one of the most haunted in the city.

An open gas jet in a kitchen stove was listed as the cause of the fire that destroyed Lahey's Tavern and the top two floors of the Lukeman Clothing Company building on the east side of the square on March 16, 1969. About 40 firemen from Jacksonville, South Jacksonville, White Hall and Chapin fought the blaze for more than four hours in sub-freezing temperatures before it was brought under control. The investigation that followed discovered that the gas jet, accidentally left on "simmer," overheated an adjacent deep fryer, igniting the entire stove. The fire then spread to a hood mounted over the stove and up to a tin exhaust pipe to the roof. The pipe became so hot that it ignited the flooring material on the unoccupied second floor of the building. A second trail of flames ran from the stove to a staircase. The exhaust pipe on top of the brick tavern then ignited the frame of a sealed window on the vacant third floor of the Lukeman building and spread, undetected, through the walls and roof of the second structure for more than a half-hour. Hard work on the part of the firefighters kept the fire from spreading to any of the other buildings on the block.

On July 4, 1975, fire caused more than $300,000 in damage at Lovekamp's Carpet Warehouse on East Morton Avenue. In August 1983, fire destroyed Bill's Star Market on West State Street. Two house fires occurred in March and October of 1986, killing four people at the Rosedale boarding house on Brown Street, and two more at a home on Tendick Street. On March 17, 1987, fire destroyed Cohen's Furniture Store on West Morton Avenue, causing more than $1 million in damage.

Meanwhile, the Jacksonville Fire Department had come into its own, adding a substation on West Lafayette Avenue in August 1973, and bringing its equipment into the modern era. Today the department has 24 full-time firefighters on duty, all trained in ways that were never imagined by the men who formed two social clubs to fight fires in the 1850s. Bucket brigades and hand-pumps pulled by horses have been replaced by state-of-the-art trucks, aerial platforms, rescue trucks, tankers, special rescue equipment, and even a HazMat operations trailer. The department is a long way from its roots in the nineteenth century, and yet, its dedication to the people of Jacksonville remains the same.

The 1966 Arson Fires

In the fall of 1966, a series of what turned out to be arson fires ignited in the city of Jacksonville, costing more than $1 million in damage. The fires ended up being the work of a "helpful bystander" who had been present at each of them, and he was only stopped after six fires had already taken place.

During the early morning hours of September 20, 1966, a fire destroyed the old Routt High School building on East State Street. Earlier that evening, another blaze, which swept through a professor's office on the ground floor of MacMurray College's Main Hall, was also put out by Jacksonville firefighters. It wasn't long before investigators recognized the similarities between the two fires and realized that they had an arsonist on their hands.

The Routt fire, which occurred about a week after the opening of the new Routt High School building, ended with the destruction of the top floor and attic of the building. Flames shot out as high as 20 feet above the building's roof. It was first reported at 2:20 a.m., and it burned for more than two hours before firefighters could get it under control. The roof of the building, built in 1905, collapsed and spread the flames through the entire third floor and attic. Seeping into the walls, the flames spread all of the way down to the building's basement, where more damage occurred.

After the fire was eventually brought under control around 4:30 a.m., the Dominican sisters who lived in the convent directly to the east of the school were forced to evacuate. Smoke was blowing directly into the home, making it impossible for them to breathe.

It was the second fire that evening, and it was at Routt where Fire Chief Dale Bond began to suspect arson. The fire had started at three different places at the east end of the building, which was suspicious in itself, and he now began to believe that the earlier fire at MacMurray had been a diversion from the larger blaze at the high school. The fire at MacMurray, reported a couple of hours before the Routt fire, started when someone tossed a brick through a window to get access to the building. Once inside, they set a fire using papers and several books. The damage turned out to be slight, mostly caused by smoke and water, but the fire had apparently been a distraction.

Two months later, on November 16, 1966, four separate fires damaged four different buildings. Firefighters received their first call at 9:55 p.m. at the William Cole residence on West State Street; followed by a blaze at the Jonathan

Turner Junior High at 10:03 p.m.; then the First Baptist Church at 10:28 p.m. Later, a false alarm was recorded on Marion Street at 11:42 p.m.; followed by the discovery of a fire at Washington Elementary School at 12:11 a.m., and another false alarm at the Little Theater at MacMurray College at 1:41 a.m.

The fire at the Cole home had been set in six different rooms - three upstairs and three downstairs. The damage to the house was primarily in those rooms, where the fires had been started near the curtains. There was no sign of forced entry into the residence because the door had been unlocked at the time. Firefighters only spent about 15 minutes dousing the flames at the junior high. The door had been standing wide open when they arrived. The fire at the church had been started after someone broke a window in back to gain entry. The church was half-way through a six-week remodeling and redecorating program, but the damage to the structure was so bad that the church had to be torn down.

Police detectives and fire investigators knew that an arsonist was on the loose in Jacksonville, and they were determined to track him down before any further damage could be done, or worse, someone was killed or injured in the blazes. They began putting together a series of clues, interviewing witnesses, and trying to put together a list of people who had been on the scene of the fires. One name began appearing on every list - a young man named Danny Shutt. As with some arsonists, Shutt was present at each fire and was terribly interested, and even helpful, in seeing the blazes put out. On September 20, he had been present at the Routt fire and had even helped firemen pull hose into the interior of the building. He was soaking wet when he came out of the building and a newsman on the scene loaned him a raincoat to put on. Newspaper reporters also remembered seeing him at the fire at the Baptist Church. The police received reports from witnesses on the night of the fire about a motorcycle leaving the Jonathan Turner area at a high rate of speed. Shutt was the owner of a motorcycle and was seen riding it that same night. Photographs taken at the fire scenes showed Shutt's face at every one of them.

Police Chief Charles Runkel later told the newspapers, "At the church fire, our investigators went into the building while it was still burning and collected evidence. We took fingerprints from the church fire and, at one of the other fires, the person who set the fire had left behind a gas can, which was used to start the fire. The fingerprints all matched those of Danny."

Initially, Shutt entered a not guilty plea to the charges that were filed against him, but on March 29, 1967, he withdrew the plea and confessed to the crimes. He was sentenced to between four and 20 years in prison on the six counts of arson. He was released on parole on February 16, 1970 and returned to Jacksonville. His parole ended on February 1, 1972.

The Bob Hawks Extortion Fires

One of the most dramatic blazes to occur in Jacksonville over the last few decades broke out on September 13, 1997, when Bob Hawks Auto Body was destroyed by fire. The fire was extinguished - and ruled accidental - but it soon became the first in a series of strange crimes that were all aimed at the owner of the business by a competitor, Raymond D. Lindsey, owner of Majestic Auto Enterprises, Inc.

Hawks' garage became the first casualty in the war, but it would not be the last. On September 25, 1997, shortly before midnight, Hawks' truck, which was parked in his driveway, mysteriously burst into flames and was ruined. Although the auto body garage fire was ruled accidental by the Illinois State Fire Marshal's Office on September 29, and the truck fire was also ruled accidental by state fire marshals on October 2, a third fire that appeared to be aimed at Hawks brought those findings into question.

Just after midnight on October 12, Hawks' 1986 Nordic Crestliner boat caught on fire while parked on a trailer in his backyard. After investigating the boat fire, the authorities began to suspect that something criminal was in the works. "A boat on a trailer just doesn't burn," said Captain Dave Tavender of the Jacksonville Fire Department.

About a week after the boat fire, another truck fire occurred, but this time it was not a vehicle owned by Hawks. This fiery wreck of a truck belonged to Michael Heady, a team mate and business associate of Hawks in the race car circuit.

A short time later, the perpetrators changed tactics - and became even more deadly. In November, the home of Kenneth Vasconcellos, a business associate of Hawks', was shot at with deer slugs during a drive-by shooting. Soon after, a second house, located nearby and owned by Dave Banks, was also shot at, presumably in a case of mistaken identity.

The weird events ended in December when Lindsey and Scott C. Sims were arrested, each on a charge of armed robbery after holding up the Fanco service station at the corner of Westgate and Morton Avenues. While being held on those charges, the Jacksonville police built a case that linked the two men to the arson fires. After a series of legal maneuvers, more charges and more arrests, five men were eventually charged with arson, robbery, criminal damage, and reckless discharge of a firearm. They included Lindsey and Sims, along with Thatcher Floyd, Robert Hoos III, and Jeremiah Glover. All of them received various prison sentences, and all have since been paroled from the Illinois Correctional system.

Haunted Jacksonville

6. "THE SHOW MUST GO ON"
History and Hauntings of Jacksonville Theaters

In the early days of Jacksonville, the city had no real theaters to speak of, but there were a number of meeting places and halls where local children performed one-act plays and pageants and where speeches were given, bands played, and where traveling shows often took the make-shift stage.

Strawn's Opera House

The first real theater in town was the Strawn Opera House, which became the focal point of the community after it was finished in 1861. The theater was built by Jacob Strawn, Morgan County's reigning "cattle king," who amassed a great fortune starting in the early days of the Civil War. By 1862, half of the 165 million pounds of beef that entered the market in New York City came from Illinois, and Morgan County led the state. With the Texas cattle trade closed because of the war, beef prices rose, and Morgan County cattlemen worked feverishly to keep up with the Union demand for beef.

With the money he made, Strawn gave back to the community and built the Opera House. Located on the south side of the square, it hosted touring lectures, symphonies, and theater and opera groups. The building's imposing presence on the square symbolized the kind of genteel life that Jacksonville's middle class had so proudly nurtured over the years. But there was also no question that the Opera House emerged during very turbulent times.

Strawn Opera House on the Jacksonville Square

The paint had barely dried on the walls inside of the Opera House when America was ripped apart by the Civil War. On the evening of April 15, the day that Confederate guns fired on Fort Sumter, the people of Jacksonville crowded into the new theater to hear their political leaders dedicate the city to the war effort. The meeting was organized "without distinction of party" and both Republican and Democratic leaders addressed the crowd in a carefully balanced program. Two military companies were raised from volunteers who enlisted after the mass meeting, and each day, people gathered outside of the Opera House and waited for the latest war news over the telegraph.

When it came time for the Jacksonville soldiers to depart for Springfield, they were given a send-off at the Opera House. On Sunday, April 26, a community religious service was held in their honor. The volunteers were seated prominently in the front. The audience in the packed hall listened quietly as Jacksonville's Philharmonic Society played and Professor Sanders of Illinois College delivered a reverent patriotic speech. A second meeting held later on that evening featured community religious and political leaders and they made a charitable plea that citizens not persecute their southern neighbors in Jacksonville, "who were probably loyal to the Union, but yet held sympathies for

195

the southern people." Enthusiastic applause indicated that the appeal for tolerance would be heeded - at least for a little while.

By July 1861, a third company of Jacksonville volunteers was raised under George McConnell and sent to Cairo to help suppress the threats of secession in Southern Illinois. As the war dragged on, more young men joined the army, and by March 1862, nearly 650 Jacksonville men had enlisted.

As the people of Jacksonville came to realize the war was more about sacrifice and death than mere faith in the country, the community's patriotic ardor became even more intense. The first wartime Fourth of July was celebrated with unprecedented scale and grandeur. A huge procession began early in the morning and the festivities went on long into the night. Feelings ran strong in the city and the first cracks began to appear in the local peace between Republicans and Democrats and Southerners. Behind the veil of patriotic union, sectional tensions flared over the war and its purpose. Pro-Southern students at Illinois College lampooned the Union during the fall of 1861, parading about the square with their coats turned inside-out, sticks over their shoulders, stovepipe hats, a banner, and a brass horn. When some of their classmates proposed delivering an anti-abolitionist commencement speech in June 1862, their professor cautiously forbade it. Students who protested his decision had their diplomas withheld. Outraged Southerners and sympathetic Democrats gave the students a public forum by renting out Strawn's Opera House and inviting the public to attend.

This put the theater in the center of the controversy that enveloped Jacksonville during the war, for things were even more militant outside of the city. Southern sympathizers in Illinois formed a secret society called the Knights of the Golden Circle. Their stronghold was in Southern Illinois but pro-Southerners in every part of the state joined in with the civil strife they created, even in Jacksonville. In September 1863, between 200 and 400 heavily armed Knights swarmed into Jacksonville and gathered on the square. Their mission was to rescue their leader, John Husted, who had beaten a man who had informed on Knights' activities at the railroad station and was now being held in the local jail. The Knights arrived in Jacksonville, making the claim that several thousand armed horsemen were waiting at Mauvaisterre Creek, ready to attack unless assurances were given that Husted would receive a fair trial.

Jacksonville's Republicans had anticipated violence. They had their own secret society, the Union League, ready to do battle if needed. On the morning of Husted's trial, the streets of Jacksonville were filled with Union League men. Bank clerks on the square strapped on pistols, staff members at the opera house bolted the doors and the pressmen at the *Journal* newspaper, twice burned, prepared for danger. A telegram was sent to Camp Butler outside Springfield to ask for army support and orders were given to bring out repeating rifles to defend the town. At the courthouse, though, Husted's trial was brief. He was bound over to the circuit court under a $500 bond and the Knights on the square returned home with the satisfaction that justice had been done. The editor at the *Journal* denounced the Knights, but they caused little trouble in Jacksonville during the remainder of the war.

The Opera House, like Jacksonville itself, endured the war. After the last celebrations over the end of the fighting were completed, the theater settled into a comfortable routine of music and traveling performers that continued until June 27, 1887, when a fire broke out in the nearby Wright Furniture store and largely destroyed the Opera House, along with three other buildings. The losses on the theater were said to be around $85,000.

The Opera House was rebuilt, but in December 1922, another fire broke out and caused extensive damage to the building. By that time, the years of live shows in America were fading, beginning to be replaced by a new form of public entertainment - the movies. Strawn's was rebuilt, but the building was smaller and became a retail outlet, replacing the theater. In the 1920s, it became home to Kline's department store, one of many in a chain of stores in the eastern United States, and it remained in operation until the decline of the downtown square.

Sadly, on May 20, 1988, the Strawn building collapsed, completely destroying the structure. This brought an end to the former theater's long history in downtown Jacksonville.

Grand Opera House & the Illinois Theater

The Grand Opera House was located at the northeast corner of the downtown square, where North Mauvaisterre and East Court Street came together. While it is now occupied by the Illinois Theater, this site actually has a long theater history in Jacksonville.

The Grand was constructed in 1885. The four-story structure, built from stone and brick, was designed and erected by the same firm, F.W. Menke Stone Co., which helped build the Greene County Courthouse in Carrollton and the Presbyterian Church and Public Library in Jacksonville. The Grand building originally contained seven stores, a basement restaurant, and 60 offices, as well as a large lobby and an auditorium that could seat 1,400 people. Patrons had their choice of floor, gallery or private seating boxes. In the early 1900s, the Grand Hotel was also opened in the building. During part of this time, the hotel was operated by Harry Hofmann, who also operated the Hofmann Floral Co. on the square.

But the real draw for the building was the theater. It was ornately decorated. The lobby had natural wood on the walls, a tile floor and a frescoed ceiling. The

The Grand Opera House was located on the southeast corner of the square

theater was lighted with 500 gas fixtures and nearly as many electric lights on the stage and in the hall. The stage was so magnificent that a number of performers exclaimed that it was "if anything, a little too large," wrote a *Journal* reporter of the era.

Over the years, the Grand Opera House offered a venue for many famous people, including three-time presidential candidate William Jennings Bryan, Admiral George Dewey, Eugene V. Debs, poet James Whitcomb Riley, and Sarah Bernhardt.

By the 1910s, live shows and vaudeville began to fade in popularity, the Grand did what so many other theaters of the time did - they began showing moving pictures. In the late 1920s, they installed a sound system and started showing the first "talkies" in Jacksonville. Even though the old stage still remained hidden behind the movie screen, it was never used again. In 1927, the owners abandoned live shows altogether and became a movie house. They also changed the name to the Illinois Theatre, ushering in a new era for the place, but one that only lasted 11 more years.

In 1938, the old building was torn down and was replaced with a brand new building that is still home to the Illinois Theatre today. Although its seen many changes, including being turned into a double-screened, twin theater in the 1970s, and a number of different owners over the years, many things here have stayed the same - including some of the resident ghosts.

The Illinois Theatre replaced the old opera house in 1938, but stories say that the ghosts remain.

One of the most commonly reported incidents about the Illinois is the presence of apparitions in clothing from the late 1800s and early 1900s. Theaters are common places to find ghosts, perhaps more because of the residual energy that is left behind at the location than for dire events or unexpected deaths. Nearly every range of human emotion - from happiness to sadness, terror, grief and despair - has been experienced in a theater. If such emotions leave an impression behind like an old recording, then perhaps it's possible that those recordings replay themselves at times, producing sounds like footsteps, applause, laughter, and weeping or even visual sightings of people who don't seem to be aware that they are in another place and time. All of these things - and more -- have been reported at the Illinois Theater.

Times Theater

The Times Theater opened at 231 East State Street in Jacksonville on Christmas Day 1940. For many, it was like receiving a brand new brick and mortar Christmas present. Adults paid a quarter and children a dime to get into a packed house to see Joan Bennett in "The Housekeeper's Daughter" and Jackie Coogan in "Streets of New York."

Kenneth Childs, from Streator, spent more than $40,000 to build the times, which originally had seats for 680 people in the auditorium. In May 1941, less than five months after it had opened, Childs announced that he had arranged for the Times to be operated by Fox Midwest Theaters, which already operated the Illinois Theatre. The Times was closed a short time later so that air conditioning could be installed, but it soon re-opened to big crowds.

At that time, Jacksonville had three movie theaters - the Illinois, the Times and the Majestic, the latter two both on East State Street. George Hunter, manager of the Illinois, said in 1941: "The Times will present mainly first-run attractions at popular prices. The Majestic will operate as a popular priced family theater, playing the pick of outstanding second-run features. The new policy will give Jacksonville a wide range of attractions to choose from, as well as an admission price to please every type of patron."

In 1953, Fox sold the Times to El Fran Theater Corp., which was owned by Ben Montee and Howard Busey, both local Jacksonville men. The partners named the business after their wives - Eleanor Montee and Frances Busey. Both men had a great love for the theater business and Busey remained involved with the Times for many years, even after it was put up for sale in 1960. After the Times was sold to Frisina Theaters, he worked for the new company, dividing his time between managing the Times and the 67 Drive-In Theatre, which he, Ed Bonacorsi and Elmore Suter built in 1949. He was a member of the Church of Our Savior, Knights of Columbus and the Elks Club. Like his partner, he also served in World War II. Howard Busey passed away in 1980.

His partner, Ben Montee, also loved the Times. A well-known local businessman and very active in the Lutheran Church, he began working for Fox Theaters in Southern Illinois after World War II. He eventually came to Jacksonville and decided to settle in town. In addition to co-owning the Times with Busey, he also founded Cater-Vend, a Jacksonville vending machine business. After the Times was sold in 1960, he bought the Jacksonville Coca-Cola bottling plant, retiring in 1981. He served as president of the Passavant Hospital Board, director of the Elliott State Bank, president of the Jacksonville Chamber of Commerce and was a life member of the Elks Lodge. Montee was also a generous supporter of Illinois and MacMurray Colleges. He died in 1992, outliving his partner by 12 years.

The most dramatic incident to occur at the Times Theater took place on September 20, 1953. A fire broke out behind the screen during an evening showing of "South Sea Woman," starring Burt Lancaster and Virginia Mayo and sent 600 people fleeing from the theater. Phillip Busey, Howard's son, recalled that night very well nearly 50 years later. "When the fire started, my father was at the Times," he said. "I was with my mother, probably at the drive-in. I remember riding in the car with my mother up South Main and we could see that there was a fire in downtown Jacksonville. After the fire was out, but before the fire department left, we were allowed to go just inside the doors. The lobby, concession area, offices and projection booth survived. The damage was to the auditorium." The interior of the theater had sustained major damage, due to a combination of fire, water and smoke. While the Times was repaired, Busey and Montee leased the Majestic, which had closed down the year before.

Frisina Theaters gave the Times a major makeover in 1972, installing a new soundproof ceiling, screen, projection equipment, and curtain controls. Eventually, they sold the theater, and it was taken over by Mid America Theatres, which declared bankruptcy in 1982. They were closing theaters all over the region and were forced to cancel their plans to build a new twin drive-in at the site of Howard Busey's old 67 Drive-In outside of town. The Times sat empty

The Times Theater in the summer of 2014

until the following year, when it was taken over by Kerasotes Theatres of Springfield. They remodeled the building and re-opened the Times as a twin theater.

In July 2008, the Times and Illinois Theatres were purchased by Great Dreams Theatres, a partnership between Dr. Peter Karras, of Springfield, and Joe Avampato, of Delavan, Wisconsin. After the change in ownership, both theaters underwent a series of renovations. But changes in the theater industry in the early 2010s forced movie houses all over America to make an expensive switch to digital projection equipment. Only the Illinois Theatre survived this costly - and mandatory - overhaul. The Times closed down in January 2011. But even though the building sat silent and dark, based on the eerie stories that have circulated about the theater for many years, one has to wonder if it has ever been truly empty.

When peeking into the front doors of the building, one would immediately notice the long stretch of mirror that adorns the back wall of the lobby. Numerous employees of the theater describe the same woman who has shown herself in that mirror - the "lady in the lobby". She is a young woman wearing late 1800's dress and her light brown hair is pulled back in a delicate bun on top of her head. In one account, a new employee was asked to clean the mirror while the manager went upstairs to take care of the nightly paperwork. The employee obliged, but while cleaning the mirror, he saw a young woman with an old-time dress and a bun in her hair, standing right behind him. The figure took three steps and disappeared right before the young man's eyes. Struck with terror, the employee scrambled up the stairs to the manager's office. After several minutes of collecting his thoughts and catching his breath, he described the incident to his manager. Although the manager was not surprised, having heard of this occurring many times before, she agreed to stay with the new employee in the lobby while he finished his work. A similar event took place when a new employee had a run in with the lady in the lobby for the first time. He was so petrified that he left the building without locking the doors and never returned for his second night on the job.

Although he did not run away, one employee, a janitor, saw his job a little differently after some encouragement from the lady in the lobby. The manager had been noticing that this janitor was often cutting corners and leaving tasks unfinished. While alone in the lobby one afternoon, the manager, speaking out loud to herself, decided that she needed to talk with the janitor and persuade him to straighten up. That night, after "cleaning" the auditoriums and lobby, the man entered the stairwell to turn off all of the lights before going home. As he quickly glanced over his shoulder to confirm the lights were all out, he immediately noticed a large amount of popcorn had been thrown all over the lobby floor. Knowing he was the only living person in the building at the time, he took the hint as he cleaned up the mess. After this event, the man was a much more thorough janitor.

Most employees never felt any fear or malevolent sensations from the lady in the lobby. In fact, one manager felt she was quite protective. She recalls one night when she felt unusually unsafe in the building. She was overcome with anxiety and felt as though the spirit wanted her out, and fast! She decided that she could come back in the morning and complete the work she had left unfinished. That night, soon after the manager locked up the building to go home, a burglar broke into the building. The manager was convinced that a spirit within the building was concerned for her safety and had warned her to leave.

Who is this lady in the lobby? Some believe that she could have connections to the Rialto Theater that once stood on the same plot of land that the Times Theater now occupies. Perhaps she is there to see a show, or maybe an actress waiting for her curtain call. Very little is known about the Rialto Theatre and the identity of the young woman remains a mystery.

The lobby is not the only area of this historic building with ghostly activity. The upper floor of the Times Theater has its fair share of paranormal happenings as well. There have been multiple reports of spectral entities that haunt the projection booths. In the first, a calming spirit. One former employee recalls the overwhelming sensation of calm she would sometimes experience in the first projection booth, as well as memorable time a spirit whispered in her ear. Right outside of Booth 1, a manager recalls clearly hearing voices on the stairwell, as if a full conversation was taking place through the wall that connected the Times Theater to the golf store next door. The manager was so convinced of what she heard that she entered the building next door the following day to determine what was on the other side of that wall. She found nothing. No staircase. No electrical equipment. Nothing that could explain her experience. As if that wasn't enough, the manager was teased and tormented by the sounds of stomping footsteps coming up the stairs while she worked in the office. Turning in anticipation to see which employee was coming up to the office, many times she found that it was no one, or at least no one that she could see.

The second projection booth on the west side of the building is home to a particularly active prankster. This spirit, presumed by theatre staff over the years to be a small boy, was notorious for moving objects about the room or making them disappear altogether, not to be found for hours, or even days! This spirit would create so much havoc that the desperate staff decided to put some toys in the projection booth, a teddy bear and some wooden blocks. They hoped that the entity would occupy his time with the toys rather than the projection equipment and cleaning materials he so often disturbed and removed. Although the activity did not cease, staff members claimed their plan did work for a while.

Before a movie could be shown to the public, there was much work to be done. Each film would arrive to the theater on multiple reels, each about 20-30 minutes long. It was the projectionist's job to "splice", or piece together, the reels into one large continuous strip of film. To ensure continuity and quality, the theater employees would screen the film prior to its release date. In case an issue presented itself, the staff members would sit near the back of the auditorium. Often times the employees would see the heads of spectral moviegoers sitting in the seats in the middle of the auditorium. One employee, being an amateur ghost hunter, once caught an electronic voice phenomenon EVP on a digital recorder that said either "screen" or "scream".

After sitting empty until late August 2014, new owners, Josh and McKea Jones took over the theater with new plans to for the space focusing on physical fitness and nutrition - not the movie industry. Since the purchase, the owners have experienced voices calling down the long hall to the second auditorium. With so many renovations taking place, could this stir up the spirits that call this theater their home?

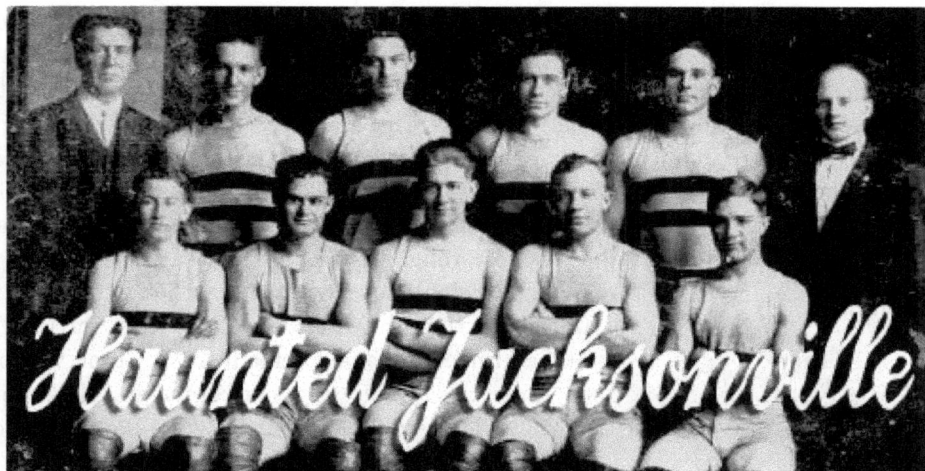

7. A GATHERING OF SPIRITS

History & Hauntings of Our Saviour Rectory

Almost from the start, the "Athens of the West" was regarded on the frontier as a bastion of higher learning. The men who came from New England to found one of the greatest universities in the region, Illinois College, were thinkers, dreamers, and philosophers. They brought with them ideas and beliefs that would shape the city of Jacksonville. They also brought with them their thoughts on religion and spirituality, beliefs that would also become a major part of the growing city. As more and more settlers flocked to the area, the energy and enterprise that turned Jacksonville into a political and cultural center was also present in the city's religious beliefs.

Soon after arriving in the area, the early settlers began forming religious groups. The first, a group of Methodists, gathered in the home of James Deaton, who lived about three and a half miles north of what is now Jacksonville. The "church" consisted of only four members: Deaton and his wife and Abraham Johnson and his wife. The Deaton house continued to be a meeting house for the next 18 years and eventually became the start of the Mount Zion Methodist Church.

In Jacksonville, the first organized congregation was also Methodist and met at the home of John Jordan, whose cabin stood where the Church of Our Saviour stands today. The group evolved into Centenary Methodist Church, which was arguably the most prominent church in the early years of the town because of its early start and the fact that most of the town's most prominent citizens were members.

The first Presbyterians in the community followed a short time after the Methodists. The church formed in 1827 with 12 members, and their first meeting place was Judge John Leeper's barn, located on what is Hardin Avenue today. All of the early groups met in members' homes, but many later moved to a log schoolhouse that was built near Central Park and used as a meeting place presumably at alternating times for religious societies until 1833.

Reverend Barton W. Stone

The early 1830s saw the formation of the Central Christian Church when the Reverend Barton W. Stone arrived in Jacksonville in 1832. Stone was one of America's great religious reformers of the era. Born in Maryland in 1772, he was one of the co-founders of the Christian Church Disciples of Christ , and in the midst of a great religious revival in 1801, Stone and four other ministers renounced Calvinism, a drastic change in religious beliefs in the early nineteenth century. The Calvinist principle espoused that God would save only a chosen, pre-ordained few for entry into Heaven, and that no amount of prayer or good works would change that. Stone was among the first ministers to start a new movement that came from the belief that all men were sinners, and that anyone could achieve salvation by praying to God for forgiveness. This was against the principles of Calvinism and many older church officials considered it blasphemous. Stone then withdrew from the Presbyterian Church and organized a new church at Cane Ridge, Kentucky, which he named "Christian." Stone and his followers appealed for a church that was based on "an individualized, non-partisan adherence to Christ, with one name, and one source of literal authority, the Bible." Reverend Stone spent much of the early nineteenth century doing evangelical work and establishing new churches in Kentucky and Ohio.

He came to Jacksonville in 1832 and decided to settle in the fledgling community. Soon after his arrival, he helped unite another faction of the Christian Church, the "Campbellites," with his own followers, who were known as the "Stonenites." The union of the two similar religious societies resulted in the founding of Jacksonville's Central Christian Church.

Stone remained in the area, eventually settling on a farm southeast of town near what is now Lake Jacksonville, until his death in 1844.

Mount Emory Baptist Church was founded in 1837 by Reverend John Livingston and Reverend Samuel Bull. The church's early founding was brought about by the large number of free blacks in the area, even in those early days. In fact, until about 1877, there were many more Black Baptists in Jacksonville than white.

The Presbyterians were the first to build their own church. Dedicated in 1831, the building was only 30 feet wide and 40 feet long, but it was purportedly the first Presbyterian church in the state that had pews on which the congregation could sit.

All of the churches were small in number, though. In the 1830 census, there were only 466 people in Jacksonville, so none of them could support a full-time preacher. Because of this, each of the various denominations were served by circuit riders, itinerant ministers who went from town to town preaching the gospel. The circuit riders were a rough, often daring bunch. The land was primitive and often dangerous, and the preachers carried weapons and were known to fend off hostile threats from bandits with guns and knives. They also had to brave the weather, which could be deadly. The first Presbyterian circuit rider that served Jacksonville, John Birch, covered a circuit that stretched from Edwardsville to Galena. He died during a winter storm in the "wilds of one of the northern counties of the state."

The Church of Our Saviour began with just five of six families in 1851 and was not large enough to justify having its own priest. A priest actually came from Springfield to celebrate Mass, at times under extremely hard conditions. One Christmas morning, after celebrating two Masses in Springfield, he rented a handcar and traveled by rail to Jacksonville, pumping the handles to power the car so that he could offer Christmas Mass to Catholics in our city. The ordeal was made even more difficult because, at the time, priests had to fast beginning at midnight before a Mass.

Our Saviour was one of many churches in town that were founded, or at least enlarged, by immigrants. In the middle nineteenth century, Jacksonville saw several large waves of new arrivals, including the Portuguese, which created two Presbyterian churches, the first in 1850, and the Germans, who created Salem Lutheran in 1858.

As the town grew and congregations were able to start paying full-time ministers, the competition for membership became intense. A series of religious revivals swept through the country in the 1840s and 1850s, and all of them had an impact on Jacksonville. They shook the spiritual foundations of the city and produced hundreds of new converts. Revivals, a staple of evangelical Christianity, usually involved long meetings that were held on a nightly basis for days, even weeks, at a time. In the winter of 1848, Illinois College professor Julian Sturtevant reported that meetings were held in most of the churches in town every single night for almost two months.

Led by the Methodists, the other churches quickly followed suit in the search for converts and new members. The meetings could be wild and disorienting events. One witness, a minister named James Finley, wrote that they "exhibited nothing to the spectators but a scene of confusion, such as scarcely could be put into human language." A typical revival meeting of the 1840s began in a low-key, solemn way. A preacher often a traveling minister brought in for the event gave a sermon of welcome and led a prayer of peace for the community. This was followed by the singing of several hymns. Then there would be more sermons. Gradually, as the hours went by, the atmosphere changed. The preachers became livelier and the audience grew more excited. One attendee recalled" "The order of the preaching was for the first speaker to be somewhat logical, and to show forth to the listening audience his great learning and wisdom; for the last speaker was left the sensational. He would 'get happy,' clap his hands, froth at the mouth; the congregation responding, some groaning, some crying loudly, 'Amen,' some calling 'glory, glory, glory to God!'" The sermons could go on for hours, but those who attended usually felt revived by the spirit.

And it didn't end there. As mentioned, the revivals could go on for days and weeks. With each passing night, the sermons grew increasingly more sensational and impassioned, and the excited response of the crowd became more prolonged. As days passed, people cried out during the sermons, shouted prayers and wept openly. Some grabbed their neighbors and desperately pleaded with them to repent. They sobbed uncontrollably and ran in terror through the church.

As the services grew more frenzied, people often fell to the ground, overcome by the spirit. Ministers referred to this as the "falling exercise." Reverend Barton Stone, who participated in many revival meetings in his time, described the falling exercise as "very common among all classes, the saints and sinners of every age and every grade, from the philosopher to the clown. The subject of this exercise would, generally, with a piercing scream, fall like a log on the floor and appear as dead." They might remain that way for minutes, or hours. At some meetings, they were set aside where they could be laid out and not stepped on by others. When they awoke, they often wept loudly or screamed out for God, or spoke in what Stone described as "language almost superhuman... I have heard them agonizing in tears and strong crying for mercy to be shown to sinners, and speaking like angels to all around."

Those that didn't fall might experience the jerks - a compulsive movement that would begin in the arms and shoulders and then spread through the body. Stone wrote, "When the head alone was affected, it would be jerked backward and forward, or from side to side, so quickly that the features of the face could not be distinguished. When the whole system was affected, I have seen the person stand in one place and jerk backward and forward in quick succession, their head nearly touching the floor behind and before."

Related to the jerks was the "rolling exercise." People would start by twisting their heads from side to side and rapidly nodding and snapping their heads back. Then they would hurl themselves to the floor ad start rolling over and over like dogs. Sometimes they writhed and screamed as if they were being stabbed with hot pokers. Then they would bounce up and down and shake convulsively as if they were flying apart.

There was also the "dancing exercise," a weird, somber sequence of steps and retreats; the "laughing exercise," which provoked gales of laughter in the most somber church-goer; and the "singing exercise," which occurred uncontrollably. Others would run wildly through the church, shoving people aside, or jump up and down, usually calling on God as they did so.

The reader can imagine that such meetings could be an unnerving experience for those who had never experienced such things before - but there was no question that they led to many conversions as many were awed - or terrified - by what appeared to be a spiritual power that was present at the revivals.

Some denominations were undoubtedly more restrained than others, so the revivals of the period varied greatly in their intensity. At one revival led by the legendary circuit rider Peter Cartwright, who helped found what would become MacMurray College, a young man from the Methodist's national organization insisted on helping Cartwright, who was well-known as a wild, firebrand preacher. The polite young man began to read carefully from a prepared sermon to the Jacksonville audience, which soon grew boring. Saving the situation, Cartwright jumped in and began working up the meeting with a quick fire-and-brimstone sermon that was meant to terrify the sinners in the crowd. An enormous man suddenly jumped up out of his seat and began crying out to God, but the young preacher told him to "be composed." However, Cartwright ignored him and bellowed at the man to "Pray on brother, pray on... there's no composure in hell or damnation!" In his ecstasy, the large man grabbed a hold of the young man, lifted him up off the floor and jumped from bench to bench around the room, knocking people down as he went. Cartwright thought of advising the terrified young preacher to "be composed," but as soon as the man escaped, he fled the church, presumably to return back east.

The revivals of the middle nineteenth century had a controlling effect on the people of Jacksonville. Many members of the community "mended their ways" during this period, and those that didn't often found themselves answering to church officials. The Christian Church, for example, brought charges against a member, John Fisher, for going to the theater, playing cards, and showing disrespect toward the elderly and malice toward fellow members. Apparently, to build up his courage, Fisher had several drinks before his hearing and at one point, threatened to "shoot or horsewhip one of his accusers." The elders of the church took his behavior as proof that he was "manifesting the spirit of Satan" and kicked him out of the congregation.

Such enforcement of religious morality became common among Jacksonville churches. A group at Our Saviour enforced piety similar to the evangelical Protestant churches in town. The Catholic Men's Association prohibited intemperance and gambling and transgressors had to confess their sins before the Association's board. The first several meetings of the association were entirely filled with the confessions of backsliding members. When Thomas Mulready and Matthew Rogers, both board members, failed to attend the first meeting, the board became convinced that the men were drunk and expelled them. Another board member, Jeremiah Clancy, was seen passing the day in a saloon and he was accused of gambling. He told the board that he had declined to play cards because he was a member of the Association, but admitted that he had bankrolled a friend to take his place in a game. When Clancy used the same excuse on another occasion, the board decided that it violated the spirit of the group's by-laws and kicked him out.

As the churches became more established and their congregations grew, they built large and more impressive houses of worship. The symbol of this grandeur was along West State Street where, between 1831 and 1967, there were no fewer than nine church sites that were home to 13 congregations at various times. The sites saw periods of many changes, as congregations split, formed, re-formed and merged. The most active spot was on the northwest corner of Church and State Streets, which was home to several Presbyterian denominations, a Universalist church, a Methodist, and a Baptist church.

Such activity even continues today, and now, as it was then, the turmoil is unsettling to the people involved. But now, as then, the disagreements over theology are signs of an active and intense religious atmosphere that still permeates through Jacksonville after all of these years.

A Rebellious Congregation

There was one church in Jacksonville that became infamous for breaking the rules. The Congregational Church was once known as the "abolitionist church," and that was not a name of admiration. In fact, it was once spat out in contempt for the members. But such derision was nothing new to the leaders of the church for the very founding of the society ruined the New England hierarchy of the church's plans for frontier expansion.

In 1801, the Eastern leaders of the Presbyterian and Congregational Churches formed an agreement called "A Plan of Union." Each town in the west would have either a Presbyterian or a Congregational Church, and members of both denominations were free to attend each other's church, depending on what was available in the community. The church kept its name and general beliefs, but welcomed members of other churches. The idea behind the plan was to save money. Rather than pour resources into competitive situations in the new towns being settled on the western frontier, the two churches were able to serve all their members with just one building and one minister. The Plan of Union did not specifically prohibit Congregational Churches in the west, but for some reason, nearly all of the churches formed west of northeastern Ohio were Presbyterian.

In April 1833, Jacksonville had a Presbyterian church, but it served a number of Congregationalists, including many of the leaders of the recently founded Illinois College. In fact, Julian Sturtevant, the college's second president, served as the interim pastor of the church for several weeks when he was a professor at the school. But Sturtevant was becoming disenchanted with the Presbyterian church and found himself more in sympathy with the Congregationalists. Two friends, Edward Beecher, the first Illinois College president, and Theron Baldwin, a college trustee, urged him to be patient because they believed the Presbyterian church was soon going to split over slavery and other issues.

Soon after, however, Sturtevant, Beecher, and another colleague, William Kirby, found themselves accused of heresy by a local pastor, William J. Fraser, who was the minister of the Providence Church in Virginia. The charges are sketchy since the men were simply charged with "unsound teaching." Sturtevant was accused of having views contrary to Presbyterian doctrine and contrary to its reading of the biblical scripture. Whatever the alleged offenses actually were, the men were all cleared fairly quickly. Reverend Fraser was suspended from his duties, partially because of a slander charge stemming from a letter he had published in the *Illinois Herald* newspaper in Springfield. The heresy charge didn't cause Sturtevant to help form a Congregational Church, but it did speed things along.

Later that same year, two people who wanted to start a Congregational Church approached Sturtevant and Beecher. The two Illinois College men hesitated at first, but by December, they had consented. In early 1833, there was only one Illinois town, the northern community of Princeton, with a Congregational church. Two other churches in Mendon and Timewell soon followed, but the church in Timewell later turned back to Presbyterianism. However, the churches in Quincy and Jacksonville did not.

211

The Quincy Presbyterian church reorganized later that year under the leadership of Illinois College Trustee, Asa Turner. While the changes in Quincy undoubtedly upset the leaders in New England, the reorganization in Jacksonville unsettled and angered them. The Jacksonville church did not change from Presbyterian to Congregationalist - the organizers formed a rival church. The competition meant to be avoided by the Plan of Union had now been created by the new church. It was the first to be organized in the west outside of the Presbyterian church, and it was roundly condemned by both sides. Not only were the Presbyterians upset but, for many years, it was regarded as an outlaw body by the New England Congregationalists.

Jacksonville's rebellion against the carefully organized church hierarchy in the east opened the door for the nationalization of the Congregational Church and the Plan of Union was dismantled in 1837 - at the same time that the Jacksonville congregation jumped into the fight against slavery.

For decades before the Civil War, the city had been a haven for abolitionists, mainly because of the New England men who came west to found Illinois College. Many Illinois College students and staff members worked hard to help slaves escape from bondage in the South and many of them were arrested for their efforts.

But the city of Jacksonville could not really be considered an abolitionist community. The city had a large number of settlers who came from Kentucky, Tennessee, and other southern states. Many of them had relatives who owned slaves or profited from slavery themselves and had no interest in hearing Yankee talk about how slaves should be freed. Julia Wolcott Carter, the daughter of one of the founders of the Congregationalist Church, wrote: "There was always a strong southern sentiment in Jacksonville - people who had grown up amidst slavery, some who still held slaves in the south and lived upon the proceeds of their toil and many who had relatives in the south." At the very least, many Jacksonville residents didn't want their city to be known as an "abolitionist town," regardless of how they personally felt about the issue.

With that said, the actions of many of the church's members - helping slaves escape and using church funds to pay for the legal and living expenses of escaped slaves who were suing for their freedom - probably angered many people in Jacksonville.

But does this come as a surprise, given the history of the church? They may have taken the side of the minority, upsetting the people of Jacksonville, but since their very presence was a sore point to the leaders of the denomination back east, one more offense hardly seemed to matter.

The Four Corner Churches,
Jacksonville, Illinois

GRACE METHODIST CHURCH

STATE STREET PRESBYTERIAN CHURCH

TRINITY CHURCH

FIRST BAPTIST CHURCH

When Ripley's "Believe it or Not" Got it Wrong

It was a 1967 photograph that debunked one of the greatest legends in Jacksonville history.

A photograph that was published in the *Journal and Courier* on January 18, 1967, showing the demolition of the 171-foot spire of the Central Baptist Church, was transmitted in the United Press International wire and was sent out with the following caption:

1 18 67 - Jacksonville, Ill.: The church steeple of the Central Baptist Church begins its descent and crashes to the ground, ending what residents claim is the only intersection in the world with a church on all four corners. The 81-year-old church will be replaced on another site.

It only took a few days for the people of Jacksonville to discover that one of the symbols of the city was a myth. The legendary "four-church corner" at West State and Church Streets was unusual, but it definitely wasn't unique. The *Journal* office received at least two letters, one from St. Petersburg, Florida and another from Rochester, New York, stating that the city of Palmyra, New York also had an intersection with churches on all four corners.

It wasn't as though the people of Jacksonville purposely lied about their churches - they had been misled by none other than Robert L. Ripley himself, the creator of the famous newspaper column, "Ripley's Believe It or Not." Ripley, the famous reporter of the weird, odd and bizarre, visited Jacksonville and was so fascinated with the "four-church corner" that he included it in his column, complete with a sketch of the churches, in 1939. But it turned out Ripley was wrong - there was at least one other four-church corner in America.

But that didn't make ours any less special to the people of Jacksonville. The corner had a long history, dating back a half-century before Ripley's "discovery." The Central Baptist Church building, the first to be torn down, was the most imposing of the four churches and the one that created the four-church corner. It had been constructed in 1885 as the State Street Presbyterian Church and remained so until it was sold in 1952 to the Central Baptist organization. The State Street Presbyterians merged with the Westminster Presbyterians to form the First Presbyterian Church. The Lincoln Avenue Baptist and Westfair Baptist congregations trace their roots back to the Central Baptist Church.

The other corner churches included the First Baptist Church, which was built between 1871 and 1874 as a Presbyterian church; Grace United Methodist Church, built in 1909; and Trinity Episcopal Church, built in 1919-1920. While the Grace Methodist and Trinity Episcopal buildings still stand, the First Baptist Church met an unfortunate end in November 1966 when it burned during the city's series of arson fires. The church's sanctuary and 80-foot tower were gutted in the blaze, but its brick walls remained standing after the Central Baptist building was razed in 1967, making it the second of the four-corners churches to fall.

Hauntings of the Our Saviour Rectory

There is likely no building in Jacksonville that captures the imaginations of ghost enthusiasts like that of the former rectory used by the Church of Our Saviour. While there are no tales of violent death or terror in the long history of the building, there is no question that many claim to have had a large number of eerie experiences within its brick walls. What make this place so haunted? Like the city of Jacksonville itself, perhaps it's a place from which the dead simply don't want to leave.

The Church of Our Savior was founded in 1851. At the time, there were only a handful of Catholic families in Jacksonville. The first Mass in Jacksonville was celebrated in 1851 by Father Gifford of Springfield, in a private residence with five or six families in attendance. A short time later, land was donated to the church by Murray McConnel at the southeast corner of West Lafayette Avenue and North Sandy Street. The congregation raised enough money to build a small brick church.

The church was too small to be able to have its own priest, so Father Quigley of Springfield visited the church at intervals, including the Christmas day that he traveled 30 miles by handcar to say Mass. The first pastor was P.T. McElhern, followed by Fathers Brennan, Mangan, O'Halloran and Clifford. Father Joseph

214

Costa followed in 1866 and began looking for land on which to build a new church. Unfortunately, he found that anti-Catholic sentiment in the community was so strong that he found difficulty obtaining a site. No one wanted to sell land to the Catholic church, so he ended up going through a third party, former Governor Richard Yates, to buy land on East State Street.

The anti-Catholic movement was one of the plagues of nineteenth century America, claiming that Catholics only offered allegiance to the church and so a Catholic was incapable of being a "good American." The prejudiced and misunderstandings continued for years, but the influx of immigrants to Jacksonville helped to form a local Catholic community and the stereotypes of the past were soon proven to be untrue. The Church of Our Saviour dedicated its new church in 1868. Father Costa also completed a rectory later to be a convent and started St. Patrick's School.

His successor, Father Mackin, secured the Dominican sisters of St. Catherine's convent in Kentucky. The nuns moved into a small inadequate cottage next to the school, but they only remained for two years. Father Mackin moved out of the rectory and into a small house nearby and moved the sisters into the larger home. Father Mackin was followed by Father Hickey, who built Liberty Hall next to the grade school and in 1877, was instrumental in securing the former Yates residence as a home of the Dominican sisters. They remained in the house until they moved to Springfield in 1893.

In 1883, Father John W. Crowe came to Springfield and by 1895, he had completely remodeled the church and had built a new rectory. In 1896, he secured the Sisters of the Holy Cross to prepare a new hospital, which was located at the remodeled convent that had been abandoned by the Dominican nuns. He also bought a home for the Routt Club and in 1902, built Routt High School on East State Street, where it stood until destroyed by fire in 1966.

He was succeeded by Reverend Francis Formaz, who built the new grad school, which is still used today. Monsignor Michael Driscoll arrived after the passing of Father Formaz in 1960 and would oversee the building of a new Routt High School, a new convent and homes for the pastor and his assistant. In 1995, Father Ken Venvertloh took over the reins of the parish and continues to serve today.

The Church of Our Saviour has a long history in the city of Jacksonville and one portion of it - the rectory built by Father Crowe - touches on the bizarre and, many believe, the supernatural.

The land on which the rectory is now located was first purchased in November 1823 by William S. Jordan and his wife, Elisa. In November 1835, they sold the land to attorney John J. Hardin, who was killed during the Mexican War in 1847. After Hardin's death, his law partner and the executor of his estate,

David A. Smith, sold most of Hardin's land to Richard Yates, who studied law under Hardin. Yates would go on to serve as the Illinois governor during the Civil War. Yates sold the property to James Ewing in December 1849. Ewing was a carpenter by trade and he built the first home on the property. On July 4, 1865, he sold the house to Elbert Sharp, his sister, Elizabeth Berry, and their father, Martin Sharp. Elbert Sharp had come to Illinois with his father in 1828. They settled on a farm northeast of Jacksonville before purchasing the home at 462 East State Street. Sharp became a carpenter and then entered the grocery business in 1872. When Martin Sharp died in 1872, Elbert bought his father's share of the house and later bought out his sister's share in 1884. Tragically, he died in an accident just one year later, but his wife, Mary, remained in the home until 1895. At that time, the house was purchased by the Church of Our Saviour for $5,000.

In August 1895, the Sharp house was torn down and replaced by a new rectory for the church. The first priest to live there was Father John W. Crowe, who arrived in Jacksonville in 1883. Over the span of 12 years, he had managed to raise the funds to remodel the church and build the new two-story Queen Anne-style rectory. While the rectory was being built, Father Crowe lived in the Yates mansion, which stood east of the church and had been used previously by the Dominican sisters as a convent. After the rectory was completed, the Yates mansion was remodeled and turned into Our Saviour's Hospital, which opened in November 1896. Father Crowe lived in the new rectory until his death in 1916.

After Father Crowe's death, he was succeeded by Reverend Francis Formaz, who had served under Crowe as assistant pastor since 1901. It was during his tenure that three bells were installed in the tower of the old church and the church acquired an organ. Both the bells and the organ were moved to the new church, which now stands east of the rectory, in 1977.

The last priest to live in the rectory was Monsignor Michael Driscoll, who was installed as pastor after Father Formaz's death in 1960.

The rectory was closed in 1995 and within a few years, stories began to emerge from the building of strange sights and sounds that were connected to the history of the place. Many claimed that the stories had been around for years - even when the rectory was still being used by pastors from the Church of Our Saviour - and were not a recent invention at all. In fact, Monsignor Michael Driscoll was said to be a great believer in the spirit world, and some that we have spoken with claim that the first stories of the rectory's ghosts were told while he was in residence there. Father Driscoll often told people that he believed that a person would smell the scent of lilac or lavender when a ghost was present. Did he come by such knowledge first-hand?

The former Our Saviour Church Rectory

There are many who believe that he did, for the first spirit said to be connected to the rectory is that of Father Francis Formaz, who began living there as an assistant pastor in 1901 and remained until his death 59 years later. And many claim, that he still hasn't left the building.

Not long after he died, there were reports of the smell of a man's cologne in the rectory when no one wearing cologne was present. A radio often mysteriously turned itself to St. Louis Cardinals' games Father Formaz's favorite team and the sound of a man walking was often heard in a hallway. Some even claimed that they saw the ghost of Father Formaz.

At that time, the altar boys from the church were responsible for cleaning the rectory. They had heard the rumors about a resident ghost, and for this reason, some of them were afraid to go inside. Apprehension turned to outright terror, though, after one of the boys had an encounter with Father Formaz himself. The young man said that he was cleaning the priest's former bedroom and had the distinct feeling that he was being watched. Slowly turning around, he looked out the window and saw an elderly man looking into the room with his hands pressed against the glass next to his face. The boy ran from the room in horror, vowing to never return. Of course, such a story could easily be explained by saying that someone who was aware of the boy's nervousness was simply playing a trick on him - until it's explained that the window in question was on the second floor of the house and no one could have stood outside of it and looked in!

As the years passed, the story of the altar boy was repeated time and time again, and soon more tales were told, often claiming the man's face had started to be seen inside of the house, looking out toward the street - when the house was empty and silent. Our friend Loren Hamilton even had a group of people at the rectory one night and a number of them saw the eerie face peering out at them.

Who was the old man? Members of the local parish have long been divided as to the spirit's identity. Most believe that Father Formaz is the ghost of the rectory, but others believe that it might be another resident, or even a guest who once stayed a night or two in the building. Whoever it might be, it's likely that his residency pre-dated that of Monsignor Driscoll, who almost assuredly encountered one of the rectory's unearthly occupants during his tenancy. But could he have remained behind himself? Driscoll did die on the premises and perhaps his interest in the spirit world also caused him to linger behind. If so, does he walk here alone?

Many people don't believe that he does. Based on the experiences of those who have been able to spend time at the house -- from the authors to Loren Hamilton and many of our guests over the last few years -- we've come to believe that this actively haunted place is home to a number of different spirits. In addition to Father Formaz, who has been seen on numerous occasions, it is thought that Monsignor Driscoll is still watching over the place. As Loren has pointed out, a lot of the activity that occurs in the house happens in the room where he died. Many of us have heard knocking sounds in the room, have heard doors slam and felt inexplicable cold chills that seem to come from nowhere. During investigations, recordings have picked up a man's voice and on one occasion, a man's image was captured on film. Many who have entered the room claim to feel sick and short of breath, even though they have no knowledge of what occurred in the room.

Much activity has taken place in an upstairs bedroom down the hall from the room in which Monsignor Driscoll passed. During one investigation, our team experienced many unexplained spikes on the EMF and KII meters that suggested there was an increase in the energy within the room. In addition to this new age ghost hunting technology, our team had also decided to experiment with dowsing rods. Dowsing for water, mineral deposits, oil, and even missing persons is a technique that goes back to ancient times. During this investigation, we asked any spirit who was present to communicate with us by crossing the two rods for "yes" and separating them for "no." Although we were skeptical at first, the spirit in this particular bedroom was quite fond of communicating using the rods and was able to cross and uncross the rods on command. In addition, this spirit was able to turn my flashlight on and off at my request. By using these various means of communication, the team discovered that the spirit was that of a young girl. Why was there a young girl haunting the living place of the Catholic priests? Thankfully, before the end of the investigation, the young girl exposed that she was not connected to the building itself, but rather to the bed we had been sitting on throughout the entire investigation. Did this young girl meet an early end beneath those sheets? Or was the bed a place of joy and comfort in the afterlife, just as it was for her before her death? Once we better understood the young girl's spirit connection, the activity began to fade. But before she said goodnight, I felt a chilly, small hand placed on my lap, almost as if thanking me for our visit.

After the investigation, the team spoke with a church member who remembers when a donation of furniture was made to the church to furnish the extra bedrooms in the home, including the items in this particular bedroom. We also had the pleasure of speaking with a psychic who had previously investigated in the rectory. She asked me, "Did you meet the little girl in the back bedroom? Isn't she darling?"

The former rectory for the Church of Our Saviour is undoubtedly one of the eeriest spots in Jacksonville, plagued by decades of weird stories and ghostly tales. Is it truly haunted? Do spirits of previous residents still linger behind? Years of unexplainable happenings and first-hand accounts seem to suggest that the building is inhabited by a number of spirits. Do you believe? Perhaps - or perhaps not, but remember that there have been more skeptics that have left the old rectory as believers in ghosts than most of the allegedly haunted places in Jacksonville combined.

8. MEDICINE ON THE PRAIRIE

History & Hauntings of Jacksonville's Asylums and Hospitals

The city of Jacksonville did everything that it could in the nineteenth century to live up to its reputation as the "Athens of the West," establishing schools like Illinois College, the Illinois Conference Female Academy, State School for the Deaf and the Illinois State School for the Blind and at one time, boasting as many as eight hospitals, including Passavant Memorial Hospital, Our Saviour's Hospital, five private institutions and the State Hospital for the Insane. The thriving community had a long history of medical "firsts," which included Illinois' first medical school, the first county medical society formed in 1846, and the first mental hospital in the state.

As early as the 1840s, leading residents of Jacksonville worked hard to make the city a medical center on the Illinois prairie. However, Jacksonville's first doctor was a land speculator named Ero Chandler, who established a house and office in 1821 before the town was officially founded. Dr. Chandler helped organized the Presbyterian Church in town and in 1833 gave the land behind his home to establish the Jacksonville Female Academy. His years as a doctor in the city were short-lived. In 1836, he moved to Hancock County and gave up medicine to become a farmer.

In the early days of Illinois College, trustees decided to establish a medical school. It opened in 1843 with a 16-week course of instruction. In order to graduate, students had to pass an examination before a board of doctors who had already earned their degree. Since there were so few actual doctors in the area, one of the first acts of Illinois College's Medical School was to confer an M.D. degree on several doctors that were already practicing in Jacksonville. The Medical School only lasted until 1848.

The faculty of the school was more distinguished, however. At least two of them achieved national recognition. David Prince was a professor of anatomy and surgery. Except during the time of his service in the Civil War, he remained in Jacksonville and was a pioneer in plastic and orthopedic surgery. He invented a new method for restoring the lower lip and face. He was also well-respected, even beloved, in the community. His medical knowledge far exceeded most doctors of the day and included literature in several foreign languages. He was active in many medical organizations, became Vice President of the American Medical Association, a founder of the American Surgical Association and of the Illinois State Medical Society, as well as a delegate to two international medical congresses in Europe. After returning from the war, Price built Jacksonville's first private hospital, the Jacksonville Surgical Infirmary. Better known as the Prince Sanitarium, it opened in 1867 on South Sandy Street. Prince was far ahead of his time. He incorporated a system of air locks in the infirmary that sealed off the operating room from other parts of the building. A similar system is used in modern operating rooms today.

Another private hospital in Jacksonville was the New Home Sanitarium, which was founded in 1909 by Alonzo Home Kenniebrew. It was located on West Morgan Street and was operated by one of the few African-American physicians to have practiced in Jacksonville. Dr. Kenniebrew was a graduate of Meharry Medical College, where he also taught. He also served on the staff at Tuskegee Institute and was the private physician of Booker T. Washington.

Dr. James Allmond Day also operated a private hospital in Jacksonville for a short time. It was located at 1008 West State Street and he specialized in surgery. Day opened his first office in Jacksonville in 1903. He had practiced medicine in Winchester for about a decade prior to going to Vienna, Berlin and Paris, where he and many other doctors observed, studied, and assisted with surgeries of all kinds. When he returned to Jacksonville, he moved into a room at the Dunlap Hotel and began renewing acquaintances with former patients and colleagues. A number of doctors in the area were generous with referrals and welcomed Day's new expertise in surgery. Before long, he had a busy practice at Passavant and Our Saviour's Hospitals.

In 1911, Dr. Day bought a large brick house on State Street, which he converted into a 30-bed private surgical hospital. It was an immediate success and he usually performed three or four surgeries every weekday morning. He did brain surgery, removed lungs and kidneys, repaired compound fractures and removed diseased parts from any and all organs. Hospital stays were much

Dr. Day's hospital on West State Street

longer in those days. New mothers might convalesce for a week. Someone who had their appendix removed might stay for two weeks. Part of the reason for the long stays was the lack of smooth, paved roads and comfortable vehicles. One could not bump along a rough and rutted road in a wagon until the incision from an operation was properly healed.

Around the same time that he opened the hospital, Dr. Day married Frances Wilmot, a woman that he had known in Winchester. They soon bought a house on West North Street now West Douglas Street , just a couple of blocks from the hospital. The new responsibilities of family, in addition to the hospital, were almost more than Dr. Day could handle. The demands from his practice were extreme. His workload had become staggering and the stress of daily surgery, postoperative care, office visits and financial administration weighed heavily on him. In 1917, completely overwhelmed, Dr. Day decided to close the hospital and move to Springfield and perform operations in the hospitals there. He continued to practice in Springfield until 1939, when he retired at age 70. He passed away in 1968.

Passavant Hospital

The voluntary non-profit hospital system in Jacksonville began with Passavant Hospital. The original building was located on East State Street and was acquired by Eliza Ayers in 1868. Mrs. Ayers encouraged Reverend William

Passavant Hospital in the 1960s

Passavant to use the property to start a hospital. When he died in 1894, the hospital was named in his honor.

In the early days, the hospital consisted of four rooms: a men's ward, a women's ward, a laundry and kitchen, and an operating and reception room. Reverend Passavant arranged to have people from the Lutheran Association for the Works of Mercy sent to operate the hospital. The institution operated just as it was until 1902, when the Passavant School of Nursing was established. In 1913, Samuel W. Nichols donated funds to build a Nurses' Home on the hospital campus.

By 1945, the hospital's capacity had reached its limits. Even with new construction over the years, patients were now being turned away for lack of beds. At this time, a group of residents began raising funds to build a 140-bed facility on West Walnut Street, on farmland donated to the new hospital by Charles A. Rowe. The new Passavant Memorial Hospital opened in 1953.

By the 1960s, Passavant was continuing to grow and overshadowing the other hospital in town, which was Our Saviour's Hospital, re-named Holy Cross in 1964 and later, Norris Hospital. It was determined that the city would be best-served by one hospital, so Norris was first taken over by the Passavant Association and later, closed and absorbed by Passavant Memorial. The community then put all investments toward one hospital, rather than duplicating staff, equipment and other expenses. The ownership was also extended to all area churches at that time and Passavant Memorial Area Hospital Association was incorporated on August 29, 1979.

The 1953 building has been renovated many times over the years. In 1975, a major addition was completed that housed outpatient, emergency, and diagnostic and treatment departments. The south addition in 1981 added new surgical areas, business office, Intensive Care Unit, meeting rooms, a lobby, entrance to the hospital, and two nursing units. The radiology wing was added in 1989, along with a new cafeteria. In 1992, the Ambulatory Care Center was completed, bringing together all of the outpatient services. In 1999, the Maternity center was renovated, adding rooms for private labor, for delivery and recovery, and a delivery room was added to allow Caesarean sections to be done in the obstetrics unit. In the years since, Passavant had added same-day surgery services, an MRI system, physical therapy and much more.

The dreams of the people of Jacksonville in the nineteenth century for modern medical care have truly been made real in the twenty-first century at Passavant Hospital.

Our Saviour's and Norris Hospital

Although now closed and abandoned - and long regarded as one of the most haunted buildings in Jacksonville - Norris Hospital has a long history in the city. It began life as the Yates Mansion, then became a convent, and finally, a hospital. Cobbled together from three separate structures, it served the city for many years as a place of care and healing before falling into disrepair and ruin after it was closed down.

The original residence of Richard Yates, who later became governor of Illinois, was built in 1839 and served as the home of the young law graduate and his wife, Catherine. The house on East State Street was expanded several times, growing in prominence with the lawyer turned politician. When he passed away in 1873, his wife was left alone in the old house. It had been Governor Yates who had appointed Ulysses S. Grant to the military post that led him to Civil War victory and later, to the White House. When Grant toured the country in 1879, he stopped a parade that was held in his honor in Jacksonville so that he could visit the widow of Governor Yates, who sat watching out the drawing room window.

Grant had another connection to a woman who would have a history in the house. In 1874, at the unveiling of the Lincoln Monument in Springfield, Grant invited two nuns from Jacksonville to attend the ceremony. Dominicans Sister Josephine and Sister Rachel both served as nurses during the Civil War, and the former general asked them to represent the hundreds of Catholic sisters from 20 religious orders who nursed the wounded and dying during the war.

Sister Josephine was superior of six Dominican sisters who were brought to Jacksonville by Father Mackin from their motherhouse, St. Catherine's Convent, near Lexington, Kentucky. They were tasked with teaching at Our Saviour's

Our Saviour's Hospital after several additions. The original Yates mansion can be seen on the right side, with new additions added over time.

parochial school and establishing a motherhouse in Jacksonville. The seven newcomers established themselves in a cottage that stood at the site of MacMurray College's Little Theater.

When the Sisters negotiated the purchase of the Yates property in 1885 for St. Rose's Academy and for a motherhouse, Charles Routt provided $5,000 to help work out the sale. The Sisters borrowed the remaining $3,000 needed. The following year, the new owners replaced the center and western sections of the home with a three-story brick structure. The new school was soon open and thriving and the enlarged Yates drawing room became the center of the cultural life at the academy.

The Dominican motherhouse and academy were transferred to Springfield in 1892, but the Sisters maintained their convent on East Court Street. For many years, they taught in the building that was later occupied by the Holy Cross Cultural School of Nursing.

After a short period of time when the building was used as a parish rectory and Routt Club, it next saw the arrival of the Sisters of the Holy Cross in 1896 to establish Our Saviour's Hospital. Charles Routt, who had passed away the previous year, had left a legacy of $12,800 for the founding of a sister's hospital in Jacksonville. When word of this spread, nine local doctors petitioned the pastor of Our Saviour's parish, Father John Crowe, to assist in the establishment of this much-needed community institution. The Sisters of the Holy Cross of Notre

225

Dame in Indiana were chosen to organize the hospital and they arrived in Jacksonville on August 26, 1896. The founders of Our Saviour Hospital were Sister Lydia, the mother superior, and Sisters DeSales, Theodora, Angelus, Joachim, Louis and Ermin.

Unfortunately, the building was so unprepared that they were not ready when the first demand for nursing care came to them. A great many changes were needed to convert the former Yates home into a hospital: "installing toilets and bathtubs, preparing an operating room, and installing an elevator which is worked by electric power; the elevator alone costing $1,000." But in the midst of that hard work, the Sisters had their first patients.

On October 22, 1896, a young doctor named Gillett brought three typhoid fever patients, children of a widower named Edward Corrigan, to the new hospital. The former Yates drawing room, which had been the heart of St. Rose's Academy, now became the heart of the hospital. The Sisters set up three beds for the children, John, age 14, Mary, 11, and Maggie, 9. Simple curtains were placed around the beds and the Sisters cared for the children and nursed them back to health. All three of them survived under the round-the-clock watch of Sister Ermin.

And the hospital thrived. Although its first quarters were small, 138 patients were cared for between the opening date and July 1, 1897. It soon became apparent that the hospital was growing and needed additional space. The Sisters appealed to William Routt, the son of the man who had originally helped to purchase the Yates property, and came to their aid with a generous contribution. In October 1897, construction began on the first addition and it was completed in May of the following year. It was three and two-thirds stories high, contained all of the modern conveniences of steam heating, gas and electric lights and cost approximately $10,000 to build.

Although there was no formal medical staff in those days, approximately 20 doctors cared for the patients, taught the sisters and gave material support to the hospital. A Ladies Aid Society, which was a volunteer service of local women, gave generously of their time and at one period contributed enough canned and preserved fruit to serve the patients for six weeks.

The Holy Cross Sisters in Jacksonville continued the traditions established during the Civil War. Sister Lydia and Sister DeSales had been among 63 Holy Cross Sisters who served as U.S. Army nurses in nine hospitals from Missouri to Washington, D.C. Sister Victoria, also an army nurse, came to Our Savior's Hospital at a later date. Sister Lydia's time in Jacksonville was interrupted by the Spanish-American War. This veteran of the Civil War was appointed Chief of Army Nurses at Camp Hamilton near Lexington, Kentucky, which made her responsible for other Holy Cross Sisters, Sisters of St. Joseph, Sisters of Charity and the "trained female contract nurses." Sister Lydia's assignment later took her to Cuba and to Washington to report directly to the president. In recognition for her service, she was awarded the Army Medal for Distinguished Service.

In 1903, Sister Lydia returned to Jacksonville, and as the hospital superintendent, made plans to tackle the problem of the adequate preparation of nurses. During her first year, she purchased textbooks, but there was little time for their use. The nurses were working 12 hours a day, as were all of the other employees of the hospital. Sister Lydia's return to the hospital was directly on the heels of an epidemic of typhoid fever that swept through Jacksonville, increasing the number of patient admissions at Our Saviour's to 302. It lasted for eight months, during which there were sometimes as many as 14 cases in the hospital at one time.

In May 1921, the nurse's home was opened and two months later, a second addition to the original building was begun. This was the only major construction undertaken until the Frank A. Norris wing was constructed and the original Yates mansion buildings were razed. The nurses' school was not the first attempt at training nurses at the hospital. The first training school had opened in 1908 under the care of Sister Cordelia, an Army nurse who had worked with Sister Lydia at Camp Hamilton. But due to scarcity of time, personnel and materials, the first class of four nurses didn't complete their studies until 1921. The training school was opened again and was registered with the Illinois State Board in January 1922. The first new class of students graduated in May 1924.

The hospital continued to grow. Radiographic equipment was purchased in the 1920s, but there was no radiologist on staff until many years later. Dr. Garm Norbury was the first physician to assume responsibility for the pathology department of the hospital. Modern equipment was obtained for the hospital's surgery and its adequately furnished and staffed laboratory, X-ray and emergency room. With the addition of the F.A. Norris East Wing and the renovated west wing, the hospital grew to offer 130 patient beds to serve the needs of the community before the hospital's name was changed to Holy Cross in 1964. In 1968, it became Norris Hospital before being taken over as a unit for Passavant Hospital.

Norris was modernized during the 1970s, but in 1983, it was closed and the property was sold to MacMurray College. The college used the former hospital to support their growing nursing program. Students had access to equipment and materials left behind, such as beds and wheelchairs, and the environment alone made this the perfect location to study nursing. The Criminal Justice department was also housed in the building and the Art department used the several rooms for classes and personal studio space for upperclassmen.

The older section of Norris Hospital today

A former student of MacMurray recalls the many late nights spent working in his studio in the east wing of the third floor. By this time, the west part of the building was deemed unsafe and was no longer being used. Although no one was allowed past the door in the middle of the hallway, this student would hear deep voices, moaning sounds, and worst of all, screams coming from the other side of the building. When he would venture outside of his studio to investigate the source of the ruckus, no one was found. He was alone - or so he hoped. This sort of event occurred so frequently that the student began to get used to the shouting and pleas for help. It was rumored that the west side of that floor was once used to house patients in need of psychiatric care. This student was aware of the rumor but declared the spirits would not bother him as long as they kept to themselves. But that all changed late one night, while working in the quiet of his studio, he began to hear, again, the crying and moaning from the other side of the third floor. This time, he heard the door in the middle of the two hallways unlatch as if someone was coming through the door to the east part of the hallway. Petrified, he listened as he heard a shuffle of labored footfalls approaching his studio door. Feeling confident that he would soon come face to face with the suffering spirit, he steadied himself in the frame of the third story

228

window and jumped. He first landed on a lower roof one and a half floors down, leaped atop an awning, and finally landed safely on the gravel lot below. He did not return to his studio for several days, and even when he did, he decided he would work during the day from then on.

On the top floor of the hospital, formerly used as the tuberculosis unit, Teri Moore, our friend Hannah Grey's mother and a former Art professor for the college, had her own personal studio space. As an American Hauntings tour guide, Hannah often describes her many personal experiences to the visitors. While visiting her mother, she would witness the strange happenings on the fourth floor of the building: doors opening and closing on their own, the water faucet turning on full blast while no one was in the restroom, and the eerie impression that she was not alone. She could even hear the muffled, distant sounding voices of people talking down the hall, but upon investigation, she found no one.

Like many artists, Teri would spend many late nights working in her studio. She even spent the night in the building on regular occasions. Each morning, when exiting the room to head to her first class of the day, Teri would notice a small mound of smoked cigarettes piled outside of her studio door. Teri was not a smoker nor was anyone smoking in the building. In fact, no one visited the east side of the building because it was in such disrepair. Each time, Teri would sweep up the pile of cigarettes and throw them in the garbage. The next time she spent the night, she would discover the same pile of cigarettes waiting for her in the morning. Was this the work of a spirit recanting the pain and frustration of a serious lung condition?

There is one personal experience from Norris Hospital that I will never forget. While doing an investigation, the team and I meandered through the building, not coming across any kind of significant activity at all, that is, until we reached the first floor. While walking over rolls of carpet and dodging fallen ceiling tiles, I noticed as the lights on my K-II meter began to flicker. The team decided to stop for an EVP session. With meters, flashlights, and digital recorders around the circle, we began asking questions, hoping an intelligent spirit was in our presence. To our delight, the spirit in the hallway with us at that time was very energetic, and responded to our questions by lighting up the lights on the K-II meter in my hand. We discovered that the spirit was that of a little girl, a happy little girl. As we sat there in the dark, we could each feel the breeze brush by our skin as the girl playfully weaved in and out of each of person in the circle. We even witnessed the various meters scattered between us would light up one at a time as the energy traveled around the group. After several minutes of fun, the lights began to fall dim. I asked the spirit if she was done playing. At the time, I had no idea that I had received a clear answer on the digital recorder- "yes." When the activity had faded away, we decided to move along down the hall. It was then that I felt a sudden, firm set of small hands grasp my lower leg. I called out to the other members of the group to observe the flare of my jean pressed tightly around my calf. Pictures were snapped, digital audio was recorded, and meters were in hand, yet no other evidence appeared besides the visible grasp around my pant leg. After a couple of minutes, which seemed like a very long time to me, the tiny grip released my leg and never returned.

Are these the spirits of former patients who still linger at Norris Hospital? Or could the specters be much older? Could they be the Sisters who once nursed and cared for the sick and dying who were placed under their watch? Or perhaps one lingering ghost might be that of Richard Yates himself, wandering the place that was built over the ruins of his former home? We may never know the identities of those who walk here, but one thing is sure, no single spirit in Norris Hospital walks alone.

Broken Spirits
History and Hauntings of the State Hospital for the Insane

If spirits are truly the personalities of those who once lived, then wouldn't these spirits reflect whatever turmoil might have plagued them in life? And if hauntings can sometimes be the effects of trauma being imprinted on the atmosphere of a place, then wouldn't places where terror and insanity were commonplace be especially prone to these hauntings? As an answer to both of these questions, we need point no further than to the crumbling remains of the former state hospitals that dot the landscape of Illinois - including the city of Jacksonville.

In its final years of operations at our old state hospital, after the last patients had departed, staff members in the building started to report some odd occurrences. Could events of days gone by still be lingering here? What macabre history has occurred in these now crumbling building? There are many tales to tell about this sad and forlorn place. It is a strange story that is filled with social reform, insanity, ghosts, and it even maintains a connection to a supernatural incident that is known all over America.

We tend to think of mental hospitals of the past as places of terror, hells of chaos and misery, squalor, abuse, and brutality. Most of them now, shuttered and abandoned - we experience a shiver of horror as we contemplate being confined in such a place. Before the middle nineteenth century, the mentally ill were hidden away from the rest of us, kept out of sight from the "decent folk" and often hidden in cold basements, locked in cages or chained to walls. Mental health

230

care barely existed. In those days, anyone suffering from a mental disorder was simply locked away from society in an asylum. Many of these hospitals were filthy places of confinement where patients were often left in straitjackets, locked in restraint chairs, or even placed in crates or cages if they were especially disturbed. Many of them spent every day in shackles and chains and even the so-called "treatments" were barbaric.

Not surprisingly, such techniques brought little success and patients rarely improved. In those days before psychiatry and medication, most mental patients spent their entire lives locked up inside of an asylum. There was little preparation for them to return to life outside, because no one ever expected them to be freed. After years in the asylum, residents became "institutionalized," and no longer desired, or could no longer face, the outside world. They lived in the state hospitals for decades, died in them, and were buried on the grounds. Under such conditions, it was inevitable that the asylum population would grow and individual asylums, often large to begin with, came to resemble small towns. It was inevitable too, that wilth a large inmate population, and inadequate funding and staffing, that state hospitals fell short of their original ideals. By the latter years of the nineteenth century, they had fallen into states of squalor and negligence and were often run by inept, corrupt, or even sadistic bureaucrats - a problem that persisted into the twentieth century.

But most state hospitals did not start out to be places of squalor and fear. The first hospitals were often palatial buildings with high ceilings, lofty windows, and spacious grounds, providing abundant light, fresh air, exercise, and a varied diet. Most asylums were self-supporting and grew and raised their own food. Inmates would work in the fields and dairies, work being considered a form of therapy for them, as well as supporting the hospital. There were gigantic kitchens and laundries and there, like the gardens and livestock, provided work and therapy for the patients, as well as an opportunity to learn life skills. These were things that many, withdrawn into their illnesses, might never have acquired before. Community and companionship, too, were vital for patients who would be otherwise isolated in their own mental worlds, driven by their own obsessions or hallucinations. Thanks to this, even when things became so dismal in the 1950s, some of the good aspects of asylum life could still be found in them. There were often, even in the worst hospitals, pockets of human decency and kindness. By the start of the twentieth century, asylums were no longer places of isolation, but rather meant to be places of comfort and safety for the mentally ill.

And often they were, enjoying a sort of "golden age" between the latter part of the nineteenth century and into the years of the Great Depression. But things would change and conditions, in many hospitals, began to deteriorate, declining back to the days when mental illness was a stigma and when the insane were kept away from the "normal people."

The 1950s brought the advent of specific antipsychotic drugs, which seemed to promise, if not a "cure," at least an effective alleviation or suppression of psychotic symptoms. The availability of these drugs strengthened the idea that hospitalization need not be for life. If a short stay in a hospital could "break" a psychosis and be followed by patients returning to their own communities, where they could be maintained on medication and monitored as outpatients, then it was felt, the prognosis, the whole history of mental illness, might be transformed and the vast and hopeless populations of asylums drastically reduced.

During the 1960s, a number of new state hospitals were built with this idea in mind, dedicated to short-term admissions. Sadly, though, the new hospitals found themselves soon overwhelmed by the influx of patients from older hospitals that were now being closed down. Legal changes followed, now making it illegal for the patients to work. This meant that instead of doing useful activities in the laundry, or outdoors, they were now left sitting zombie-like in open wards, in front of now never-turned-off televisions. With many patients filled full of drugs, their complacency allowed them to be released, or "deinstitutionalized," to use one of the psychiatric catch-phrases of the day. And what started as a trickle of released patients in the 1960s became a flood in the 1980s, even though it was clear by then that it was creating as many problems as it solved. Every major city was filled with daily reminders of those problems in the form of untreated patients wandering the streets. There was no way to deal with the hundreds of thousands of inmates who had been turned away by the few state hospitals that remained. Most of the hospitals had, by then, been closed down by federal budget cuts that swept the nation.

By the 1990s, it was clear that the system had overreacted and that the wholesale closure of state hospitals had proceeded far too rapidly, with no alternatives in place. It was not closure that the hospitals needed, but fixing: a plan to deal with overcrowding, understaffing, negligence, and brutality. Simply treating the problems with drugs was not enough. The benign aspects of the asylum had been forgotten, and they had stopped offering the safe haven that the first state hospitals were meant to provide.

The Illinois State Hospital for the Insane

In the 1840s, Illinois did not have a system in place for the care of the state's mentally ill citizens, who were then either living with their families or kept in the local poor house. The catalyst for the creation of Illinois' first asylum - as well as asylums in other states - was schoolteacher-turned-reformer Dorothea Dix, who, beginning in the early 1840s, traveled across America lobbying states

232

to build hospitals for the proper care of the "indigent insane." She knew just how bad things were. Her tours of America's asylums revealed that people with mental illness were often treated no better than criminals and were often kept in jails and cages. The insane asylums that did exist were a slightly better option, but offered no treatment.

Dix's humanitarian appeals were persuasive and they were well timed: expansionist America was eager to create large civic institutions that would serve as models to an enlightened society. Public schools, universities, prisons and asylums were all part of this agenda, though the high-minded rhetoric was not always matched by the less-than-altruistic motives of politicians. Regardless, Dix bullied and cajoled one state legislature after another until they bent to her will. In Illinois, she addressed the state legislature in December 1946, asking for an institution to be founded to serve people with mental illnesses.

On March 1, 1847, the legislature established the Illinois State Asylum and Hospital for the Insane with a nine-member board of trustees that was empowered to appoint a superintendent, purchase land within four miles of Jacksonville, and construct facilities. At the time, only two other states had state-operated facilities for the mentally ill. The hospital was created to shift the economic burden of the mentally ill onto the state, which paid all of the patients' expenses. However, patients or their county of residence remained responsible for transportation, clothing and incidentals.

The original board hired James M. Higgins as the Superintendent and purchased 160 acres of land for $3,270 on the south side of Jacksonville, along what is now Morton Avenue. Construction began in 1848 and although Dorothea Dix expressed the wish that the Jacksonville State Hospital be opened by 1849, it actually took more than three years, thanks to constriction problems and other delays.

Dix was the catalyst for the first wave of asylum building, but it was Thomas Story Kirkbride who provided the blueprint for their expansion. Kirkbride, who served as the superintendent of the Pennsylvania Hospital for the Insane in Philadelphia, drew on his own experience and travels in Europe to devise the model asylum. As a skilled administrator, he was obsessed with asylum design and management. He believed that a well-designed and beautifully landscaped hospital could heal mental illness. If the insane were placed in a peaceful, structured environment, he believed, they had a much better chance of returning to the outside world as an improved individual. His belief - and the design that he created - helped to spread the idea that lunacy could be cured in a hospital, not at home.

The asylum building was the cornerstone of Kirkbride's idea. It consisted of a central administration building flanked symmetrically by linked pavilions, each

The Illinois State Hospital for the Insane

stepping back to create a "V, like a formation of birds in flight, or as some have called it, a "bat-wing design." The layout was designed by sex, illness and social class. The most disturbed patients were housed in the outermost wards, while those more socially adjusted lived closer to the center, where the staff lived. The stepped arrangement of the wards made the hospital easier to manage, while at the same time, admitted an abundance of light with views of the outdoors. The location of the planned asylums - like the hospital in Jacksonville - was meant to be in the country, away from the city, offering privacy and land for farming and gardening. The land immediately around the asylum was used for pleasure, where the patients could take a relaxing stroll and admire picturesque views.

The "Kirkbride Plan" was an American invention and the state hospital brought this design to Jacksonville. For many local residents, especially those who had never been to a major city, the Kirkbride building on the state hospital grounds would be the largest building they would ever see. Building the asylum required enormous state expenditures and an army of workers who lived on-site during the construction. It was a technological marvel of the time, offering modern amenities such as fireproof construction, central heating, plumbing, and gaslight. But it was not a hospital in the modern sense of the word. On the outside, it exuded grandeur but inside, it resembled a dormitory. Each pavilion in the structure was three stories high, with one ward per floor. The ward consisted of a long, wide hallway, lined by small bedrooms. Each ward also contained a dining room, a parlor or sitting room, bathrooms, storage closets and rooms for attendants. Patients spent most of their time in the hallways or common areas, not in the bedrooms, which were locked during the day and used only for sleeping.

The Illinois State Hospital in Jacksonville finally opened on November 3, 1851. Only two of the wards were ready for occupancy, but that day saw the first patient arrive at the asylum's doors. Sophronia McElhiney, of McLean County, was admitted with a disagnosis of "extreme jealousy." She remained at the hospital for the next 16 years.

The requirements that allowed people to be admitted to the hospital in those days would be totally unacceptable in the modern age. The "supposed exciting causes of insanity," as they were called at the time, ranged from "novel reading" to "abortion." According to the hospital's 11th biennial report, there were 623 patients admitted between 1866 and 1868. The "exciting causes" of four of those were "jealousy," seven were admitted for "overexertion" and 30 for religious excitement. Early treatment emphasized fresh air, activities and exercise. More sophisticated treatment methods, including any kind of medication, were extremely limited. Many of the residents remained at the hospital for decades and new patients continued to be admitted on a regular basis.

Elizabeth Packard

In 1860, a patient was admitted that would not only become one of the most famous to ever come to the Jacksonville hospital, but she would go on to lead a campaign that would change laws in at least three states as to who could be admitted to an asylum and, most importantly, why they were placed there. Her name was Elizabeth P.A. Packard, and she was committed to the Jacksonville hospital against her will by her husband because they had a disagreement over her religious beliefs. At the time, Illinois law allowed a husband to confine his wife to an asylum for basically any reason that he wanted to and no hearing was required. Mrs. Packard would spend three years locked away from the world at the state hospital in Jacksonville.

Elizabeth Parsons Ware was born in Kankakee County, Illinois, in December 1816. At the insistence of her parents, she married Reverend Theophilis Packard

Elizabeth Packard

in May 1839. The couple had six children, and lived quietly for many years, and appeared to have a peaceful marriage. However, Reverend Packard had very rigid religious beliefs and after many years of marriage, Elizabeth began to question her husband's teachings and began expressing opinions that did not agree with his. While the main subject of their dispute was religion, the couple also began to disagree on child rearing, family finances, and the issue of slavery.

At the time the state asylum in Jacksonville opened, the Illinois legislature passed a law that required a public hearing before a person could be committed to the hospital against his or her will. There was one exception to this law, though: a husband could have his wife committed without either a public hearing or her consent. In 1860, Theophilis Packard judged that his wife was "slightly insane" and arranged for a doctor, J.W. Brown, to speak with her. The doctor came to the house pretending to be a sewing machine salesman. The doctor prodded her with leading questions, pushing Elizabeth into admitted that she was unhappy with her husband and upset with his accusations to others that she was insane. Dr. Brown reported this conversation to her husband along with the observation that Mrs. Packard "exhibited a great dislike toward me" and Reverend Packard decided to have his wife committed to the asylum. She only learned of this decision on June 18, 1860, when the county sheriff arrived at the Packard home to take her into custody.

Elizabeth Packard spent the next three years at the Jacksonville Insane Asylum in Jacksonville. She was regularly questioned by her doctors, but she refused to agree that she was insane or to change her religious views. Finally, after public pressure, Mrs. Packard was brought for a jury trial before Judge Starr of Kankakee; the jury declared her falsely imprisoned, and she was released. In 1863, in part due to pressure from her children who wished her released, the doctors declared that she was incurable and discharged her.

When Elizabeth returned to the home she had shared with her husband in Manteno, Illinois, she found that on the night before her release, her husband had rented their home to another family, sold her furniture, and had taken her money, notes, wardrobe, and children and left the state. She appealed to both the Supreme Court of Chicago and Boston, where her husband had taken her children, but had no legal recourse, as married women in those states at the time had no legal rights to their property or children. But Elizabeth was determined to change all that and she sued her husband.

At the subsequent trial, her husband's lawyers produced witnesses from his family who testified that Elizabeth had argued with her husband and had tried to withdraw from his congregation. These witnesses concurred with Reverend Packard that this was a sign of insanity. The record from the Illinois State Hospital stating that Mrs. Packard's condition was "incurable" was also entered into the court record.

Elizabeth's lawyers, Stephen Moore and John W. Orr, responded by calling witnesses from the neighborhood that knew the Packards, but were not members of reverend's church. These witnesses testified they never saw Elizabeth exhibit any signs of insanity, while discussing religion or otherwise. The final witness was Dr. Duncanson, who was both a physician and a theologian. Dr. Duncanson had interviewed Elizabeth Packard and he testified that while he was not necessarily in agreement with all her religious beliefs, "I do not call people insane because they differ with me. I pronounce her a sane woman and wish we had a nation of such women."

The jury took only seven minutes to find in Elizabeth Packard's favor. She was legally declared sane, and Judge Charles Starr issued an order that she should not be further confined.

Elizabeth did not return home after the trial. Even though she and her husband never formally divorced, they remained separated for the rest of their lives. Elizabeth remained close to her children, and while she did not have custody of them when they were young, they supported her throughout their lives.

Elizabeth realized how narrow her legal victory had been. While she had escaped confinement, it was largely a measure of luck. The underlying social principles that had led to her confinement still existed. She decided to try and do something to not only change the law, but the public's perception of what was happening in some cases with legal commitments to asylums. She founded the Anti-Insane Asylum Society and published several books, including *Marital Power Exemplified, or Three Years Imprisonment for Religious Belief* 1864 , *Great Disclosure of Spiritual Wickedness in High Places* 1865 , *The Mystic Key or the Asylum Secret Unlocked* 1866 , and *The Prisoners' Hidden Life, Or Insane Asylums Unveiled* 1868 . In 1867, the State of Illinois passed a "Bill for the Protection of Personal Liberty," which guaranteed all people accused of insanity, including wives, had the right to a public hearing. She also saw similar laws passed in three other states.

Jacksonville and the "Watseka Wonder"

In 1865, the state asylum in Jacksonville received another patient who, although she was unknown at the time, would go on to achieve fame as one of the greatest enigmas in American supernatural history. Her name was Mary Roff, and she and her family lived in Watseka, Illinois. The young woman had been pronounced incurable by all of the doctors in their area where she lived. They could not explain the strange trances and spells that plagued her - or an obsession with blood that nearly killed her.

Mary Roff was born on October 8, 1846 in Warren County, Indiana, a little less than a year before Asa and Dorothy Ann Roff and their family came to Illinois and settled in the town that would become Watseka. Starting at the age of six months, Mary began to suffer from seizures, which over the course of her

Mary Roff

life gradually increased in violence. When the attacks began, she was a tiny infant and her condition paralyzed the Roffs with fear, especially after the earlier deaths of two of their children, William and George. Strangely, though, even though Mary lay in a coma-like state for several days, she soon recovered and, within a few weeks, seemed perfectly fine.

Unfortunately, her periods of good health would not last. A few weeks later, another spell seized her. Her pupils would dilate, her body would become very stiff and her muscles would twitch uncontrollably for a short time. The seizure would then be followed by a period of eerie calm that could last for minutes, hours or even days. Once it came to an end, she would behave normally, as if no illness afflicted her --- at least until she suffered from another bout with the puzzling illness. The spells came every three to five weeks, and as she grew older, they became more violent and more prolonged.

As Mary grew older, and the seizures became more horrifying, she began to complain of hearing mysterious voices in her head. The voices, she said, came from nowhere and told her to do things that she knew she shouldn't. Even her periods of good health seemed to be marked by a depression and despondency that should not have been present in a beautiful young girl who was dearly loved by her parents and her sister, Minerva. Mary could often be found sitting in the parlor of their home, playing mournful music and singing sad songs. A feeling of doom seemed to linger about her, as if she knew terrible events were coming.

By the time Mary was 15, her health had grown worse. The Roffs had taken her to see doctors all over the region, including Dr. Jesse Bennett and Dr. Franklin Blades of Watseka, and several prominent physicians in Chicago, including Dr. N.S. Davis. Davis was a professor at the Northwestern University Medical School and a well-known homeopathic physician. He not only helped to charter a homeopathic medical college in Chicago but also pressed for reforms for the city's healthcare system. He led the campaign in 1862 for the city to hire a health officer and to start a citywide board of health. Asa Roff spared no expense in trying to get treatment for Mary, seeking out the best Illinois medical men of the time, but it was all to no avail. No one could discover what was wrong with her. It eventually was suggested that she be sent to a sanitarium run by a Dr. Nevins in Peoria for treatment.

238

The sanitarium was similar to many that dotted the American landscape during the 1850s and 1860s. It was known simply as a "water cure," or hydropathic institution, and it offered an alternative to the usual practice of medicine by promising a healthier life through simple, natural, drug-free means. It was based on the use of pure, soft, mineral-free water in various forms of baths, wet wraps, and internal cleansing. Treatment also included other "natural" treatments like exercise, fresh air, and a vegetarian diet that was rich in fruits and grains. The use of alcohol and tobacco was strictly prohibited, and ladies who came to the clinic were encouraged to cast off the tight-fitting corsets that were fashionable at the time and to wear loose-fitting clothing.

By this time, Mary's doctors had come to believe that her spells and seizures were caused by some sort of "female ailment" and so a water cure seemed to be the perfect answer. Water cure sanitariums held a special appeal for women. Most members of the medical community at this time treated women's issues, like menstruation, childbirth, and menopause as unnatural occurrences to be dealt with aggressively, but the water cure advocates treated them as natural events that they believed could be eased by exercise, diet, calmness, and baths. In addition, there were usually female doctors on staff to attend to the ladies, since hydropathic medical schools were among the only places that women who wanted to study medicine found acceptance.

Patients like Mary who came for a water cure were instructed to bring with them certain items that were needed for treatment: two large wool blankets, three comforters, two coarse cotton sheets, one coarse linen sheet, six towels and pieces of cotton for bandages. During the course of water treatments, Mary was immersed naked into a tub of water and then placed into a tub of very hot water. She would also receive a cold water douche and wet sheets were wrapped tightly around her body to restrict her circulation, followed by vigorous rubbing to restore her circulation to normal. She would later go for a strenuous walk and then return to her room for a nap, where she would be wrapped with several blankets and comforters, leaving only her face exposed.

There were few illnesses that could not be "treated" by a water cure, which purported to cure colds, weak constitutions, fevers, poor circulation, gout, alcoholism, and even seizures and insanity. And while the treatment may seem harsh, or even shocking, it was preferable to most general medicine of the day, which relied heavily on purgatives, enemas, laxatives, and bloodletting for treating illnesses. The water cure was not only gentler but could actually be effective.

Mary remained at Dr. Nevins' sanitarium for 18 months, during which time she improved and relapsed several times. Her weird seizures continued, frightening the other patients, until finally, in the late spring of 1864, she was markedly improved and the doctor was able to send her home to Watseka. He truly believed that she had been cured and Mary finally seemed to be well --- at least for a time.

As summer approached, Mary began to complain of sharp, stabbing pains in her head. She called it a "lump of pain" and the only way that she seemed to be able to alleviate the discomfort was by cutting herself. She developed an obsession with blood and began stabbing herself with pins and cutting herself with a straight razor. A local doctor and druggist, F. Conrad Secrest, was called in and he began applying leeches to Mary.

Bloodletting was a part of medical practice that dated back to ancient times and became particularly popular in America during the middle part of the 1800s. It was believed that by draining the blood, balance could be restored to the body. It was accomplished in two ways - either by cutting into a vein and letting blood escape, or by applying leeches, which took blood at a slow, predictable rate and then fell off when full.

Leeches were used for bloodletting in ancient Greece and Rome, and they continued to be a part of European medical practice throughout the ages. The word "leech" even comes from an Old English word for physician. The practice remained popular for years and with the dawn of science, leeches became even more widely used. In the first half of the nineteenth century, scientific journals were full of articles extolling their virtues and trade in medicinal leeches became a major industry.

The use of leeches was often quite gruesome. They could be applied almost anywhere, including the gums, lips, nose, fingers, breasts, and even "the mouth of the womb." They were most commonly applied to the temples and prolonged use would leave the patient with small x-shaped scars where the leeches had fed. Dozens of leeches could be applied at a time. When they were full, they were stored in special jars until they were ready to be used again. Sometimes, a patient would be bled continuously for days at a time.

For some reason, Dr. Secrest left a supply of leeches at the Roff home and Mary would apply them to herself whenever she felt anxious or complained of a headache. She applied them to her temples and it was said that she treated them like pets. A bleeding session, which could last for 35 minutes or so, usually alleviated whatever pain she was feeling.

But on some days, the small amount of blood drawn by a leech or a straight pin was not enough. On Saturday morning, July 16, 1864, Mary took a knife and slipped outside to a hiding place in the backyard. She began cutting her arm and lost so much blood that she fainted. She was found several hours later and was carried into the house. It was some time before she stirred but when she did, she began to thrash violently about and scream as though she were being tortured.

Her convulsions and screams continued almost non-stop for the next five days and nights. Mary only weighed about 100 pounds, but the Roffs required the almost constant services of five strong men to hold her down on the bed. The girl bucked and kicked, punched and thrashed throughout the night and into the daylight hours. No one could explain the brutal force being manifested by this slender girl.

Finally, on the fifth day, the ravings ceased and Mary's demeanor became strangely serene. She regained consciousness and appeared to be quite normal, expect for one thing - she claimed not to recognize anyone in her family, nor her doctors, friends or neighbors. The house was filled with well-meaning acquaintances, as well as friends of Asa Roff, but Mary did not appear to know any of them. In addition to this peculiar development, Mary was able to speak of places where she had never been, often with uncanny accuracy. In addition, she was reportedly able to predict future events and she knew things about people that she should have had no way of knowing.

She also began to manifest a very strange, clairvoyant ability that allowed her to read and do anything else that she normally did in the course of her daily life, all while wearing a blindfold. Her eyes covered by a heavy blindfold, Mary would dress, stand before the mirror, open and search drawers, pick up various items and do whatever she customarily did.

The Roffs and their friends were amazed by this startling new ability and Mary was frequently put to the test by various ministers, newspaper reporters, and "all of the prominent citizens of Watseka at that time."

During one of these tests, Mary was handed a thick medical encyclopedia and asked to find a listing for "blood." She turned to the index, while blindfolded, traced her fingers along the thousands of entries, pointed to the word "blood" and then opened the book to the page that was indicated and managed to read the entry. On another occasion, she took a box of letters that had been sent to her by friends and sat down, with a blindfold on, and read them aloud for the doctors, ministers, and businessmen who were present. When the Reverend J.H. Rhea, newspaper editor A.G. Smith, Asa Roff, and several others added some of their own letters to those that had been written to Mary, she proceeded to pull out these letters and examine them. If any were turned wrong-side up, she would reverse them, read aloud the addresses that were written on them and violently toss aside any letter that was not her own.

No one could explain how she was able to do these things. They were as mysterious as the spells that had been troubling her since she was an infant. Most of the physicians who treated Mary referred to her condition as catalepsy, a popular diagnosis of the nineteenth century.

Catalepsy is a condition that is characterized by rigid muscles and limbs, a loss of muscle control and a slowing down of bodily functions, like breathing. For this reason, many sufferers were mistakenly declared dead and this allegedly led to many premature burials in years past. In modern times, it has been learned that catalepsy does not appear of its own accord and instead, manifests as one of many symptom caused by disorders that have physical causes, ranging from Parkinson's disease to epilepsy. In some cases, isolated cataleptic instances can also be precipitated by extreme emotional shock, but this is rare.

Most medical professionals in years past, especially those in the time of Mary Roff, believed that catalepsy was caused by a mental disorder. For this reason, they suspected that Mary was slipping into a cataleptic trance whenever she was by seized by one of her spells. However, this diagnosis did not explain how she obtained knowledge that she should not have had, was able to foresee future events, and could use clairvoyant powers to see and read through a blindfold. All of these "symptoms" remained unexplained.

For just this reason, some of the ministers who were called to the Roff home to examine Mary and witness her strange feats called her powers "a mystery of God's providence." They could find no explanation for how she was accomplishing the uncanny things she did and merely left the answers to the mysteries of divine intervention.

Perhaps the most perplexed by what was occurring were the newspaper editors and writers who came to visit the Roffs. These men could not look toward medical science for answers and their cynicism kept them from simply leaving the mystery in the hands of God. They knew that Mary's abilities, and her illness, were the result of some unaccountable phenomenon, but just what that was, they were unprepared to say.

Mary remained in what was referred to as her "clairvoyant state" for three or four days, still not recognizing anyone, and then finally, she seemed to regain her wits and began acting like herself again. She was once again conscious of those around her, recognized her family and friends, and lost the ability to psychically "see" through a blindfold. Unfortunately, her return to what passed for normalcy meant the loss of the serene calmness that had accompanied her clairvoyant abilities and the return of her violent seizures.

The episodes came over and over again, causing Mary great pain and distress, and she would sometimes remain unconscious and rigid on the floor, or in her bed, for hours or days at a time. She never moved except when she was first seized by a spell, which often elicited horrifying screams. Her return to consciousness was often accompanied by the violent thrashing about that sometimes required several men to hold her down.

After coming out of her seizures, Mary began to speak of what she saw when she was unconscious. Angels and spirits spoke to her and traveled with her as she looked over places that she had never before visited. In time, she began to claim that these beings accompanied her back from "the other side" and were present in the Roff house. When Mary spoke with them, her friends and family saw nothing and never heard the other side of the conversations that she claimed to be having with the spirits.

Mary's condition worsened until finally, feeling they had no other choice, Asa and Dorothy Ann Roff accepted the advice that they had been given by several of Mary's doctors: they would place the girl in an insane asylum. All of the other possible avenues had been exhausted. No doctor could find a cure for her bizarre problem and, in fact, none of them could even agree on what the problem actually was. Despite the eerie abilities that Mary manifested for a time, there seemed to be no explanation for what was wrong with her other than that she was mentally ill.

Arrangements were made to send her away and all of this was carried out with the Roffs never realizing that Mary would not return home alive.

Placing Mary in an insane asylum was not a step that the Roffs took lightly. They had done everything that they could think of to find a cure for her baffling condition. They had allowed her to stay at Dr. Nevins' water cure facility, at great expense, for nearly 18 months and had spent a small fortune on doctors, treatments and possible solutions. All of it had been to no avail and they had little choice but to consider the idea that Mary was mentally ill.

Tragically, though, sending her to the asylum offered little chance for a cure. The Illinois State Hospital for the Insane in Jacksonville was able to warehouse and confine patients but there were few methods of treatment. Conditions at the asylum - while not barbaric - were far from what Mary was used to at home, and it's likely that the young woman found it to be a terrifying ordeal. Her physical health began to fail as she continued to endure her seizures while being subjected to the grim conditions of the hospital.

Asa and Dorothy Roff made as many trips to see their daughter as possible. Visiting time was restricted by hospital officials, but the Roffs were able to come on successive days if they stayed somewhere locally. On July 5, 1865, they were on the third day of a visit to the hospital when Mary died. She had been able to sit down with them for breakfast but soon after had returned to her room for a nap. She drifted off to sleep, but a few minutes later, she began to let out the familiar screams. They were the same bloodcurdling cries that came before Mary was gripped by one of her spells. Her parents were summoned, in hopes that they might be able to calm her down, but by the time they arrived at her room, the girl had gone quiet.

Mary had died. At the age of 18, Mary Roff had been taken from this world, leaving a scar on her parent's hearts that was so deep that they turned to the Spiritualist movement to make sense of what had happened to her.

Twelve years later, Mary Roff was an almost forgotten footnote in Watseka history. It's likely that, except for her parents and a few close friends, Mary would have been forgotten if not for what happened in July 1877. It was at this time that the so-called "Watseka Wonder" left an indelible mark on this sleepy farm community - and the name of Mary Roff came as a shocking reminder to the residents of the town.

Lurancy Vennum

On July 11, a 13-year-old girl named Lurancy Vennum first fell into a mysterious, catatonic trance during which she claimed that she was able to speak to angels and the spirits of the dead. The strange spells would often occur many times each day and some of them would last for hours. During the trances, Lurancy would speak in different voices and tell of places far away that she had no real knowledge about. When she woke up, she wouldn't remember anything that she said or did while she was under the influence of these spells. Word quickly spread around town that odd things were happening at the home of Thomas and Lurinda Vennum, and soon the news began to spread out of town, to Chicago and around the state. Soon, many visitors began to arrive in Watseka, all hoping to see the young girl.

The news of these strange trances gained much attention within the Spiritualist community, for many believed that Lurancy was manifesting mediumistic abilities during her trances. Soon, Spiritualists from all over Illinois, and from throughout the country, came to Watseka to see if the stories were true.

The Vennum family was not interested in mediums and Spiritualists, however. They were only concerned with the health and welfare of their daughter. They took her to one physician after another in hopes that someone would be able to help her. The doctors could find nothing physically wrong with Lurancy, and they eventually diagnosed her as being mentally ill. It was recommended that she be sent to the state insane asylum. Heartbroken, the Vennums felt they had no other choice, and after the holiday season of 1877, they began to make arrangements to have their daughter committed. They knew there was little chance that Lurancy would ever come home again.

But before Lurancy could be sent away, in January 1878, a man named Asa Roff arrived at the Vennum home. He explained to them that his own daughter, Mary, had been afflicted with the same condition that Lurancy was suffering from. He begged the Vennums not to send Lurancy to the asylum. He had mistakenly sent his own daughter away years before and she had later died. Despite her death, though, he was convinced that his daughter's spirit still existed. Little did he know, however, that it would soon become apparent to many that his daughter's spirit was now inside of the body of Lurancy Vennum.

This was the beginning of a series of strange and fantastic events that rocked the little town of Watseka and created a mystery that remains unsolved to this day.

Mary Lurancy Vennum, or "Rancy" as she was usually called, was born on April 16, 1864, in Milford, a small community about seven miles south of Watseka. After living in Iowa for a year, the Vennums returned to Milford, and a few years later, when Lurancy, was about seven, they moved to Watseka. This was long after Mary Roff's brief notoriety in town and her tragic death. The Vennum family knew nothing of the girl, her strange illness, or anything about the Roff family. The only acquaintance between the two families came during one brief call that Mrs. Roff made on Mrs. Vennum after they moved to Watseka in 1871. Mr. Roff and Mr. Vennum were on formal speaking terms but that was all. The families lived on opposite sides of town.

Lurancy was the daughter of Thomas Jefferson Vennum, who was born in Washington County, Pennsylvania, in 1832. He had come to Illinois with his family when he was still a child, and a number of Vennums were some of the first settlers of Iroquois County. His wife, Lurinda J. Smith, was born in Indiana in 1837, and they were married in Fayette County, Iowa, in 1855. Thomas Vennum had been a farmer all of his life but his wife had asked him to move the family into town after he received a small inheritance from the sale of a farm in Iowa. Vennum was well liked in the community when his family's trouble began in July 1877.

Lurancy had never been a sickly girl, nor an especially imaginative one. For both reasons, her family was surprised when the strange events began. Save for a bout with measles in 1873, she had never been seriously ill and until 1877, she had never made up stories or told fanciful tales about much of anything at all. However, in the early days of July, she began speaking of mysterious voices that came to her in the night.

According to her story, they had roused her from her sleep. She stated: "There were persons in my room last night, and they called 'Rancy, Rancy...' and I felt their breath upon my face." She seemed to be frightened by what had occurred and was convinced that she had not dreamed it. Her parents had never known her to lie but, not believing in such things, they were not inclined to give credence to her story. They merely assumed that their daughter had experienced a very vivid nightmare, one so real that she believed that she was awake when it happened.

The following night, the same thing happened again. Lurancy was terrified and refused to stay in her room. She rose in the dead of night and nervously paced the parlor, too frightened to return to her second-floor bedroom. She told her mother that each time she tried to sleep, the presences would return, whispering her name. Finally, Lurinda took Lurancy back to her room and they lay down together on the bed. She wrapped her arms around her daughter and coaxed her back to sleep. The rest of the night passed without incident.

But on July 11, 1877, the possession truly began.

On that otherwise ordinary morning, Lurancy got out of bed feeling dizzy and nauseated. She complained to her mother about feeling sick but went about her household chores as usual. Around six o'clock that evening, after the day's heat had begun to fade, Lurinda asked Lurancy to help her start supper. Lurancy had been sewing a carpet that afternoon, and she put aside her things and rose to come into the kitchen.

Suddenly, she spoke: "Ma, I feel bad. I feel so queer." She grabbed at her left breast with her hand, then collapsed to the floor. She was so quiet that she seemed to be dead and every muscle in her body had gone rigid and cold.

She stayed in a deep, catatonic sleep for the next five hours but when she woke up, she said she felt fine. The following day, Lurancy again slipped into a trance-like sleep but this time was different. This time, as she lay perfectly still, she began to speak out loud, talking of visions and spirits and carrying on conversations with people that no one else could see. She told her family that she was in heaven and that she could see and hear spirits. She described them and called some of them by name. Among them was her brother, who she affectionately called "Bertie." He had died when Lurancy was only three years old.

In the days and weeks that followed, Lurancy's spells came more and more frequently, and they sometimes lasted for more than eight hours at a time. While she was in her trance state, she continued to speak about her visions, which were sometimes terrifying. She began to see more and more spirits, including those who had terrorized her at night in her bedroom. So many of them were unfamiliar and frightening to her and she would cry out while in the midst of her spells. At times, Lurancy reportedly spoke in other languages, or at least spouted nonsense words that no one could understand. She lapsed into lengthy trances that would sometimes last for hours each day. When she awoke, she would remember nothing of what had happened during the trance and was always ignorant of her weird ramblings.

The frightening trances lasted throughout the summer months but at some point in September 1877, they stopped. Lurancy seemed to be herself again. Although her mother watched her cautiously for several weeks, the bizarre illness seemed to be gone. Gradually, life in the Vennum household began to return to normal.

But these times of normalcy were not destined to last.

On November 27, 1877, Lurancy began to complain of a violent pain in her stomach. The pain remained a dull, throbbing ache, but several times each day, it became excruciating. The sharp, stabbing pain would always come on quite suddenly, making Lurancy scream and moan in torment. She would fall to the floor, her teeth grinding in agony, as the pain ripped through her body. It was later reported: "In these painful paroxysms, she would double herself back until her head and feet actually touched."

These horrendous episodes went on for about two weeks, only coming to an end on December 11, when Lurancy slipped once more into one of the dreaded trances that her parents thought had gone away. She was seized by one of these spells and slowly sank to the floor, completely unconscious. Her body rigidly remained in the same position for the next several hours. When she awakened, the abdominal pains were gone.

Unfortunately, though, the spells had returned. For the next several weeks, the trances came over her and lasted for two hours, three hours, or even as long as eight hours. They occurred as many as twelve times each day, sending Lurancy into a place where she once again began to speak with the spirits that she saw there. She called them "angels" and held long eerie conversations with them, of which she would remember nothing when she finally regained consciousness.

Shortly after the trances had begun, Lurancy was placed under the care of Dr. L.N. Pittwood, who was one of the city's best-known medical practitioners. He could find nothing physically wrong with her. The family turned to a physician called Dr. Jewett for answers after the stomach pains and new spells, but he was also at a loss as to what was causing the illness. Many of the friends and family members of the Vennums believed that Lurancy had gone insane, and the family's minister, the Reverend B.M. Baker from the Methodist church, went as far as to contact the state asylum in Jacksonville to see if the girl could be admitted there. It was the general opinion among those whose counsel the Vennums valued, that the girl should be institutionalized.

Stories and rumors about Lurancy and her visions began to circulate in Watseka. People were talking about the weird happenings and the local newspaper printed stories about them. No one followed the case more closely than Asa Roff. During his own daughter's illness, she had also claimed to communicate with spirits and she fell into long, sometimes violent, trances. He became convinced that Lurancy Vennum was suffering with the same affliction that Mary had. In spite of this, Roff said nothing until the Vennum family had exhausted every known cure for Lurancy and it appeared that she was going to be sent away to the asylum. At this point, he became determined to try and help.

Asa Roff called on the Vennum family in late January 1878. The family was naturally skeptical of the reason for his visit. Roff had little more than a casual acquaintance with Thomas Vennum, but he explained that he had become interested in Lurancy's case after hearing the rumors that were going around town. Lurancy claimed to have had contact with the spirits of the dead, the possibility of which, being a devout Spiritualist, he did not doubt in the slightest. However, his real interest was concerning her illness. His late daughter Mary had suffered from an identical condition and she had also given incontrovertible evidence of supernatural powers in the form of clairvoyance. In her time, Mary had also been regarded as insane, although now, years later, Roff was convinced that she had been of sound mind but had been the victim of a "spirit infestation." He believed that the same could be said of Lurancy and he begged the Vennums not to send her to an asylum.

He believed there was a way to help the girl and he convinced the Vennums to allow him to call in one more physician. If there was nothing that this man could do, then they could take whatever steps they believed were necessary to try and help Lurancy. With some reluctance, the Vennums agreed to his plea. Although they didn't know it at the time, their lives would never be the same again.

Roff returned to the Vennum house in the company of Dr. E. Winchester Stevens on January 31. Dr. Stevens was a physician from Janesville, Wisconsin, who, like Roff, was a devout Spiritualist. He was curious about the case, having visited Watseka a few times and had heard about it during the preceding fall. He wanted to offer whatever help he could to the beleaguered family. His interest had been piqued by the medical aspects of the case and by the possibility that Lurancy might be "spirit infested," as he had come to believe that his friend's daughter, Mary Roff, had been.

Stevens and Roff were considering the idea that Lurancy was a sort of vessel through which the dead were communicating. Roff only wished that he had seen

248

the same evidence in his own daughter years before. He believed that if Mary had actually been insane, that she had been driven to madness by the bizarre gifts and abilities that she possessed. No one had been able to help Mary but he believed that Stevens could help Lurancy Vennum. He didn't want to see what had happened to Mary befall someone else's daughter, and so he had brought Dr. Stevens to Watseka in order for him to examine Lurancy.

When they arrived at the house that afternoon, Dr. Stevens found Lurancy sitting in the kitchen next to the stove. She sat in a chair with her feet curled up under her. Her chin was in her hands and her elbows rested on her knees. She was slumped over, staring at the stove as though entranced by something in the dancing flames. Mrs. Vennum spoke to her but she did not respond. She remained with her eyes fixed straight ahead, as if she was unaware of anyone else in the room.

When he was finally able to get her attention, Lurancy first claimed that she was not herself, but rather an old German woman with a surly demeanor. During this dialogue, Lurancy's demeanor had changed. She hunched herself over in the chair and her voice cracked, as though she really was an old woman. Then, she changed again. Guiltily, she admitted that she was not a woman but a young man who had lost his life and now was a spirit inside of Lurancy. The discussion between them became antagonistic and then Lurancy began to grow quiet and sullen, refusing to talk or answer any questions that Dr. Stevens asked of her. This went on for several minutes and then, perhaps believing that the girl was too tired to continue, Stevens got up to leave. As he did, Lurancy also stood up. Almost immediately, her hands fluttered in the air and her eyes rolled back into her head. Her body stiffened and she fell, crashing to the hard wooden floor. Her body was rigid and it appeared that she had gone into another of her mysterious trances.

Mr. Vennum and Mr. Roff managed to get Lurancy back into her chair and Dr. Stevens sat down in front of her again. He managed to pry her hands, which were stiffly held against her chest, away from her body and took them into his own. His voice lowered to a soft, even tone and he began to speak to her, stroking her hands and easing her out of the control of the spell. Soon, Lurancy's voice became her own and she began to speak to Dr. Stevens, maintaining that while her body was in the Vennum house, her consciousness was in heaven, where she was conversing with angels.

In this hypnotized condition, Lurancy answered the doctor's questions and spoke of her seemingly insane condition and the influences that were controlling her. She told him that she regretted allowing some of the spirits around her to take control over her body; they were evil and forced her to do and say horrible things. Stevens explained to her that she was able to control what spirits influenced her and then asked her that, if she was going to be controlled by spirits, wouldn't it be better to be controlled by a happier, more intelligent and rational being? Lurancy agreed that this would be preferable if she could do it.

Lurancy sat for several minutes in eerie silence. By this time, the winter sun had long since set and the Vennum kitchen was dimly lighted by the fire from the stove and one kerosene lamp that had been placed on the table. The lengthening shadows danced across the room as Lurancy waited, then let out a long sigh before she spoke again. She said that she had looked about, and had inquired of those around her, to find someone who would prevent the cruel and insane spirits on the other side from returning to annoy her and her family.

She said: "There are a great many spirits here who would be glad to come."

Lurancy proceeded to give names and descriptions of people that Dr. Stevens wrote were "long since deceased" and who were unknown to the girl but often recognized by the older people who were present. Lurancy waited for several more minutes and then explained that she had found one spirit who wanted to come with her. The spirit was a young woman who believed that she could help Lurancy in a way that no other spirit could.

Dr. Stevens asked her the name of the spirit and her whispered reply echoed in the kitchen. Lurancy spoke: "Her name is Mary Roff."

While the name of Mary Roff may have sent shivers down the spines of some of the adults who were present, the name meant nothing to Lurancy herself. She had never heard of the girl and could not have known what had happened to her years before. Even if we take into consideration that rumors may have circulated about the Roff family and their crazy daughter that they once had to lock up in an asylum and who had subsequently died, it's likely that Lurancy would not have been exposed to them. The Roff and Vennum families had never had any real contact with one another and Lurancy had been a very young child when Mary had died.

Asa Roff soon recovered from the surprise of hearing his daughter's name on Lurancy's lips. He quickly assured the girl that Mary had been a good and intelligent young woman and would certainly help her in any way that she could. He added that Mary had once suffered from an affliction much like the one that was now bothering Lurancy.

Silence again filled the kitchen as Lurancy's unconscious mind appeared to deliberate about Mary's presence. Finally, she agreed that Mary would take the place of the troubled and disturbed spirits who had initially possessed her body.

Dr. Stevens and Mr. Roff left from the house a few hours later. Dr. Stevens wrote: "Leaving the family satisfied that a new fountain of light and source of help had been reached. A new beam of truth reached and touched the hearts of the sorrowing family. And to use the language of Mary Roff, 'Dr. Stevens opened the gate for her,' and for the inflowing light where before was darkness."

Lurancy remained in her trance for the rest of the evening and into the next day. During this time, she claimed to be Mary Roff. She was not a spirit inhabiting another girl's body; she insisted that she actually was Mary! She claimed that she had no idea where she was, was unable to recognize the Vennum house, which was a place where Mary Roff had never been. She wanted to go home, she said, which meant back to the Roff house.

Lurancy was so insistent about this that on the following morning, Friday, February 1, Thomas Vennum called at the office of Asa Roff and explained to him what was happening. He said that his daughter continued to claim that she was Mary and demanded that she be allowed to go home. Vennum said: "She seems like a child real homesick, wants to see her pa and ma and her brothers."

The Vennums had mixed feelings about these latest developments. They were happy to see that the rigid, corpse-like spells, excruciating pain and weird trances had passed but now they faced having had a stranger on their hands. She was very polite, mild and docile but she constantly begged the Vennums to let her go home. They tried to convince her, as did Mr. Roff, that she was already at home but the girl was having none of it. She would not be pacified. The Vennums were becoming more and more convinced that this girl was no longer their daughter.

The news of this amazing new development quickly spread, and when Mrs. Roff heard what had happened, she hurried to the Vennum house in the company of her married daughter, Minerva Alter. The two women hurried up the sidewalk of the Vennum house and saw Lurancy sitting by the window. When she saw them approaching, she cried out: "Here comes Ma and Nervie!" As they came into the house, she hugged and kissed the surprised women and wept for joy. It was said that no one had called Minerva by the nickname "Nervie" since Mary's death in 1865.

From this time on, Lurancy seemed even more homesick than before, frantically wanting to leave and go home with the Roffs. It now seemed entirely possible to everyone involved that Mary Roff had taken control of Lurancy. Even though the girl still looked like Lurancy Vennum, she knew everything about the Roff family and she treated them as her loved ones. To the Vennums, she was distantly polite, as though they were strangers. The Vennums were understandably shocked and unnerved by the turn of events. Their daughter had become someone completely unknown to them.

Finally, some friends of the family insisted that the Vennums allow the girl to go home with the Roffs for a time. The Vennums were reluctant to do so. They were still befuddled by what was going on and they felt that it would be an imposition to send their daughter to be cared for by strangers, no matter whom she claimed to be. But after a few more days of the girl's weeping and begging to "go home," the Vennums decided to discuss the situation with the Roffs. It was a delicate problem but one that Mr. and Mrs. Roff agreed to take on. Braving the ridicule of people in town, and with no other motive but one of kindness, they opened their home to receive Lurancy.

On February 11, Lurancy --- or rather "Mary" --- was allowed to go to the Roff home. The Vennums agreed that this arrangement would be for the best, at least temporarily. They desperately hoped that Lurancy would regain her true identity. The Roffs, meanwhile, saw the possession as a "miracle," as though Mary had returned from the grave. They took Lurancy across town, and as they were riding in the buggy, they passed by the former Roff home, where they had been living when Mary died. The home now belonged to Minerva and her husband, Henry Alter. The girl demanded to know why they were not stopping there and the Roffs had to explain that they had moved several years before to a brick home on Fifth Street. The young woman's lack of knowledge about this move, as well as her identification of the old house, was further proof to the Roffs that Lurancy had been possessed by their dead daughter.

Lurancy's arrival in the Roff home, as Mary, was met with great excitement. She immediately began calling the Roffs "ma and pa" and recognized each member of the family. Even though Lurancy knew none of them herself, she greeted them, as Mary, with affection. One of them asked her how long she would stay and she replied: "The angels will let me stay until sometime in May."

For the next several months, Lurancy lived as Mary and seemed to have forgotten about her former life. As the days passed, Lurancy continued to show that she knew more about the Roff family, their possessions, and their habits than she could have possibly known if she had been merely faking. Many of the incidents that she referred to had taken place years before Lurancy had been born. Her physical condition began to improve while staying with the Roffs and she no longer suffered from the frightening attacks that had plagued her.

She appeared to be quite contented while living in the Roff home, and she recognized and called by name many of the neighbors and family friends known to Mary during her lifetime. In contrast, she claimed not to recognize any family members, friends or associates of the Vennums. Even though the Vennums allowed their daughter to live with the Roff family, they visited her often. Lurancy, while living as Mary, soon learned to love these "strangers" as friends.

Her day-to-day life in the Roff home was anything but unusual. She was easygoing, affable and hardworking, helping with the household chores, cooking and cleaning and going about the activities of any young girl of the time. She liked to read and sing, as Mary always had, and she loved sitting with her father and talking about anything that came to her mind. One day she asked him: "Pa, who was it that used to say 'confound it'?" She began laughing when she realized that the saying was one that he often used when Mary was a young girl --- nearly 20 years before.

One day, she met an old friend and neighbor of the Roffs, who had been a widow with the surname Lord when Mary was a girl. Some years after Mary had died, the woman had married a Mr. Wagoner. This seemed to be unknown to the girl. When the two were reunited, Lurancy hugged her tightly and called her by the last name of her late husband. She did not seem to be able to comprehend that this family friend had remarried.

A few weeks after Lurancy was settled into the Roff home, Mrs. Parker, who lived next door to the Roff family in 1852, moved and then lived next door to them again in 1860, came to the house with her daughter-in-law, Nellie Parker. Lurancy -- or Mary -- recognized both women immediately, calling Mrs. Parker "Auntie Parker," and the other "Nellie," just as she had known them years before. Mary sat down to speak to the two ladies and right away, she asked Mrs. Parker, "Do you remember how Nervie and I used to come to your house and sing?"

Mrs. Parker said that she did and she would later recall this incident and swear that no one had mentioned this to Lurancy before her visit. The young girl had brought it up on her own. She testified that Mary and Minerva often visited her house and loved to sing "Mary had a Little Lamb." Minerva also recalled doing this and added that they came to Mrs. Parker's house during the time when Mr. Roff was the town's postmaster, before 1852. This would have been more than a decade before Lurancy Vennum was born.

One evening in late March, Mr. Roff was reading a newspaper and drinking tea. He asked his wife if she could find a certain velvet head-dress that Mary had worn before she had died. If she knew where it was, he asked her to bring it out and say nothing of it, but to wait and see if Lurancy recognized it. Dorothy Ann quickly found the piece and placed it where she had been instructed. Lurancy was outside at the time but she soon came in and glanced over as she passed the stand where the head-dress was. She immediately exclaimed: "Oh, there is my head-dress that I wore when my hair was short!"

Lurancy took the velvet piece and lovingly caressed it. The Roffs were pleased and amazed, seeing this as further evidence that the spirit of Mary was alive within the body of Lurancy. It was yet another thing that Lurancy could not have known anything about, and such a trivial matter that even the cleverest hoaxer could not have uncovered it if she planned to try and fool the family. But Lurancy, or Mary, was not finished yet.

She turned to Mrs. Roff: "Ma, where is my box of letters? Have you got them yet?"

Mrs. Roff found a box filled with letters that had been saved after Mary had died. They were the same letters that Mary had been able to read blindfolded during the eerie tests that she had been subjected to by her father, the ministers and the newspapermen.

Lurancy began to examine them: "Oh, Ma, here is the collar I tatted! Why did you not show me my letters and things before?"

The collar had been preserved among the things that had been saved as mementoes of a lost child and it was something that Mary had made long before Lurancy had even been born. Like so many other things from her childhood, the spirit of Mary recognized it and spoke of it through the voice and body of another girl. The Roffs needed no further convincing. This was their daughter Mary, no matter what physical form she might be in.

Of course, not everyone in Watseka believed that Lurancy had been possessed by the spirit of Mary Roff. The Vennums' minister, Reverend Baker, after learning that Lurancy was staying with the Roffs, pleaded with the family once again to have the girl committed to the state asylum. He told them: "I think you will see the time when you will wish that you had sent her to the asylum." He said others in the congregation shared his opinion, and added: "I would sooner follow a girl of mine to the grave than have her go to the Roffs' and be made a Spiritualist."

Several of the doctors who had attempted to treat Lurancy started spreading scathing rumors about Dr. Stevens and dismissed the case as nothing more than catalepsy and "humbug." They believed that Lurancy was faking the whole thing and making fools of her parents and the Roff family. Of course, no one who voiced these opinions in Watseka had actually visited either family and had no in-depth knowledge of the situation. This ignorance did not stop the rumors from being spread, though, and the Roffs and Vennums were ridiculed by many in the community. For the most part, they ignored the laughter and the disdain, believing that something truly authentic and supernatural was taking place.

On May 7, Lurancy as Mary called Mrs. Roff to a private room and there, in tears, informed her that Lurancy Vennum would be coming back soon. She could feel the other girl's spirit returning and she had no idea whether or not Lurancy would be staying or not. If Mary was going to be released from the body, then she hoped that she would have time to see Allie, Minerva and Henry so that she could tell them goodbye. The girl wept as she told these things to Mrs. Roff and it was almost as if, no matter how much she wanted to help Lurancy, Mary didn't want to let go of the earthly form that she had managed to obtain.

The young woman sat down in a chair and over the course of the next few minutes, a battle took place for control of her physical form. Her eyes slowly closed and her face shifted expressions several times before her eyes fluttered open again. The girl, confused, looked wildly about before exclaiming: "Where am I? I have never been here before!"

Lurancy Vennum had returned.

Mrs. Roff sat down next to the girl and held her hand, gently rubbing her arm. She tried to calm the girl: "You are at Mr. Roff's, brought here by Mary to cure your body."

Lurancy burst into tears. "I want to go home!"

Mrs. Roff soothed her and told her that someone would send for her parents. She then asked the girl if she felt any pain in her breast. Lurancy, or Mary, had been complaining of the pain for a few days, continually holding her left breast and pressing on it with her fingers .

Lurancy looked puzzled for a moment and then seemed surprised when she spoke with some confusion: "No, but Mary did."

Lurancy remained with Mrs. Roff for only a few minutes and then a subtle change seemed to sweep over her body and her features. A quiet humming sound came from the girl's lips and then softly turned into song. It was "We are Coming, Sister Mary," a childhood favorite of Mary Roff's. The dead girl had returned to the body of Lurancy Vennum.

Mary's return was marked by sadness. Everyone knew that, after the brief return of Lurancy, it was nearly time for her to leave. Over the next two weeks, a battle raged for the control of Lurancy's body. At one moment, Lurancy would announce that she had to leave and at the next she would cling to her father and cry at the idea of leaving him. She spent nearly every day going from one family member to another, hugging them and touching them at every opportunity. She became increasingly upset with each passing day, weeping at the thought of leaving her "real family."

Dr. Stevens returned to town to have as much contact with Mary as he could before she was gone. He found that over the last two weeks, she seemed to be more aware of not only her past life as Mary Roff but also about the fact that she was masquerading, as it were, in a borrowed form. One day, Stevens asked her: "Do you remember the time you cut your arm?"

Lurancy or Mary admitted that she did and she rolled up her sleeve to show him the scar. She started to speak and then paused in confusion, saying: "Oh, this is not the arm; that one is in the ground." Then, she went on to describe the spot where Mary had been buried and the circumstances of her funeral.

The spirit of Mary, dwelling in Lurancy, seemed also to have held on to the clairvoyant abilities that Mary manifested before her death. One afternoon, Lurancy came to her mother and told her that Mary's brother, Frank, had to be carefully watched over during the coming night. He was going to become very sick and he could die if he was not properly cared for. At the time of this announcement, Frank was feeling just fine and, in fact, was uptown playing in a band that had been put together by the Roff brothers and their friends. That same evening, Dr. Stevens had stopped by to visit the family but then had left by 9:30 p.m.

During the early morning hours, Frank was suddenly afflicted with something like spasms and a terrible chill, which caused him to tremble and shake so badly that he almost fainted. Lurancy rushed into his room and saw the situation exactly as she had predicted it. She told her father: "Send to Mr. Marsh's for Dr. Stevens."

Roff replied: "No, Dr. Stevens is at the old town."

Mary shook her head: "No, he is at Mr. Marsh's, go quick for him, Pa!"

Mr. Roff ran from the house and went next door to the Marsh's. Here, he found Dr. Stevens but by the time the doctor could get dressed and hurry to the Roff home, Lurancy had things well in hand. She had made Mrs. Roff sit down, had provided hot water and cloths for Frank, and was doing all that could be done for him. The doctor agreed with her methods and allowed her to continue. Mary's spirit, working through Lurancy, had likely saved the young man's life.

The girl also told Dr. Stevens of seeing some of his deceased children on the other side. They were about Mary's age but had been there longer than she had. She told him that she was with them quite often and even traveled to the doctor's home with them. She correctly described his home in Wisconsin, even though she had never been there, gave the names and ages of his children, and as evidence that she was telling the truth, told the doctor of a supernatural experience that had occurred to Mrs. E.W. Wood, one of the doctor's married daughters. Stevens never revealed the details behind the story but attested to the fact that what Lurancy told him had actually taken place.

As more time passed, Lurancy's control over her own body began to slowly return. Mary's spirit would sometimes recede for a time. Mary's identity was not lost, nor did Lurancy's personality return, but it was enough to provide evidence that she was slowly returning to her own body.

On the afternoon of Sunday, May 19, Lurancy was sitting in the parlor with Mr. Roff. Henry Vennum, Lurancy's brother, was seated in a chair in the hallway. Other members of the Roff family waited with him in the corridor. He had come to the house to visit his sister and Roff, based on recent experiences, felt that Lurancy's spirit was near. It soon turned out that he was correct in his assumptions. In a matter of moments, Mary departed and Lurancy took control of her body again. Henry was called in and when he stepped into the room, Lurancy wrapped her arms around his neck, kissed his cheek and burst into tears. She was so happy to see him that Henry started to cry, which caused everyone else in the household to weep.

Mr. Roff asked Lurancy if she would be able to stay with them until someone could go to the Vennum house and bring back her mother. Lurancy answered that she could not, but if her mother were brought over, she would come again and be able to talk with her. Her eyes seemed to waver for a moment and her body shook slightly --- Lurancy was gone. It was obvious to everyone gathered in the parlor that Mary had returned. However, Lurinda Vennum was brought to the Roff house within the hour and when she came into the parlor, Lurancy once again regained full control of her body. Mother and daughter embraced one another, kissed and wept until everyone assembled was crying in sympathy. Lurancy stayed for a few minutes and then, as mysteriously as she had gone, Mary Roff returned and Mrs. Vennum was a beloved stranger once more.

But it would not stay that way for much longer.

On the morning of May 21, Asa Roff wrote to Dr. Stevens that Mary was planning to leave Lurancy's body that very day. He penned, "She is bidding neighbors and friends good-bye. Rancy is to return home all right today. Mary came from her room upstairs where she was sleeping, at ten o'clock last night, lay down by us, hugged and kissed us, and cried because she must bid us goodbye, telling us to give all her pictures, marbles and cards, and twenty-five cents Mrs. Vennum had given her, to Rancy, and had us promise to visit Rancy often." She told her father to tell Dr. Stevens that she was returning to heaven and that Rancy was coming home."

Mary sent word to her sister, Minerva, to come to the Roff house and stay with her for an hour so that she could say goodbye. After that, when Lurancy returned, Minerva was to take the girl to Mr. Roff's office and then he would take her to the Vennums. Mary said: "I will come in spirit as close to you as I can, and comfort you in sorrow, and you will feel me near you sometimes."

As 11:00 a.m. approached, Mary seemed to fight the idea of leaving and allowing Lurancy to return. Minerva was a little upset with her. She spoke, saying, "Mary, you have always done the things that you said you would, but as I don't understand these things, will you please let Lurancy come back just now, and then you can come again if you want to?"

Mary agreed that she would and kissed her mother and sister goodbye. The girl's eyes rolled back for an instant and immediately, she was Lurancy Vennum again. She found herself walking outside with Minerva, starting toward Mr. Roff's office. Lurancy asked Minerva: "Why Mrs. Alter, where are we going?" The girl then paused for a moment and smiled slightly to herself before she spoke again: "Oh yes, I know, Mary told me."

On the way, they met Mrs. Marsh and Mrs. Hoober, who were the nearest neighbors and some of Mary's closest friends. Lurancy did not recognize either of the women, but she was polite to them and greeted them warmly. When she

257

and Minerva walked on, she remarked: "Mary thinks so much of these neighbors."

She then turned to Minerva, with whom Lurancy had been only slightly acquainted two years before, and said: "Mrs. Alter, Mary can come and talk to you nearly all the way home, if you want her to, and then I will come back."

Minerva agreed: "I have trusted you in the past, and of course, I would love to talk with my sister."

Mary's spirit enveloped Lurancy again and according to Minerva, the two of them talked about many things and family matters as they walked. As the hour for Mary's departure finally arrived, Lurancy returned. She told Minerva and Mr. Roff that she felt as though she had been asleep for a very long time, yet knew that she had not. She asked Mr. Roff if he would take her home and he immediately agreed to do so.

Lurancy returned home to the Vennum house. She displayed none of the strange symptoms of her earlier illness and her parents were convinced that she had somehow been cured, thanks to the intervention of the spirit of Mary Roff. She soon became a healthy and happy young woman, suffering no ill effects from her strange experience. She had no memories of the possession, other than of those things that Mary allowed her to know. It was as if the months that she spent as Mary Roff had never happened at all.

In June 1878, Dr. Stevens returned to Watseka to renew his friendship with the Roff and Vennum families. He was especially curious as to whether or not any of Lurancy's spells or trances had returned and whether Mary Roff had actually managed to cure the girl of her affliction.

On Sunday, June 2, Stevens met with Lurancy and her parents at the house of a friend, who lived about two miles away from the Vennums. Lurancy was introduced to him by her father. She was sure that she had never met the man before and came across as a little shy, as one might expect from a young girl meeting a stranger for the first time. They spoke very little that day and Stevens left the meeting feeling both disappointed that he could learn nothing more from the girl and excited that she truly seemed to have been the victim of a possession. She remembered nothing of meeting the doctor during the time that she was living as Mary Roff.

The next day, June 3, brought him a great surprise. Without any notice to anyone as to where he was going that day, Dr. Stevens stopped unannounced at the home of a friend, a noted attorney in Watseka. As he was entering the gate, Lurancy Vennum walked up beside him and greeted him warmly. The doctor was surprised by her presence, especially as she had seemed so reluctant to talk with him the previous day. Lurancy said: "How do you do, Doctor? Mary Roff told me to come here and meet you. Somehow she makes me feel that you have been a very kind friend to me." Lurancy then went on to deliver a long message for the doctor that she claimed to have received from Mary.

Dr. Stevens later wrote that since the June 3 meeting, he had seen Lurancy many times and on every occasion, she was very friendly and forthcoming. Something about her demeanor had changed and he was convinced that it was because of the intervention of Mary Roff.

As weeks passed, everyone involved in the case watched very closely to see how Lurancy behaved. Would they see a return of the strange seizures and spells? Would they see the possession by Mary Roff return? We can only imagine the anxiety that must have filled the hearts of the Vennums, and even those of the Roffs, who had come to consider Lurancy almost a part of their own family.

Needless to say, the two families involved were not the only ones with an interest in the strange story. The people of Watseka had watched avidly as this curious drama played out in their city. But it was not until three months after the affair had ended that the public at large obtained any knowledge about it. Newspapers in Watseka, and in the surrounding area, had quickly reported the final outcome of the case.

The editor for the *Iroquois County Times*, under a banner of "Mesmeric Mysteries" wrote of Lurancy Vennum:

It was hard for even the most skeptical not to believe there was something supernatural about her. If she was not prompted by the spirit of Mary Roff, how could she know so much about the family, people with whom she was not acquainted, and whom she had never visited? No stranger would have suspected her of being the victim of disease, though her eyes were unusually bright.

There are yet numberless mysteries in this world, though science has dissipated many wonders, and philosophy has made plain many marvels. There is much that is unaccountable in the actions of Spiritualistic mediums, and they do many things which puzzle the greatest philosophers. Skeptical and unbelieving as we are, and slight as our evidence has been, we have seen enough to convince us that Spiritualism is not all humbug. The case of Lurancy Vennum, a bright young girl of fourteen years, has been the subject of much discussion in Watseka during the past year, and there is a good deal in it beyond human comprehension...

The first news of the story, outside of local newspapers, came from two articles that were contributed by Dr. Stevens to the August 3 and 10, 1878, issues of the *Religio-Philosophical Journal*, one of the leading Spiritualist newspapers of the day. In the articles, Stevens discussed the case in great detail, emphasizing the fact that, as of the time of writing, no return of the ailments, trances and

259

spells had returned to bother Lurancy. Stevens said he was convinced that the spirit of Mary Roff had returned to earth to possess Lurancy Vennum and had been the instrument of her cure.

But not everyone was as convinced. While Spiritualists were more than willing to believe in the possibility of Lurancy being possessed and healed by Mary's spirit, many members of the general public were not so easily impressed. A number of letters appeared in newspapers, insinuating and openly alleging that Dr. Steven's narrative of the case was nothing more than a work of fiction.

The veracity of the Roffs was also attacked. Letters were forwarded to Asa Roff from the editors of the Journal, inquiring as to the truthfulness of Stevens' account of what he called "The Watseka Wonder." Some of them merely wanted to hear Roff's side of things but others accused him of collaborating with Stevens to fool the public.

Roff was indignant over the content of many of the letters he received, including those that were so rude that he never shared their content with anyone. He knew what he and his family had experienced and was convinced of the authenticity of the events. He felt he had no need to defend himself but as a believer in the wonders of Spiritualism, and in defense of his friend, Dr. Stevens, and the reputations of Lurancy and Mary, he wrote a lengthy letter to the editors of the *Religio-Philosophical Journal* that served as his reply to the many critics who attacked him, his family, Dr. Stevens and the Vennums.

The letter appeared in the August 31 edition of the *Journal* and the editors followed it with a number of statements attesting to the reputation of Asa B. Roff. The writers of these testimonials included Matthew H. Peters, the mayor of Watseka; Charles H. Wood, a former judge of the Twentieth Circuit of Illinois; O.F. McNeill, a former county judge; O.C. Munhall, the Watseka postmaster; attorney Robert Doyle; attorney John W. Riggs; Henry Butzow, circuit clerk; Thomas Vennum not Lurancy's father , who was the former circuit clerk; Franklin Blades, a judge on the Eleventh Judicial Circuit, and former county judge M.B. Wright.

The letters were followed by an announcement from Colonel J.C. Bundy, the editor of the *Journal.* He wrote to the effect that he had "entire confidence in the truthfulness of the narrative, and believes from his knowledge of the witnesses that the account is unimpeachable, in every particular." As for Dr. Stevens, Colonel Bundy stated that he had been personally acquainted with the physician for many years and had "implicit confidence in his veracity."

After all of this, accusations of perjury and deception were obviously futile, and aside from saying that it was simply "fraud" which no one could explain , there were no adequate interpretations for the events that took place in Watseka.

Lurancy remained in touch with the Roff family for the rest of her life. Although she had no real memories of her time as Mary, she still felt a curious closeness to them that she could never explain. On January 1, 1882, Lurancy married George Binning, a farmer who lived about three miles west of Watseka. In 1884, they moved west to Rawlins County, Kansas, in the northwestern corner of the state.

The Roffs visited with Lurancy often, and saw her at least once each year after she moved to Kansas. Whenever she returned home to Watseka to see her parents, she always stayed with the Roffs for part of the time. During these visits, she would allow Mary to take control of her, just as she did when living with them in 1878.

Aside from this, Lurancy had little occasion to use the mediumistic skills that she had acquired. Her parents rarely spoke with her on the subject, fearing that it would cause a return of the "spells" that plagued her before she was possessed by Mary. Her husband had no interest in Spiritualism and Asa Roff wrote rather disapprovingly that he "furnished poor conditions for further development in that direction." This, combined with her household chores and care of her children, made her spirit possessions and talking with the dead things of the past.

Oddly, Lurancy told the Roffs that she was never sick a day in her life after Mary cured her in 1878.

Lurancy lived in Kansas until the death of her husband when he was in his 50s. After that, she moved to Oklahoma for a time and then eventually settled down in Long Beach, California, in 1910. She died there, at the age of 88, in 1952. She raised eleven children but it was said that none of them knew of her strange time as the "Watseka Wonder" until they were informed of it after her death by a cousin.

The Vennum family stayed on in Watseka for many years, but after the death of her husband, Lurinda Vennum moved to Kansas to live with Lurancy and her grandchildren. Both of the Vennums are buried in Oak Hill Cemetery in Watseka.

Dr. Stevens lectured on the "Watseka Wonder" for eight years before dying in Chicago in 1886. He was convinced that what had occurred had been genuine and that Mary Roff had actually taken over the body of Lurancy Vennum for a time.

Minerva Alter wrote a short follow-up article to Dr. Stevens' accounts in 1908, when she was sixty-four years old. In it, she stated that neither she nor her family had any interest in deceiving or misleading people. She vowed the possession had been real, and talked about the great joy that she and her parents had felt when they were reunited with a daughter and a sister who had been dead for twelve years. At the time of the writing, she stated that Lurancy was a healthy, middle-aged woman with eleven children, respected as a neighbor and honored as a friend. She added: "Of the part she played in a great drama staged by heaven and earth, and of what she experienced, she has but a dim remembrance."

Asa and Dorothy Ann Roff received hundreds of letters, from believers and skeptics alike, after the story of the possession was printed in newspapers and appeared in magazines all over the country. In 1879, Roff was elected as justice of the peace in Watseka but resigned the position in June of that same year. Without much explanation, he moved to Garden City, Kansas, where his sons lived and where the family had invested considerable amounts of money. He invested in farmland but found that the climate was too dry for it to be profitable and moved to Emporia, Kansas, where he and his wife lived for a year. From Kansas, Roff moved to Council Bluffs, Iowa for two years and then moved to Kansas City, where he lived for several more years.

In 1885, Roff moved back to Watseka and there he and his wife lived the rest of their lives. In the spring of 1889, he was elected police magistrate for a term of four years and once more served as justice of the peace. He and Dorothy Ann were both buried in Oak Hill Cemetery.

The story of the Watseka Wonder remains one of the strangest unsolved mysteries in the annals of American history. What really happened in this small Illinois town in 1878? Did the spirit of Mary Roff really possess the body of Lurancy Vennum? It seems almost impossible to believe, but the families of both young women, as well as hundreds of friends and supporters, certainly believed that it happened. One thing is certain --- something extraordinary happened in Watseka involving Lurancy Vennum, her family and the family of a dead girl named Mary Roff. Was it a true spirit possession, a case of mental illness, or the most elaborate and carefully constructed hoax of the 1870s?

The reader will have to decide what they choose to believe. As for our thoughts on this mysterious case? Well, we still don't know. We do believe that something amazing occurred in Watseka in the spring of 1878 and believe that it permanently affected not only the Vennum and Roff families, but also the entire town of Watseka itself.

Was Lurancy actually possessed by the spirit of Mary Roff? Logic tells us that it couldn't have happened, but this case certainly gives us pause. The story of the "Watseka Wonder" can make just about anyone wonder if we know as much about the unexplained as we think we do.

It certainly inspires that feeling in us.

The Rise and Fall of the Jacksonville State Hospital

Like so many lofty ideals, the state hospitals often failed to live up to their expectations. Jacksonville's asylum was no exception. It soon became overcrowded by an influx of the poor, many of them immigrants, who did not respond well to "moral treatment," which was biased by class. The elderly and the chronically ill - two groups that would never get better - began filling up the wards. As the population of the place began to expand, the need for control prevailed, making the treatment more custodial than curative. The hospital was held accountable to the state legislature for its expenditures and so the financial panics of 1873, 1893, and 1907, as well as periods of recession, took their toll, leading to budget cuts and staff shortages. Low wages, high turnover rates and inexperienced attendants led to patient abuse and corruption.

By the latter part of the 1850s, the hospital had outgrown the Old Main building, its only building, which had been built to accommodate 250 patients, but held many more. In 1858, the west wing was added to the main building. An east wing was added in 1867, as the hospital's population rose to 450. By 1876, the hospital had 1,200 residents and the need for another building was apparent. The Annex was built in 1886 and expanded in 1892. At three stories high and a quarter-mile long, it briefly held the distinction of being the longest continuous three-story building in the world.

When the Board of State Commissioners of Public Charities was abolished in 1909, the institute was reorganized and renamed Jacksonville State Hospital. In 1917, the Department of Public Welfare assumed responsibility for the hospital and retained control until the creation of the Illinois Department of Mental Health in 1961.

The hospital's population reached its peak in 1952 with 3,616 residents. Keeping the inmates busy was a priority. A broom shop, print shop, carpentry shop, greenhouse, and gazebos were all constructed for the patient's diversion. Patients worked for free, supplementing the work done by employees, and allowing the ever-shrinking budget of the hospital to stretch further. They grew crops, raised cattle, pigs and chickens, and made furniture and clothing. The hospital, with thousands of patients and staff, along with hundreds of acres of land, functioned more like a work farm than a medical facility.

Just caring for all those people's basic needs was a massive undertaking. The facility was almost like a city. There were 100 buildings on the campus, which had its own dairy farm, butcher, kitchen, fire station, bowling alley, and power plant. The complex even had its own medical hospital, known as the Acute Care Hospital and later as the Bowen Building. There was a morgue and an existing cemetery on Lincoln Avenue, where residents who died at the facility were buried.

Just before the decline of the Jacksonville State Hospital

After a peak in the middle 1950s, the patient population began to decline steadily after the introduction if psychotropic drugs, changes in commitment laws, and a shift in policy about community-based care. Medications that were effective in treating involuntary behavior became available at this time, leading to the discharge of many patients who otherwise would have remained institutionalized for the rest of their lives. A series of court decisions confirmed a constitutional right to treatment and establishing minimum standards of care. This ultimately resulted in the loss of patient labor and deprived the hospital of its important inmate work force. This delivered a fatal blow to the hospital's economic viability.

Thanks to this, population at the Jacksonville institution began to decline. By 1967, there were 1,699 residents, and in 1972, the population dropped to 591. It continued to drop during its remaining years in operation.

In the early 1970s, the state hospital wound down its agricultural and manufacturing programs. Shops closed, services were contracted to the private sector, and farms were sold off to help pay for mandated services. Buildings already in disrepair were left to deteriorate further, too expensive to renovate and bring up to code.

In 1970, the facility was renamed the Jacksonville Mental Health and Developmental Center, and later, the Jacksonville Developmental Center JDC , to reflect its declining psychiatric population and its rising population of developmentally disabled residents. The facility closed its last unit for the mentally ill in 1976. Today, most people with mental illnesses are treated within their own communities. For those who are committed, their stays are usually numbered in days instead of months and years. Hospitalization is a last resort.

Much of the hospital's acreage was sold off or donated to other public agencies, including the 62 acres that were given to the city for Jacksonville's Community Park in 1982. In September 2011, Governor Pat Quinn announced a plan to close the facility in February 2012 due to budget issues. The last residents moved out in November 2012.

These days, there are only a scattering of buildings from the old hospital still in existence. Many buildings, including the Annex and the Old Main, have been demolished. While many are gone, others have been renovated and have been put back into limited use. The empty structures stand forlorn and abandoned, slowly crumbling on land that once was home to a thriving hospital.

They continue to stand, silent and dark - but are they empty?

Hauntings

The debris of decades still remain in many of them. As the buildings decayed, packed with vast amounts of old patient files that were left to gather mold and dust in dank forgotten basements and broken pieces of furniture that haven't been used in decades, we wonder about the patients that once lived and died within these walls. But what else has been left behind?

With decades of trauma being experienced within these walls by patients who faced both their own mental afflictions and forced treatments in search of a "cure," it's no surprise that the psychic "debris" of decades remains behind as well. Imprints of their disturbed thoughts and erratic emotions are eerily strong in the buildings where the insane were house and strange disturbances are common. Hospitals have long been regarded as places were the spirits of the dead can linger. Are there lost and broken souls trapped in the abandoned halls of these crumbling buildings? Are they truly the personalities of those who once lived here? Or are they simply spooky ideas conjured up by staff members and visitors who venture into these forbidding places? The atmosphere of many of the buildings at JDC is more than enough to justify the reports of apparitions and ghostly encounters, but we'll leave the truth to such tales up to the reader to decide.

Those who have worked in the buildings that remain at the site, renovated and used for other businesses and agencies after being abandoned by the

265

The last buildings of the Jacksonville Developmental Center have now been abandoned - but are they truly empty?

developmental center, have unnerving stories to tell of ghosts - phantom footsteps, tapping and knocking sounds, voices, and shadowy figures that seem to be solid and yet disappear without warning.

And some encounters are more personal.

Jacksonville native Betsy Thornton was employed by an agency that worked with people with developmental disabilities in the Winslow Building on the grounds of the former hospital. Overall, the building seemed like a normal old building, except for a few buildings - the kitchen and the laundry room. Part of Betsy's job was to wash dishes and clean the area every afternoon. She told us, "I could never shake the feeling that I needed to look over my shoulder and watch my back. It was a very uneasy feeling every day. "

One day as she was washing ditches, she heard someone say something in the dining room. She went to the door to see who it was and found there was no one there. Thinking that the voice came from further down the hallway, she went to check and found that place was also empty. The person nearest to her was in a distant bathroom and they had not spoken. Thinking that it was simply her imagination, she went back to work in the kitchen. But as she stuck her hands into the sink, she felt a knife sticking straight up in the water - a knife that had not been there before! Panicked, she looked to her left at the far end of the counter, where the knives were always left for last. She waited to wash them, fearing that she might cut herself. Somehow while looking for the source of the mysterious voice, two knives she had left there had moved on their own and ended up in the sink. Betsy had no explanation for how - or why - the knives were moved. "Was it done by whatever had always made me feel uncomfortable in that part of the building as though my presence was unwanted in this area to try and injure me?" she asked. "Or is there another explanation, I don't know. But it's still something I'll never forget."

Another experience occurred in the same building when she went to get a drink while on break. She recalled that it was eerily quiet. She didn't see anyone in the building, but as she was putting her money into the vending machine, she heard a deep, low growl coming not far from her left ear. She turned quickly, but there was no one there. She froze in place and then literally ran out of the building, not looking back. Who had made the menacing sound from behind her? Betsy had a theory. "Residents were frequently rewarded with soda or tea, so I can't help but question if it was the spirit of a former resident who waits around hoping to get another soda or tea. Sadly, that was the highlight of most of their days."

Other staff members had their own experiences in the same building. Some claimed that they felt that it was hard to breathe in there. One room was particularly troublesome for everyone. Whenever they tried to open the door, it always felt like someone was holding it from the other side. No one ever was. The room was used as a craft supply room in recent years, but it had a bathtub in it, so it was likely used for other things in days past.

There were also times when the phone would ring and there wouldn't be anyone on the other end of the line. This would not have been so strange, but there were other oddities connected to that particular telephone. A supervisor confessed to the fact that she would often get calls at home from the Winslow building - mysterious calls that came in between 1:00 and 3:00 a.m. There was no one in the building at that time. It was locked up tight all night and security guards patrolled the grounds. The calls were never explained.

Who still lingers in the remaining buildings of the old Jacksonville State Hospital? Spectral patients or lingering staff members from days gone by? We may never know, but we can certainly all agree that its past is filled with some of the strangest stories in the annals of Jacksonville history.

Oak Lawn Retreat

Oak Lawn Retreat, which was also known as McFarland's Insane Retreat, was a private asylum for the mentally ill that was located on a 60-acre site that fronted Morton Avenue on the east side of the city. Unlike the state hospital, Oak Lawn was not hampered by strict budgets or oversight from the Illinois legislature. Opened by Dr. Andrew McFarland in 1872, the hospital, which was modeled after a Scottish abbey, provided care and treatment that could not be offered in the state institution. For this reason, it attracted patients from all over the Midwest and from states as far away as Colorado, Wyoming and Oklahoma, which was then Indian Territory. It had room for about 20 patients at a time, each of them from backgrounds that were as diverse as their ailments.

Dr. McFarland was the son of a Concord, Massachusetts clergyman named Asa McFarland and his wife, Elizabeth Kneeland McFarland. Born in July 1817,

Oak Lawn Retreat, Dr. McFarland's private sanitarium, was located east of Jacksonville. McFarland had no idea when he opened it that he would eventually became a patient in his own asylum.

he attended Dartmouth College and lectured at Jefferson Medical College in Philadelphia in 1843. He then practiced at Sandwich and Laconia, New Hampshire, and was appointed as the superintendent of the New Hampshire Asylum for the Insane in August 1845. He resigned in November 1852 and traveled to Europe, where he visited and worked in a number of insane asylums, hoping to bring back new ideas for the treatment of the mentally ill in America.

In 1854, he came west and became the third superintendent of the Illinois State Asylum for the Insane in Jacksonville. It was during this time that he met and attempted to ease the "insanity" of Elizabeth Packard, the woman who had been committed against her will because she argued with her husband's religious teachings. In 1867, Dr. McFarland would be one of the people that she filed suit against during her heavily publicized trial. The trial and the investigation surrounding it earned McFarland a terrible reputation all over the country. Until that time, he had been known as an expert on the treatment of mental health and had consulted on cases across the country. Following the accusations by Mrs. Packard, he began to be seen, as the newspapers called it, "as a fiend in human form." According to his family, his health was shattered by the trial and he remained at the state hospital only a short time longer before resigning. In 1872, he opened his private asylum, Oak Lawn Retreat.

The hospital was a great success and Dr. McFarland finally seemed to himself again, but an injury he suffered in September 1887 finally ruined his health for good. A fire broke out at the three-story hospital on September 21, and while all of the patients and staff got out of the building safely, McFarland was badly hurt when a piece of furniture that was tossed out of an upstairs window landed on his head. His skull was fractured and doctors feared that he would not survive. Somehow, though, he managed to pull through, but he was never the same again.

After stepping down from the day-to-day operations of the asylum, he turned the management of it over to his son, Dr. George McFarland, and his granddaughter, Dr. Annette McFarland, a graduate of the Rush Medical College in Chicago. Gradually, as his health declined, his personality changed, causing violent mood swings. In time, he became a resident at the hospital that he had started 20 years before.

By November 1891, McFarland's moods were so dangerous that he often had to be locked away. Toward the end of the month, though, he began to seem more like his old self and he was given the freedom of the building. On November 23, McFarland had dinner with his son and then excused himself when he was finished so that he could go and visit with one of the inmates with whom he had a special regard. Nothing more was seen of him until later that night, when his body was discovered hanging in the doorway of an empty room in the asylum. Dr. McFarland had twisted a bed sheet into a rope, tied it through a transom above the door and then took his own life.

The newspapers stated that he was "wearied of existence," but he left no note behind or any indication that he planned to commit suicide. It was ironic that, after all of the people he had helped over the years, there was no one there to try and save him from his own mental demons.

Oak Lawn Retreat remained in operation for more than twenty more years, operated by McFarland's son and granddaughter. By the early 1900s, the focus of the hospital had changed from strictly a mental hospital to a sanatorium for those who were both wealthy and ill. According to advertisements in the early 1900s, they were specializing in the treatment of diseases that were generally considered to be incurable: Bright's disease, hardening of the arteries, Diabetes, high blood pressure, uremia, asthma, various forms of rheumatism, blood poisoning, pyorrhea, acute and chronic ulcers, stomach, heart and kidney diseases, eczema and hay fever. The hospital boasted of being "especially equipped with scientific hydrotherophy," which could apparently cure just about anything.

The fad of using mineral baths and retreats such as Oak Lawn lasted into the early 1910s and began to fade from popularity. In time, the hospital closed, only to see new life a few years later, when tuberculosis was sweeping the nation and new hospitals were opening for treatment of the disease on a weekly basis.

During the nineteenth and early twentieth centuries, America was ravaged by tuberculosis, or "consumption," as it was often called. This terrifying plague, for which no cure existed before antibiotics were discovered, claimed entire families and occasionally entire towns. After tuberculosis was determined to be contagious in the 1880s, campaigns were started to stop people from spitting in public places and the infected were "encouraged" to enter sanatoriums where they could be quarantined and treated.

Treatments for tuberculosis were sometimes as bad as the disease itself. Some of the experiments that were conducted in search of a cure seem barbaric by today's standards but others are now common practice. Patient's lungs were exposed to ultraviolet light to try and stop the spread of bacteria. This was done in "sun rooms," using artificial light in place of sunlight, or on outside porches and patios. Since fresh air was thought to also be a possible cure, patients were often placed in front of huge windows or on open porches, no matter what the season. Old photographs show patients lounging in chairs, taking in the fresh air, while literally covered with snow.

Other treatments were less pleasant --- and much bloodier. Balloons would be surgically implanted in the lungs and then filled with air to expand them. Needless to say, this often had disastrous results, as did an operation where muscles and ribs were removed from a patient's chest to allow the lungs to expand further and let in more oxygen. This blood-soaked procedure was seen as a "last resort" and many patients did not survive it. Overall, there were few patients who actually survived their stays in the sanatoriums of the time. It was not until the 1930s that cases of tuberculosis began to decline, thanks to the discovery of antibiotics, which could treat the illness.

In the early 1900s, Jacksonville was just as terrified of tuberculosis as other towns across the country. One of those leading the fight against the disease at this time was Dr. T.O. Hardesty, who helped organize the Morgan County Anti-Tuberculosis Society in 1905, the second such group in Illinois. A few years later, Hardesty established a clinic and began treating patients with tuberculosis. Hardesty lobbied the state of Illinois for help and the legislature passed a bill authorizing county governments to levy a tax for the purpose of establishing and maintaining tuberculosis sanatoriums. The tax dollars helped Hardesty's organization buy the empty Oak Lawn Retreat in 1917. After the association remodeled the building, they renamed it Oaklawn and it began to serve as Morgan County's tuberculosis sanatorium.

Few drugs were used in the early years of the sanatorium. In fact, of 78 patients treated one year, only $476.58 was spent for medication. Sick patients would have their beds wheeled onto a porch on the south side of Oaklawn, where they would be exposed, even in cold weather, to fresh air and sunlight, which were thought to improve the patients' health. An average stay at Oaklawn was from 18 months to two years - if they survived that long. The main use for the hospital was to isolate those who had come down with the disease and to keep them away from those who were still healthy. Families were tragically divided with parents, and even children, forced into the sanatorium with little contact with their loved ones.

After antibiotics were developed, the patient count at Oaklawn began to decline. By the 1960s, Oaklawn was turning more to prevention and early diagnosis, as fewer patients were hospitalized at Oaklawn each year. In 1969, the clinic was moved to the Medical Center on West Walnut Street, and the old sanatorium was torn down in 1981.

During the last years that the buildings stood in ruins on Country Club Road, just off Morton Avenue, rumors ran rampant that the former hospital was haunted. Stories were often told of strange sights and sounds and even a wandering apparition that might have been Dr. McFarland himself - or perhaps one of the scores of patients and inmates who called the place home over the years.

Norbury Sanatorium

A second private hospital for the mentally ill opened in Jacksonville in 1901. The Norbury Sanatorium consisted of two different structures - the Maplewood Sanatorium on South Diamond Street and later, a second unit on Mound Avenue. They were founded by Dr. Frank Parsons Norbury, who had started his medical practice in Jacksonville in 1888. He was trained in Neurology and Psychiatry and later worked at both the state hospital and Oak Lawn Retreat before opening his own hospital to serve the needs of the mentally ill.

Dr. Norbury was born in Beardstown, Illinois, in August 1863, the youngest son of Charles Joseph Norbury and Elizabeth Peters Norbury. They had 13 children altogether, six sons and seven daughters. As a child, Frank attended public schools and graduated high school in Beardstown in 1881. Immediately after graduation, he became an office and field assistant to Captain R.A. Brown, U.S. Engineer Corps, engaged in improving the Illinois River. He served for five years, and during the winter, when work was stopped, he attended classes at Illinois College in Jacksonville. He eventually

Dr. Frank P. Norbury

271

took up the study of medicine, working for Captain Brown during the summer. In 1886, he entered the Medico-Chirurgical College in Philadelphia and then spent his senior year at Long Island College Hospital in Brooklyn, New York, from which he received his medical degree. Soon after, he took a position on the residence staff of the Pennsylvania Training School for Feebleminded Children, near Philadelphia. The institution, with over 800 inmates, gave Norbury the chance to train in clinical neurology, neuropathology, and the mental illness in children. His training continued until he decided to return home to Illinois and accept an appointment on the residence staff of the Illinois State Hospital for the Insane in Jacksonville. In addition to his private practice, he remained on staff at the state hospital for five years.

In October 1890, he married Mary Garm, one of his graduating classmates from Beardstown High School, and they made their home at the state hospital for three years. It was there that their son, Frank Garm, was born in January 1892.

In July 1893, Norbury resigned from state service to work full-time in private practice in Jacksonville. During this time, he helped to establish Our Saviour's Hospital and was for many years an attending physician and a lecturer at the Training School for Nurses. In July 1893, he also began teaching and was a professor of mental and nervous diseases at the Keokuk Medical College. Later, in 1895, he moved to St. Louis and accepted an appointment to the chair of internal medicine at the St. Louis College of Physicians and Surgeons and also as professor of mental and nervous diseases at the Women's Medical College. It was during this time that he also became an editor for a medical journal, a position that he held for 10 years.

Dr. Norbury remained in St. Louis for only one year before coming back to Jacksonville. He returned to his private practice and he also took a physician's position at Oak Lawn Retreat and at the Illinois State School for the Blind. In addition, he continued teaching at Keokuk Medical College, took a teaching position at Illinois College, and a third position at Drake University in Des Moines, Iowa. Then, in 1901, having resigned from Oak Lawn Retreat, he established the Norbury Sanatorium on South Diamond Street in Jacksonville.

The new sanatorium was Dr. Norbury's brainchild. He recognized the need for more defined and individual private care for mentally ill patients - the kind of care that they certainly couldn't get in the state facility and which was lacking at Oak Lawn in the years following the death of Dr. McFarland. Norbury felt that advancements were needed in the mental health field and by opening a private hospital that did not depend on state funds was the best way to keep step with, and contribute to, those advancements. He took on two partners to be his Board of Directors, his son, Dr. Frank G. Norbury and Dr. Albert H. Dollear, a

The center entrance of Dr. Norbury's Hospital on South Diamond Street. The remaining structure has been turned into apartments today.

student of Norbury's who graduated from the St. Louis University's Medical Department in 1904.

The hospital began modestly with only 15 patients in a building at 806 South Diamond Street, a home that had been remodeled to meet the requirements of hospital service. As the hospital grew, eventually reaching a capacity of 100 patients, more buildings were added at the South Diamond Street location. The four buildings - three for patients and one for nurses - were dubbed Maplewood and were situated on 13 acres of ground on what was then the outskirts of the city.

A second department, meant for women only and known as Maplecrest, was located at 1631 Mound Avenue, west of the city on Route 36. It was located on the highest point in Morgan County, with 31 acres of landscaped grounds. It also offered four independent units of 10 rooms, each with individual bath services. Physical therapy was supplied by hydrotherapeutic equipment, electro-therapy, occupational therapy, and an X-ray machine located in the basement. A concrete tennis court was located on the lawn. The general offices were located at Maplecrest, as were the laundry, gardens, orchard and chicken farm.

As the sanatorium grew, it became necessary to add more doctors and staff, and Norbury himself never stopped traveling, teaching and attended conferences that would advance his skills and techniques. He was very active in the social welfare work of the state and served as the president of the Illinois State Conference of Charities and Corrections for 12 years. Illinois Governor Charles S. Deneen also appointed him superintendent of the Kankakee State Hospital in 1909, and he served there two years. At the end of that time, the governor then asked him to serve as the medical member of the Board of Administration of

One of the private patient rooms at the Norbury hospital

Illinois. This forced him to move to Springfield and he appointed Dr. Dollear to take his place as administrator of the Norbury Sanatorium in Jacksonville.

Dr. Norbury continued medical work on a state and national level until 1917, when he was sent overseas during World War I to study conditions there by the Surgeon General's Office of the Army. He served in various capacities with the military until returning to Springfield in May 1919. At this time, he was called upon to assist in organizing the care and treatment of mental cases in returning soldiers.

Although he was seldom not working in some capacity in the medical field, he eventually settled down in Springfield and in 1922, began limiting his work to consultations and the Sanatorium in Jacksonville. He passed away in 1939, having achieved more during his decades of service than most doctors could ever dream of. Three generations of Norbury doctors dedicated their lives to the people of Jacksonville. Frank Garm Norbury and his son, Frank Barnes Norbury, continued the tradition started by their father and grandfather. Together, they provided over 100 years of medical service to others.

As for the hospitals created by Dr. Norbury, they lasted until 1967, when the Norbury and Dollear families finally closed them down. The Maplecrest site on Mound Avenue was later replaced by the First Baptist Church and private homes. The hospital buildings on South Diamond Street, though, still exist today and went on to become an apartment building.

And it seems that the years of mental anguish and death that occurred within those walls have left an indelible mark behind. Over the years, many of the residents have told stories of a haunting at the former hospital. The most common paranormal experiences to be reported are the voices in the hallways, both shouting and calming tones, knocking sounds, slamming doors, and the bone chilling sight of a tall, slender shadow figure that roams the building. In one account, a tenant recalls the shadow figure visiting her bedroom in the night, once lifting her from the bed and pulling her around the room.

274

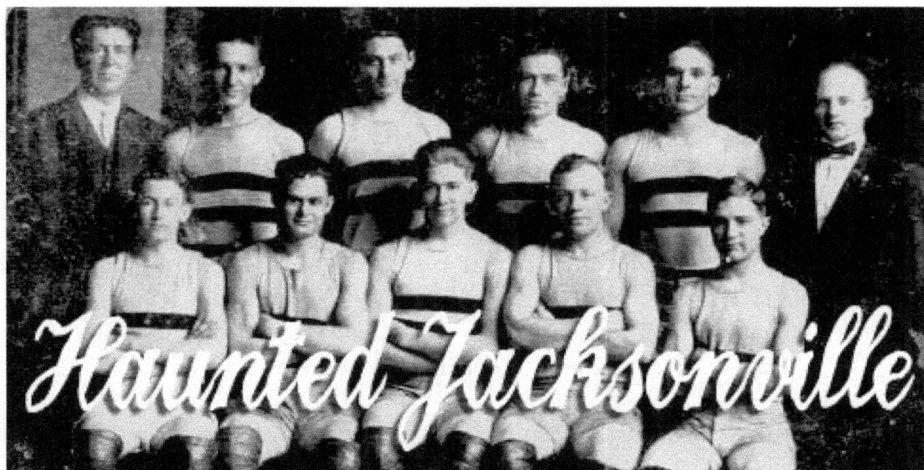
Haunted Jacksonville

9. SCHOOL SPIRITS

History & Hauntings of Jacksonville's Schools and Colleges

Why do schools become haunted? That's a question that has been bothering most ghost enthusiasts for decades. It seems that almost every college, and even many grade schools, have a ghost story or two floating around the campus. Many are tales of murdered coeds who never actually existed , suicides of which no records can be found or teachers who simply refuse to leave which might be more believable .

Many have surmised - for obvious reasons - that ghost stories from schools are simply the product of overactive imaginations and are the result of students who are far too susceptible to stories of spooks and spirits. But what about the stories told by not only students, but by teachers, professors, and staff members? Are these ghostly tales simply wild imaginations at work?

Perhaps some of these stories are simply the mixture of fact and fancy. Perhaps the ghostly lore that surrounds school is just that - folklore. But perhaps the story was created to explain something that was truly supernatural and our human need for an explanation created a story of yet another murdered coed or spectral teacher. What if our academic ghost stories are real? What if the pent-up energy of having hundreds of students together in one place not only attracts spirits, but conjures up a haunting? Perhaps some of these ghosts really are the spirits of former students, teachers, principals and maintenance men who have some sort of unfinished business in this world - or perhaps the suicides and deaths that have become so much a part of our local lore actually took place. What if their traumatic lives and deaths actually caused their spirits to linger behind?

Many would argue and say that such stories cannot be true. But if you have ever lived or spent time at some of the schools that will be mentioned in the pages ahead, you might admit that you heard some very odd stories on campus - or you might have experienced them for yourself. The type of "school spirit" that can be found in some of Jacksonville's hallowed halls of learning may not be what some people think of when they recall their alma mater, but let us assure you there is more to some of our local schools and colleges than first meets the eye.

Truth or legend? You'll have to decide that one for yourself.

Even before the arrival of the New Englanders who wanted to bring culture to the frontier and mold the city into the "Athens of the West," the early settlers of Jacksonville felt the need to make sure their children received a good education. Even though what became Jacksonville's public school district would not come along for another 40 years, school first went into session in town beginning in the winter of 1826.

The first teacher in town was a man without a schoolhouse. He was a young man named Carson, who had been hired to teach summer school at the courthouse, but left after "not meeting with much encouragement as he thought would pay." In other words, he offered classes but had no students to attend them at the time.

The first school, purchased for $50, was located on the south side of College Avenue between East and Mauvaisterre Streets, in what was then the southeast part of town. It opened on the first Monday in December 1826, and the teacher was Judge William Thomas. At the time, he had run out of money to pay for room and board and was looking for a job, so he began teaching on the subscriber method, meaning that families who signed up did so for a small fee and sent all the children to him that they could spare from farm work. He taught anywhere from 30-50 children each day and worked 10-12 hours a day. It is not clear from historical records how much he was paid because most of his fees were in "cash or produce, pork, cattle or hogs at cash prices." We do know that he made $52 in three months, because after that time he was able to pay for lodging for a year, which was $1 per week. Some of Thomas' later writings also indicate that he had money to spare for stamps and other expenses.

In 1825, the Illinois legislature passed a law creating schools free to children ages 5 to 21, paid for by a general tax on property. The Jacksonville school district was organized under this law, which was as unpopular then as it is today. In 1827, though, the legislature passed another law that said that no one could be taxed to pay for schools "except upon his written consent." The law further said that no more than one-half of the school's budget could be generated through property taxes; the rest had to come from tuition. Various attempts were made at reviving the free school law and Jacksonville leaders - which over the next decades would have the faculty members of two colleges, a deaf school, and a blind school championing the cause of education - were among the strongest lobbyists. More laws came and went, creating a bureaucratic nightmare of mammoth proportions, and even today, funding for schools remains a controversial issue.

Even with all of the public money that had been spent on the school since 1826, it was not until 1840 that Jacksonville was recognized as having a free public school, ranking it in a tie with Springfield for third in the state. Chicago and Alton had established their schools in 1834 and 1837.

The second Jacksonville school was established in 1848, when school trustees bought a site at the northwest corner of State and Fayette Streets. West Jacksonville School opened in 1850 with Newton Bateman, who would later become the state superintendent of education, as principal.

By 1866, there were four separate school districts in Jacksonville, each with a three-member school board and all overseen by a single school commissioner. The four schools were West Jacksonville, which was the largest in the city with 600 students and seven teachers; Locust Grove School, on the north side of East College Street between Mauvaisterre and East Streets; Jefferson School, located on what is now Douglas Avenue between Mauvaisterre and East Streets; and Washington School, where the current Washington Elementary School stands.

At the time it was built, Washington cost a then-exorbitant sum of $50,000 and boasted an "airy basement for a gymnasium and playground in wet weather in addition to all the other conveniences of other schools." The school, which is also considered to be the district's first high school, was deemed one of the finest in the state at that time.

The state legislature gave the city council power to act in all matters related to education and the council decided that it wanted to consolidate the schools. The Jacksonville School District commenced on September 9, 1867, with 942 students attending many more reported later after harvest farm work ended . The superintendent was Israel Wilkinson, who made $1,800 a year. However, in his first report to the school board, he pointed out that the superintendent in Springfield made $3,100 a year. There is no record to say that Wilkinson received the raise that he obviously felt he deserved, but we hope that he did.

The four districts in town became four wards. A fifth school, for black children only, was added on Anna Street and it remained open until 1876. There were 2,500 white children and 110 black children in school in 1868.

The first rules passed by the school board included a prohibition on tobacco, and students were warned that if they brought firearms and knives to school, they would be suspended. Coal and wood were at a premium in schools and a rule was passed that stated that room temperatures in the winter time could not be above 65 degrees.

If students missed more than four half-days in four weeks without a note from their parents, they forfeited their seats. This was a big deal in a classroom that might have 75 students in it and only 30-35 seats. It did not take long for parents to realize that some of their children were not only standing, but were shoulder-to-shoulder in the classrooms. When he heard the complaints, Superintendent Wilkinson had little sympathy. He issued a rather blunt statement that basically said that parents either needed to cough up more money for the schools, or they needed to stop having children. He advised them to "veto the rapid increase of children," because if they were born, they needed to be educated.

Over the next five years, though, sites were purchased for four more schools, which began to ease the overcrowding issues, but not the lack of funds. Even in the nineteenth century, teachers from District 117 were already worried about how the bills were going to be paid.

High School Apartments

Whether or not the city of Jacksonville can boast the first high school in the state of Illinois is a subject of some debate. Jacksonville's first recognized high school was established in 1867 at the site where Washington Elementary School now stands. Chicago had established its high school in 1865 - two years before. But, while you couldn't technically attend high school in Jacksonville until 1867, you could receive the equivalent of a high school degree as early as 1851.

Newton Bateman, who was the principal of West Jacksonville School, organized "college grade courses" in his school in 1851, after seeing the trend that was taking place on America's east coast. Cities like Boston and New York had established high schools during the first half of the nineteenth century, and Bateman decided to bring this new plan to the west. The high school department at West Jacksonville School became so popular that three other school districts in town decided to implement similar plans. Each of them followed the same list of courses: algebra, geometry, trigonometry, conic sections, navigation, surveying, Latin grammar, Caesar, Euclid, Virgil, natural philosophy, chemistry, astronomy, political economy, constitutional law, botany, physiology, and physical geography.

The high school was finally established in 1867, but it was not until 1878 that it was approved by voters. Some citizens were upset because all high school

The original Jacksonville High School, which burned down in 1918

students were transferred away from their ward schools to one building. Others were upset because the curriculum didn't include any kind of religious training. These opponents periodically demanded that the board abolish the high school, and so in 1878, the board called their bluff and put the question up for a vote. The referendum asking whether to keep the high school passed easily, 1,973-293.

The original building lasted until 1900, when a new building costing $75,000 and boasting a second-floor study hall that could house 400 students was constructed on West State Street at the site of what is now the High School Apartments. The building lasted just 18 years and was destroyed by fire on March 14, 1918. The blaze broke out in the basement during the early morning hours and swept through the building, also destroying the nearby Trinity Episcopal Church.

The nearby David Prince Junior High School, which survived the fire, was placed into double-duty. The junior high students attended school from 7:30 a.m. to 12:30 p.m. and the high school students would attend from 1:00 p.m. to 6:00 p.m. The laboratories at Illinois College and Illinois Women's College were used as well. But that didn't last long. Given the events of the day, it turned out that the school buildings were not necessary during the coming winter of 1918 - when the Spanish Flu Epidemic raged through the city and the entire nation. Jacksonville students were banned from coming to school at all from early October through the holiday season.

The flu epidemic followed World War I, which had been considered the "War to End All Wars" when America joined the fight in 1917. The first outbreak of what became known as the Spanish Flu occurred in Haskell County, Kansas, in January 1918, just nine months after the United States had declared war on Germany. Within weeks, the flu spread to Camp Funston, which was located at Fort Riley, near Manhattan, Kansas. The camp was one of the country's largest military facilities, quickly put together to train soldiers for the war. The wartime conditions provided a perfect breeding ground for influenza, because America's entrance into the conflict brought together large groups of soldiers and sailors to encampments and naval installations across the country. From these locations, troops were transported across the Atlantic to the front lines in France. Some of the ships literally became death traps and thousands of flu victims were buried at sea. Freighters and troop ships from other countries then served as carriers of the disease, connecting the battlefields to other cities and countries around the world.

Although the first cases of the disease were discovered in the United States and the rest of Europe long before getting to Spain, the epidemic received its nickname of "Spanish Flu" because Spain, a neutral country in World War I, had no special wartime censorship for news about the disease and the accompanying death toll. Since it received reliable press coverage in Spain, people got the false impression that Spain was the most - if not the only - affected country.

The first European outbreak of the flu occurred in April in Brest, France, the principal port of disembarkation for American troops in Europe. From there, the disease spread across the continent, then on toward Asia and Africa. By the fall of 1918, the disease had reached a lethal stage. Army leaders were unprepared for such a monumental health crisis and largely ignored the warnings about troop movements since they were more concerned about building up strength in Europe for a final thrust against Germany. Despite General John J. Pershing's request for more troops, the draft was canceled in October. On the other side of the lines, the flu contributed to Germany's failure to stop the final Allied assault in late 1918. Germany agreed to an armistice on November 11.

The second wave of the 1918 pandemic was much deadlier than the first. The first wave had resembled typical flu epidemics; those most at risk were the sick and elderly, while younger, healthier people recovered easily. But in August, when the second wave swept across the United States, the virus had mutated to a much deadlier form.

Thousands died. The new wave of the disease was spread by soldiers returning from Europe, and for Americans, the flu turned out to be more devastating than the war that accompanied it. By the fall of 1918, the Surgeon General of the Army reported that the disease had "exploded" in port cities where soldiers were entering the United States from overseas. In the early stages of the illness, the epidemic had been largely ignored by the public health departments and was regarded as merely a minor outbreak. Most doctors cited pneumonia on the death certificates of those killed, since flu came first and weakened the resistance of those who were sick. Pneumonia usually followed and was the eventual cause of death for most.

Late in the year, though, as port cities and naval bases began to report large numbers of illnesses and death, the public began to realize that something was very wrong. However, little was done to curb the spread of the virus. Doctors warned local health departments to quarantine the sick and to restrict attendance at large public gatherings. However, most towns, in the grip of patriotic fervor, resisted the advice and held rallies and parades for returning soldiers. In Philadelphia, a massive Liberty Loan parade was held in October, despite the pleas of some medical officials to cancel it. The city paid a horrible price for continuing with the event, as fatalities soon approached one thousand per week.

In the days and weeks that followed, the disease began to spread to the interior parts of the country. The Navy carried the flu from coast to coast on their troop ships and the Army did the same via the railways. Soldiers packed into tight quarters on the trains guaranteed the rapid spread of respiratory illnesses, and when they arrived in the various stations, they passed the flu on to all who came into contact with them.

Large public gatherings in support of the war, such as parades, bond rallies and loan drives, brought masses of people together and they quickly spread the flu even further. The people simply did not appreciate the amount of danger they were in, and they ignored orders calling for the closure of schools, churches, theaters, and other public meeting places. Most cities refused to halt their public transportation services until hundreds of transit authority workers fell ill and forced them to do so. Soon, those who collected the dead and interred them found themselves overwhelmed in some cities. The accumulation of corpses then served to create secondary epidemics, making the larger cities the hardest hit by the flu.

As the death toll mounted around the country, the social fabric of many communities began to unravel. In San Francisco, schools were closed for six weeks; in Philadelphia, bodies were "stacked like cordwood" and went uncollected. The police were forced to remove bodies from homes and families had to dig graves for their loved ones, as gravediggers refused to work. Factories closed due to high absence rates.

The people's indifference to the flu led directly to the rapid and deadly spread of the disease. Most considered the flu as merely a side note to the terrible war and, in those days, epidemics of one sort or another were a common part of life. Most people had already lived through an epidemic of some sort, although usually on a much smaller scale. Influenza moved quickly. It arrived in a town, flourished for a time and then left before most people had the opportunity to realize how great the danger was. Also, the flu did not always kill and when it did, it killed quickly, especially young adults. Normally the healthiest of age groups, individuals in their twenties, had the highest rate of mortality from the Spanish flu. Many of their deaths were agonizing. Historian John Barry described a flu death: "Blood poured from their noses, ears and eye sockets; some victims lay in agony; delirium took others away while living." Coughing was sometimes so violent that the muscles of the rib cage were torn apart. When the extremities such as lips and cheeks turned black, death followed soon after. In some cases, victims who were fine in the morning were dead by evening.

Nearly one-fourth of all Americans caught the flu between the fall of 1918 and the late winter of 1919. Even if sufficient numbers of doctors had been available, they could have done little to intercede. No flu vaccines existed at the time and caregivers could do little but encourage patients to drink plenty of fluids, hand out aspirin, and keep the dying comfortable. Emergency Red Cross hospitals were set up from coast to coast, but doctors and nurses were scarce, as the war effort had taken many of them into the military and to France. Despite frantic appeals, calls for more nurses went unanswered.

In many cases, entire families were incapacitated with illness, unaided by doctors and avoided by their neighbors, who refused to enter homes that had "Influenza" signs nailed to the front door. Some cities required people to wear surgical masks, which were actually ineffective to the microscopic virus. Because death rates were highest among people in their twenties, many of whom were parents, the flu produced thousands of young orphans around the country.

The federal government offered little assistance to flu victims. The U.S. Public Health Service, aside from issuing a handful of warnings, played a very small role in the epidemic. This was in part because President Woodrow Wilson did not publicly acknowledge it. His priorities in 1918 were the defeat of Germany and the supervision of the peace settlement when the war was over. Following the president's lead, American newspapers downplayed the epidemic, urging citizens to not become fearful and pumping up the patriotic fervor that came with the end of the war. The deliberate suppression of bad news during the war helps to explain why the Spanish Flu epidemic received so little attention when compared with other catastrophes that struck the United States during the twentieth century.

After Germany surrendered, President Wilson went to France as the head of the American delegation for the peace negotiations held at Versailles. In April 1919, the president contracted the flu, which came on very suddenly. He later recalled that night was "one of the worst through which I have ever passed." Prior to getting sick, Wilson had resisted the Allied demands to punish Germany, but even before he was fully recovered, he changed his mind and went along with the Allied position, including the imposition of expensive financial reparations on Germany. It's unknown just how much effect the flu had on Wilson's reversal but some believe that it may have contributed to his debilitating stroke the following September, an event that clouded his judgment when the Senate considered the ratification of the Versailles Treaty.

The flu may, or may not, have had an effect on world politics but it's certain that it had an impact on the social history of the United States, as well as the role of medical research in years to come. The epidemic was slowly brought under control and almost seemed to vanish as a few more months passed. By then, however, the damage was done. Millions were dead around the world, entire families were wiped out, towns had been laid waste and never recovered, and American history had been altered in a way that had never happened before. And all because of the flu...

In Jacksonville, the influenza raged for several weeks and reached its peak period between the middle of October and early November 1918. By the time public health officials issued an order to stop all public gatherings there were over 300,000 confirmed cases of the flu in Illinois and several thousand of them were in Jacksonville.

In October, an order was issued stating that all schools, theaters, billiard rooms, and dance halls would be closed until further notice. This included all classes and sporting events at the colleges and at all of the public schools. The order also banned all church services and all meetings and gatherings of "social, patriotic, religious or educational nature." All children were told to stay inside of their homes and were not allowed to mingle with other children in the neighborhood.

On October 18, a similar order was issued by Illinois' Governor Lowden, who allowed for some gatherings to take place, but only those directly related to the war effort. However, the following rules had to be applied to any such meetings: "crowding would not be permitted... persons affected by colds would not be admitted... coughers, sneezers and spitters would be expelled... and the premises had to be ventilated, heated and cleaned."

Bans began to be lifted the following month, and on November 11, the Armistice was signed and the Great War was officially over. Reports of new outbreaks of the flu had dropped significantly, and it was believed safe for the public to gather once more. The people of Jacksonville celebrated into the early morning hours. Blowing whistles spread the news and people left their homes and ran out into the streets. An unofficial parade was held downtown and was marked by crowds of citizens singing, screaming, blowing whistles and horns,

The High School Apartments today

and banging pots and pans. The night became bedlam and lasted into the following day.

The public schools were re-opened after the holidays and officials worked hard to insure that high school students still received their education. In 1920, a new school was built on the site and it still stands today, not as a high school, but as an apartment building. The last class to graduate from that school was in 1982, and then it was later turned to private use as apartments - apartments with a reputation for being haunted.

There is a perplexing question about who haunts the former high school today. According to records, no one died in the fire that occurred on the site in the original building in 1918. There isn't even record to say that anyone died in the school at any point over the years and yet, for whatever reason, strange reports make their way out of the building today. Former students or staff? Teachers who chose to linger behind? No one knows, but stories and first-hand encounters are often told.

As legend has it, one tenant would often hear the laughter of a little girl in her apartment. She lived alone with her cat and there were no children in the apartments nearby. Her neighbors told her that it was not unusual to hear children playing in the hallway, but this tenant felt like the voices were a lot closer than that. One night while trying to sleep, her cat sat at the bedroom door whimpering and continuously pestered her weary owner. Tired and annoyed, she tossed the cat out into the living room, closed the bedroom door, and climbed back into bed. Throughout the night, she heard the faint sounds of laughter and voices coming from outside of her bedroom. As if that wasn't enough to disturb her slumber, she also heard the sound of the cat scratching at the bedroom door, begging to be let back in, or so she thought. After a restless night sleep, she awoke the next morning to find the door to her bedroom was covered with crayon marks.

Other accounts are not as playful. One tenant, who still shaken by his experiences, recalls the many unsettling occurrences that took place while living in the high school apartments. On a good day, the only activity that might take place in the apartment would be objects moving about the room on their own, like a bottle cap flying off of the coffee table or a dirty sock leaving the laundry basket and landing in the hallway. But all too often, the spirit residing here would make itself known in a more dramatic way. On one occasion, while the tenant's brother was visiting, they narrowly escaped a knife that levitated from the countertop flew through the air right between the tenant and his brothers faces, and stuck in the wall behind them.

But the most disturbing of nights left his tenant looking for a new place to live after he met his resident spirit face to shadowy face. Sleeping soundly in bed the man awoke with a start, feeling an eerie presence around him. This was not out of the ordinary, however on this night the powerful presence overwhelmed that man with fear. Even though he knew it would do no good, he reached for a baseball bat and held it close. Sitting on the side of his bed, knuckles white and teeth clenched, the man prepared himself for a spiritual battle that would last all night long. At one point, a figure started to appear on the screen of his television. The television was turned off and it was obvious this was no reflection. At another point in the night, he felt a heavy weight press down on the bed near where he was sitting. And the climax of this battle began when he heard the slow, heavy footsteps right outside of his bedroom door. He was certain that whatever was out there would soon show itself. He was right. Standing in the doorway was a large shadowy figure. Staring at one another, the man was too scared to move from his spot on the bed. He recalls having the desire to run but literally could not move an inch. What occurred after this is still quite fuzzy to the man. The next thing he remembers is sprinting from his bed, leaving his apartment without getting dressed, and exiting the building to seek comfort elsewhere. He returned only to pack his belongings.

The School that Hides a Graveyard

Perhaps one of the strangest stories of a Jacksonville school dates back to 1955, although its origins in the city go back much further. In August 1955, workers who were digging the foundations of Jonathan Turner Junior High made a gruesome discovery. They found two cast-iron coffins containing a man and a woman as the excavation crew prepared to remove a tree. The caskets were in excellent condition and each contained a plate glass window that was set in lead. The two corpses were plainly visible and according to Ed Cooper, the sexton of Diamond Grove Cemetery where the caskets were reinterred at the time, the color of their skin was a dull gold. They were well-preserved, but the identities of the couple remains a mystery.

So, how did two bodies end up in the middle of a building site for a new school? The answer to that goes back to the 1830s, and the really interesting part of it is that there may have been a lot more than just two of them - and many of them might still be there under the school today.

What would someday be Jonathan Turner Junior High started out as the Illinois College Burying Ground, which was established by the college's trustees in 1838. The cemetery faced County Street - later named Lincoln Avenue - and it was abandoned in the late 1860s or early 1870s.

In the early years of the college, trustees saw the need for a cemetery on the grounds and also recognized the opportunity to generate some revenue for the school with the sale of burial plots. The college owned a great deal of land south of the campus, so dedicating a few acres to the cemetery seemed practical. Lots were offered for sale and the ones that were sold more than paid for the land. The New Englanders brought with them their traditions for a burying ground, placing the graves very close together with the headstone of one being next to the foot of another. The only issue? No one bothered to keep any records as to how many people were buried there or who they were. Even though historians have managed to identify 38 people they believe were buried there, there are scores of people never identified.

Perhaps the most famous of the known burials in the cemetery was Augustine Frederick Prevost, a stepson of Aaron Burr, the third vice president of the United States and the man that killed Alexander Hamilton in a duel. In 1834, when Prevost was 68 years old, he moved his family to Morgan County from Westford, New York. They built a log cabin and settled on a 240-acre farm just south of present-day Concord, where family members lived for several years after Prevost's death in 1842. Years later, when the cemetery was closed, Prevost's remains were exhumed and moved to Diamond Grove Cemetery, which opened some distance from the city limits of that time in the late 1860s.

At some point, it was realized that the location was not really suitable for a cemetery and it was closed. Bodies began to be removed as early as 1867. A story in the *Jacksonville Journal* in April 1867 read, "The College Grave Yard has now been abandoned, the space allotted to it being filled and the situation of the land unfavorable to improvement and enlargement. Many bodies and monuments have been moved from it to the new one." The "new one" is presumably a reference to Diamond Grove Cemetery.

If the college cemetery was as full as the newspaper article implies, then it held far more than the 38 bodies that historians have been able to discover. After all, city records indicate that Illinois College officials staked out a cemetery that was 655 feet long, north to south, and 340 feet wide.

After the 1867 closure, the stories of how and when the bodies were removed from the burial ground gets a little hazy. Local cemetery records show that remains were still being exhumed from the college cemetery as late as 1874, and yet a newspaper story from a decade later mentioned that still more had not been moved. In 1884, a *Journal* reporter wrote, "It is a pity all of the bodies cannot be removed from this ancient resting place of the dead and reinterred in one of the two city cemeteries."

So, were all of the bodies - at least the bodies that could be found with no records to aid in the search - actually moved in the years after 1884? Or was the cemetery merely forgotten? An effort had undoubtedly been made to discover the last of the remains, but based on the discovery made by construction workers in 1955, not all of them were found.

And if two of them were missed, just how many more might be out there, waiting to be found - under the halls, classrooms and offices of Jonathan Turner Junior High?

Spectral Ladies
The Fiery History & Hauntings of MacMurray College

We were standing in the dark one night, just after Halloween, crowded into a dorm room in MacMurray College's Rutledge Hall, waiting for something to happen. It had been an uneventful night so far. For several years, we had been coming to Rutledge Hall to take part in an evening of ghost hunting with some of the students and residence advisors that lived there during the school year. Strange things had happened in years past, but this year had been quiet - until we got to "Pam's" room.

According to Rutledge lore, Pam had been a student at MacMurray in the early 1970s and had passed away in her suite, which contained two sleeping rooms with a bathroom between them. Ever since that time, her ghost was said to haunt the room. Students who had been unlucky enough to end up there had eerie stories to tell of unexplainable sounds, voices, moving objects and on many occasions, the apparition of Pam herself, walking from one room to the next and disappearing in and out of the bathroom.

Haunted Rutledge Hall on the MacMurray College campus

On this particular night, we had divided the students into groups and the authors had taken one group which included two young women who lived in the room at the time to Pam's room. They each had weird stories to tell, including many hair-raising incidents that had occurred during the few months that they had been living in the suite that semester. Some of them - like the night one of the young women woke up and saw a woman draped in shadow appear from the doorway to the bathroom - were enough to make them leave the room and stay elsewhere for a night.

While the stories certainly set the stage for something spooky to happen, nothing did - at least at first.

For our night of ghost hunting with the students, we always bring along as many electrical gadgets as possible. Some are worthwhile, some are not, but all are interesting. One such gadget was a device that measured the level of electromagnetic energy in a room some researchers believe that ghosts can change or manipulate this type of radiation in a location. Can they? Jury's still out on that one and it also measured the ambient temperature too. Nearly everyone who has an interest in ghosts has read about "cold spots" and it's believed that this is a significant sign that a spirit is present. And while perhaps that's not scientific, researchers have believed this for over 150 years, which seems to give it some credibility.

So, after moving from one room of the suite to the bathroom - and crowding six people into the tiny bathroom where Pam died- and then onto the second bedroom, we all sat down to wait in the dark for that "something" to occur. We placed several gadgets and recording devices around the room, hoping to capture whatever might take place, including the device that measured the electromagnetic fields and the temperature in room, which, by the way, was a balmy 76 degrees on November 2.

We didn't have long to wait. It started off with asking questions to whatever spirit might be present presumably Pam and waiting a few seconds to see if a spectral reply might turn up on the recorder when it was played back. We didn't hear anything and all of the devices stayed dark. A couple of additional devices to measure the room's energy had been placed on a nearby table, not far from the device that has already been described. The rather one-sided conversation that we were having with thin air trailed off after a few minutes and we began talking about past ghost hunting nights at Rutledge Hall and some of the odd things that had occurred. Lisa mentioned that after the previous year's outing, strange things also began happening in her home. She blamed them on Pam...

Almost as soon as she mentioned Pam's name, one of the young women present hissed, "Did you hear that?" We hadn't, but she later said that it sounded like a woman crying. But we didn't get a chance to think about it. Almost immediately, the lights on *all* of the measuring devices flared to life. None of them had been touched. No one passed near them. They hadn't been moved in any way. And yet, not only did all of the lights go on, signaling a sudden change in the room's atmosphere, but the digital temperature read-out on the main device inexplicably dropped almost 20 degrees!

Pam, it seemed, had come to visit.

The Early Days

The story of MacMurray College stretches all of the way back to the days of the Illinois frontier, when any higher education offered for women was extremely hard to find. In those days, nearly all education was promoted by religious groups and so the schools for women that did exist had largely been founded so that ministers and educated laymen could find more suitable wives.

During the 1830s and 1840s, the largest Protestant denomination in the state was the Methodist Church. It had established McKendree College in 1829, as well as several elementary and secondary schools. In keeping with the general theme of educating young women to make better wives, the Illinois Conference of the Methodist Church voted to establish a female academy in Jacksonville on September 23, 1846. The school was to be called the Illinois Conference Female Academy, and on October 10, 1846, the first meeting of its Board of Trustees was held at East Charge Church, located on East State Street where the Times Theater now stands.

Nine men, all of whom would be regarded for their generosity and organization, made up the new Board. Five of them were clergymen and the other four were laymen. The two men who were best-known among them were Peter Akers, a Methodist minister and the chairman of the education committee of the Illinois Conference who was most responsible for the school's establishment, and Peter Cartwright, the famous Methodist circuit rider and the board's first president. The other founders were clergymen W.D.R. Trotter, W.C. Stribbling, William J. Rutledge, and laymen William Thomas, William Brown, Matthew Stacy and Nicholas Milburn.

The college's first president
James F. Jaquess

At the meeting, the Board instructed its new prudential committee to secure a lot and make plans for constructing a building. The committee found five acres available on East State Street and they purchased it for the bargain price of $500. The Board immediately began raising funds for a building, but their efforts fell far short of their goal. Undeterred, though, they decided to start the school in a rented space. The next plan was to find a president for the school, and after a long and difficult search, they decided on a 29-year-old Methodist minister from Springfield named James F. Jaquess. The school opened on October 1, 1848, and classes were held in the basement of the East Charge Church with most of the students being housed with Methodist families throughout Jacksonville.

Jaquess served as the school's first president for seven years. Under his leadership, the Academy expanded to a size that was unusual for colleges for women in those days 282 enrollments in 1855 alone and retained a good faculty despite many financial setbacks. In the opinion of many, he also raised the academic level of the school to equal that of the men's colleges of the time. It was an amazing accomplishment and an uphill battle. In 1851, the academy's name was changed to Illinois Conference Female College to reflect its advanced status. This made it one of two women's schools of collegiate rank in the western United States.

In the midst of these exciting changes, the actual school building was being constructed. The cornerstone had been laid in 1849, and it was finally completed in the winter of 1852. The brick structure was four stories tall, with an observatory on top. Combining Georgian architecture with a classical style that was more common in the southern states, its most striking feature was the four

Main Hall, the first building on campus

massive Corinthian columns that decorated the front. The building encompassed all functions of the school - classrooms, library, chapel, dining hall, and living space for teachers, students, and the president's family. It soon became recognized as "one of the best college buildings in the west." In 1855, a five-story wing was added to the west side to accommodate dormitory space for an increasing enrollment. The school's reputation was attracting students from all over the region - but that wasn't the only reason for the influx of new students.

The college seemed to be constantly in debt. Money had to be borrowed to complete the building, and fund-raising efforts by various agents had been disappointing from the start. It was at this time that President Jaquess came up with the idea of "perpetual scholarships" to reduce the debt. Scholarships were sold for $100 each, and the holder had the right to keep one person at a time in school, with the scholarship paying the tuition fees. This right could be passed on to an heir, then another, perpetually. Ten-year scholarships were sold for $25. Scholarships were sold to Methodist clergymen for half price, but they were the only ones to receive the discount. The result of the perpetual and ten-year scholarships was a dramatic increase in attendance, thus requiring a new wing to be added on to the original building, but also brought the college to the brink of bankruptcy.

By 1855, the debt was more than $28,000 and by 1857, had increased to $40,000. The perpetual scholarship plan brought in money in the short term, but then it was gone and there was no room for new students or more scholarships

291

to be sold. Things were so bad at times that President Jaquess had to go out and solicit not only funds for the school, but fuel for the furnaces and food for the students. He wrote, "Things are in a desperate condition." By 1855, he had not been paid a full salary in quite some time and when he resigned that same year, he and his wife only received one-third of the salary that was due them.

Unfortunately, Jaquess' administration began a recurring pattern for the college of continued growth and academic excellence, but tough times when it came to finances.

The years before and immediately after the Civil War were dark days for the college - and for most colleges and academies in the north and south. It was a time when men and boys went away to fight the war, emptying nearly every school, and when young women were expected to go and take care of things at home while the men were away. Nearly every college, seminary, and academy for women closed down during the war and the era of Reconstruction.

Dr. Charles Adams was the president of the Illinois Conference Female College during this time and made a heroic effort to keep things running. He would eventually be highly praised for his administration, even though he had to deal with a difficult time in history, and he had also inherited the college's overwhelming debt and all of the problems that accompanied it. Interest charges alone were $4,000 per year and pressure from creditors grew worse with each passing month.

In 1860, the Illinois Conference met in Jacksonville. With the country on the brink of a civil war and the financial future of the college uncertain, the Conference was considering the idea of closing the school and selling off the property to pay its outstanding debts. It turned out to be a simple woman from Carlinville who changed the mind of the Board. Her name was Ann Dumville and she was a poor and uneducated housekeeper who had nevertheless managed to send two of her three daughters to the college. In those days, women did not hold any leadership positions in the Methodist Church. They rarely attended the annual conference and, if they did, they never spoke. However, this woman, described as "saintly" and who "gave what little she had to the church and charity," dared to speak up when it was suggested that the college be closed. Her speech was brief, but wonderfully effective, and it stirred the hearts of everyone in attendance. It was said that the ministers present "shouted and wept and rallied to the rescue and the college was not sold."

This crisis was narrowly averted, with the college still heavily in debt, but a new crisis occurred the following year when a fire destroyed the west wing of the building. The blaze occurred in November 1861, and while no one was hurt, the loss was about $40,000 and, of course, the college had no insurance.

To save the college from bankruptcy, an arrangement was made with the creditors in which certain trustees would purchase the college and all of the assets at a sheriff's sale, and they in turn would assume all of the debt. It was a risky, yet generous move on the part of the school's supporters. Under a new financial agent, Colin D. James, a tremendous fund-raising effort was started and money was contributed by the trustees, ministers of the Illinois Conference, Jacksonville businessmen, and even farmers in the surrounding area. Future college president Dr. W.F. Short sold his horse and buggy and his only cow to meet the payments of his promised contribution. Mrs. Dumville donated her $100 life savings. Peter Cartwright donated the equivalent of four years' salary from the church. The Board which now had 29 trustees contributed 90 percent of the funds that were raised.

The subscribers in this great effort became known as the "Founders of 1862" or the "Second Founders." They had literally saved the college from ruin. By October 1862, the Board was able to report to the Illinois Conference that the school was free from debt.

In January 1863, the college was incorporated with a new charter and a new name: Illinois Female College. In addition to being free from debt, the school was also free of all obligation to honor the perpetual scholarships that had raised short time cash, but proved to be a financial hardship for the school. However, at the first meeting of the new Board, a vote was taken to allow for their partial use. This decision reduced the income from tuition for many years some were used as late as 1910 , but the Board felt bound to honor the scholarships purchased in some manner. The Board also voted to begin the task of rebuilding the west wing, which was completed in 1864, three years after the fire.

Life at the college was not one of leisure. Behind the main buildings were the barns, stables, and outhouses. Horses, pigs and cows were kept where Rutledge Hall is located today. The horses were used for recruitment trips to visit prospective students and for plowing the large garden. The garden was used to both feed the students and also to raise money from the sale of produce to the community. During his presidency, Jaquess made soap for the college and President Adams chopped wood for heat and personally hauled it to the various floors of the building using a hand-operated elevator. He also owned a horticulture business on the side and sold a variety of trees.

The students also worked hard, at their studies and household chores. There were strict rules of conduct and a strict daily schedule, rising early in the morning and remaining in continual motion from classroom to study hall to dining room to dorm room for "lights out." They would start over again the following day. The curriculum included science physical geography, geology, astronomy, physics, chemistry, botany, zoology, and physiology , social science ancient and modern history, American history, ancient and modern geography, political science and economy , mathematics geometry, algebra, trigonometry, and conic sections , rhetoric grammar, composition and literature and philosophy and religion ethics, logic, psychology and evidences of Christianity . Latin was required and French, German and Greek were also offered, along with training in harmony, musical composition, piano and voice, art, domestic economy, and gymnastics. This was a true college, not a finishing school that taught sewing and manners to young ladies. Those lucky enough to attend the Illinois Female College received a true education.

Campus Fires

The new era that the college enjoyed after the war was shattered by two more fires - and they would not be the last. The first occurred on February 28, 1870, when a blaze destroyed the main building. It was thought that the fire was caused by a defective chimney flue. The building was insured this time, but the contents were not. The undamaged west wing was large enough to house the displaced students and classes were once again held in the basement of Centenary Church formerly East Charge Church. It had been renamed in 1866 . Construction costs exceeded the insurance recovery and the trustees were forced to borrow, partly from the college's small endowment. They also voted to lease lots south of College Avenue where Rutledge Hall now stands . The school's charter did not allow the land to be sold, so it was leased for 99 years at the price of $2,600.

The new building finally went up in January 1871. Built on the same foundation, it was three stories tall, with three towers and a mansard roof. Lit by gas and heated by steam, it contained parlors, a chapel, classrooms, offices, dorm rooms, and an apartment for the president and his family. One feature added was the gymnasium in the basement. Best of all, it was built to be fireproof - a claim that it failed to prove when it burned again on November 18, 1872.

This time, the fire was thought to have started in the "dust shaft," extending from the basement to the tower, which was constructed to make the removal of refuse from sweeping more convenient. A burning match, or friction caused by a mouse, was blamed for the blaze. The dust shaft acted as a chimney and spread the fire over the entire building.

After three destructive fires, there had to have been some of those involved with the college who wondered if the school was truly meant to be. With three fires in 26 years, plus the prospect of going into debt once again, a mass meeting was called at Centenary Church to discuss the future of the school. In spite of the doubts, though, board members and supporters refused to give up. Peter Akers, then 82 years old, was among the leaders insisting that the school had to go on. President William H. DeMotte, still grieving over the death of his wife just a few months before, cheered on the others. He had no intention of closing the college, even temporarily.

Offers of support flooded in, including from Chaddock College in Quincy, which offered the use of its buildings. But once again, the college returned to the basement at Centenary Church and also used other empty rooms around the neighborhood. Students who could not be placed in the west wing were given rooms in town. Benefit concerts were held to raise funds and donations poured in. The loss of the main building was valued at $40,000. Insurance coverage was for $35,000 but since some of the materials could be re-used, not all of it was needed. The new main building, the third built by the college called Main Hall by generations of alumni , was constructed using the same plans as the last that burned and was ready for use in December 1873.

Over a period of 25 years between 1868 and 1893, the college was forced to survive on the income that came in from tuition, fees, and board. Various plans to raise an endowment were tried, but the results were poor. And what money was raised was nearly always borrowed back by the school to pay for fire damage, supplies and various shortfalls. The Board even attempted to speculate in railroad land out west, with the college earning a commission on sales, but there is no record of any profit being made. The college had been free from debt, but the money troubles were far from over.

One of the problems with fundraising was that so many people considered the school a private institution owned by the president. It's easy to understand how they got that idea. In 1866, the Board of trustees, to protect themselves financially after the school nearly closed four years earlier, gave the president complete financial responsibility aside from building costs. He paid the teachers, the cost of boarding, furniture, repairs, and insurance; in return, he received the entire income. Certainly this arrangement was more beneficial to the Conference and trustees than to the presidents. Another reason for the money problems was that minister's daughters received free tuition and other students were still attending on the perpetual scholarships that were still being honored.

During this same period, collegiate enrollment steadily declined, though other departments such as primary and preparatory, which had generally been part of the school's curriculum since its inception, helped to even out the total enrollment. To appeal to a broader range of students, a kindergarten program was even organized in 1881. The most inspired addition to the curriculum was the founding of an Academy of Music and Art in 1875, with the right granted by the state legislature to give diplomas for completion of the required course work. The first diplomas were granted in 1879, with the college being the first in the state to do so. From that point on, music and art became increasingly more important to the college and the Academy of Art was judged as an equal to the finest conservatories in the country. The Art Department also drew a large number of students and in 1888, a Department of Elocution was added. The program of lectures and concerts at Strawn's Opera House was another attraction for students. Among the lecturers featured were Ralph Waldo Emerson, Henry Ward Beecher, Susan B. Anthony, Frederick Douglass, Oscar Wilde, and Mark Twain.

The Golden Age Begins

A turning point came for the college in 1893. It was in this year that Dr. Joseph R. Harker became president of the school, and under his administration, closer relations were established between the college and the former students of the school. An Alumni Association had been started in 1893 to fill six of the 24 seats on the Board of Trustees. By changing the president's financial contract with the Board placing the risks back with the Board and making his position a salaried one , he also established better relations with the Illinois Conference of the Methodist Church and accomplished an important milestone in progressing towards a modern college. In 1899, the school's name was changed to the Illinois Women's College, "in keeping with the progressive spirit of the times and the advanced standing of the institution."

The changes led to greater opportunities for fund-raising. As a "traveling salesman" for the college, Dr. Harker began the laborious task of gathering money for the expansion, endowment, and for another attempt at retiring past debt. By 1903, with the help of alumni, trustees and friends of the college, he had collected $30,000 and had a surplus of income over expenses of $37,000. With this, the college purchased two properties adjoining the campus and made three additions to the main hall. The additions were constructed on the east and west of the building and the third addition extended the west front, bringing the old wing rebuilt in 1864 after the first fire out to the line of the main building. In January 1907, a Music Hall located east of the main hall was completed. Financed by a $25,000 matching gift from Andrew Carnegie and funds raised by alumni and student organizations, it housed rooms for music and art and a large auditorium. In April 1908, even after all of the new construction, Dr. Harker was able to report to the trustees that the college was free from debt - and had $50,000 in endowment.

Dr. Harker was not finished with his grand plans. Around this same time, he achieved another goal for the college, which was raising the school to a four-year college that could grant bachelor's degrees. He established the required curriculum in 1907 and the following year, the school was recognized by the Methodist Senate as a standard four-year college. In 1909, it received full

Illinois Women's College

accreditation from the North Central Association of Colleges and the first Bachelor of Arts degrees were awarded.

As enrollment increased, more classroom and dormitory space was needed. In the fall of 1909, a five-story building was constructed to fill both those needs. Connected to the main hall by corridors, it was named Harker Hall by an act of the board of trustees in recognition of the president's tireless service.

The last structure built during Dr. Harker's presidency was the gymnasium, which was built in 1917. It did not receive the name Harker Gymnasium until 1936. On the main floor were the basketball court and the stage for dramatic productions. The basement contained a swimming pool and a bowling alley.

Among President Harker's many talents was his ability to interest prominent businessmen in the college. The greater the businessman, he knew, the deeper the pockets. Two of the donors to the college were Andrew Carnegie and Dr. C.E. Welch, head of the grape juice corporation. The most important, though, was James E. MacMurray, president of the Acme Steel Corporation in Chicago and a one-time Illinois Senator. An active member of the Methodist Church, he had sent his daughter, Miriam, to Illinois Women's College. President Harker encouraged his interest in the school by upgrading to a four-year institution. In 1916, MacMurray became a member of the Board of Trustees and, in 1921, became president of the Board. By the time Dr. Harker retired in 1925, Senator MacMurray had donated about $45,000 to the college.

Under the subsequent president, Clarence P. McClelland, MacMurray's interest in the school stayed strong. MacMurray Science Hall was built in 1928 with $125,000 matching funds from the senator and an equal amount raised by alumni and supporters of the college.

The Gymnasium Fire

Hardtner Gymnasium, where the deadly fire took place in 1929.

Tragedy returned to the college on February 22, 1929. It was on that evening that the school's fourth - and first deadly - fire occurred. At a Washington's Birthday party in the gymnasium, a photographer was taking pictures of the party-goers in their costumes. The powder from an exploding flashbulb apparently ignited a curtain on the stage. The flames spread quickly, causing an intense wave of heat to sweep across the balcony. Although the fire caused little damage to the building, three people were killed and fifteen students and faculty members were seriously injured by the flames and in accidents while trying to escape the building. Among the dead were a student who was killed when she jumped from an upper floor to escape the flames and two staff members, including the college's librarian, who were burned to death. Mrs. McClelland, wife of the college's president, was hospitalized for a month from a complicated leg fracture caused by her fall from a window to the pavement below.

The college was closed for two weeks after the fire. The gym was eventually repaired, but the impact of the tragedy lingered much longer - and it became the scene of some of the college's first ghost stories. Accounts soon circulated of hearing footsteps in the empty gym, voices and even the screams of those who died in the fire. As time passed, though, the stories began to fade, as if the remnants of horror that had been imprinted on the place slowly dissipated as months and years went by.

The MacMurray Years

As enrollment at the college continued to grow, more living and dining space was needed. As a gift to the college, Senator MacMurray financed the construction of Jane Hall named after his wife and McClelland Dining Hall, both completed in the spring of 1930. Soon after, President McClelland proposed a name change for the school to MacMurray College for Women. It receive the unanimous approval of the Board of Trustees.

Even with the generosity of Senator MacMurray, the early 1930s were a difficult time for the school. This was during the lowest years of

James E. MacMurray

the Great Depression and few could afford to feed their families, let alone contribute to the college. Building plans and even desperately needed repairs were postponed. Even the salary budget was reduced and yet the college began sinking into debt. The school began using the endowment and annuity funds for operating expenses and that income decreased also. But, once again, James MacMurray came to the college's rescue. Between 1934 and 1939, he provided either full or partial funding to pay off the deficit, refurbish Main and Harker Halls, build Ann Rutledge Hall in 1937, and add two wings to Jane Hall in 1939. In 1938 and 1941, he made gifts to the college's endowment that totaled over $3 million. In 1940, the college purchased Liberty Hall the gymnasium and recreation hall for neighboring Our Saviour's School and converted it into the Little Theatre.

James MacMurray died in 1942, still president of the Board of Trustees at the time of his death. Under President McClelland's administration, he donated more than $4 million to the college. In 1947, Kathryn Hall was built and named for his widow Jane had died in 1937 , marking the last major gift that he made to the school. More than anyone, James MacMurray changed the face of the campus and made it possible for the college to reach and exceed its goals of expansion. It seems only right that it continues to bear his name today.

The senator would not be the last prominent friend of the college. Another benefactor emerged in 1943, a well-known New York philanthropist named Mrs. Annie Merner Pfeiffer. After being contacted by President McClelland to support the building of a library, Mrs. Pfeiffer agreed to give the college $100,000 if the school could raise the same amount. The Henry Pfeiffer Memorial Library named for her late husband was completed in 1941. The clock tower and chimes were donated by the members of that year's graduating class.

In 1944, Mrs. Pfeiffer agreed to donate $125,000 in matching funds for the construction of a chapel, which was desperately needed by the college. A growing enrollment had forced moving it from the East Annex of Music Hall to the Music Hall in Orr's Auditorium, to Centenary Church and finally to Grace Methodist Church. Named Annie Merner Chapel, it became the college's centennial project and was completed in 1949. A tradition on campus states that nothing will ever be built on the Rutledge lawn so that Henry Pfeiffer and Annie Merner will always be able to see one another. The front doors of the two buildings are exactly in line with each other - connected the husband and wife, even in death.

During this same time period, the academic quality of the college was raised yet again. In 1942, a graduate school was started. Master's Degrees were granted in psychology, physical education, and special education. The program earned national recognition and continued through 1961.

More changes soon arrived at MacMurray College. The late 1930s and early 1940s were years of more relaxed rules for dormitory hours, required chapel, smoking, and "weekend permission." Playing bridge was the most popular informal pastime. This period was also noted for the development of the women's initiation ceremony, which has become known as the "Green Ribbon."

The 1940s were occupied with activities in support of American efforts in World War II, but by the latter part of the decade, the campus had returned to normal and student life came to be characterized by such events as presentation of the senior song, senior cut day, the Lantern Drill, and the highlight of the year, the Faculty Show, which was sort of a combination of follies and a talent show.

But it was during the presidency of Dr. Louis W. Norris that an unsettling trend began to be realized in America. Due to a lower birth rate during the Depression, students were now entering colleges in fewer numbers. Fewer yet were entering schools that were designed for women - or men - only. Public high schools had been coeducational for decades, but most colleges had not. All-female colleges around the country were experiencing enrollment and retention problems and MacMurray was no exception. Young women were enrolling in sufficient numbers, but few of them stayed for the entire four years. Most were busy getting married and starting a family in the wake of World War II.

Men and Women Together

On October 9, 1955, on a motion made by Milburn Peter Akers, the great-grandson of founder Peter Akers, the Board voted to establish the MacMurray College for Men as a coordinate college to the existing school. Other coordinating colleges existed at the time, but MacMurray was the first in the Midwest. The college would not be completely co-educational, as it is today, until 1969. From

1957, when the first class of men were enrolled, until 1969, there were two MacMurray Colleges, one for men and one for women. The men had the same professors, but for the first two years, had separate classes. Initially, there were two separate student newspapers, two student governments and even two yearbooks. Separate housing and dining halls were also needed. The men and women did eat together on Thursday and Sunday evenings, however, formal attire was

Even though men were enrolled starting in 1957, MacMurray College remained two separate schools - one for men and one for women - until 1969.

required. The men's campus grew up around Chambers and Hardin Avenues and as far from the women as possible. Their dorms were even given a "contemporary" design to make them look different than the women's. Blackstock House was built in 1957 and three others, Norris House, Kendall House, and Michalson House followed over the next nine years. Over time, men's sports were added, including soccer, basketball, baseball, track, golf, wrestling, and finally, football in 1984.

By the time the first men's class graduated in 1961, men and women were working together in music, drama, and at the campus radio station. The 1961 yearbook was the first to be jointly issued. The Hub, a popular student meeting place located in the basement of Rutledge Hall, soon became inadequate and was moved to the new Campus Center in 1965. The dining rooms in the basements of Norris and Blackstock were closed and, in 1967, men joined women for meals on a regular basis. In time, as a natural course of events and by the student's choice, coordinate education was finally dropped and, in 1969, the trustees officially declared MacMurray to be a coeducational college.

Following the turbulent 1960s and 1970s, the 1980s ushered in a period of relative calm on college campuses across the country, including at MacMurray. For many students, their attention became focused on career preparation and graduate school placement, and new programs were started to meet these needs. Academic emphasis returned to the liberal arts in the form of a new general education program, otherwise known as MacMurray's Core Curriculum, the

301

"Ideas in Perspective" sequence. The general education program included studies in humanities, religion, history, and literature.

Throughout its history, financial hardship was a general theme. Another crisis occurred in 1980s. When Dr. Edward J. Mitchell became president in 1986, the college's financial situation was critical once again. After a period of more than 45 years, the college's endowment had been slowly consumed to finance each year's operating expenses. During the 1970s, rapidly increasing interest rates fueled rapidly increasing debts, and by 1986, the college's working endowment reached a low of $500,000 and external debt reached a peak of $7.2 million. Rumors spread that the college would close, but by reducing all budgets, decreasing faculty and staff, and holding salaries at the same level for four years, Dr. Mitchell was able to lead the college to recovery. After a disagreement with the college's Board of Trustees, though, Dr. Mitchell resigned on the eve of MacMurray's 150th anniversary.

The college's 14th president, Dr. Lawrence D. Bryan, took over in 1997, and within a few years had added a combination music and art building. In 2007, Dr. Colleen Hester became the first female president in the college's history.

MacMurray College today is among a select group of American colleges that has been in existence for nearly 170 years - and given its often troubled history, that's a remarkable achievement. Time and again, the college has proven itself to be a survivor, adapting to meet the changes of time, turning trials into triumph through hard work, sacrifice and sometimes, amazing luck. There is no question that MacMurray has had an often exciting, tragic, and colorful history - and its one in which ghosts and hauntings have long been a part.

Hauntings at MacMurray College

There is no question that MacMurray College has had its brushes with strangeness over the years. One of them involved a psychic prediction of a murder that was going to take place at the college, made by none other than famous psychic Jeane Dixon, who supposedly predicted the election and assassination of John F. Kennedy in 1960, among other things. Of course, she also predicted that World War III would start in 1958 and that the Russians would put the first man on the moon.

Regardless, Dixon predicted that a ghastly murder would take place in a small, Midwestern town with two colleges and a state hospital. The horrific axe murder would occur on a rainy day in April and on the steps of a dormitory with pillars that faced to the east. Many became convinced that this was MacMurray College, even though a university in Missouri also fit the description. The year the murder was supposed to take place? 1978 - So we can rest assured that we're safe on this one.

302

Another erroneous legend, although probably the most famous, is the story of the infamous "Blue Lady" of MacMurray College. The tale dates back to the late 1800s and involves a young student who attended a dance or some other social gathering one night and was supposed to meet her lover there. Unfortunately, he never showed and she returned to her dorm room in Rutledge Hall very upset and depressed. The Blue Lady - who would be so named because of the color of the gown she wore to impress her date that night - walked into her room to find her lover and her roommate together. She was so enraged that she murdered both of them and then flung herself from the window of the room, which was located high on an upper floor of the building. To this day, the Blue Lady lurks in a haunted room in Rutledge Hall and she stalks the campus with a black rose in her hand. If she approaches a young man and hands him the rose, he is soon to die.

It's an eerie story - but one rife with problems. In the late 1800s, the college was still an all-female school and it's unlikely that any co-ed dances would have taken place or that a young man could have easily have been smuggled into one of the dorm rooms. In addition, there is no record of any murders or a suicide taking place on the campus at that time. The biggest problem, though? Even though there is a room in Rutledge Hall that has been dubbed the "Blue Lady Room," which is said to be haunted by her spirit, the building wasn't actually constructed until 1937, long after the story is said to have taken place. So, while the tale of the "Blue Lady" is a great story, it's unfortunately that - just a story. But that does not mean that Rutledge Hall is not haunted. And it also does not mean that a tough-to-track-down story can't have some basis in fact.

The haunted history in the Blue Lady's room is, however, very real. So real, in fact, that the college recognizes the room as haunted and has not assigned any student to live there for many years. Students who live in dorm rooms nearby have heard noises inside the room, much like if someone where living in the room. Voices and footsteps, the sound of items be shuffled around, even the sound of a telephone ringing when there is no telephone inside the room. One student even recalls hearing a typewriter at work when walking passed the room. He put his ear to the door, and sure enough the sound was coming from inside.

Even during our investigations, we have had our fair share of occurrences in the Blue Lady's room. During one late night investigation, the voice of a woman came through the only walkie-talkie that was not yet powered down and very clearly asked "Can you hear me?" Another time, when asked to make a knocking sound, the spirit responded with two very loud and clear knocks on the chest of drawers positioned under the room's one window. One student will certainly never forget the time one investigator left a trigger object on top of a storage tote in the room. She asked the spirit to move it while she was gone. The trigger object, a small Q-tip she found in the closet earlier, was later discovered on the floor, on the other side of the room, under the seat of a colossal MacMurray football player. He ran from the room screaming. But one experience I will never forget was one of the most frustrating. Our team had arrived on campus for the annual investigation of Rutledge Hall with the students. The one room the students were dying to investigate was, of course, the Blue Lady's room. The room is normally locked and the students, except for the Resident Director, do not have access to this part of the third floor. When we arrived to the Blue Lady's room, the RD could not get the door to open. It seemed to be stuck. Campus security came by to give it a try but could not get the door to budge! It was unlocked, but would not open. Something was keeping it closed but we could not see what it was. Finally, the security officer was granted permission to enter the dorm room next door to gain entry through the adjoining bathroom, using the master key owned only by campus security. Upon entering the room, it was clear why the door would not open. An additional safety latch attached to the back of the door had been secured preventing the door from opening even when the knob was unlocked. Since this added security measure can only be locked and unlocked from inside the room, who locked it? Perhaps the spirit within was not welcoming guests that night.

Visits with Pam

Although the legend of the Blue Lady has been passed down through the generations, her room is not the most active space in Rutledge Hall. The story of Pam may not be famous and while we have had a lot of trouble tracking down the real "Pam" of the story, there is definitely something going on in the suite of rooms where she allegedly once lived that cannot be easily explained. As noted in the introduction to this section about MacMurray College, Pam was said to have lived in Rutledge in the early 1970s. As the story goes, Pam, who was very involved in campus activities, was absent at choir practice that night. Since this was so unusual for Pam, a friend decided to stop by to check in on her. When she arrived, she discovered Pam's lifeless body lying on the floor of the bathroom.

Her friends remember her as being joyful, funny, and a bit of a prankster. Recent residents of Rutledge Hall would agree. Some of the students find Pam's spirit to be fun loving, while others are quite disturbed by her antics. Some of her favorite tricks include turning on the water in the students' restrooms and taking items and replacing them in other parts of the room or building. For quite some time, Pam fixated on a large rubber exercise ball that belonged to one of the students who lived in her former room. This exercise ball would be moved to different locations in the building, once being found in the shower, in the hall, in the dorm rooms of other students, and even once it was found in the Blue Lady's room. Students report these kinds of happenings almost daily, and while Pam makes her presence known throughout the building, the most active location is the suite in which she took her final breaths.

In this room, the girls who have lived there over the years have had numerous encounters. One young woman recalls one evening playing a workout game on her Xbox Connect, which essentially films the player and registers their movement onto the screen. When she was done playing and only her silhouette was left on the snowy screen, she noticed a second silhouette standing just behind her. When she turned to look, there was no one there.

On another student investigation, one team member wanted to try placing another trigger object, remembering the success she had with this in the Blue Lady's room. This time she included the young woman who lived in Pam's room in the plan. She instructed her to choose one small object to place on the desk and then ask Pam to move the object while they were out of the room. The student opened a desk drawer and pulled out a packet of mustard from her stash and placed it on the corner of the desk. After asking Pam to show herself by participating in their experiment, the two left the room, locking the door behind them. When the whole group returned about an hour later, the young woman screamed with excitement and fear. The mustard packet that she placed on the corner of the desk had been left undisturbed, but the desk drawer was open and a dozen mustard packets had been strewn across the floor.

In the fall of 2013, both authors returned to MacMurray and Rutledge Hall for another outing with the students in search of the resident ghosts. We chased down the legends, checked out the "Blue Lady's" room and settled down in Pam's room to see if she might be around. As described earlier, we're both convinced that she was. No matter how many questions might remain about the validity of using scientific and electrical devices to search for ghosts, we can't offer a reasonable explanation for how the temperature dropped so suddenly in the bedroom, or why the lights and alarms on all of those meters went off at the same time, signaling a drastic change in the magnetic atmosphere of the room. We're sure that a hardened skeptic might be able to come up with something, but would it be any more believable than the possibility that it was a ghost? We don't think so.

Once the reaction of those devices are combined with literally years of eyewitness testimony about strange experiences in the rooms, then it's hard to dismiss at least the chance that it's truly haunted. We believe it's better than a mere chance that a ghost makes her presence known there but, of course, the truth of such things remains for the reader to decide.

But if "Pam" - or whoever the spirit might be - truly does linger in her former dorm room, why does she stay? A tragic life ended too soon? Some sort of unfinished business that she still need to complete? No one can say, at least so far. Perhaps one day, we'll find out. We hope that we'll be around when she decides to let us know.

Ghosts of Illinois College
History and Hauntings of the School that Made us the "Athens of the West"

It was education that provided the foundation for the city of Jacksonville. The frontier town was not even five years old when it gained its first institution and arguably, it's greatest one. Illinois College was founded in 1829 by Reverend John M. Ellis, a Presbyterian minister who felt a "seminary of learning" was needed in the new frontier state of Illinois. His plans came to the attention of a group of students at Yale University in New England and seven of them - the fabled "Yale Band" - came west to help establish the college. It became one of the first institutes of higher learning in Illinois, and it became nationally known in the years prior to the Civil War. Illinois College was one of only two colleges to be marked in "Mitchell's Geography" in 1839. Harvard University was the other.

Even the first graduates of Illinois College made a mark in history. The first two men to graduate were Richard Yates, who became the Civil War governor of Illinois and later a U.S. Senator, and Jonathan Edward Spilman, the man who composed the now-familiar music to Robert Burns' immortal poem, "Flow Gently, Sweet Afton." Both men received their baccalaureate degree from Illinois College in 1835.

Nine students met for the first class at Illinois College on January 4, 1830. Julian Sturtevant, the school's first instructor and the second president, reported, "We had come there that morning to open a fountain for future generations to drink at." Shortly after, Edward Beecher left the Park Street Church in Boston to serve the new college as its first president. He created a strong college and retained close intellectual ties with New England. His brother, Henry Ward Beecher, preached and lectured at Illinois College, and his sister, Harriet Beecher Stowe, who wrote the controversial book *Uncle Tom's Cabin*, was an occasional visitor. His brother, Thomas, graduated from Illinois College in 1843. Ralph Waldo Emerson, Mark Twain, Horace Greeley, and Wendell Phillips were among the college's visitors and lecturers in the early years.

In 1843 and 1845, two of the college's seven literary societies were formed. Possibly unique in the Midwest today, these societies have continued in their roles as centers for debate and criticism. Abraham Lincoln was one of many speakers appearing on the campus under the sponsorship of a literary society.

In the years leading up to the Civil War, Illinois College became heavily involved with America's abolitionist movement. Thanks to the family of President Beecher, it seems nearly impossible for the college to have avoided the entanglement. Illinois College is still widely regarded as having been a station on the Underground Railroad, and rumors abound that slaves were hidden at the Smith and Fayerweather houses on campus. Over time, the school gained a reputation as an "abolitionist college" and its name was spoken with contempt by pro-slavery activists. And the students were often just as involved as Edward Beecher was in protesting against slavery. Many of them lost the respect of their families. An irate southern father once complained that the college was turning his son into an "abolitionist pup" and disowned him. Other students even ran into trouble with the law.

But the leaders of Illinois College were torn between a cause they believed in and getting the young college mired in a heated political debate. Julian Sturtevant, the college's second president, hated slavery but never enough to satisfy the die-hard abolitionists. He once wrote, "I went too far against slavery to win the favor of its advocates, and not far enough to gain the approbation of its assailants."

In 1837, Professor Sturtevant counseled Elijah Lovejoy, the abolitionist editor from Alton, against purchasing another printing press after a mob had destroyed his previous ones. He said that it would result in disaster. Lovejoy was killed just a few days later, trying to prevent a mob from destroying his new press. Edward Beecher, who was president at the time, was with Lovejoy on the night before he was killed. He had just reluctantly agreed to chair an anti-slavery convention, still worrying about the effect on the school. He needn't have worried. Lovejoy's murder further inflamed the passions of the students and professors at Illinois College, leading to its first brush with the slavery laws of the era.

A year later, when armed Jacksonville men kidnapped a slave, Bob Logan, and placed him on a steamboat heading south, the protests increased. Logan had claimed his freedom four years earlier after his master brought him to Illinois. Logan's sister, Emily, managed to escape and successfully sued for her freedom in Sangamon County court in 1840. The leader of the kidnappers, who were relatives of the people who hid the Logans, was acquitted at trial, further angering the anti-slavery protesters at Illinois College.

In 1843, a student named Samuel Willard was arrested for harboring a fugitive slave and attempting to escort her to freedom. They learned of the young woman's plight when a former slave the Willards helped free came to their door one night and begged them to help the other woman, Judy Green. She was owned by a Louisiana woman who was visiting friends in Illinois. The laws weren't clear at that time about the status of slaves when they were brought into free states. Abolitionists said they were free the moment they stepped into places like Illinois, but pro-slavery advocates, obviously, disagreed.

Julius Willard took the slave and headed to Greenfield, where friends would then escort Miss Green to safety. But a group of armed men, organized by the family of the slave's owner, began searching for her. They began raiding homes in the black section of the town until someone informed on the Willards.

Both of the Willards were arrested and thrown in jail, and they later took their case to the Illinois Supreme Court, where they lost. Julius Willard was fined $20, plus court costs, and Samuel was fined $1. Unfortunately, Judy Green was later captured and returned to Louisiana.

The actions of the Willards and the court case, though, served as a call to arms for the anti-slavery proponents. However, it also raised the anger of a lot of Jacksonville people who wanted the college and other anti-slavery activists to stay out of the south's business. At worst, there was talk of tarring and feathering the Willards as retribution. There were 36 citizens that signed a petition condemning the fact that a visitor to Jacksonville had had her "property" taken away from her. These 36 citizens were members of the newly-formed Anti-Negro Stealing Society, and they wrote in their petition, "An outrage has been committed upon the property of a widow lady visiting our town." But the pro-slavery outbursts were short-lived - and there's no record that the Anti-Negro Stealing Society ever held another meeting.

Nervous members of the Illinois College Board of Trustees toyed with the idea of expelling Samuel Willard, who was a senior that year. However, every faculty member came to the young man's support and he was allowed to stay. He graduated from the Illinois Medical College in 1848 and later became a surgeon during the Civil War. After being seriously wounded in the fighting, he retired from medicine and became the superintendent of schools in Springfield and later taught in Chicago. He died in 1913 at the age of 91.

In the years following the Civil War, graduates contributed with distinction to the national scene. Among these was William Jennings Bryan, who within 15 years after graduating was the Democratic candidate for the U.S. presidency in the race with William McKinley. He continued with a prominent role in politics even after being defeated in the election.

Hauntings at Illinois College

Illinois College, continuing its founders' progressive way of thinking, began accepting women in 1903. There have been many prominent graduates of the school over the years, both men and women, and it has maintained an outstanding program of scholarship.

In addition, it has maintained a long history with the supernatural as well. Like many other historic spots in Illinois, the events of the past have certainly left their mark on Illinois College. These events come back to "haunt" students and faculty members today, and there are many who have encountered the ghosts of yesterday face to face.

Beecher Hall, the oldest building on Illinois College's campus - and some say, the most haunted

One place where strange events have been reported is in Beecher Hall, which was built in 1829. This two-level building is now used as a meeting hall for two of the school's literary societies, Sigma Pi and Phi Alpha. The Sigs meet on the upper floor and the Phis meet in the lower part of the building. The majority of the encounters here seem to involve the groups who frequent the upper floor. The most commonly reported events are ghostly footsteps that can be distinctly heard in one room, always coming from another. If a curious witness follows the sound, the footsteps will suddenly be heard in the other room instead. Years ago, this was a medical building and cadavers were stored in the attic above the upper floor. Some believe that this may explain the ghostly activity. Campus legend has it that the students were not actually supposed to have the cadavers that were secreted away in the building. Supposedly, they were so dedicated to collecting medical knowledge that they stole corpses from local hospitals and cemeteries, introducing the art of "body snatching" to Illinois College. The corpses were said

309

to have been hidden in the attic until the stench of decaying flesh alerted college officials to their presence.

Other legends claim that the ghost is that of Williams Jennings Bryan, who has returned to haunt his old school. He was a member of Sigma Pi and was often in the building during his years at Illinois College. There are others who say that it might be Abraham Lincoln's ghost instead. He was an honorary Phi Alpha and while he did not attend the school, he spoke at Beecher Hall on occasion. In addition, William Berry Lincoln's partner at new Salem , William H. Herndon his law partner , and Ann Rutledge's brother, David, all attended Illinois College.

The David A. Smith House

Another allegedly haunted spot on campus is the David A. Smith House, built in 1854. Today, the structure is home to three of the women's literary societies, the Gamma Deltas, the Chi Betas and Sigma Phi Epsilon. There is a parlor for all of them, but the Delts use a room on the main floor while the Betas and the Sig Phips have rooms on the second floor. The attic is used by all of the groups, and there is also a dining room, a kitchen, and an apartment at the back of the house.

There are several versions of the historic legend concerning the ghost in this house, but all of them claim that she is the daughter of the original owner and that her name was Effie Smith. The story goes that Effie was being courted by a young man from town and they became engaged. When he proposed to her, he gave her a diamond ring and she was said to have scratched the stone against her bedroom window to see if it was real. When she realized that it was, she etched her signature into the glass where it remained for many years afterward. The window has recently been removed and this small and unusual piece of history has been lost.

Then, the story begins to take different paths. In one version, David Smith disapproved of his daughter's fiancée and he locked Effie into a closet one day when the man came calling. Fearful of her father's wrath, the young man hid himself in a small room that was only accessible from the attic. For some reason, he nailed himself in and later died there. According to students who have been in the attic, the nails are still visible there today on the inside of the door. It is

310

said that when Effie learned of her lover's cruel fate, she threw herself from an upstairs window and died in the fall.

In the second version of the story, Effie's young man went off to fight in the Civil War. Every day, Effie climbed up to the attic and sat in a rocking chair by the window, watching for him to return. When she learned that he had been killed in battle, she committed suicide by jumping out of the attic window. Yet another variation of the legend has Effie being jilted by her lover, at which point she committed suicide. Regardless of what happened, the story claims that she has since returned to haunt the house.

Effie's rocking chair is still in the attic and the stories say that if you move it away from the window where it sits facing out, then leave the attic and return later, the chair will have returned to its original position. This window is located in a storage area for the Chi Beta society and every year, they test the chair and discover that the story is true - or so the story goes. One young woman walked into the room one day and the door suddenly slammed closed behind her. It is also not uncommon for cold air to suddenly fill this room, even though for years, the windows were painted shut. It was said that an icy cold wind would often come from the window that had Effie's name etched on the glass.

Another reportedly ghostly location is Whipple Hall, which was constructed in 1882. The spectral occupant of this place is known only as the "Gray Ghost." The building, which was once a preparatory school, has been updated and renovated many times over the years. The upper part once served as the meeting hall for the Alpha Phi Omega society and the Eta Sigma chapter, a national service fraternity, as well as the location of the security office. The lower part housed the meeting hall of the Pi Pi Rho Literary Society. More recently, though, it is home to the Al Habtoor Leadership Center, Congressman Paul Findley's Congressional Office, and the Communication and Rhetorical Studies department.

Perhaps the most famous sighting on campus of the Gray Ghost occurred to a girl who was leaving a Pi Pi Rho party one night and had to retrieve something from

Whipple Hall

the Alpha Phi Omega hall. She had been drinking but later insisted that she was not drunk . She said she had started climbing the curved staircase and as she reached the middle of the curve of the stairs, she looked up to the top landing and saw a man standing there. He was dressed all in gray and she quickly realized that he was not a security officer. As she peered into the shadows, she also realized something else -- he had no face! She began screaming and ran back down the staircase and out of the building. Due to the noise of the party, no one heard her screams and the revelers wouldn't learn of the strange experience until later.

A room that is located on the third floor of Illinois College's Ellis Hall is also rumored to be infested with ghosts. According to reports, no one lives there if they don't absolutely have to. Rumor has it that a girl hanged herself in the room's closet around 1986 after failing to get a bid from a literary society. It is said that doors open and close on their own, appliances and radios turn on and off and that windows have a habit of going up and down under their own power. Or at least that's one version of the story....

Other students and alumni of Illinois College claim that the girl who haunts Room 303 was a young woman named Gail who died of natural causes in the room. Apparently, her parents were aware that she was terminally ill when she went to school, but since attending college had always been her dream, they allowed her to go anyway. She died while living in Ellis Hall and a small plaque is mounted on the door of the room in her memory. It is said that her ghost is a mischievous one, opening doors and hiding things. Legend has it that if third floor residents lose anything, they will call out to Gail and ask her to return it. The missing item is usually found a short time later.

A former student at the college who lived for two years in Ellis Hall, wrote to tell me of her experiences while living below the "haunted room." She said that she often heard knocking sounds coming from the other side of the wall, even

Fayerweather House

though there was nothing there. It was the outer wall of the building and there were no trees nearby.

The college is said to have other haunted places, but stories from some of these sites are much sketchier. One of them is Fayerweather House, a residence hall for women. It has been said that windows and doors open and shut on their own and that lights turn on and off without explanation. Stories say that a girl hanged herself in the house, committing suicide in the closet of Room 5, which is located on the stairway landing between the first and second floors of the house. "Susie," as she has been called, is noisy and can often be heard walking around the house, opening doors in the middle of the night and scratching on walls.

Many legends claimed that the attic of the Fayerweather house was converted into dorm rooms that were never used. The stories claimed that the rooms were closed when too many strange things started to happen to the students who lived there. This was not the case, but the rooms were indeed haunted. Several students that we interviewed told of doors slamming, lights turning on and off, and objects that purportedly moved about on their own.

Sturtevant Hall

Another haunted site is Sturtevant Hall, one of the most famous spots on campus. Sturtevant was the third building on the Illinois College campus and is said to be the structure that truly gave the school its identity. Beecher Hall was the first college building on campus and in the state of Illinois and while it gave the college its life, it's the top of the main tower at Sturtevant that is pictured in the campus logo, and it gave the school credibility. Beecher Hall had been criticized for being plain and awkward and so President Julian Sturtevant wanted to provide the campus with a "suitable, commodious, elegant building."

The Romanesque Revival-style building, prominent in public buildings from about 1840 through 1900, has two asymmetrical towers, one square and one round. It is a grand building and when fundraising slowed, it delayed its completion until 1857. When it opened, it was known simply as "The College Building" but in 1888, two years after President Sturtevant's death, it was named in his honor.

The building came about as the result of a disaster. A four-story dormitory once stood on this site and it was destroyed by fire on December 30, 1852. Apparently, Jacksonville had a new fire engine that winter, but no one knew how to use it and the building was destroyed. President Sturtevant disliked dormitories. He felt that the young men of Illinois College would be better served by boarding with upstanding, local families. So, even though it replaced a four-story dormitory, Sturtevant Hall did not have a single bedroom inside of it. The plans instead called for a chapel, library, lecture rooms, five classrooms and the college's science rooms.

In 1920, the building caught fire, destroying the roof and most of the interior. The inside was rebuilt, the science labs updated, and the chapel moved to Jones Memorial Hall. In 1965, the building was remodeled and the science labs were moved to the Crispin Science Building. Sturtevant became a building for classes and faculty offices. In 1993, it was renovated again, adding air-conditioning, an elevator, new light fixtures, windows, and restrooms.

At one time, the building housed the Pi Pi Rho Literary Society, and for years, members maintained that the toilets in the place often flushed by themselves. This may have been the first ghostly stories told about Sturtevant Hall, but they would not be the last. Recent stories say that a ghostly young man in a Civil War uniform is sometimes seen here. In addition, it is said to be nearly impossible to find someone who is willing to spend the night in the north tower of the building due to strange noises that haunt the place.

Crampton Hall

Crampton Hall, which was built in 1873, is also believed to be home to a ghost. The residence was built to house 69 men, and it was named in honor of Rufus C. Crampton, a former professor and president of the college. According to the story, there was a male student who left a party one night and was later found hanged in his closet. Rumors still state that he was hanged in a way that he could not have done it himself. His former room is believed to be haunted.

And apparently closets in Crampton Hall are as mysterious as the stories that revolve around them. One student told me of three of the residents who were waiting for a fourth friend to get ready so that they could all go somewhere together. Finally, they tired of waiting and went to check on him, only to find that he was hanging upside down in the closet, stark naked, and so frightened that he was almost incoherent. The student went on to say that he lived in Crampton Hall for one semester and would never live there again. One night, he said he fell asleep with his lights on only to be awakened by a noise. When he looked up, he saw a man standing there looking at him. The man quickly turned and vanished into the closet.

Another resident haunt can be found in the McGaw performing arts building. It has been reported that you will never find anyone who is willing to be alone in the auditorium at night. The place is allegedly haunted by the ghost of a man dressed in clothing from the 1940s. People on the stage are said to glimpse him out of the corners of their eyes.

Rammelkamp Chapel allegedly has a haunted basement. Some of the students tell stories of classroom doors that open suddenly and then slam shut, sometimes in the middle of lectures. The classrooms are located on both sides of a long hall. By looking out the door, it is possible to see into the classroom across the hall. One day, during a class, a student reportedly became quite upset when she looked across the hall and spotted a woman in white in the adjoining classroom. This would not have been so strange if the woman had not vanished in front of her eyes.

315

Bibliography

Cole, Arthur Charles - Illinois: The Era of the Civil War 1848-1870; 1919
Doyle, Don Harrison, Social Order of a Frontier Community: Jacksonville, Illinois 1825-1870; 1983
Eames, Charles M. - Historic Morgan and Classic Jacksonville; 1885
Fernandes, Vernon R. Q. - The People of Jacksonville; 1991
Fliege, Stu - Tales and Trails of Illinois; 2002
Jacksonville City Directories   various years
Kay, Betty Carlson & Gary Jacks Barwick - Jacksonville, Illinois; 1999
Howard, Robert P. - Illinois: A History of the Prairie State; 1972
May, Allan - The Race Wire Service; 2009
Morgan County Historical Society - Greetings From Jacksonville, Illinois; 2010
Margolies, John - Home Away from Home; 1995
Pease, Theodore Calvin - Illinois: The Frontier State 1818-1848; 1918
Sandlin, Lee - Wicked River; 2010
Personal Interviews and Correspondence

Newspapers:
Alton Telegraph
Chicago Inter-Ocean
Chicago Tribune

Decatur Daily Herald
Decatur Daily Republican
Decatur Daily Review
Jacksonville Courier
Jacksonville Daily Journal
Jacksonville Journal-Courier
Jacksonville Weekly Journal

Special Thanks to:
George Taylor - Special Research Advisor
Lois Taylor - Editing and Proofreading
April Slaughter - Cover Design
Staff at the Jacksonville Public Library
Staff at the Morgan County Genealogical Society
Morgan County Historical Society
Students and Staff at MacMurray College
Students and Staff at Illinois College
Hannah Grey
Loren Hamilton
Misty Taylor
J.R. Manker
Greg Olson
Kyle and Lux Horton
Haven and Helayna Taylor

ABOUT THE AUTHORS

TROY TAYLOR

Troy Taylor is a crime buff, supernatural historian and the author of more than 100 books on ghosts, hauntings, crime, and the unexplained in America. He is also the founder of the American Hauntings Tour Company. When not traveling to the far-flung reaches of the country in search of the unusual, Troy resides somewhere among the cornfields of Illinois.

LISA TAYLOR HORTON

Lisa Taylor Horton is a Jacksonville native, elementary school teacher, and Illinois College graduate, with a Master's Degree in Education. She is the Tour Coordinator and Marketing Director for the American Hauntings Tour Company and the host of the Haunted Jacksonville Tours. A long-time ghost enthusiast and researcher, she has spent most of her life searching for the ghost stories and hauntings of the area. She lives in Jacksonville.

And no, they are not related.

HAUNTED JACKSONVILLE TOURS
History & Hauntings of the "Athens of the West"

The Haunted Jacksonville Book was the inspiration for the Haunted Jacksonville Tours of the city! Each tour takes guess to spirited sites in the old downtown area and lasts approximately three hours. The tour will include not only the ghost stories behind each of the reputedly haunted sites, but their history as well. Popular with ghost enthusiasts and history buffs alike, the tour includes visits to a number of haunted locations   number depends on availability , odd and unusual stories about the city and more!

Public tours are offered during the spring, summer and fall, with special tours during the Halloween season. All tickets are sold on a reservations-only basis and spots are reserved on a first come   first served basis. Spaces are limited for all tours!

Take a journey back in time to the early days of Jacksonville history and explore the ghostly tales that have long haunted the city! This is not just a ghost tour - escape from the ordinary and discover the secret side of the city with the Haunted Jacksonville Tour!

Get More Information and reservations at
www.hauntedjacksonville.com

How we keep these dead souls in our hearts. Each one of us carries within himself his necropolis.
Gustave Flaubert